Beyond the American Dream

Also by Charles D. Hayes

Self-University

Proving You're Qualified

Beyond the American Dream:

Lifelong Learning and the Search for Meaning in a Postmodern World

Autodidactic Press

Library of Congress Catalog No. 98-92545
Publisher's Cataloging in Publication

(Prepared by Quality Books)

Hayes, Charles D.
Beyond the American dream : lifelong learning and the search
    for meaning in a postmodern world / [by Charles D. Hayes]. –
    1st ed.
    p. cm.
    Includes bibliographical references and index.
    Preassigned LCCN: 98-92545
    ISBN: 0-9621979-2-0
    1. Self-culture. 2. Non-formal education—United
    States. 3. Postmodernism and education—United States.
I. Title.
LC32.H39 1998 374
QB198-209

Printed in the United States of America

10 9 8 7 6 5 4 3 2 1

First Edition

This book is printed on recycled paper

Autodidactic Press
P. O. Box 872749
Wasilla, AK 99687
www.autodidactic.com

This book is dedicated to my granddaughter, Lauren Emily Hayes, and to the memory of Eduard C. Lindeman, who proposed the simple idea that lifelong learning creates new reasons for living. This insight can move us far beyond the American Dream to a better world.

Acknowledgments

This book has been nearly a decade in the making with far more drafts and revisions than I care to remember. Enough material has been discarded for at least another book or two. I wish to thank a number of people who, over the years, have read either the whole manuscript or sections in various stages and who have offered valuable advice. They are: Walter Truett Anderson, Fern Channdonet, Mike Chmielewski, Jorge Fernandez, James R. Fisher Jr., Ronald Gross, Robert M. Pirsig, Jack Roderick, Earl Shorris, Philip Slater, Bob Talbott, my sister Cheryl Wright, and my wife Nancy. I'm also grateful to the many authors whose works I've referenced to make my case for lifelong learning. Readers should understand that the quotations I've selected are for the sake of my own arguments and mine alone. It should in no way be inferred that the authors quoted either agree or disagree with my positions. The contradictions in this work remain my property and my principle preoccupation.

I am indebted most of all to my editor, LuAnne Dowling, without whose tact, patience, and ability to turn convoluted wording into clear statements this book would likely have never made it into print.

Table of Contents

x

xi

Preface

The world is so full of wonderful things we should all, if we were taught how to appreciate it, be far richer than kings.[1]

—Ashley Montagu

Richer than kings indeed! In the world of ideas we can all find riches far more enjoyable and far longer lasting than any pleasures money can buy. The joys of vibrant thought can never be lost. Continuous, self-directed learning is the greatest means we have to navigate our way through life.

More and more we hear the term "lifelong learning" used in connection with the kind of learning required to earn a living, but this misses the point. What I've discovered is really quite simple: knowledge sought critically and passionately, for its own sake, gives purpose and meaning to living. This seems like common sense, except it is not common in our society to relate well to others or to really know what you want to do with your life. Those who are searching for satisfaction tend to dabble with self-help material in bits and pieces without ever fully embracing the idea that they are seeing to their own education. The few who whole-heartedly buy into taking charge of their own self-education find that the process profoundly changes their expectations.

Unfortunately, the negative aspects of traditional education keep many people from ever considering that quality of life hinges on continuous learning. We see countless examples of people who graduate from college more confused than when they began. They are often terribly disappointed to discover they don't seem at all suited for a career in their major area of study.

They've allowed themselves to be molded into a shape that doesn't fit them because they haven't learned to think for themselves. Worse, people trained in rigid scientific disciplines for their professional lives use no such criteria in their personal lives, blindly following the first guru that comes along with a preposterous story to tell.

When we fail to take charge of our education, we fail to take charge of our lives. The result is that we give away our power by letting others decide our fate. Self-directed inquiry, the process of taking charge of your own education, is an empowering experience. It is the lifeblood of democracy, the key to controlling your life, and a means to living your life to its fullest.[2] Education has as much to do with how well we succeed in our personal lives as it does with the satisfaction and rewards we get from work. And, as you will see, self-education helps us to define which projects are worthy of the term *work*. Our capacity for education is rooted in our ability to develop reasoning skills, which is what makes us unique as human beings. Quite simply, the practice of learning is the process of becoming more human. Learning is growth, and growth is a way of experiencing quality of life. Dropping out of learning is equivalent to dropping out of life.

Beyond the American Dream aims to demonstrate that we humans are unique contradictions: we are overconfident, yet we can be easily discouraged. Without thinking, we will adopt a social standard of measurement—no matter how bizarre—and use it as a yardstick to measure ourselves and others. We are self-deceptive and easily prejudiced, yet we're capable of giving up our lives for a stranger without a moment's hesitation. We confuse knowledge and perception. Many of us are too easily fooled by our culture into believing that thinking is for others. As a result, we allow ourselves to miss the greatest part of living. Within these pages I hope to inspire you to reexamine the whole purpose of education. Doing so can be pivotal in your search for fulfillment, just as it was for me. I am more convinced than ever that education for the sake of understanding life is one of the most liberating activities that adults can engage in.

I was past 40 when I discovered what I really wanted to do for a living. Yet, had I known at 25 what I know today, I could easily have figured it out then. If the schools I attended had focused on helping me discover my strengths at age 10, I could have had an even earlier head start. But all that is hindsight. Raised in a racist community, I became a police officer at the age of 23. Racism among my fellow officers was not the exception, it was the norm. Not until I was in my thirties did I choose to begin my own self-education, and it changed my life completely. I now know that if I hadn't started questioning what I saw and heard, and hadn't chosen to figure out the answers for myself, I would have cheated myself out of the best life has to offer.

Lately I've come to realize that if you can't occasionally make people angry, you probably don't have much to say. This book, like others I've published, is heavily biased and highly opinionated in favor of the ideas I've assimilated through my own education. Though it is not my intention to offend, rare will be the reader who is not annoyed or even outraged by something written here. You might find the book infuriating. At the very least I hope you find it provocative. Some of the ideas I posit are counter intuitive, some are slippery, others threaten tradition. My purpose is not to solicit agreement, but to create situations where meaningful reflection is the only escape and critical thinking the only alternative. Meaningful reflection requires you to use your own experience and observations to consider and to thoroughly examine any issue. Critical thinking means you must place your inquiry outside or beyond your own interest and be willing to test assumptions or ask any question.

In the spirit of Franz Kafka, who once said, "If the book we're reading doesn't wake us up with a blow on the head, what are we reading it for?" I invite you to stick with me through this text. Regardless of whether you agree with my observations or not, I promise you alarm, illumination, inspiration, and your money's worth of material worthy of reflection. This book has a dark side and a bright side. How much of each you find will be up to you.

Beyond the American Dream is not a "how to" book; it is a "why to." More than enough books today promise much and deliver little. They fill page after page with useless lists and numbered steps so generalized that they have little to do with real-life situations. In finding the power that drives self-education, how-to is not nearly as important as the simple desire to know. A strong sense of purpose will naturally produce its own how-to's. This book is not intended as a recipe for good living, but as a smorgasbord of intellective morsels so arranged as to create a craving for more—in full appreciation of the fact that purpose inspires method.

In the preface to *Don Quixote*, Miguel de Cervantes offers a warning about the use of maxims and quotations from other sources, concerned that an author could stultify the reader with amazement and obscure the lessons yielded by actual living experience. Cervantes' protagonist Don Quixote, himself driven mad from over-influence by the literature of chivalry, tilts his lance at windmills, mistaking them for giant monsters. As the novel progresses, Don Quixote becomes a tragic figure, due, in part, to his society's refusal to accept any deviance from accepted norms of behavior. The story is a profound representation of both cultural and individual self-awareness.

My own works, including this one, make liberal use of quotations from authors whose words have added meaning to my personal search for knowledge. I offer them to you here as veins in a gold mine. Your own choices will lead you to the motherlode: when a quotation strikes a nerve, you will know where to begin your own search. Some of the quotations I have selected as important to the theme of this book convey a sexist bias in tone though not in intent. I hope readers will not be offended by them. Sympathetic as I am to the assertion that the pervasive usage of *he* to stand for humankind has contributed in cumulative effect to diminish the power and status of women, I have nonetheless found it necessary to respect the words of thinkers from earlier times.

Education in the fullest sense—education, that is, to live, work, and play in a global economic society—increasingly depends upon a *radical awareness* of one's being in the world, an awareness that comes from learning beyond our respective cultures and even calls for occasionally tilting at windmills. The gist of all serious study in disciplines of human interest, we find, is that life is not what it appears to be; true knowledge is often deeply hidden from the surface of life. Clearly, book learning by itself is not sufficient, but if you fail to develop your own thirst for knowledge, culture will overwhelm your efforts. The record of history is very clear on this point.

To realize that we as individuals have a choice about how to live our lives—a real choice, independent of what our peers think of our actions—comes as something of a shock because examples occur so rarely. Don Quixote may have been a fool *par excellence*, but many scholars believe he demonstrated greater character than his one-dimensional countrymen. I offer you the quotations in this work as part of an educational dialog, not to amaze or impress you, but to serve as the lances of those who've had courage enough to joust at the absurdities of popular culture. Fortunately, everything worth knowing is free for the learning, if you have the desire to learn.

The purpose of *Beyond the American Dream* is to urge you to question some of your most cherished opinions, using the process that worked for me. I am certain you'll feel better for having done so. When you take charge of your education, you take charge of your life, and you shape your own American Dream. The counterbalance of personal freedom is responsibility. Self-education can decrease your dependence upon authority, allowing you to develop more confidence in your own judgment. This, in turn, can inspire you to take active responsibility in addressing the problems faced by our society. In practice, then, learning becomes the greatest act of self-determination, the ultimate act of freedom. It is central if we are to move beyond the American Dream and live lives far richer than kings.

Introduction

Dreams are the touchstones of our character.[1]
—Henry David Thoreau

The start of a new millennium represents for many a time of optimism about the future—a clean slate, if you will, on which to cast fresh hopes and dreams. For others, it signals a time to take stock, to own up to past mistakes and to reassess what really matters. Even if this second view seems more realistic, it needn't be devoid of hope. Obviously, the slate can't be brushed completely clean, but there's a chance new tools can be shaped for imprinting the next thousand years with truly positive outcomes.

We live in an age of great paradox, filled with technological magic and social blunder. Economic conditions are changing faster than ever before in our history. Millions of people in America are working harder, grasping for more and more of what appears to be less and less. Where one wage earner per family used to be enough, now two are needed. Value seems to be slipping away along with our ability to define it. We celebrate growth as the ultimate measure of our success, even though an integral part of that growth depends on sending billions of pounds of contaminants into our air and water supplies each year. The structure of our economy demands that we grow, but the current rate of global pollution lends credence to the environmentalists' slogan, "Uncontrolled growth is the ideology of a cancer cell."

Almost every major American city has a section that resembles a war zone, where thousands of people are living the "American nightmare" instead of the dream. Their ranks grow

1

daily, while conservatives and liberals argue over the reasons. If we heed the lessons of history, demographics suggest that the growth of "have nots" in our society is rapidly becoming a threat to national security. Similar conditions throughout the past have left a clear record of revolution and disintegration. Poverty in and of itself does not cause revolution, but resentment of poverty does.

The physical infrastructures of our society—our roads, dams, bridges, and underground water systems—are rapidly deteriorating to the degree that they are becoming dangerous, yet our political leaders fear asking us to pay for the needed repairs. They know the penalty for asking for higher taxes and the peril that focusing on past spending practices might bring. For them, far more can be gained politically by simply diverting our attention to emotional "flag-waving" issues.

Millions feel powerless in a society founded upon the premise that real power lies with the people. We allow our system to define us rather than perceiving ourselves as having the power to define the system. For decades we have called ourselves the greatest nation on earth while many of our citizens died (and still do) from lack of affordable health care. We spend more money to maintain people in prison than it would cost to send them to the best universities in the country, yet millions of hardworking citizens cannot afford to go to college. We treat higher learning in America as if it were a scarce resource, and in the next breath speak in awe of an information explosion.

We have grossly misunderstood the objective of education, allowing our institutions to focus on credentialing instead of on the fundamental need for learning that can sustain a democracy and enable people to live their lives to the fullest. The external motivators at the heart of our educational system cause people to conclude that an education is something you can "finish," even though the knowledge necessary to maintain a democracy in a highly technological society escalates daily.

That education is primarily a means to an economic end, and is more important than education for living itself, is a foolish assumption. It is a lowly aspiration for human beings. Our ability to reason separates us from animals (at least in degree), making intellectual endeavor the key to experiencing one's humanity. Indeed, at the threshold of a new millennium we find ourselves in predicaments where the only way out is *thinking*—thinking at a depth to which most Americans are completely unaccustomed. If we are to move beyond the American Dream to a vision which is capable of enduring the century ahead, that vision must acknowledge and honor the biological world, the social realm, and the world of ideas.

The nine chapters in this book lay the groundwork for such a vision. Chapter One takes a cursory glance at American history in 50-year increments to get a sense of past American dreams and aspirations. Here I present the analogy of a king-of-the-mountain game to describe the characteristics of our illusionary meritocracy, the nature of competition, and how we define worth. The pathology of king-of-the-mountain values is characterized as mountain fever, and poverty is portrayed as residing at the bottom of the mountain. Chapter Two suggests an escape from both the game and poverty through knowledge, self-directed inquiry, and expanded awareness. In Chapter Three an examination of the philosophy of history brings fresh perspective to the present for survival in an increasingly media-driven culture. It's my assumption that where we are and where we are going are tied to the knowledge contained in our history, or where we have been. Chapter Four is a look at belief and perception, how they shape and suppress inquiry, and how the ubiquitous use of the term *postmodernism* has come to describe everything from nihilism to utopia.

Our biological predisposition toward specific self-deceptive and ethnocentric behaviors is the subject of Chapter Five. Since these proclivities affect the environment and shape the future of humanity, Chapter Six goes on to discuss how we might override our antiquated biological predispositions in order to achieve a more dynamic society. Chapter Seven examines economics in the sense that the term *economy* is really a euphemism for moral value, and that understanding it as such is a requisite for human prosperity. Chapter Eight shows what it means to truly rise to the occasion of one's culture. Intellect creates culture, and those who live well enough to better their culture can create a life truly worth living. Finally, Chapter Nine shows how accepting responsibility for the future means facing our greatest fears head-on, and how doing so can take us beyond the American Dream to a quality of life earlier generations could have neither dreamed of nor imagined.

It would be an understatement to say the views expressed in my books are not exactly mainstream. Then again, my whole point is that mainstream has unintentionally come to represent shallow water. Mainstream America is dying of thirst—a thirst for knowledge, purpose, and meaning.

I have been greatly influenced by many of the authors whose sharply contrasting works are mentioned in this book. Barbara Ehrenreich, Carol Gilligan, Hazel Henderson, Walter Truett Anderson, Mihaly Csikszentmihalyi, James R. Fisher Jr., Charles Handy, Richard Garner, Kenneth J. Gergen, Todd Gitlin, Michael Lewis, Neil Postman, Earl Shorris, John F. Schumaker, Philip Slater, and Robert Wright slice through the membrane of social discourse as if they were surgeons of postmodern reality. Morris Berman makes much more than just another compelling case for paying attention to what really matters in this life. And Robert M. Pirsig provides a model framework with which we can comprehend the enormous scope and complexity of the problems humanity will face in the new millennium. But sometimes it is to the people with whom we most disagree that we are most indebted. Francis Fukuyama's book *The End of History and the Last Man* has afforded me a much better understanding of what I really believe about the conception of the American Dream, precisely because I disagree with his brilliantly argued conclusions.

Beyond the American Dream is about vision and values, the thesis being that what we envision with relish becomes valuable simply because we see it that way. In other words, vision and value are so closely related that they very nearly amount to the same thing. Dreams shape our future, and the American Dream shapes America. But dreams occur because something thought desirable is missing. Our failure to thoroughly comprehend this enigma may explain why we seem to have traded a sense of virtue, based upon self-reliance when material goods were scarce in the nineteenth century, for something called "values," when material goods are abundant and most of us now consider ourselves victims of one kind or another.

You will find in these pages a continuing discussion about the nature of education. Many ideas appear more than once in slightly different contexts in order to drive a point home. When I began this journey, it was my intention to move from simple, to compound, to complex ideas as the text progressed. But, as can happen in pursuits of this kind, sometimes the reverse obtains. Therefore, let me urge you to continue reading, even if your impressions seem fuzzy. Trust the process and, on reflection, the full picture will come clear. Surely, if our dreams and aspirations disclose our character, then we have projected the quality of our enterprise into the present and toward the future. Now, as we face the new millennium, what looms on tomorrow's horizon appears to be less than we've hoped for. It's time to move beyond the dream.

Chapter One

American Dreams

In oneself lies the whole world and if you know how to look and learn, then the door is there and the key is in your hand. Nobody on earth can give you either the key or the door to open, except yourself.[1]

—*J. Krishnamurti*

That each of us holds the key to our own world is a profoundly simple idea, but it could be the most formidable barrier to living any of us will ever face. To imagine that we have such power as individuals puts us at odds with our culture. It's a conflict that may last a lifetime, even though our culture pretends to give each and every one of us precisely this kind of power. This battle and how to win it are what living a successful life is about. A satisfying life presupposes the mastery of culture. If we're going to move beyond the American Dream, as we must, the first requirement is to awaken from it. And the only way to wake up is to understand how it is that the spell of our culture lulled us to sleep in the first place.

Origins

America is built upon dreams. There have been more American dreams than stars in the milky way. Indeed, each citizen is raised with the expectation of being the shaper of his or her own dream. Dreams express the quality of our lives and of our society, but they also betray our character. If America is to be a great country, if we are to live meaningful lives, we must dream great dreams. And yet, signs everywhere suggest the American Dream is in peril. It has become a daily ritual for media pundits to dis-

7

parage today's young people, saying they will not be able to live as well as their parents. I intend to show that this notion is one of the greatest absurdities of the twentieth century and that it is true only if we can be duped into believing it.

To begin this journey we must gain some perspective from the past about the American Dream. Without a close reading of history we are easily deceived about social values and the lessons of everyday living. Historian James Lincoln Collier put it this way:

> ...there is a general feeling among Americans today that all ages before our times were "puritanical" and that the line of history has always been from greater repressiveness in personal behavior to greater freedom. This is not the case. Over history, at least in the so-called Western world, there has been a steady swing of the pendulum between times of greater and lesser restriction on sexuality, gambling, drinking, dancing, and other of the sensual pleasures.[2]

An historical record of social values is of primary importance because it is the fundamental source of any culture's moral sense of right and wrong. Each age produces endless historical interpretations and re-interpretations of what the times were really all about. But this is how we develop knowledge from history. This is how we gain perspective. A survey of everyday life in the recent past is a rich resource for better understanding the realities of today. The review of our history that follows will, of necessity, be cursory, and it will be arbitrary because you can begin anywhere, at any time, and achieve a similar result. In this example, we will go back 200 years from the 1996 presidential election and come forward in 50-year increments, to begin to appreciate what American dreams are made of.

1796

In 1796, George Washington was president. There were roughly five million people in America. The British economist Thomas Malthus was busy formulating a theory concerning global population. Life for most was hard. Everyday life was nothing like the aesthetic, serene depiction of order pictured in American cinema. "The physical texture of American life was far closer to that in the villages of many third-world countries today than to anything in the present-day United States."[3] The seventeenth century philosopher Thomas Hobbes once characterized life in a "state of nature" as "solitary, poor, nasty, brutish, and short." Philosophers have been taking issue with his assertion ever since, but in eighteenth century America, many ordinary citizens would have argued that they themselves lived, if not in, at least very near such a state. The exception was that of being solitary; very few people lived alone. Not long before, it had been *illegal* to live by oneself in America.

More than 80 percent of the population were in some way engaged in farming. Homes were small, poorly insulated and widely scattered. Few houses had many windows. The two-story homes that have survived from the eighteenth and nineteenth centuries are the exceptions, not the rule.[4]

Many farm families shared living space with chickens and livestock. People seldom bathed. Even in cities, people threw their garbage into the streets to be devoured by free-roaming pigs.[5] By today's standards the stench of life in 1796 would defy description. Both men and women went barefooted in the summer.[6] Walking was the most common form of transportation. Far fewer people owned horses than is suggested by American arts and media. Wild game was still an important food source for many rural families.[7]

Nights in eighteenth-century America brought their own special problems: most beds had at least two occupants, and bedfellows often extended beyond one's family. Bedbugs were ubiquitous. Candles were a sign of wealth. Few people read books. For those who did, catching reading material on fire was a common occurrence. All this in the midst of nights so bright with starlight as to cast a mystical shadow of awe over all of creation.

Men and women had clear duties in the domain of work (this was less true of slaves) except during harvest time. Domestic work paid only one-third to one-fourth what agricultural work did,[8] even though cooking was a back-breaking effort, with pots and kettles made of iron.[9] A large part of local economies consisted of a labor-commodity exchange, what today we would call bartering. "The negro-whip was the south's most distinctive tool of agriculture."[10] Planting and growing cycles were ruled by the zodiac; according to the stars, there was a time for everything.

Birth rates were high; the average household contained six people (slaves not included). Orphans and children from very poor families were indentured for work in more prosperous households.[11] "In the 1780s and 1790s nearly one-third of rural New England brides were already with child."[12] Death in childbirth was common to women of all social standings. One child in three died in infancy. Children born to slave families were considered a "return on investment." State-of-the-art medicine was often no better than what was offered as remedy by illiterate faith healers.[13] Plagues and deadly epidemics struck often, without warning. Doctors purged patients of bodily fluids (blood) just as they had in ancient times. The most healthful aspect of living was that daily life demanded strenuous exercise. The taste of many foods was much harsher than the food we eat today (although some was probably better) due to the excess of salt as a preservative. Smoking, chewing, and spitting of tobacco was so popular that evidence of the habit was hard to avoid. One had to step carefully. Alcohol consumption estimates for the period range from nearly four [14] to six gallons[15] per year per person. Most white children spent some time in school, but not nearly as much as they do today.[16] Some didn't go at all. Illiteracy was common. Teaching slaves to read and write was a serious crime. The classroom was occasionally a place of violence where teenage boys were sometimes known to beat up teachers and run them off. Public brawling was a vicious activity often erupting with an implicit attempt to cause permanent injury. Criminals were publicly flogged and maimed.[17] Public executions were festive occasions, drawing large crowds of enthusiastic gawkers.

And, tough as life was during these times, we musn't overlook that conditions were worse, much worse, for slaves. "Americans of the 18th century, from the top of the social system to the bottom, were less religious than we are today."[18] Political reality did not include African-Americans, Native Americans, or women. In 1796, Americans dreamed of better times.

1846

In 1846, James Polk was president. Abraham Lincoln was elected to Congress. Henry David Thoreau was living alone in the woods at Walden Pond, and Ralph Waldo Emerson was busy on the lecture circuit. The population stood at 22 million. America was at war with Mexico. Cities had grown nearly eightfold since 1796, but few would be considered urban in any modern sense of the word.[19,20] The rise of the middle class had ushered in what would later be called Victorian values, characterized as "a pose" by Robert M. Pirsig in his book *Lila*.[21] Victorianism, James Lincoln Collier writes, "was a revolution in thought, attitude, and manner which touched virtually every aspect of ordinary life."[22] Though regarded as a genteel model of refinement, Victorian values were in part a product of Freud's "narcissism of minor differences," an attempt to adopt standards of behavior which would distinguish the small but growing middle class from the ever-increasing influx of immigrants. [23]

But there was also a more positive aspect of Victorianism. Collier writes that "Victorianism was really about...order and decency."[24] It produced a movement of self-education and a focus on self-control and self-discipline. Victorianism resulted in improved personal hygiene and cleanliness in general. Homes and yards were better kept, neatness became fashionable. The emphasis on self-control caused alcohol consumption to drop to less than a gallon and a half per person per year.[25] There was movement toward genuine civility. Public executions were discontinued.[26] The amount of reading material available skyrocketed. In cities, ice boxes dramatically improved food storage for those who could afford them. Cookstoves and cookbooks were gaining popularity. Ready-made shoes and clothing were widely available. Attitudes about sex were changing—fewer pregnant brides appeared at the altar.

Barter was giving way to a cash economy, and with it the bonds of community were loosened.[27] During the next 150 years, this commercialization from human relations to market relationships would alter the associations of Americans from those focused on community to those increasingly dissipated in cyberspace. And yet, Victorian values were well suited to the proliferation of a conforming, organized workplace. Textile mills and factories were springing up everywhere, and with them came the 12-hour workday and an increasingly sharper division of two types of work: blue-collar and white-collar. The Morse telegraph created a communication revolution.[28] Medical practice improved, but only marginally. All this improvement on the cusp of the Civil War, which would be the bloodiest war in American history. Political reality still did not include African-Americans, Native Americans, or women, though the former dreamed of freedom and the latter of voting. In 1846, the great westward expansion was underway. Settlers envisaged new beginnings in lands of milk and honey. Manifest Destiny awaited.

1896

In 1896, William McKinley, running on a pro-business platform, defeated William Jennings Bryan in the presidential election. Grover Cleveland would finish the year in his final term as president. The country was in the grip of an economic depression. The frontier period of American history was itself history. The Indian wars were over, the buffalo herds were gone, and the great plains were settled. A ship could now cross the Atlantic in only a week.[29] The population had swelled to 75 million. My grandfather was seven years old. The industrialization of America was in full reign. Andrew Carnegie, Jay Gould, George Pullman, J.P. Morgan and John D. Rockefeller were cutting deals and creating empires. Thomas Alva Edison and George Westinghouse were locked in a battle to out-genuis one another. The telephone took the communication revolution to a level of frenzy which continues and escalates to this day. The incandescent lamp and the phonograph changed the reality of ordinary living. In the coming years, artificial lamplight would blot out the mystical awe of starlight.

The industrialization of the economy had produced a clear demarcation of haves versus have nots. And yet, the middle class was growing rapidly. The modern day corporation had arrived. The industrialization of work also created a sharp division between work and play. While play had been a built-in component of work in the agrarian economy—harvest time was a socially festive occasion—such was not so in the factory. As a result, for the first time, recreation for the masses became "an activity of its own, rather than...an adjunct to a task, a celebration."[30] Spontaneity was out. In the factory everyone worked 52 weeks per year.[31] Retail wars plagued the 1890s as small store owners complained that giant stores were driving them out of business—the same cry we hear today.[32]

People who broke the Victorian codes of behavior were suspected of being of inferior immigrant stock.[33] Victorians considered visual advertising to be a lowbrow activity; some thought that department store window displays were fraudulent and decadent because they promised things (goods out of season) which could not be delivered. [34]And yet, gawking was catching on. People began to anticipate new storefront offerings; crowds formed and sometimes broke into riots while waiting for the curtains to be removed from the latest shop window displays.[35] In the years to come, retailers would adopt the use of religious iconography to inspire Christmas buying.[36] The business of fashion was becoming the business of business. If the affluent, growing middle class could be persuaded to respond positively to fashion, if self-denial could be diminished, if having the latest products could become a necessity, then people would have to be perpetual customers in order to be seen as successful. Citizens would eventually be reduced to consumers. Buying on credit had been unheard of, lending for profit frowned on, but in 1896, Wanamaker's, a New York department store, opened 2500 charge accounts.[37]

The Civil War had ended slavery in Dixie, but oppression of terroristic proportions continued. On May 18, 1896, the U.S. Supreme Court upheld Plessy v. Ferguson, paving the way for an oppressive segregation which would reign with government sanction for 58 years. Throughout the South the lynching of black men would become so common that Mark Twain once referred to America as the "United States of Lyncherdom."[38]

Citizens were confused; rampant money-making was occurring in the industrial economy while farm families were growing poorer by the day. Corrupt government and the underhanded influence of special interests dominated political conversation. Efforts to create a third party (populist) smoldered with varying degrees of enthusiasm, but never quite caught fire. Except among the growing middle class, and even though an economic depression still held sway, there was a crisp sense of excitement in the air about a future rife with possibilities. Psychologist William James gave his address, "The Will to Believe," at Brown and Yale universities wherein he championed the power of the mind to create the kind of future it believed in.[39]

In 1896, seeds of the ethic of consumerism were taking root. And, for the adventurous soul, riches were a distinct possibility: gold was discovered in the Klondike. Self-denial would be on the wane until the Great Depression of the 1930s, which would bring the precept home to the American population with a vengeance. In 1896 Americans began to dream of a material prosperity barely imaginable a century earlier.

1946

In 1946, Harry Truman was president. I was 3 years old; my grandfather, 57. The population had doubled in 50 years to 150 million people. World War II, the war to end all wars, was over. The automobile, the two-week vacation, and the cross-cultural influence experienced overseas by formerly naïve servicemen brought a cataclysmic reshaping to everyday reality. The usual fear of a post-war economic downturn was overcome by pent-up demand; spending increased dramatically. During the war, 20 million American family victory gardens had produced one-third of the nation's vegetables.

A Cold War was beginning, which would waste an incomprehensible amount of natural and human resources during the next 50 years. Still, the dream of what it meant to be a successful American was gaining rapid consensus, and it had everything to do with ownership as status. But nothing in the twentieth century would overshadow the impact of commercial television beginning in 1946. Commercial television would become a major player in defining American Dreams.

1996

In 1996, William Jefferson Clinton was president. My grandfather had passed away 15 years earlier. I was 53, and my granddaughter was two years old. The population had grown to nearly 260 million. The history of 1796 was long forgotten. Out-of-wedlock births were occurring in 1996 as often as they had two hundred years before, although there was less advantage for the parents to marry. In 1996 politicians championed family values, but their policies failed to value families: married couples paid tax penalties for their union. Millions could not afford decent health care, and yet the professions were alarmed that there were too many doctors. The half-century from 1946 to 1996 saw a tremendous transfer of the tax burden from corporations to individuals, as paid lobbyists earned their keep peddling influence on Capitol Hill just as they had in 1896. In the early 1990s, the long-heralded promises of technological efficiency, stemming from the early days of the assembly line, began paying dividends by displacing industrial employees in the same way that agricultural workers were replaced in 1896. Shortly after the arrival of the desktop computer, millions of workers were downsized (fired) from good-paying jobs under the rubric of reengineering, while the growth of telecommunications emulated the heydays of the great railroad expansion. And, as it had a century before, a third-party populism smoldered with resentment.

In 1996, social critics lamented a loss of social capital (the common bond of community) which holds society together. Reasons for the perceived demise of community abounded: the "time is money" mind-set, welfare, the media, divorce, downsizing, social mobility, economic pressure, inadequate education, and the emergence of a global economy. There appeared to be no obvious explanation for the loss of community spirit, and yet few would say it hadn't lessened. What was clearly missing was the social-economic equity that once enabled people (though they worked very hard) to see that there was time enough to attend to the human needs of community. Prior to 1946, there were few latch-key children, and the elderly were not routinely warehoused in institutions. Census data tell us that in 1996 a third of all full-time jobs paid less than $20,000 per year.

In 1996, American politics revealed a conspicuous contempt for the poor, which in many cases betrayed a racially motivated hatred. Lost was virtually any historical recognition or even acknowledgment that the hard labor of impoverished slaves once lifted young America up by its agricultural bootstraps. If anyone of any race had made such a claim in public in 1796, 1896, or 1996 he or she would likely have incurred looks of incredulity befitting visitors from some distant planet.

Now, if you were to go back 50 years beyond my brief critique of history, to create your own essay for 1746, you might change your view of what America could, would, or should be about. Dig into details deep enough and you'll find a country permeated with social ferment bordering on anarchy, a country where, over time, thousands of homeless children have lived in the streets and back alleys, though these have escaped the popular texts of twentieth-century classroom history. My point is simple: Seeing through the veil of culture in the past is difficult without extraordinary effort, but if the past remains effectively obscured, the present is corrupt by design.

Until postmodern times, reviews of history such as this one generally conveyed a sense of struggle between opposing worldviews: one sacred—tribal, communial, organic, and holistic—with an emphasis on inner creativity and inspiration; the other centered on reason, enlightenment, objectivity, and logic with a focus on outer progress. The former is the romanticist or traditionalist worldview; the latter is the modernist or rejectionist perspective. In popular culture, we use the term left-brain right-brain to frame the issue, with little regard to its attenuated past. In his book *The Saturated Self*, psychology professor Kenneth J. Gergen puts this discrepancy in perspective:

> Largely from the nineteenth century, we have inherited a *romanticist* view of the self, one that attributes to each person characteristics of personal depth: passion, soul, creativity, and moral fiber. This vocabulary is essential to the formation of deeply committed relations, dedicated friendships, and life purposes. But since the rise of the *modernist* worldview beginning in the early twentieth century, the romantic vocabulary has been threatened.... As we enter the

postmodern era, all previous beliefs about the self are placed in jeopardy, and with them the patterns of action they sustain.... Postmodernism seems to the romanticist little short of nihilism: All intrinsic properties of the human being, along with moral worth and personal commitment, are lost from view, leaving nothing to believe in. Similarly, the modernist reviles the romanticist for sentimentalism, head-in-the-sand impracticality, and the replacement of objective decision making by highfalutin morality, while decrying postmodernism's threats to truth and objectivity. To give up these virtues, the modernist maintains, is to revert to medievalism, to open the culture to the tyrannies of rhetoric, to deny us the optimistic sense of progress, and to reduce life to so many parlor games.[40]

Today's ubiquitous use of the word postmodernism seems to be a complex effort to announce the simple conclusion that this cultural battle is over and that *there is no clear winner.* Reality suggests that today's American Dream has become the residue of media technology, that millions of us tune in for instructions on what to buy, wear, think about, and value—even what we should dream. Indeed, for now, we must take time to examine some current realities before we can delve further into dreams.

King of the Mountain

In spite of the fact that our economy is based on the dynamics of competition, we like to think of ourselves as a society noted for helping others. In many cases we do lend assistance, but the competitive nature of our economy is so strong, and our focus on winning so compelling, that we create a perpetual demand for a large number of losers. The need to keep our own progress in perspective means we must continually compare ourselves with the progress of others. Even those who may seek intellectually to help others can rarely do so without simultaneously feeling some sense of satisfaction and pride at having reached a decided advantage over those they are trying to help.

We are taught from birth that we are citizens of a democracy where equality of opportunity exists; we use the idea of merit to try to ensure equality of opportunity by measuring effort. The assumption is that effort leads to greater ability, and that as one's ability increases so does one's worth to society. Observers have termed this approach a "meritocracy."[41] Meritocracy and competition in America can be likened to a game of king of the mountain, a game you may remember playing as a child. Upon finding a hill or steep gravel pile, the first in the group to run to the top tries to keep others from reaching the top by pushing them back down. The first lesson the players learn is that it is far easier to keep others from reaching the top when you are there than it is to reach the top when the position is already occupied. A meritocracy acts in much the same manner, except that the methods of keeping people from reaching the top are less overt and not always consciously employed by those who are already there.

Imagine our whole social process being played out as a massive version of this game. You can visualize groups of people—from the street dwellers on the ground to the most influential leaders on top—occupying many ridges of relative comfort in between. The mountain is a hierarchy delineated with lines of class and authority, as though all of us were long-time members of a giant corporation.[42] Each level, regardless of how it is defined, bears its own style of speech, dress, labels, symbols, roles, social etiquette, and definitive behavioral codes that mark the boundaries demanded for membership.[43]

The history of culture suggests that, once humans assume an identity with a social class, the roots run so deep as to be analogous with the salmon imprinted at birth with instructions on where to die. Regardless of our levels of personal achievement, we humans carry the imprint of our social class with us to our graves. At the same time, however, the American Dream derives largely from the idea that anyone at the bottom can, through hard work and persistence, climb all the way to the top. Individual stories from the past and present show that a few people have always managed to do this, but the evidence also suggests that the level a person is born into is a better indicator of that person's ability to advance than any other.

Paradoxically, the higher the level of social position reached on the mountain, the more the people on that level seem blinded by the relative advantage of their position. For example, the middle class expects the bottom level to simply go out and get a job, failing to see the distinct advantage they themselves maintain through quality of education and social connections. The typical middle-class businessman tends to forget that Uncle John helped him get a plum job or loaned him the money to start a business. In time, he stops remembering such assistance entirely and concludes that he is where he is simply because of his own hard work. He sees himself as deserving while he sees those at lower economic levels as being lazy and undeserving.

The Race to the Top

The trouble with a meritocracy is that requirements are set as a means of measuring ability, and yet the process of meeting those qualifications is not in and of itself sufficient to prove ability. In other words, just because a person has completed the qualifying educational steps to become a teacher does not guarantee that the person will in fact be a good teacher.

The competitive nature of our society, the external need to qualify, has permeated so much of life in America that all aspects of life, school, work, and leisure are dominated by "results." There is a tendency not to engage in activities for their own sake. People whose motivation is primarily external anchor their existence on a pose, which is another way of saying that their existence is based on nonexistence. External motivation edges out intrinsic satisfaction. Life is punctuated by reaching plateaus which are not by themselves desirable—they exist only to prompt us to make the next move. In economic terms we focus on what we call the bottom line, but, when all is said and done, the bottom line is a hard place to live. It is nothing but an abstraction. When human beings become abstract they are devalued to the status of statistics.

Normally we don't think of competition as being antithetical to creativity because of the constant arrival of new products on the store shelves. On a different level, however, competition actually discourages creativity and encourages imitation. Individual sports competition is a case in point: because the risk of losing is too great, performance becomes confined to a narrow range of effort where people behave in pretty much the same way. The gymnast or figure skater doesn't want to be seen taking a risk which will upset the judges; conservative efforts minimize the possibility of great loss. Another example is the movie industry where producers prefer to use only the formulas they've already tested. Movie sequels substitute for innovation.

In America we think of competition and capitalism as being so closely related that they amount to the same thing, but the Japanese operate within a capitalistic economic structure which is based strongly on cooperation. American society is founded first on a *situational* or *structural* competition, which requires a win/lose proposition, and second on *intentional* competition, which simply reflects our attitudes about how competitive we are as individuals.[44] We grow up with a myriad of mixed messages about competition. When do we compete? How much is too much competition? Where do we draw the line between the profound need to think of ourselves as winners and the overt acts that will cause others to be losers? We are taught that competition builds character, but the evidence suggests that, more often than not, competition is antithetical to building character.[45] Crippled egos often require the crutch of prejudice to achieve, maintain, or justify status.

Our culture still considers the word "struggle" to be synonymous with competition, as in a species' struggle for survival, but recent data clearly suggest the two are not the same.[46] Struggle and survival appear to depend much more on cooperation than on competition. For example, we think of our own history of the American West as a telling model of competitive struggle and triumph, but in fact the frontier was profoundly cooperative in practice. Frontier families shared their labor and crops with others in a strong communal sense.

Failure to understand the inherent nature of competition is a significant barrier to solving many of our social problems. The problem of "homelessness" and misconceptions about competition in America amount to a general contempt for the homeless because they appear to be poor competitors. An old-fashioned home or shelter raising for the homeless would seem socialistic to some, but our history shows it to be an American thing to do: neighbor helping neighbor.

When real life experience is very different from what we have come to believe, an objective understanding of competition is necessary to keep one's well-being and self-esteem in proper perspective. What we think of ourselves as people strongly depends on what we believe about the nature of competition and how we see ourselves functioning as competitors. The lesson we must learn about competition is profoundly simple: competition is a means and not an end. If the race to the top of the mountain consumes the climber, the trip is not worthwhile.

Merit and Value

The drive to prove merit often blinds us to the intrinsic value of education. The need to be seen as qualified, and thus deserving, has so externalized higher education in America that credentials take on the attributes of admission tickets or passports. You can be incompetent and get a good job as long as you have a degree, but in many fields of work you can be extremely talented and never get an opportunity to prove it if you are degreeless. (Fortunately, in many disciplines the current velocity of technological change, combined with increased competition, is changing this situation dramatically.) The need to qualify is so overwhelming that millions of people never understand their individual rights in the context of what it means to be a citizen. The only value they can relate to is economic. Hierarchical economic power distorts perceptions of value. If only economically powerful people are viewed as successful, then only rich people have the capacity to define value.

Education for the sake of better understanding life could mitigate the tendency to base our self-esteem on the perpetual need to win or to prove our worth through consumption. In other words, a liberal education that goes far beyond economics can lead us to discover we have "value" based on who we are, not on what we do or how much we spend. But such is our system of extrinsic rewards that we habitually favor action over inactivity which might be attributed to thinking. We focus on answers in school but spend little time developing the ability to think critically and independently. The call for action is so pronounced that even to be associated with a thinking profession such as teaching is to many people contemptible. Professors don't do, goes the logic, they think. What could they possibly know without practical experience?

Most people will agree that a meritocracy is a fair description of what we are attempting with our elaborate educational system, but there is little agreement about how we actually create a meritocracy. We spend billions of dollars to qualify people for employment with little emphasis given to demonstrated ability other than the use of short-term memory. People whose educational credentials allow them the franchise of a profession form professional associations, and then these groups begin to lean toward restricting entry into the profession instead of holding their members to professional standards. The field of medicine is a case in point. Television news magazines repeatedly feature doctors who have harmed scores of patients and still practice medicine, even after their exploits have become nationally known. The reason corrective action is seldom taken in these cases is not that proof of incompetence is hard to find, but that one can't delve very far into this subject without threatening the very foundation of the way credentials are awarded in the first place.

Here, our education system strikes a parallel with the king-of-the-mountain game in our economic structure. When the bonds of loyalty get wrapped up in borrowed opinion, formally educated people assume a posture of expectation and a sense of privileged status based on what they have been exposed to rather than what they can do in actual practice. Likewise, competent people without degrees feel guilty for not having been exposed to a classroom exercise, even if their expertise clearly demonstrates the exercise wasn't necessary. Put differently, a degree, no matter how remotely related to the task at hand, can entitle the holder to perform that job poorly, while someone without a degree but with demonstrated competence is prevented from doing the job at all.

When we put credentials and competition in perspective by stripping away the mystique, it becomes easy to see that much of what passes for meritocracy is really a simple, though expensive, means of maintaining an advantage. Many competent people judge themselves harshly because they lack credentials which are arbitrary and have nothing to do with their work. Perhaps the greatest error we make, however, is that we are so focused on the hierarchical structure of our society, so caught up in what we construe to be the game of life, that we concentrate on the finger instead of where it points. We mistake form for substance, means for ends. Thus, it's not surprising that our system for determining merit is a greater measure of economic power than it is of competence.

Through all of history we have held men and women in high esteem because of their adherence to principles, yet today we measure their success primarily by the size of their pocketbooks or the prominence of their credentials. As long as our economic system holds precedence over our most cherished ideals, we have little hope of achieving anything that might resemble genuine progress. As long as we live in the shadow of a king-of-the-mountain society, where external motivation obliterates the desire to discover what we really care about—so much so that we remain convinced contentment is only for cows—we learn how to *do*, but not how to *be*. We lose sight of how to find purpose and meaning in the context of our daily lives.

In the movie classic *Doctor Zhivago*, Yurii Andreievich (played by Omar Sharif), is making his way to a country dacha to be with his family and escape the political strife of the Bolshevik Revolution when he is stopped and asked what he and his family will do once they get there. He replies, "Just live." This was an ideological answer frowned upon in both communist and capitalistic countries, because to not appear to be striving toward some external aspiration does not acknowledge the authority of the person or party in power at the time. But, to my mind, "just living" is not a lowly ambition—unless one does it poorly. Contentment poses a threat to a consumer-driven society, but being content, as we shall see, necessarily involves a willingness to take responsibility.

Evaluation of Worth

Surely the external thrust of our economically obsessed culture helps to manufacture the prejudice that enables Americans to sit idly by while millions of dark-skinned people in the world slowly starve to death. It keeps us from becoming concerned enough to use our political influence to make certain that worldwide food problems are solved. If the world were sufficiently outraged, death from starvation would disappear.

The picture becomes more complicated than it seems because of our tendency to favor *doing* over *thinking*. I am fascinated by the fact that our society prefers action to the extent that incorrect action will allow for forgiveness, but inaction based on thinking through an issue (with a subsequent conclusion that no action should be taken) is scorned. Because the people who are starving to death are not seen as doers, they have no value as beings in our view. But if these people were highly literate, they would qualify as thinkers; we could not help but see them differently, even though they weren't doers. Imagine the difference in public perception if starving Ethiopians or Somalis were featured on television discussing economic theory and making eloquent pleas for assistance. Without being consciously aware that we were attributing value to the thinking side of humanity, we would recognize that these people have value. They would be human beings instead of having the non-being status they've been relegated to. (This image is so disturbing and so uncomfortable that I have excised it from this text numerous times, but it is such an important point that I always feel compelled to put it back in.) Now, contrast the "reality of human starvation" and the "reality of political power" with the fact that in recent years several American companies have been successfully marketing diet pet food. Surely it suggests too much doing somewhere and too little thinking.

Or, consider the problem of doing versus thinking in another context. Viewed in terms of economics, it appears that if resources (which represent doing) are scarce, then conservation (which represents thinking) should have a value equal to—or, in most cases, greater than—consumption. Simply put, thinking provides a significant portion of the vision required to sustain humanity; societies that lose their sense of purpose cease to exist. Thinking is the stuff dreams are made of. One might argue that it is possible to reason and come up with a poor sense of purpose, but almost any effort at all beats a system driven by appetite alone.

Thomas Jefferson envisioned a nation where independence would be the very essence of liberty, a state which would clearly require as much emphasis on thinking as on doing. The evidence overwhelmingly suggests that we have internalized the philosophical values of our economic system to the exclusion of humanity, in that we value human doings but not human beings. We have "replaced culture with wealth."[47] Our economic king-of-the-mountain ethos has become the basis of ultimate value, supplanting and proving eminently more forceful than the role once held by religion.

Medical heroics are a good example of our bias for action versus not thinking things through. Doctors save brain-dead people from dying while able-bodied people die from lack of medical treatment. The heroic action involved in reviving a drowning victim who has suffered severe brain damage is far easier to deal with than drawing the line on treatment, pulling the plug on a respirator, or figuring out how to provide poor people with medical care. Think about the value that is lost. Our culture attributes so much value to the ideology of freedom that we are thoughtless during the times when evaluating worth ought to be most critical. If someone attempts suicide in public, the full weight of the law will be used to see that the person is kept alive. Yet, if someone with no health insurance desperately needs an operation, that person will be allowed to die quietly.

Now, what if we ripped away the veil, let the rabbit out of the hat, and just for a moment pretended that thinking *is* doing! Value assumes a new identity and the whole world looks different: Thinking is suddenly important. Ambiguity is no longer scorned and avoided. The necessities of life change. There is an immediate shift from a psychology of scarcity to a psychology of abundance. Life becomes a university. Thinking something through now has a value all its own. Human beings have value. We immediately begin to emulate those whom we have long celebrated for being wise (almost everyone respects Socrates for this reason, but few have aspired to develop his wisdom). Imagine what kind of society we would have today if thinking had always held a position on a par with the concept of hard work. What kind of decisions would such values yield? The search for truth by examining our most cherished beliefs would become not only a common, natural thing to do, it would be expected.

Mountain Fever

Our game of king of the mountain embodies seldom acknowledged cultural aspirations. One is reminiscent of an observation by Ernest Becker in *The Denial of Death:*

> When we appreciate how natural it is for man to strive to be a hero, how deeply it goes in his evolutionary and organismic constitution, how openly he shows it as a child, then it is all the more curious how ignorant most of us are, consciously, of what we really want and need. In our culture anyway, especially in modern times, the heroic seems too big for us, or we too small for it. Tell a young man that he is entitled to be a hero and he will blush. We disguise our struggle by piling up figures in a bank book to reflect privately our sense of heroic worth. Or by having only a little better home in the neighborhood, a bigger car, brighter children. But underneath throbs the ache of cosmic specialness, no matter how we mask it in concerns of smaller scope.[48]

Most of us come closest to realizing this need by the simple societal tug to "be somebody." In *Realty Isn't What It Used To Be*, Walter Truett Anderson makes this point in his description of Lee Harvey Oswald's mother in an interview with reporters.

> She told the press: "I am an important person. I will be remembered." Mrs. Oswald was not trying to get any laws passed, and she was not crazy....She knew that once she was part of the immense story that was unfolding on millions of TV screens ... she would be *real*. She would have met the requirement the modern era imposed on us all—the demand that we be somebody. And she understood that the more people there are who think you are somebody, the more somebody you are.[49]

Anderson continues:

> We all live now in the political theater, but we have no ethic for it and little real understanding of what we can accomplish in it or what it does to us. And all we know for sure

about our leaders—left, right, or center—is that they have managed to get good speaking parts.[50]

It's debatable whether this need to be a hero or somebody important is inborn, a result of our culture, or another way of dealing with our mortality, but we cannot deny that our culture exacerbates the tendency. Millions of people define themselves solely by the king-of-the-mountain ethos or external nature of our society. Indeed, the most common form of mountain fever is born of the daily struggle to succeed. In his book *Going Nowhere Fast*, psychologist Melvyn Kinder writes:

> I find many people acting on the assumptions that life is a series of self-improvements, the sum total of which is equated with happiness. But when we attempt to find happiness in this way, we engage in a never-ending quest that subtly and inevitably makes us even more unhappy! What starts out as a positive attempt to better our lives, gradually and insidiously grows negative and psychologically toxic. It seems the harder we try to achieve fulfillment, the more we are driven by the fear of not reaching these goals. We end up frustrated, going nowhere fast.[51]

Kinder continues:

> We are blindly and dangerously pursuing happiness without, perhaps, understanding what it is. Happiness is not about having what you want, but wanting what we have. In many ways, happiness is within us waiting to be discovered. But this message is one that most of us fail to recognize or at best realize later than is necessary. Instead of peace of mind, we've learned the language of pursuit and unceasing self-improvement.[52]

Mountain fever is the phenomenon that causes millions of people to shop without specific regard to goods, but as a substitute for loneliness or a way to alleviate boredom. John Dewey said, "I own, therefore I am," expressing a truer psychology than the Cartesian "I think, therefore I am."[53]

Runaway mountain fever leads to a vicious confusion over self-worth and one's ability to consume. Plato argued that "poverty consists, not in the decrease of one's possessions, but in the increase of one's greed." And, in *Our Kind*, Marvin Harris characterizes the plight of the yuppies, a special breed of consumer first identified in the 1980s:

> Yuppies are much maligned because their purchasing of symbols of wealth and power is not another example of a weird propensity to emulate at any cost. Rather, it is an unrelenting condition of success imposed from above in a society where wealth and power depend on mass consumption. Only people who prove themselves legal to the ethos of consumerism are admitted to the higher circles of consumer society. For upwardly mobile youth (or even for youth who merely wish not to fall to lower social ranks), conspicuous consumption is less a benefit than a cost of success.[54]

A friend of mine suggested that when a person is living on automatic pilot and catches mountain fever the result is, "Stockpile, stockpile, stockpile, oops: death." Without a thorough investment in introspection and reflection, few are immune from mountain fever or are ready for the next step of reaching for purpose and meaning instead of higher ground. Eric Hoffer has pointed out that "our frustration is greater when we have much and want more than when we have nothing and want some."[55] The mid-range on our king-of-the-mountain model reveals a middle class held together not so much by a common bond as through a shared fear of falling off the mountain and ending up with nothing. The Ethiopians, Somalis, and Rwandans seem to embody the consequences of such a fall, even if there is no such reality in America. Mountain fever is epidemic when the ethos of consumption coalesces with the Romantic notion of the self as "infinite possibility: the unending search for new and intense experiences."[56] In *The Culture of Cynicism*, Richard Stivers explains:

> When life-style is reduced to consumption, the consumption of life-style becomes the consumption of consumption. This represents consumption taken to its logical and absurd conclusion....In any society where consumption becomes an end in itself, the meaning of life, the human being is persuaded to become an image/object. This happens in two ways. First, there is an implicit pantheism in the rhetoric of

consumption: I become what I consume; the powers of the objects of consumption become my powers. Second, the reified human being becomes a mere role player who puts himself on display for others to consume. [57]

Climbing Strategies

Getting to the top in a king-of-the-mountain society requires some know-how and some know-who. Appearance is important. To begin one's ascent the need to fit in is intense. It helps tremendously if one can speak and dress the part one seeks. Sometimes we are hesitant to admit that the need can be so formidable. We attempt to place emphasis on skill and competence, but the need to fit in drives people all over the world to develop accents like the specific groups of people with whom they want to associate.

Don't misunderstand my message here. I'm not saying our purpose in life should always be to fit in. On the contrary, I believe that differences give rise to quality, but if you are going to climb the mountain economically you have to understand how the game is played. If you expect to overcome resistance, you must anticipate and understand it. Posture in this context is simply your action based on an assessment of your place on the mountain.

Another subtle way to appreciate how pervasively we want to be "like" and not unlike those in our immediate group is to watch old television shows and notice how strange everyone looks. Fashion is the lace of conformity. The players' hairstyles, their clothing, and even their choice of words may seem strange in comparison to the way we dress and talk today. We don't see the impetus behind the acceptability of current styles, yet the power exists with such a force that it makes the hierarchical structure of king of the mountain seem absolutely normal. Such subtleties are not observable at all except when contrasted with different times.

The most vivid example of the external nature of our culture is found in the phenomenon of the beauty pageant. Everything the contestants say and do is based upon what they think the judges want to hear and see. So, in a sense, the winners are, by definition, those who can best prove that as individuals they do not exist. The winner, who has no individuality, is presented as the "most real" individual, and the losers, who were less adept at shaking their individuality, will feel they do not exist because they did not win. In other words, the cultural ethos we adopt in order to function successfully within an economic hierarchy has its own special incentive for making things as they are seem right. Moreover, it is our collective misfortune that prejudice is the most common gauge for checking one's progress during the climb—when altitude is so important, there must be people one can be above.

The focus on status and advantage compels us to pay three times as much for a shirt, or fifty to a hundred times as much for a watch, not because the shirt is better or the watch keeps better time, but because the labels make us appear more successful than those who wear less prestigious brands. This behavior indicates we have internalized the values of our economic system, and thereby have failed to discover the wisdom associated with learning how to live better. Our prejudices and comparative levels of advantage, offset by manic stress, suggest that we are missing more than we lay claim to, or as William James pointed out at the turn of the century, "Lives based on having are less free than lives based on doing or being."

Delusions at High Altitude

Traditional pedagogical schooling about merit and the dynamics of democracy, combined with religious beliefs that separate one group from another, causes millions of people to consciously or unconsciously assume a "just world" attitude. Translated, this means the belief that everyone is pretty much where they belong, and the fault is theirs if they are on the bottom.[58] Believing in a just world is significantly more convenient than examining issues on their own merit. And, although it is to be expected from an educational system that favors mere exposure over mastery and continued inquiry, the just world attitude is a major source of our social ills. It amounts to saying that the misfortune of others is a natural occurrence, or that people who have little have what they deserve, which justifies not checking to see if the premise is really true. John Stuart Mill despised this human tendency. He said, "Of all the vulgar modes of escaping from the consideration of the effect of social and moral influences upon the human mind, the most vulgar is that of attributing the diversities of conduct and character to inherent natural differences." Add a just world attitude to the king-of-the-mountain ethos, and you discover a society that says, if you are not naturally lucky, then you are unworthy of economic assistance. A prime example of this attitude can be found in the history of the American health insurance industry. For decades millions of Americans covered by private health insurance were under the illusion that they were medically secure (many still are), but when they became really sick, their insurance policies were canceled.

In a competition-based society, it is important to understand that when people reach higher levels of success, the impetus quickly changes—the joy of reaching the top gives way to the burden of staying on top. The problem of the game of king of the mountain is exacerbated by the ability of all participants, regardless of their place on the mountain, to see the summit, while invisible glass ceilings of prejudice form obstacles to ascending. For some this adds to a growing sense that they are where they belong, but for others it is a constant source of frustration and resentment. We are a long way from equal opportunity in America, even though we often speak as if it already exists. When large numbers of people are engaged in a struggle for survival, their reaction to the advance of those who are approaching their own level is a posture based on selfishness. Blinded by their own advantage, full of justification for being where they are, they offer a multitude of reasons for keeping others at a distance while simultaneously holding them in contempt for being at a lower level. People born into families in a relatively high position on the mountain cannot remember the climb, but they will adamantly argue that they are where they deserve to be.

When I look at the mountain as a metaphor for American society and consider the problem of balancing equity and efficiency, I cannot help but think that if the foundation of the mountain is weak, the whole structure is weakened. If people are really the backbone of society, then it stands to reason that in total we are only as strong as our weakest members. It's ironic that the jobs performed by the working people at the bottom of society are those that absolutely must be done in order to make life livable. The term "working poor" should be an oxymoron; it shouldn't exist. It seems to me a self-evident proposition that the desire of any people to form a government should include systems within which the basic human needs of its citizens are met as an elementary matter of course.

The franchise that enables business to operate freely within society is indebted to society for its very existence. Simply stated, this means that the "haves" of society have a vested interest in seeing that we are all "haves" as a means of self-preservation. Strengthen the foundation, and you ensure the stability of the structure itself.

Life at the Bottom of the Mountain

Understanding life at the bottom of the mountain is a requisite to understanding society itself. Many people (I used to be one of them) argue for the necessity of a shame-based welfare system in order to discourage people from accepting welfare. And, indeed, evolutionary psychology argues persuasively that social pressure shapes behavior. But such logic, as it pertains to social welfare in our king-of-the-mountain economic system, would assume the protection of the state of agriculture by ensuring the availability of depleted soil for future planting. Humans need to develop in a rich environment in much the same way that plants do. Plants extract nutrients from soil. Children measure their own self-worth by their surroundings. If their neighborhood is a shambles, their sense of self-worth is adversely affected. Substandard education compounds the problem. Speak eloquently about valuing human beings, in the next breath howl about the chance that someone may get something for nothing, and simultaneously demonstrate a willingness to spend more to keep people in prison than to send the poor to school, and you franchise poverty at the bottom of the mountain as surely as if you meant to do so.

People who are conditioned to receiving recognition only when they do certain things can't relate to unconditional acceptance. The very thought that someone could get something for nothing has become a deeply disturbing notion. It is ironic that people at the very top of the mountain economically have a lot in common with people at the very bottom: they are likely to be sustained by their money alone, doing very little in actual practice for their keep.[59]

I am not suggesting that we give something for nothing, but that we rethink the nature of the investment. Investment against poverty is capital for the public interest. Poverty debases capitalism as slavery does labor. Both subordinate human worth to commodities. Poverty diminishes the well-to-do, just as it does those who are most affected by it. People who cannot see beyond their own economic interests are bound like prisoners; worse, they fail to understand that their own interests when pushed to an extreme become a liability. An economic system created by people to protect their interest above and beyond that which exists in a state of nature (without some form of government) should rightfully be expected to maintain its original level of quality. It should never depreciate to such a point that normal functioning allows a large portion of its citizens to be perpetually without benefit of the equity intended—a situation reminiscent of the need that brought the association of people together to form a government in the first place.[60] In his book *A Dream Deferred*, Philip Slater adds perspective to this problem:

> Since the Bushman—one of the most economically marginal hunter-gather societies on the planet—managed to feed, shelter, and care for the nonproductive segment of their population (about 40 percent of the total) without complaining about "freeloaders" and "welfare cheats," it seems reasonable to say that any society unable to perform as well as this for its nonproductive members is a very inferior society. Few so-called primitive societies would allow any of their members to starve when food was plentiful. A society that does this is simply not doing its job. Societies exist for the benefit of all. They do not exist for the sole purpose of making a few neurotically needy people very wealthy. Surely we can envision worthier goals than this.[61]

It is strange that American society views people near the bottom of the mountain as being lazy and shiftless, even if they belong to the class of working poor. By contrast, people in the lower castes of India are considered industrious and hardworking.[62] It is even more of a mystery how we can extol duty and sacrifice as honorable American traits, fully aware that in wartime soldiers from near the bottom of the mountain always outnumber those from the upper levels.

The greatest con of the twentieth century is how those at the top of the economic mountain have convinced those in the middle that those at the bottom are the ones who keep them from moving higher. (A significant percentage of the middle class blames the poor for their own poverty.) In some individual cases this is undoubtedly true, but to declare such an assertion in general is the same as claiming the car behind you prevents you from passing the one in front of you. "It seems to be a defect in the human imagination that we always bite at the stick that hits us instead of at the hand that holds it."[63] No question, the rising cost of aid to the poor is a burden on the economy. But providing jobs for the poor requires the effort and consensus of those who are already out front. The creation of jobs presupposes wealth. Moreover, the amount of welfare paid to the poor pales in comparison to the subtle subsidies given to the wealthy under the guise of investments. In short, the psychic hydraulics of a king-of-the-mountain society depend upon the negative emotions of contempt and resentment. The former for those above, the latter for those below.

We like to think of ourselves as a classless society, but we are incredibly astute at recognizing boundaries of class. Children internalize standards about normalcy faster than they acquire language. Prejudice and bigotry franchise the trappings of class in much the same way that degrees having little to do with ability franchise opportunity. Moreover, of all subjects taught, hate is most easily learned, which is why bigotry and prejudice play such an important role when it comes to characterizing people who live at the bottom of the mountain.

Deep down at the baseline of mountain fever lies an assumption so fundamental and so taken for granted that it might be considered dormant were it not so hyperactively applicable. It constitutes the heart and perhaps the soul of the American Dream. It is what Michael Lewis characterized as "the individual-as-central sensibility." In *The Culture of Inequality* he writes:

Inequality in American life has come to be understood in light of what I have called the individual-as-central sensibility, according to which one's status and perquisites are perceived as functions of personal attributes, personal morality or immorality on the one hand and personal competence or incompetence on the other. The individual-as-central sensibility, in its hegemony over the American imagination, may free many people from social restrictions of arbitrary ascription, but in doing so it engenders widespread anxiety about the extent of one's personal achievement compared to one's aspirations. The threat to self posed by this aspiration-achievement disparity is a significantly troubling preoccupation in American society. Ultimately, it makes necessary pariahs of the disinherited—the poor, the non-white, the criminal. In the attempt to manage out of existence the threat posed by the aspiration-achievement disparity, many Americans come to view their worthiness in contradistinction to the presumed unworthiness of the disinherited. Invoking the individual-as-central sensibility—the very same sensibility that has engendered the threat to the self—many Americans make of their commonplace successes praiseworthy achievements by viewing disadvantage as the just dessert for insufficient effort born of moral infirmity or incompetence. In doing so they invest in the maintenance of inequality in American society and particularly in the perpetuation of an under-class of objectionables. In doing so they help to maintain those social problems associated with the existence of this under-class. Protestations to the contrary notwithstanding, for the many who are threatened by the aspiration-achievement disparity these problems are themselves a comfort—an indication of the insufficiencies of others to which they might also have fallen prey, but which they have, through their own praiseworthy efforts, avoided. Ultimately, the culture of inequality in American life is a closed and self-fulfilling system. It creates psychological need which only the invocation of its basic premise—the individualization of success and failure—can serve. It is sustained by the very trouble it creates.[64]

We have already witnessed the psychic price we pay for the individual-as-central sensibility through our discussion of the effects of mountain fever. People who are infected with mountain fever do not take time to create dreams of their own. Even if they did, and if their dreams came true, they would be unable to recognize them.

Although it may offer opportunity for great numbers of people, a king-of-the-mountain society is oppressive by design. Within it, the only goal of the oppressed is to become oppressors themselves, whether they realize it or not. That's a far cry from our common conception of the American Dream, and it's time our priorities shifted. The missing crucial element is *principled radical awareness*, which can lead individuals to a greater understanding of themselves and of the culture around them. Where would we be today, if aspiring to such awareness had been the object of our dreams all along? Better to ask how we can begin moving in that direction now and create new dreams for the future. The rest of this book is devoted to answering that question.

Chapter Two

Conquering Mountains

Understanding is a kind of ecstasy.[1]
—*Carl Sagan*

The Other Side of the Mountain

Conquering metaphorical mountains by finding meaning on the other side is easy in theory, but hard in practice. What it really means is conquering one's culture. It means cutting through social fabric—hearing, seeing, and thinking for ourselves. It is true, but seldom acknowledged, that we find meaning for what we call the inner life by expanding our awareness of the outer life. Spinoza put it this way, "The more we understand individual objects, the more we understand God."[2] Were it not for the trappings of culture, we would realize that science and religion do not have to be enemies to each other and that economic success does not have to be the main point of life. Culture is made up. Culture is education. Culture is science and religion. Any culture which smothers inquiry sows the seeds of its own ultimate destruction.

The trail to the other side of the mountain has been blazed by people who knew that escaping the bonds of society is inherently more important than moving from one ridge of status to the next. Thoreau took a shortcut to a higher place of meaning through the realization that, by being outside the external trappings of modern life, he was in fact at the pinnacle of his own existence. Emerson argued that a rich man was someone who had simple needs and could fill them himself.[3]

37

People often reject the external thrust of society during the period commonly referred to as midlife crisis. This life phase is a juncture of mixed circumstances for many people, but, for others, it simply amounts to the accumulation of enough conflicting life experiences that a person suddenly attains a new ability to see more clearly. Priorities change—what is truly important stands out and is usually associated with internal satisfaction instead of the external push to move up in status.

Stephen R. Covey, author of *The Seven Habits of Highly Effective People*, offers a cogent synthesis of this phenomenon as a process of maturity in which one goes from dependence to independence to interdependence. Covey's examination of success in the past 200 years suggests that the first 150 focused on the *character ethic*. In contrast, the last 50 years have focused on the *personality ethic*.[4] The character ethic is based on the Victorian principles that unite humanity: wisdom, honesty, integrity, humility, fidelity, temperance, patience, courage, fairness, justice, and modesty. (Abraham Maslow referred to these principles as Being Values.[5]) The personality ethic, on the other hand, implies that a quick motivational fix or an attitude adjustment is all that is needed to achieve a higher quality of life.[6]

I believe that the personality ethic goes deeper than this, that it is an internalization of the values of our economic system. Moreover, once one adopts this value system, one cannot help but be dependent, even though the intent is the opposite. Covey argues that "dependent people cannot choose to become interdependent. They don't have the character to do it, they don't own enough of themselves."[7] Focusing on technique without principle is like building walls without a foundation. Principle is most commonly defined as a comprehensive and fundamental law, assumption, or doctrine. Covey also says principles are not maps, but the territory itself.[8] I strongly disagree: Territory is inert. Principle is alive and apprehending. I use the term *principle* not as a notion of absolutes but as a stage of awareness, a lucid participation in the formation of one's experience, a consciously attentive intimacy, an intellectual honesty, a concern for apprehending reality to the best of one's ability, an all-encompassing familiarity, like Emerson's "instructed eye."[9] In short, principle is a willingness to *think* and not simply to act as though one is infected with a virus of shoulds and oughts passed down through the culture.

The key or essence of principle is found in the word *comprehensive*. Comprehension requires involvement through understanding—it summons responsibility. But technique, which is little more than method, requires only obedience. When technique overrides principle, heroes are replaced by celebrities. In Victorian times heroes exemplified virtue. People were admired on the basis of their character. In little more than a half-century the emphasis changed to what one has or owns, even if it's only the spotlight of attention. Today, celebrities are celebrities because they are celebrities. When technique is more important than principle in business, marketing takes precedence over product quality.

Imagine a mirror image or shadow of the mountain where we play our king-of-the-mountain game. Picture it as containing a neon-lighted version of Abraham Maslow's famous hierarchy of needs. At the bottom are the physiological needs: food, clothing, and shelter. Above those are the needs for safety and security, followed by the social needs for love and belonging, and above these are the need for self-esteem, self-respect, recognition, and social status. At the top is the need for self-actualization. Maslow argued that these needs exist in an imprecise hierarchy, but are satisfied in a hierarchical fashion. So it should be apparent that the shadow cast from the king-of-the-mountain game is consistently congruent with the game itself. People at the bottom of the mountain are dominated by the lower-level needs; people near the middle are concerned with social needs (love and belonging), while people closer to the top are preoccupied with the need for recognition and prestige.

This is not to say there are none at or near the top who give tirelessly of themselves; there are many examples of those who do. Likewise many near the top conduct themselves in ways which suggest they are above petty concerns. Maslow noted that people who are at or near the point he called self-actualization produce an almost synergistic effect toward valuing the needs of others. This is the point where real "spiritedness" kicks in. Perhaps the whole enterprise of educational psychology would have been different if Maslow had used a term like *intensified learning*, to describe this level instead of self-actualization. After all, Maslow argued that people who have achieved self-actualization have in fact learned, understood, and re-understood to such a degree that they have a clearer view of reality.[10]

When we compare our economic mountain with Maslow's hierarchy of needs, education and politics become obvious shortcuts to power. They are keys to putting this game into perspective so that, by thoroughly understanding the rules, one can win when it's important to win or when appropriate, by not playing at all. In other words, education enables us to understand the nature of our needs and to become less intimidated and controlled by them. But we seldom realize that self-mastery also means cultural mastery. Sometimes this results in the realization that goals we have been seeking are not worthy of our efforts. A large share of self-help material on the market during the past three decades amounts to little more than advanced rules for playing king of the mountain. The game itself creates a state of dependence which relies on attitude adjustments, performance tactics, and questions of *how* but not *why*. The players, by their participation, are simply admitting that the game plays the player, not the reverse. In other words, economic worth equals self-worth.

In a state of independence one learns to play by one's own rules. In a state of interdependence one learns that the rules that support humanity provide the foundation for one's own support. In *The Dual Brain, Religion, and the Unconscious*, Sim C. Liddon wrote:

> ...what becomes a person's main concern—the "ultimate concern"—is a reflection of the meaning that that person finds in his own life, which is to say it is a function of the world or cosmic view in which the individual conceives himself (herself) to be embedded. For Jung, it is only when individuals see themselves in relation to the infinite, when the "whole" of which they are a part is something infinite, that they find a meaning to life that is of "real importance."[11]

Finally, consider how complicated life becomes when millions of us play a desperate competitive social game without enough self-knowledge to know when we have won. It is ironic that when people in a competition-based society become secure (when they no longer fear falling to a lower level) because they have their own needs satisfied, they become more sensitive toward the needs of others. It often appears as if the opposite is true—that people who become more successful become more selfish. But people who appear to become more selfish haven't really satisfied their own needs. Their success becomes a means of gaining recognition, a recognition that will be lost if it does not continue; more recognition only increases the anxiety that at some point it may be lost.

Indeed, if the slopes of our mountain were not so steep or the fall not so treacherous, our system might be automatically self-nurturing. It would be both natural and normal for each of us to share a genuine concern for others. (Small, so-called primitive tribes of people share such concern for each other without question or deliberation.) But instead of those above showing an automatic concern for those still below, the middle fears the bottom and the top despises both. Imagine the possibilities for humankind if our educational system routinely produced people who were so secure with themselves that their pursuit of goodness originated from its own account, people who were not only unintimidated by divisions of class, but felt no need to be above someone else.

Purpose and Meaning vs. High Ground

There are many well-known hierarchical models depicting the human condition which fit with the king-of-the-mountain metaphor. They represent the thinking of Lawrence Kohlberg, Abraham Maslow, Erik Erickson, Jean Piaget, William Perry, Edward Deci, the VALS typology, and a myriad of similar Eastern and Western theories.[12] These models suggest three definitive spheres of social reality in America: the first being the bottom of the mountain, then the king of the mountain, followed by the other side of the mountain.

At the bottom of the mountain, people are driven by circumstances. They are locked into a time orientation of the present, expecting little in a future offset by a past not worth remembering. To use a fairy tale metaphor, people here are eaten by dragons. Religion is often the last or only hope. The popular term most commonly used for the people of this sphere is "losers." There are no heroes at this level.

The king-of-the-mountain sphere is driven by rules and laws. It is fueled by social approval and spins with conformity. The time orientation is past and future. The present is often denied, in large part because there is too little time for reflection. The fundamental approach to life at this level is to play by the rules, to use willpower and technique to win, and to win at any cost. People who thrive in this sphere invariably interpret the actions of others in terms of their own rules. For example, if they were to hear a modern-day Gandhi speak of equality, they would become suspicious and would want to know his bottom line. People in this sphere are adept at specialization; they focus on parts and destinations. They are concerned with short-term results. Religion in this sphere concentrates on rules and behavior. Technique, with a key emphasis on manipulation, is a core value. People in this sphere slay dragons and call themselves "winners." They may make significant contributions to society, but they primarily maintain their status by piling up more than they pass on, which is, after all, how they climbed to the top in the first place. Donald Trump could be called a hero in the game of king of the mountain.

The people on the other side of the mountain are noticeably out of sync with the status quo. People who have achieved financial success can prescribe rules for imitating their accomplishments, but people who live by principles inspire others to discover similar values for themselves. To follow rules is to obey. "People who lead a satisfying life, who are in tune with their past and with their future—in short, people whom we would call "happy"—are generally individuals who have lived their lives according to rules they themselves created."[13] To take actions based upon principles is to make decisions based upon an attentive awareness; a rule book is not necessary. Here, we have a commitment to truth, wisdom, and understanding, independent of a felt need to win. The focus is on wholes. The time orientation is past, present, and future with the long-term taking precedence over the short-term. Religions are observed at this level nearest the level on which they were founded. That is, the original principles remain more important than the bureaucracy of the church. People of this sphere see through dragons. Whereas in the other two spheres people are referred to as winners and losers, there is no agreed-upon name for those who derive purpose and meaning from the other side of the mountain. Indeed, most people remain unaware that a metaphoric "other side of the mountain" exists for the ordinary person. They reserve such acknowledgment for those whom we celebrate at this plane, heroes like Socrates, Spinoza, Lincoln, Gandhi, Jefferson, Emerson, Thoreau, Wallenberg, and King.[14]

Though each of these spheres of social reality contrasts sharply with the others, each maintains a broad range of experience. At the bottom of the mountain, the locus of causality is clearly impersonal. The perception is that one has little control over one's environment. Adjustment is a key concern. In the king-of-the-mountain sphere, the locus of causality is noticeably extrinsic. People pursue goals here because others say they should. They feel they have won when others say they have won. A person can be considered a complete success in the game of king of the mountain and be totally impoverished in the intellectual sphere, just as another can be enriched intellectually, gain access to the other side of the mountain, and live in austerity.

The locus of causality for those on the other side of the mountain is intrinsic. People here have developed a conscience influenced by, but independent of, the views of others. (I use the term conscience not as a metaphor for culture but as an active concern for living; if fully developed, it becomes the province of one's dreams.) The core of this sphere is nearest to Maslow's Being Values. We might call this the moral high ground, except that those who've reached it would be the first to insist that high ground in no way means being more important than others.

Morality

In centuries past, the word *morals* encompassed the whole of human subjectivity. Today, definitions of what I call the moral high ground would vary depending upon one's culture, but it's generally accepted that morality itself derives from a number of rules governing human behavior.[15] A social conscience is something one acquires in the process of living. Freud suggested that a conscience forms as the result of the imprint of nurture.[16] The behaviorists added the notion that a conscience is the result of classical conditioning. And social learning theory, or cognitive science, suggests that a conscience is at least partially born of reason.

There is truth to be found in each of these schools of thought, but my own experience leads me to have faith in the ability of reason to move us toward the high ground more than any other attribute. But—and this can hardly be overemphasized—reason must be accountable to and for the emotional contours of life. Morality can be reduced to *why*; ethics to *why not*. It is useful to think of our conscience as the crossroads where the imprint of our biological nature and our culture meet the essence of our purpose. In large part, the development of conscience is a product of chance. Fortunate are those who have been the object of concern, and who have experienced the benefits of affection in a stable environment.

Morality has three spheres of functionality. One is traditional (the way things were); one is practical (the way things are); and the third is idealistic (the way things could be). It is the nature of humans that we hold the behavior of strangers to strict, immutable standards, while we judge ourselves and our closest associates to standards deemed practical. In other words, "you have to do what you have to do to get along." But, for most, it is problematic to entertain the third realm of morality. One can't spend too much time speculating about what could be without questioning the validity of tradition or the hypocrisy of what is regarded as practical necessity.

Eighteenth-century philosopher David Hume demonstrated, in his essay *A Treatise of Human Nature,* that it is impossible to extract an authoritative "ought" from an "is." Latter day philosophers have been hard-pressed to prove him wrong. But Hume was not wishy-washy about where he thought moral authority came from. He believed morality arose from the virtue of humanness itself, and that "reason is and ought to be the slave of the passions." Thus, "oughts" are not so hard to come by for ordinary people in search of practical rules of order.

The safety of my family and yours is better assured if we can decide that we ought not to kill each other. Thinking people can easily deduce that *thou shalt not lie, cheat, steal, or kill* will serve them well as rules for human society. Coming up with these elementary guides for behavior does not require divine intervention. But, if oughts are hard to prove philosophically, it is not surprising that the greatest ideological battle of all—the one that holds a key to understanding the fundamentals of ancient and contemporary human conflict—rides on the question of where moral authority comes from. It is related to the rationalist-empiricist problem which Kant was unable to resolve (though he may have come as close as anyone ever will). Whether truth is borne of divine or natural revelation, or whether it is a process of discovery, remains the subject of endless debate.[17]

Our three spheres exist from perceptions of dependence, independence, and interdependence. If this model is to be of any use to us, it must offer some insight into why some of us settle for a life of rewards based on the approval of others, while so few seem capable or willing to live by their own principles (defined as an active living awareness) instead of someone else's rules. Study Kohlberg's theory of moral development in depth, and you can easily see how the thirst for knowledge moves one from dependence to independence to interdependence. This map is not so different from Maslow's "hierarchy of needs" model. Kohlberg's model supports Maslow's assertion that getting one's needs met predisposes one to be more concerned with the needs of others. Where most people get stalled in their climb is somewhere near the middle. In their noble effort to earn a living, they catch mountain fever. The game itself becomes more important than their original reasons for playing. They become so focused on rules, order, and the right behavior strategies (personality ethic) that they climb no higher.

Relativism

Let's dwell for a moment on why the slope of relativism is deceptively inviting. It appears to be a natural resting place: as the search for truth gets progressively harder, one can rest here because there is a degree of virtue in tolerance. But, if one is not careful, the spot becomes a haven for resting instead of a springboard for thinking. When one reaches the posture that relative opinions need to be considered and that there may be many paths that lead to truth, it is much easier to add a bit more tolerance than to continue the exploration. This seems right; we do need more tolerance, but becoming tolerant should not arrest our inquiry. Tolerance is a virtue, but the need to know, to understand, to discover what we really think and believe becomes *most* important at the point where we respect the opinions of others.

When millions of people substitute tolerance for thought, truth becomes the property of those who haven't looked very hard to find it. Thus, articulate spokesmen for any brand of gibberish can sway public opinion. The authority to enforce their version of it will be an easy task if everyone else assumes an attitude of indifference. Relativism has been popularized as the notion that one idea is as good as another, as if anyone, anywhere, ever held such a view.[18] The argument over relativism is not about truth, but over which worldviews prevail. John Stuart Mill framed the issue of effort and opinion in his 1859 essay *On Liberty*:

> He who knows only his own side of the case, knows little of that. His reasons may be good, and no one may have been able to refute them. But if he is equally unable to refute the reasons on the opposite side, if he does not so much as know what they are, he has no ground for preferring either opinion.[19]

The point is to reach a posture where one's desire to know is greater than one's need to win an argument. Paradoxically, such a position is necessary before one can admit not knowing. The desire to understand must conquer the natural tendency to form a self-justifying belief. This does not mean that one's search for truth must finally arrive at a point of rigidity, but it does mean that one must be capable of acting according to one's conscience. Moreover, this must occur in full awareness of the flimsy and arbitrary manner in which our views about reality became formed and socially solidified. Getting over the high hurdle of truth versus relativism is the first step in comprehending wisdom.

In his book *The Closing of the American Mind*, Allan Bloom excoriated Friedrich Nietzsche as the champion, if not the architect, of relativism. If you study Nietzsche in depth, however, you will realize that he would be the last person on earth to claim one opinion is as good as another, even though he said, "there are no facts, only interpretations." No one has argued more forcefully for thinking for oneself than did Nietzsche. He says,

> What, then, is truth? A mobile army of metaphors, metonyms, and anthropomorphisims—in short, a sum of human relations, which have been enhanced, transposed, and embellished poetically and rhetorically, and which after long use seem firm, canonical, and obligatory to a people: truths are illusions about which one has forgotten that this is what they are; metaphors which are worn out and without sensuous power; coins which have lost their pictures and now matter only as metal, no longer as coins.[20]

Nietzsche reasoned that people unable to infer wisdom from this statement were, in fact, too stupefied by their culture to enter into a conversation about truth.

A conscience must be based not upon internalized obedience to external authority, but upon the ability to perceive, comprehend, and judge for oneself. Both relativism and absolutism are in and of themselves antithetical to democracy. Relativism promotes tolerance, a precondition for democracy, but it is no friend of truth if it arrests further inquiry. Absolutism is intolerant by nature, since it claims to have the truth nailed down. Arthur Schlesinger Jr. writes,

> Absolutism is abstract, monistic, deductive, ahistorical, solemn, and it is intimately bound up with deference to authority. Relativism is concrete, pluralistic, inductive, historical, skeptical and intimately bound up with deference to experience. Absolutism teaches by rote; relativism by experiment. "I respect faith," that forgotten wit Wilson Mizener once said, "but doubt is what gets you an education."[21]

Conviction without the possibility of doubt is the archetype for a closed system. It's like a computer disk drive with tape over the access slot, except, in human terms, the believer becomes a tool or an instrument of power. Thus, the architects of belief create ledges on our metaphorical mountains where climbing through knowledge and understanding seems impossible. Rick Roderick offers a philosophical posture which enables a person to negotiate the deceptive slope of relativism without falling or pushing anyone else off. Roderick is a "fallibilist believing passionately in certain things but realizing that his beliefs may be wrong."[22] From this posture, "faith" could never be a justification for war.

Finding a Moral North

In the words of Irving Singer, "Traditional wisdom has always maintained that saintly and heroic lives are not only more desirable but also more meaningful than others."[23] A sharp stick in the eye would cause no more pain to Socrates or Gandhi than it would to you or me; their food would have tasted no better to them than ours does to us. They would likely have found no more satisfaction from a warm summer day than you or I. But how do you begin to measure the quality of a life lived so near the core of its inner values that the one living it would rather die than void the principles upon which it is lived? Did Socrates' decision to die for his principles mean that he was a fool, a zealot, a fanatic, a figment of Plato's imagination, or a truly wise and virtuous man? Did Socrates throw his life away, or had he pursued meaning so far into a corner as to have truth by the throat?

Perhaps we can never answer these questions, but by continuously asking them in differing ways we may advance closer to "meaning," just as a compass moves explorers closer to a "north" that they will never actually visit. Would it be fair to say that Socrates, in choosing to die for his beliefs, had reached a posture approaching the embodiment of purpose and the foundation of principle? If this sort of inquiry sheds light on the quest of living, we could propose that the other side of the mountain be called the brighter side of the mountain. This is the place where one is most likely to make a contribution that will not only add meaning to one's own life, but will also be capable of adding significance to the lives of others. Paradoxically, Socrates' surrender to his culture proved that his ideas were superior to that culture. He was physically destroyed by his culture, but by letting his critics put him to death, he has drawn eternal attention to the injustice of having social convention preside at a higher level than ideas. John Stuart Mill put it this way, "Socrates was put to death, but the Socratic philosophy rose like the sun in heaven, and spread its illumination over the whole intellectual firmament."[24]

When we speak of the need for a liberal (balanced) education, what we really mean is that learning should become intrinsic, and this cannot occur until we subdue the need to conform without question. One cannot adopt principles as one does rules without genuinely understanding and internalizing their values. To accept a rule based upon a principle is not equivalent to upholding the need for the principle. Following rules and the letter of the law is not sufficient to sustain principles. "Principles need feeding."[25] Circumstances change, making rules and the law ambiguous, but principles do not change. The United States Constitution is a draft based upon principle, but if not read, if not understood, if not upheld, if not sustained intellectually, then it is as worthless as the paper it's written on.

It is a serious mistake to underestimate the problematic nature of intrinsic versus extrinsic motivation. This is precisely why reasoning at the level of principle is so hard to achieve and why it is so important. There is very little we do as humans which is not at some nexus attached to external motivation. It may appear that we engage in art or sport for the love of the activity, and those of us who write convince ourselves that we really write for ourselves. But, if no one ever appreciated our art, observed our sport or read our writing, our enthusiasm for these efforts would diminish dramatically. Thinking this through, seeing and understanding the subtle, obscured relationships which guide our actions, affords us a much better assessment of why we really do what we do.

Moral high ground is neither won nor maintained by the posture of a superior moral stance. For decades both liberals and conservatives suffering altitude sickness have spoken eloquently of high moral principles without adopting them for themselves. Where are the politicians who will act on their own conscience without regard to the consequences? (Out of office, you say?) Indeed, where are the citizens who will make sacrifices for future generations? It is not at all difficult to imagine that, if the majority of people in America were driven by principles based upon internal values, our king-of-the-mountain game would crumble of its own weight.

Accepting a large body of doctrine without feeling the need to rise to the same level of knowledge that produced it is what keeps millions of people from dreaming their own American Dreams instead of living among the reruns from other eras. An example would be to become as knowledgeable about the affairs of government as were the founding fathers. It is self-evident that to accept doctrine without forming one's own opinion is to obey without question. Yet, in the matter of established truths, little is settled; not questioning is dangerous. When we begin our own inquiry, follow our own reason, act on and by our own principles, we meet life head on; we change *was* to *is* and balance *what* with *why*. This process overflows with purpose, as Nietzsche writes: "He who has a why to live can bear most any how." George Bernard Shaw captures the point perfectly:

> This is the true joy in life, the being used for a purpose recognized by yourself as a mighty one; the being thoroughly worn out before you are thrown on the scrap heap; the force being of nature instead of a feverish selfish little clod of ailments and grievances complaining that the world will not devote itself to make you happy.[26]

It is easy to see that the majority of people in the world are not likely to reach the core of inner values described here. It is just as easy to see, however, that the fact that they will not has nothing whatsoever to do with their individual abilities. One does not have to be president of the United States during a civil war to be like Abraham Lincoln, nor does one have to move to the woods to develop the conscience of a Henry David Thoreau. But if everyone did aspire to similar understanding, our present social institutions—even our churches—would change radically or disappear, for most of them depend upon the ethos of king of the mountain. Indeed, if the majority of humans sought to internalize truth, it would become impossible to create standing armies of people who regard the act of killing on command as "just another job." Doing one's duty would require at lot more thinking than is presently required to shoot an enemy.

If the majority of people were driven by internalized ideas of right and wrong—if they were committed to truth, equality, and justice for all—the changes in our society would be earthshaking. The surprising realization here is not so much that those at the bottom of the mountain would suddenly be independent, but that all of us would be free to make intrinsic choices. Imagine what our society would be like if everyone simply felt free not to buy what they do not need.

The trip from the middle to the other side of the mountain does not require that one climb over the top, but that one's values change from an extrinsic to an intrinsic orientation. Unfortunately, we have no great impetus for intrinsic learning as we grow older in our society, and too many people simply stop learning altogether. This leaves an enormous gap between those at the middle and those who have reached the other side: those near the middle interpret the motives of those on the other side to be the same as theirs, even though they are not based on the same criteria. For example, people motivated by money expect that everyone else is too. But people who have reached the top of Kohlberg's scale of moral development (and the other, brighter side of our mountain) parallel experts who, no longer relying on the recollection of rules, are driven by principles. They direct their own lives.

The work of Erik Erikson calls our attention to lifestage development. If we fail to mature, and the nature of our personal motivation remains extrinsic, we become in a sense "outwardly-in" focused, which means we become obsessed with ourselves (as is the case with individuals who spend hours telling others the details about their latest surgery). If we mature, if our motivation becomes intrinsic, our focus becomes inward-out; we reach Erickson's seventh stage of generativity and become concerned with what might be called our "cosmic contribution" (my term), a sincere desire to pass on some of the value we have consumed through living to those people who will still be here when we are gone.

Immanuel Kant spoke of the "moral law" within each of us. [27] A central thesis of this book is that my moral law within applies to me and me alone, and yours applies to you. (This is not to be confused with obeying the laws of the land.) I may wish you would adopt mine as a law, and I am free to argue that you should, but I cannot and will not force it upon you, nor will I let you force yours upon me. Spinoza believed (and made a very good case) that the human mind is intended as an integral union with nature. [28] When you consider these two ideas with Erikson's stage of generativity, human fulfillment resembles the biological world of living things which begin as seed, reach maturity, and produce their own seeds—only here the offspring are deeds and ideas.

Building Better Mountains

Creating a higher and better culture requires putting our current world in perspective with specific attention to biological, social, and intellectual strata of existence. In 1991, after nearly a decade and a half, Robert M. Pirsig resurrected his semi-fictional Phaedrus to present a new metaphysics of quality in *Lila: An Inquiry Into Morals.* Pirsig writes:

> Phaedrus had once called metaphysics "the high country of the mind"—an analogy to the "high country" of mountain climbing. It takes a lot of effort to get there and more effort when you arrive, but unless you make the journey you are confined to one valley of thought all your life. This high country passage through the Metaphysics of Quality allowed entry to another valley of thought in which the facts of life get a much richer interpretation. The valley spreads out into a huge fertile plain of understanding.
>
> In this plain of understanding static patterns of value are divided into four systems: inorganic patterns, biological patterns, social patterns and intellectual patterns. They are exhaustive. That's all there are. If you construct an encyclopedia of four topics—Inorganic, Biological, Social and Intellectual—nothing is left out. No "thing," that is. Only dynamic

quality, which cannot be described in any encyclopedia, is absent.[29]

Before I discuss the concept of dynamic quality, let's use Pirsig's components to construct a new model for comparison with my king-of-the-mountain metaphor. First, we establish a layer of inorganic material for our foundation. Second, we attach a strip of biological matter vertically to the left-hand corner of the foundation. Next, we attach an equal length of social matter vertically to the right-hand corner. As our final step, we lay a strip of intellectual matter across the top, joining both sides, to give us a simple square or frame. Now we have a frame for all-of-reality, elegant in its simplicity.

Does the joining of the biological and intellectual planes create society or do the biological and social planes create the individual? Sociobiologists tell us our genetic predispositions color our behavior to a far greater extent than most of us realize. On the other hand, we have seen the damage that can result from the excessive influence of our culture. This argument has been going on for decades and may never be solved. There are points to be made for each side. After all, this question of biological nature versus social nurture is surely one of degree. Pirsig suggests these four all-inclusive components—inorganic, biological, social, and intellectual—proceed upward in a moral sense (based on reason) as "a migration of static patterns" moving toward Dynamic Quality.

Although I am in general agreement with the integrity of Pirsig's model, I'm also troubled by the implications others might infer from it. Misunderstood, it might lead to the same kind of perversion that made Nietzsche's works a product of the Nazis. Clearly understood, I believe it has the potential to be a guide to the best enlightenment human reason can offer. The interdependence of these four all-encompassing patterns is so overwhelming as to temper the concept of dominance in all but the most abstract circumstances. Biological patterns are special arrangements of inorganic patterns. Social patterns and intellectual patterns cannot exist without biology, and biology cannot exist without inorganic matter. A good life without a good society is intellectually unendurable. Being itself is totally dependent upon all four patterns. Are not ideas just another term for biological expression? There is a neurochemical basis for each and every thought, but it's problematic to suggest that biological patterns will ever be fully comprehended by intellectual patterns. In *The Fourth Horseman*, Andrew Nikiforuk writes,

> The big secret to bacteria's survival is their ability to solve problems.... If a team of bacteria had written the world's history, humans would appear as a period at the end.... The real truth about bacteria reads like science fiction and is a lot more exotic than warfare. Bacteria are not only our ancestors but our number one life-support system. They clean our water, prime the atmosphere and take care of the dead.... As the planet's eldest, brightest and most numerous life-form, bacteria work in teams as one big superorganism. The art of successful living and planet regulating has taken bacteria two and a half billion years to learn....The earth's first-line defense mechanism will only tolerate so much crowding, pollution and deforestation before some of its members intervene. The superorganism, because it is the superorganism, can't behave any other way.[30]

Ideas produce vaccines, but viruses grow more and more complex in response. Indeed, could not pathological ideologies be mental viruses? Are not the thoughts which fill our heads expressions of culture? Have not ideas with the names of religions and political affiliations killed millions with as much or more vigor than the great plagues of centuries past? Will an Ebola or AIDS-like virus ultimately wipe the slate clean of human beings and by so doing achieve what Richard Preston has characterized as "revenge of the rainforest?"[31] We may be technologically literate enough for space travel, but we are still baffled by the virus of the common cold. If all of life sprang forth from a single cell, would we be correct to say that all ideas originated from one thought?

Try imaging Dynamic Quality as a sort of pristine progress that rests momentarily on the pitons and crampons of evolution. If an instance of Dynamic Quality (progress) is accepted and becomes established, it becomes static quality and we wait for yet another advance. The development of computer software is an apt analogy for how this process plays out. Ideas become system programs which remain static until overwritten. Thus, Dynamic Quality becomes the "source of all things." Intellectual patterns are the highest form of patterns. Pirsig writes,

> A human being is a collection of ideas, and these ideas take moral precedence over a society. Ideas are patterns of value. They are at a higher level of evolution than social patterns of value. Just as it is more moral for a doctor to kill a germ than a patient, so it is more moral for an idea to kill a society than it is for a society to kill an idea.[32]

From this perspective, the importance of understanding how our new model is constructed comes clear. You can't tell at first glance that one component (the intellectual plane) is morally superior. Yet, all moral progress depends upon intellectual endeavor. Unless the combined intellects of the members of our society uphold the ideas on which that society is built, we fall back to a (less caring) social posture of rules and bureaucracy that amount to static social patterns. Perhaps it's more appropriate to say that Pirsig's model works in a humanistic sense, or in a subjective way of knowing similar to that described by eighteenth-century Scottish philosopher David Hume. Humans, he said, discover conventional morality through common experience. In other words, ideas belong at the pinnacle of humanity because they evoke human aspirations in their most dramatic expression, both in the real world of everyday practicality and in our imaginations. The well-being of societies, as well as that of individuals, depends on the development and use of human intelligence. The alternative is to watch our lives unfold as if from a script: we play sterile roles and wait for someone to give us our lines.

In his book *The Evolving Self: A Psychology for the Third Millennium*, Mihaly Csikszentmihalyi writes, "Excessive acculturation leads one to see reality only through the veils of the culture. A person who invests psychic energy exclusively in goals prescribed by society is forfeiting the possibility of choice."[33] The important lesson here is that any tribe, group, country, government, society, or nation which comes together for the well-being of its members (regardless of whether its major source of influence stems from culture or biology), must—if it really values quality and truth—organize itself in such a way as to ensure that all of its members have every possible opportunity to benefit from and contribute to the intellectual plane. Too little culture results in ignorance, and too much culture produces stupidity which manifests as arrogance among its leaders.

Pirsig's model further implies that social and intellectual patterns depend on biological patterns. Our lives as individuals resemble this same hierarchical order. We are made of carbon atoms; when we are born, our biological needs dominate. Then we grow into our culture, and when we have a certain volume of experience, we enter the intellectual plane. If we master a part of our culture, and our ideas prevail, we lay down new patterns of culture. But we must understand, as William F. Allman writes in *The Stone Age Present,*

> ...the entire debate over whether *nature or nurture* has the most influence in human affairs is built on an intellectual house of cards. Culture is not an independent entity that struggles to overide human biology, but rather a reflection of that biology, as inputs from the surrounding physical and social environment combine with the evolved mechanisms in the brain to produce the full panoply of human behavior.[34]

When we apply intellectual patterns to the task of understanding biological patterns, we advance social patterns, and thus we add quality. When we apply intellectual patterns to biological patterns, we begin to understand the concept of wholeness as a representation of all four patterns. Thus, we create new cultural mountains to climb for those who come after us. Such is the character of dreams and aspirations.

It takes an extraordinary amount of thought to discern what really matters to us in this life, precisely because we have lost our visceral connection to the world of interrelatedness. If we make no effort to find our own meaning in this life, our culture will block the way. To live one's life without fully developing one's intellectual capacity is to live as if one has been infected with a cultural virus, flattened with a case of societal flu.

Deceptive Paths

Viewing humankind as capable of discovering equality as a virtuous truth has its share of articulate critics. Theories abound about the social structure of human beings. Schopenhauer believed life to be purposeless, that we are driven by the "will" to live successfully at the expense of others. Friedrich Nietzsche countered that the true nature of humans is not "will" but "will to power," suggesting that society's creative members are superior human beings and should not be subject to the same rules as members of the common flock.

It is easy to confuse the "will" with the "will to power" because they are closely related. The search for power is for some yet another means of grasping for security or assurance that one will survive. Moreover, the more power one achieves, the more power one needs. Thus, it is easy for people bent on achieving domination to assume those with power come by it naturally, and for those who succeed to see themselves as being superior to those who haven't.

In his book *In Defense of Elitism,* William A. Henry III argued that America is suffering from the over-influence of egalitarianism, that our obsession with equality comes at the expense of real merit. "If you wish to produce an elite," he says, "you must live by elite values."[35] Now, you can't get much more Nitezschean than that. Henry is right that we are living in an anti-intellectual era, and right again to suggest that some ideas are better than others, that some people and cultures have more going for them than others. He is right to rail against a new-age revival of beliefs in mysticism, medieval mumbo-jumbo, and psychobable "based on self-interest, mob politics, and fear rather than research and open-minded inquiry," and right again to say, "Opportunity does not need to be exactly equal. It only needs to exist."[36] But then he writes, "The vital thing is not to maximize everyone's performance, but to ensure maximal performance from the most talented, the ones who can make a difference."[37] We must ask, what exactly is a difference and who decides what it is? Indeed, I have argued in favor of those who bring quality to bear upon culture, but when anyone other than the individual involved decides what a difference is, or how quality of life is defined, the stage for tyranny is set. Our history proves this beyond doubt.

Livelihood in a capitalistic society is based upon some kind of performance by everyone. Will an upwardly mobile, talented elite willingly look after the rest of us? Not likely. Innate superiority is often an illusory apparition. William A. Henry III was an obsessively busy individual. Shortly before his book was published, he died of a massive heart attack. He was 44 years old. Life is not a game you win.

Survival of our species depends upon diversity. In other words, it takes all kinds of people to maintain society, and many ordinary people to produce extraordinary people. How do those who endorse a natural hierarchy based on contribution explain the genius born of ordinary parents? While some may indeed contribute more to society than others, equality is justified as much by rational, secular thinking as it is by religious morality. In other words, there is a rational basis for respecting individual members of society, regardless of what their perceived contribution to society might be.

Most theories about the virtue of human equality rise from the world's religions, but when we view mankind in terms of biological nature and take into account recent studies in psychobiology (brain science), a middle ground between Schopenhauer and Nietzsche would appear to be the "will to survive." That some people within any given society are driven to seek power is without question, but recent experience with prisoners of war and the survivors of the Nazi death camps suggest that the "will to survive" is more pervasive and far stronger in more people than the "will to power." Millions of people who went to extraordinary efforts to survive such ordeals sought little in the way of power in later years. Nietzsche's "will to power" can be as simple as an animal discharging its will to be what it is, or to do what it must in order to exist. But a "will to power" in human terms is also a result of learned behavior, which makes it a pattern of culture. A case in point: We clearly admit that knowledge is power. Now, if Nietzsche's "will to power" were literally true would this not be a planet of raging autodidacts?

The comparison between the will and the will to power could go on forever. This question lies at the heart of motivation, and it may always be a subjective call. Not long ago, while researching questions about motivation, I found 22 distinctly different defensible theories as to the true nature of motivation. I came to believe that a person's motivation must stem from a continuum made up of one's genetic, social, and learned responses. In a sense, purpose is the residue of motivation.

Viktor Frankl's experience as a prisoner in Auschwitz during World War II caused him to conclude that Schopenhauer and Nietzsche were both wrong, that neither the "will" nor the "will to power" captures the essence of human nature, but that the search for meaning is the true heart of human existence. Yet in each of our daily lives we see countless examples of people who seem hell-bent on insulating themselves from meaning in any genuine human sense. Perhaps it's more appropriate to say that there are truths to be found in the "will," in "the will to power," and in "the search for meaning," but "the will to survive" is primary. Evolutionary biologists have little trouble making a case linking us to a long line of nonhuman creatures with an undeniable "will to survive." It also seems appropriate, though simplistic in human terms, to point out the hierarchical nature of these aspirations: the will to survive is a biological predisposition, the will to power a social one, and the search for meaning is an intellectual endeavor.

Making Our Own Way

If you think of the mountain in our king-of-the-mountain model as a metaphor for a culture delineated with ridges, imagine that each ridge is wind-blown with its own rhetoric. By this I mean that at each ridge there is ample opportunity for spokesmen or gurus to rally the support of those who will go no further in seeking knowledge on their own. For example, an increasing number of radio talk shows have gained large national audiences by appealing to the ridge identified by Lawrence Kohlberg as stage four, the society-maintaining orientation. Hosts use familiar slogans, such as "America first" (a catch phrase for isolationism), to alarm their listeners to a myriad of possible foreign threats. They sustain their audiences by playing on public ignorance and fear of conspiracy. Such fears promote nationalism, ethnocentrism, bigotry, and prejudice. They ensure the status quo by creating a feeling of dread and apprehension about the future. But the way to discover purpose and meaning apart from the relentless attempt to gain economic high ground is to think these issues through for ourselves.

Self-knowledge affords the most favorable circumstances for making progress in all spheres, regardless of your personal goals. I make no pretense that I've found the other side of the mountain—I am only searching for it. But I've learned from experience that those who lay claim to high moral ground seldom stand on it. Among those who make such assertions are some of the most pretentious fools I have ever met. The properties of morality are a little like Zen: to explain Zen is to misunderstand it. To declare one is moral is to misconstrue the meaning of morality. Morality as I define it is best described by Walter Truett Anderson as:

> ... the product of hard-won wisdom, a way of being that expresses wherever a person happens to be along the (hopefully) never-ending path of understanding and reunderstanding life, constructing and reconstructing the rules of relationship between self and others.[38]

So long as individuals look to others for instructions instead of developing their own accountability, so long as rules and authority substitute for principle and conscience, society will pay a dear price. Moral crusades are never about morals. The act of proselytizing morality is almost always an attempt at to gain power. Moral virtue is best taught and learned by example. Preaching virtue is not a sign that one possesses it. This does not mean that we cannot learn from those who preach one thing and practice another. As individuals we are responsible for discerning truth on our own. Legions of authors and poets have written eloquently about lands they themselves never visited. Indeed, people who write books offering advice are often the ones most in need of it. A person who has never been to the next town can still give good directions for getting there, but perhaps not as well as the person who once got lost trying to find it. We must learn to judge for ourselves when we are getting off the right path.

The best example of moral truth is still a living example, but the greatest danger—the deep illusion—is to use the failings of others as an excuse for not having to judge the truth for ourselves. It's too easy to dismiss an argument, not on its own grounds, but on the character of the person presenting it. Thus, reducing the search for truth to name-calling amounts to abdicating responsibility. There will never be a need to form one's own opinions about divisive issues if one can always use the excuse that no one can be found to discuss them who is above reproach. Moral authority derives its ability to influence by presenting an example worthy of emulation.

Expanding Awareness

Imagine what it would be like to spend the first ten years of your life in your present home without ever being able to see or venture beyond its walls. How enlightening it would be to step through the door and observe your home from the outside. Imagine another decade confined to the community in which your home is located without being able to see or venture beyond it. How enlightening it would be to go to another town. Now, in increments of ten years imagine yourself similarly confined to your state, your country, your continent, and finally your planet. This exercise helps you to see how moving from one of these bound locations to the next leads to great leaps of understanding, expanded awareness, and insight into matters that, before, you could not even imagine. When we contrast the experience of the home-bound individual with that of the traveler to another planet, the former seems to have little more than existence and the latter seems always on the verge of meaningful discovery.

Continual learning produces the same effect, though the contrasts are more subtle. Frequently in this text I mention reality as if I know what that is, but in a literal sense I am only dimly aware of what reality might be. The limitations of my senses make me oblivious to the multitude of activities going on in and around my body at this very moment. Try to imagine for a moment what it would be like to sense of the millions of life forms on this planet who are at this very instant ripping the flesh from another living creature: the African lion dismembering the gazelle, the arctic wolfpack partially devouring the caribou before it loses its footing, hundreds of millions of perpetual predator/prey actions, the slaughter of millions of farm animals for the supermarket, or the common house cat's terrorizing of mice and rabbits in the vacant lot next door. These are harsh examples, but we are so estranged, so disembodied and removed, that this daily ritual of death would have to be heard as a perpetual scream before most of us would be able to acknowledge the fact that nature is "red in tooth and claw" and be fully aware of the fact that *life eats*.[39]

The tragedy of this lack of awareness is that we fail to see ourselves in a harsh, but very real, relationship with nature. Most of us live for decades denying the inevitability of our own death. We find it hard even to look at the dead, as evidenced by our practice of covering with a sheet or blanket the body of someone who has just died. We cannot bear to look at death for very long without acknowledging that it is a part of life. Children grow up in our culture believing that animals have human character traits, thereby forming a totally distorted view of the natural world and their own role in it. Nature is neither cruel nor kind; it simply *is*. Even so, hidden beneath a veil of beauty and a misimpression of harmony lies a seething malignancy which is not foreign to nature but is an integral part of it. We often speak of a "balance in nature," but taking a historical perspective will reveal that to be an illusion. The signature of nature is change, and this makes our environmental actions critical.

The lowest human rules over the world of animals with as much authority as a king in earlier centuries. To the beast we are god-like, to the stray dog we are as Zeus to Plato. Yet we are kin to animals, of the same flesh. To realize we are knotted to the same fate as animals, because we cannot live without them, overwhelms us with responsibility for the stewardship of our planet. Our inability to see clearly that we are a part of the process of nature and not the masters of nature is evidenced by the sorry state of the global environment.

Teacher and philosopher Joseph Campbell spoke often of the symbiotic relationship between man and animals. Tribal societies that depended on a species for food (as, for example, the American Indian depended on the buffalo) were cultures that experienced great respect for and sacred attachments to the hunted animal. In a different context, that sense of attachment is what is lacking today: we have either more respect for the animals than we have for ourselves, or none at all. The grim evidence left by ivory poachers brings an emotional cry from those who value the elephant. To save the elephant, we will kill humans if necessary, but herein lies the very crux of the problem. If we don't respect humanity enough to abolish the economic conditions that prompt people to risk death in order to poach ivory, then we have little hope of achieving the equilibrium necessary for both humans and beasts. This is not to say that even in a more just economy there would not be people who would break any law to further their own ends. But, for some Africans, the alternative to poaching is death anyway, or at best a life subordinate in economic quality to that of American family pets. Only by respecting ourselves and understanding that we are a part of the natural world are we likely to understand that to kill nature is to kill ourselves, and that to not allow our fellow humans enough equity to live with dignity amounts to the same thing.

Ever since Charles Darwin, Herbert Spencer, and Charles Pierce, we have pointed to nature for evidence to support the power of the strong over the weak. But deep within nature lies a fastener of cooperation, a lesson of profound relatedness and interdependence. Our muddled human perception is further obscured by our failure to view nature as it is designed instead of the way we would like it to be. Our tendency is to identify with the predator or the prey.

Inherent in false perception is the persistent notion that we are being objective when we aren't. There is also the fallacy that thinking is a logical process. It is not. We are adept at pattern recognition and recall, but there is nothing inherently logical in the process of thinking itself. It takes *work* to make thinking a genuine intellectual pattern. Witness a pool player striking the cue ball, and the cue ball striking the eight ball. We perceive that we see the force that causes the eight ball to move, but we do not. We see the motion of the cue ball and the subsequent motion of the eight ball, but we do not see the force that causes the eight ball to move. If this does not seem clear, I suggest thinking about it until it becomes indisputable. The exercise will help you appreciate that thinking does not naturally follow logic and the laws of physics are not necessarily discerned through appearances.

Or suppose that you are walking down the street and stop the first 30 people you meet to ask them the date of their birth. Do you think it's logical that two or more of them will have been born on the same day? Mathematical logic suggests that the odds are 2:1 in favor of at least two of them of having the same birthday, but it seems counterintuitive.[40] The point of these exercises is both simple and profound. We make millions of decisions throughout our lives based on the assumption that our thinking is naturally logical and that everything is as it appears. Not so.

To be truly aware one must be appreciative of the *memes* of culture—the memorable units of intellectual patterns which reduce thinking to a settled process. Richard Dawkins coined the term *meme* in 1976, in his book *The Selfish Gene*. He writes,

> Examples of memes are tunes, ideas, catch-phrases, clothes fashions, ways of making pots or of building arches. Just as genes propagate themselves in the gene pool by leaping from body to body via sperm or eggs, so memes propagate themselves in the meme pool by leaping from brain to brain via a process which in a broad sense, can be called imitation.[41]

Cognitive scientist Daniel C. Dennett reminds us why memes are so consequential. "Never forget the crucial point: the facts about whatever we hold dear—our highest values—are themselves very much a product of the memes that have spread most successfully."[42] Dennett reminds us that "the meme for education, for instance, is a meme that reinforces the very process of meme implantation."[43]

The disturbing yet liberating notion in all of this is that it is often much harder to be reasonable than it is to be wrong. Without a high level of awareness about the deceptive nature of perception, we have little chance of being objective about anything. The salient characteristic of the construction of reality is that, as often as not, the process is arbitrary, which means that many of our opinions are arbitrary also. We think we are being logical when there is nothing at all logical about our thinking. We often default to the notion of "common sense" when what we really mean is "common perception." The opinions (and memes) we hold about skin color, hair style, and body shape are malleable; in other words, if we are taught one is better or more beautiful than another, in time, the beauty will seem intuitively obvious.

Plato advocated not teaching logic until a person was 35 years old, but then, Plato didn't believe in democracy. If he had, I dare say he would have reduced his recommendation by at least 20 years. Why we do not teach logic (as the mechanics of argument) with as much enthusiasm as reading, writing, and arithmetic would be a mystery, were it not for the messy disruption contrary opinions bring to the classroom and to the political administration which oversees it.

Socrates argued continually that in order to achieve wisdom we must be willing to challenge our most precious beliefs. An easy way to begin is to develop a healthy skepticism for our wonderful, but frail, sense perception and to realize, above all, that "we have the power to defy the selfish genes of our birth and, when necessary, the selfish memes of our indoctrination."[44] Moreover, we must understand that while memes are the residue of intellectual patterns, they represent nothing more than social patterns. Thinking, then, by definition, must exercise enough power to break through common perception.

In *Self-University*, I quoted writer John Culkin on the nature of reality. His description is worth repeating:

> All perception is selective. We are all experts at discerning other people's patterns of selectivity. Our own is mercilessly hidden from us. Our own personal experience sets up one grid between us and reality. Our culture adds one. Our language and our media system tighten the mesh. No one man, no one culture has a privileged key to reality.[45]

Alan Watts put technological reality in perspective when he said, "The greater the scientist, the more he is impressed with his ignorance of reality, and the more he realizes that his laws and labels, descriptions and definitions, are the products of his own thought."[46] If we are going to rise to the occasion of our culture, we must make every effort to understand it and all of the other cultures with which we come into contact. We must understand that memory is often a refuge from reality, and that an event and a recollection are two separate occurrences. Thus, selective memory is often used to avoid understanding and to accept cultural assumptions without question: anything recalled similar to what culture poses as truth will be accepted as verification. Moreover, perceptual values have a way of encroaching upon memory; in time, what we value colors memory so that the past becomes idealized. Thus, cultural myths, premises that were never true, are preserved as absolute fact.[47]

Learning to Reason

Our acceptance of culture can sometimes blot out our ability to reason, leaving us with the mistaken notion that we're actually being reasonable. I can best illustrate this by offering my own experience with the study of philosophy. Even though it seemed difficult for me to understand, philosophy fascinated me with its potential for apprehending a closer view of reality. For years I had scoffed at the idea that philosophy or critical thinking had much to offer. Once I thought my way past this hurdle, I began to study in earnest. I spent many hours reading what were purported to be great works. I comprehended little of them, but I persisted. I constantly referred to the dictionary to ponder terms I barely understood, and I read lots of books that offered to simplify great works. The arguments of most of the philosophers seemed so compelling that once I felt I understood them, I could do nothing but agree with them. Thus, when I read one that contradicted another, I had no choice but to change my mind.

In time this gave way to gradual development of an ability to formulate and conduct my own arguments and to take issue with those in the books. It seems to me the reason great philosophers stand out is simply that, even though their premises may be absurd, their arguments are compelling because they appear to have legitimacy by nature of their construction. In contrast, those who consider themselves to be ordinary citizens without much experience in the construction of reasoned argument have little to offer in the intellectual arena concerning our greatest problems, except to repeat the arguments of others—or to change their minds repeatedly whenever a new, more compelling speaker rises to the podium. Each of us needs to ask ourselves which kind of person we want to be: someone who upholds and strengthens principles through a lucid awareness of one's experience and the development of one's own reasoning, or someone who simply obeys his or her way through life.

Learning to reason well requires patience and discipline. In today's world, we are presented with so much information that does not require reflection or a well-reasoned response, we begin to avoid material that does. Movies are a good example—profound and complex ideas may be presented in a movie, but observation is all that is required of the viewer. Failing to understand one scene does not prevent you from viewing the next. Contrast this with reading material that requires careful reflection upon each sentence in order to make sense of the next, and you can see how formidable the mechanics of philosophical discourse might be. But, even though reading philosophical works may seem hard, the key to understanding them is really more a matter of patience and practice than of superior intelligence. The payoff is this: the sensual pleasures of learning are inherently more satisfying than anything posing to be entertainment.

Discipline is not exactly the right word to explain what else is required for learning to reason well, but for lack of a better word it will have to do. What I mean by discipline is really more a matter of seeing, a way of observing. In the West we use the term *epistemology* to refer to the nature of knowledge and *phenomenology* to refer to the study of awareness in the philosophical sense. But these terms are, for all practical purposes, left out of the vocabulary of everyday living. This is a grave error. The ability to reason well depends in large part on the point at which one begins to reason; if we ignore the fragile nature of knowledge and awareness, we are doomed from the start. We might as well begin a journey with a map purposely mismarked so that one location has no relation to another. Similarly, reasoning well from a faulty premise does not produce the same answer as beginning from a better one. The general lack of concern on the part of Westerners about the ability to see clearly is a curiosity falling somewhere between ignorance and arrogance.

If the Eastern philosopher calls our attention to the fact that when our mind stops to focus on an object it ceases to be capable of being aware of it, we are at a loss as to how to reply. Questions like, "What is the sound of one hand clapping?" sound like mystical nonsense. My point is that, because of our culture, reasoning and seeing are bound in the same process so that one affects the other; purpose and effort are required to do either well enough to escape the bias that comes built into culture. In other words, our cultural soup is so thick that seeing, in part, is reasoning, and reasoning, in part, is seeing. To become aware of this is like being awakened from sleep. Eastern philosophy is seductive and exhilarating from the sheer novelty of its contrast with the thinking of the West. Sometimes it's profoundly wise, but it often falls far short of our human capacity to capture reality—sort of like saying, since there is not enough light in this room to see everything, it's best if we just turn off what little light we have.

The pursuit of philosophy is one the greatest ways to live purposefully, but it is not the only way. William James once wrote, "Philosophy is at once the most sublime and trivial of human pursuits."[48] In a lecture titled "What Pragmatism Means," James spoke of "a ferocious metaphysical dispute" he had once taken part in. The premise was simple: a man stands in front of a tree with a squirrel on the other side of the tree. Attempting to see the squirrel, the man circles the tree. However, the squirrel wishes to avoid the man, so he moves in a circle also, always staying on the opposite side of the tree. The metaphysical question is this: Does the man go around the squirrel? James argues that when one looks at this argument "practically" the answer is both yes and no. He said:

> If you mean passing from the north of him to the east, then to the south, then to the west, and then to the north of him again, obviously the man does go around him, for he occupies these successive positions. But if on the contrary you mean being first in front of him, then on the right of him,

then behind him, then one his left, and finally in front again, it is quite as obvious that the man fails to go around him, for by the compensating movements the squirrel makes, he keeps his belly turned toward the man all the time, and his back turned away.[49]

I believe a similar comparison can be made concerning the ability of individuals to sense a gradient quality of life. If you buy the argument I'm about to introduce in greater detail—that reason and emotion are a continuum of the same thing—then it's easy to see how depth of understanding is linked to depth of feeling. The combination of the two is what we experience and measure as quality. If we let the squirrel represent the truth and meaning of life, but never contemplate it or live in congruence with our core principles, it can be said that we have been to the north, east, south and west of life, but have never fully experienced it—we still evade the issue. In *The Evolving Self*, Mihaly Csikszentmihalyi put it this way:

> You can drive a car all your life without knowing how the engine works, because the goal of driving is to get from one place to the next, regardless of how it is done. But to live an entire life without understanding how we think, why we feel the way we feel, what directs our actions is to miss what is most important in life, which is the quality of experience itself. What ultimately counts most for each person is what happens in consciousness: the moments of joy, the times of despair added up through the years determine what life will be like. If we don't gain control over the contents of consciousness we can't live a fulfilling life, let alone contribute to a positive outcome of history. And the first step toward achieving control is understanding how the mind works.[50]

Like gold miners we sift through life in search of glitter. We seldom realize that steadfast meaning is found in the black sands of being, in understanding the finer points of everyday living. Even the most boring existence looks good when compared to the alternative.

Ralph Waldo Emerson and Fredrich Nietzsche respectively offered compelling arguments to suggest that "being" is more important than "knowing," that character is higher than the intellect. They admired the ancient Greeks, who lived more by instinct than by reason. Nietzsche argued that "life is a higher value than knowledge simply because there would be no pyramid of knowledge without forms of life."[51] To Nietzsche, being and doing are one, but I would point out that the whole context of truth is measured within the skeletal framework of the intellect. In other words, without intellectual understanding, the notion of character is meaningless.

Emerson and Nietzsche did not admire ancient savages and barbarians, but—and this is an important but—it doesn't mean they believed all savages and barbarians were without character. Just as life is necessary for the existence of intellect, so is intellect necessary for the existence of character. Kant observed that "thoughts without content are void; intuitions without conceptions, blind."[52] We often speak of the spirit found in lower animals, but not of their character. William James described character as an inner voice one hears which says, "This is the real me."[53] Instinctive action is not the single sum of character. Rather, character is shaped by instinct and is tempered by learning and knowledge. Character is the synergy of one's life; it is not so much higher than the intellect as it is a part of it. Richard Hofstadter claimed that intellect is "a unique manifestation of human dignity"[54] and that intellectuals have inherited from the clerics of centuries past "a special sense of the ultimate value in existence of the act of comprehension."[55]

History is rife with individuals who exalted intuition over reason. The irony is, they were all deep thinkers, which is a lot like the rich downplaying the importance of money. I'm not for a moment suggesting that intuition cannot be a reliable source of truth, but truth in this context is like a tent: the intellect representing the poles. Without poles there exists no form for expression in a human context. Both Emerson and Nietzsche were correct in their assertions about knowledge standing in the way of truth and intuition. People professing a whole range of religious and political ideologies let the templates of culture stop them from thinking for themselves. Emerson and Nietzsche championed intuition in theory, even as they held ideas to be higher than social convention. I believe their affection for intuition over intellect was a subtle intellectual plea for a more embodied existence. Both were onto something big: reason and emotion are deeply connected.

It's not too far fetched to argue that emotions represent biological truth and that the union of our emotions with our intellect is a healing phenomenon.[56] After all, Freud instituted what has become a multibillion-dollar business based in part on this premise. Einstein taught us that time and space are interchangeable. So too, I believe, are reason and emotion. Reason and emotion are reciprocal brain functions: thinking is a residue of both. We are happy because of context; we are sad because of context. When emotion overtakes us, reason is overwhelmed; when emotion is controlled, we reason. An infant may cry for no apparent cause and an adult may appear to do the same, but if we look deep enough we will find an explanation for both. Indeed, in a manner very much like the duality experienced in quantum mechanics, if we look for reason in an action we find it, and if we look for emotion we find it.

Reason and emotion, mind and body—all are functions of the brain. This doesn't mean that reason and emotion are not distinctively different in characteristic, but that they are still expressions from the same fount: an idea is an expression of biology. Emotion thus felt is, in part, biological understanding. Passion may exist as a continuum from an unexplainable feeling to one of complete articulate expression. Spinoza characterized emotion as "a confused idea."[57] Science writer John McCrone says, "Each emotion is a body of ideas wrapped round a relatively small kernel of sensation."[58] Emotions may result from the excretion of hormones within the brain, but upon examination we still find those excretions occurring within, or as a result of, context. Misunderstanding this issue leads to the kind of thinking that prizes an arm but sees little need for an elbow, or has a high regard for "progress" but contempt for nature. Working all of this out is what living and lifelong learning are all about. We'd be unwise to fool around with moral premises favoring only part of our brain function. We cannot cultivate a sense of justice without knowledge of the enigma of both reason and emotion. Simply put, the range from the depths of our reptilian brain stem to the core of our frontal lobes is the stage on which we play out the drama of reason versus emotion.

As a wet finger is to wind direction, so are feelings to life experience. Indeed, emotion acts as a social barometer. What we experience as quality of life as individuals and as a society represents the sum total of our personal and public integration of reason and emotion. In *Emotional Intelligence* Daniel Goleman writes,

> In a sense we have two brains, two minds—and two different kinds of intelligence: rational and emotional. How we do in life is determined by both—it is not just IQ, but emotional intelligence that matters. Indeed, intellect cannot work at its best without emotional intelligence. Ordinarily the complementarity of limbic system and neocortex, amygdala and prefrontal lobes, means each is a full partner in mental life. When these partners interact well, emotional intelligence rises—as does intellectual ability.
>
> This turns the old understanding of the tension between reason and feeling on its head: it is not that we want to do away with emotion and put reason in its place, as Erasmus had it, but instead find the intelligent balance of the two. The old paradigm held an ideal of reason freed of the pull of emotion. The new paradigm urges us to harmonize head and heart. To do that well in our lives means we must first understand more exactly what it means to use emotion intelligently.[59]

We continue to find a much stronger genetic explanation for our behavior than was previously thought possible, and yet many of our higher emotions are clearly learned. We learn when to laugh and what to laugh and cry about. Moreover, the cultural learning afforded our species is eminently more dynamic and motivating in consequence than are our genetic predispositions. Cognitive scientist Steven Pinker suggests, "Emotions are mechanisms that set the brain's highest-level goals"; they're "adaptations, well-engineered software modules that work in harmony with the intellect and are indispensable to the functioning of the whole mind."[60] But, whether or not we know for certain that reason and emotion are corresponding aspects of the same phenomenon, we must recognize the importance of acting as if they are.

This whole discussion might seem frivolous or silly, were it not for the fact that the notion of a totally separate *sense* of truth, which no one can (or need) explain, denigrates the role of *thinking* and is a major source of anti-intellectualism. Further, Richard Hofstadter adds, "At an early date, literature and learning were stigmatized as the prerogative of useless aristocracies."[61] Because the importance of knowledge and understanding in everyday life is greatly undervalued, an ever-increasing number of lunatics can lay claim to esoteric, mystic knowledge, while millions of unreflective people, who are without principle or not active participants in their own lives, heed every word and imperil their own lives through blind obedience. It is why politicians can rise to power through the use of simple cliches and slogans. If *understanding* is not a value which is sought after, bigotry and racism can serve as substitutes for thinking (simply because the feeling seems right) among those who prove willfully ignorant and easily led. This notion of reason and emotion as two separate minds is the end-run of disembodiment. When we separate reason and emotion we are truly disembodied. When we depreciate the intellect we devalue life itself.

Though related, knowledge and understanding are not exactly the same. Knowledge may be true or false just as understanding may be correct or mistaken, but understanding as truth is something of a mystery. It often arrives at the precise moment one has stopped looking for it. This leads many to erroneously conclude it is unrelated to the quest for knowledge, even though the understanding which occurred was, in fact, the product of a meaningful question.

In his book *Man's Search for Meaning*, holocaust survivor Viktor Frankl wrote:

> As each situation in life represents a challenge to man and presents a problem for him to solve, the question of the meaning of life may actually be reversed. Ultimately, man should not ask what the meaning of life is, but rather he must recognize that it is *he* who is asked. In a word, each man is questioned by life; and he can only answer to life by answering for his own life; to life he can only respond by being responsible.[62]

Frankl's point reinforces my thesis that the meaning we get from life is due in large part to the meaning we give. Most advice about meaning is meaningless because the question of the meaning of life is always secondary to the meaning *in* life. Obsessing about the meaning of life while oblivious to the meaning in your own life is like being overly concerned with the concept of wet while you are drowning. Life is meaningful because touch, taste, sound, feeling, and thought make it so. And because they are fleeting. Life is hurled against a wall of meaning because life itself comes to a screeching halt. Thus, the quality of a life is not much of an issue until the quantity of life is challenged. There are a number of diverse paths for catching a glimpse of the squirrel of truth and meaning on the other side of the tree. One path is through creativity and achievement, another is in the essence of understanding. Another is found in relationships, and still another is found through one's attitude toward suffering.[63]

While I hold that education and love of wisdom offer one key to a better quality of life, I do not mean to imply that a person cannot live a good life without the contemplation of lofty ideas. The very concept of emotional intelligence shows there is a decided difference between thinking philosophically and living philosophically. People such as Socrates, Spinoza, Voltaire, and Thoreau were successful at both living and thinking philosophically. But Francis Bacon, an eminent thinker, was guilty of unethical business dealings. Jean Jacques Rousseau wrote eloquently about child rearing but gave his own children away. Alan Watts, one of my favorite contemporary philosophers, has been called a "genuine fake" because, although his advice was often profou..d, his personal life was a mess.[64] Many "primitive" peoples, on the other hand, had no knowledge of Western philosophy, but their observations about the interdependence of our world are borne out as valid by modern physics. Some preliterate people are intuitively wise in a sense that still evades the traditional West because they live as if principle is an interest-bearing form of awareness.

Philosophy, as a rehash of timeless, unanswerable questions, may feel good but yields little practical reward. Nevertheless, philosophical inquiry as a means of expanding one's awareness dramatically enlarges one's world and the ability to experience quality and meaning from it. In *Walden Pond*, Thoreau offers us this advice, "To be a philosopher is not merely to have subtle thoughts, nor even to found a school, but to so love wisdom as to live accordingly to its dictates, a life of simplicity, independence, magnanimity, and trust."

Creating a Better Life

Aristotle argued that contemplation is the pinnacle of human existence. We still revere the "ancients" and associate their names with wisdom, even as we recognize that wisdom is less abundant today than it was in ancient times. We speak of an information or knowledge society but admit that we have made little progress in achieving wisdom. Twentieth-century medical science has given us a vast array of antibiotics to fight infection, but indiscriminate use has led to a resurgence of virulent drug-resistant bacteria. We calculate employment statistics, but we don't know the difference in value between *work* and *jobs*.

There has always been a propensity among people to reach the conclusion that some people are better than others because of what they know. Individuals with knowledge have the opportunity to make better life choices than those without knowledge, but the difference has nothing whatsoever to do with their value as people. My learning is self-improvement in the sense that it makes me a better *me*. It does not make me better than you. My intellect is the superstructure of my being, or, as Alan Watts put it, somewhere about two inches behind the eyes is where I sense that the "I" which represents the real "me" exists. [65] Regardless of whether I believe in the existence of a human soul, I have to trust, by nature of my makeup as a human being, that what I perceive to be the intellect or my thinking apparatus is very much in control of my actions. In a very real sense, I am my experience, as opposed to being separated from it. By mere thought, I can influence my emotions or lower my pulse rate. This power to think, to reason, to imagine, sets us apart from all other life forms, at least to the degree that we seem to be much better at it than they are.

Learning is a powerful way to experience our humanness, but too many of us are emptied (through traditional education) of the natural desire to learn. Aristotle said, "All men by nature desire to know." Yet it can easily be demonstrated that in modern society most people reach a level of comfort beyond which they do not wish to be aware of anything that does not fit with their established view of reality.

In the preface of *Know Thyself*, David Cernic and Linda Longmire wrote:

> The more one seeks to know himself, the more his contents change, his moods and feelings shift, his conflicts and contradictions surface. Each new awareness thus disturbs his identity, and requires a new configuration. The paradox is that instead of dispelling the mystery by exploring himself, he enhances and deepens it. The fact that he can therefore never know himself completely is not cause to lament but cause to celebrate.[66]

Anti-intellectuals argue that contemplation sets us apart from our bodies (or animal nature) and alienates us from the natural world. But, if we listen to those whom we respect for their wisdom, we will discover that the mind/body relationship is an integral part of the self and that one cannot exist in the present without the other. It's the nagging sense that emotion is less significant that devalues intellectual development. To avoid intellectual development as a purposeful means of maintaining one's human nature is ludicrous. The intellect is not only *how* but *where* we live; not to give it full rein is a recipe for mediocrity. Henry David Thoreau makes this an issue in his often-quoted piece from *Walden Pond*:

> I went to the woods because I wished to live deliberately, to front only the essential facts of life, and see if I could not learn what it had to teach, and not, when I came to die, discover that I had not lived. I did not wish to live what was not life, living is so dear; nor did I wish to practice resignation, unless it was quite necessary. I wanted to live deep and suck out all the marrow of life, to live so sturdily and spartan-like as to rout all that was not life, to cut a broad swath and shave close, to drive life into a corner, and reduce it to its lowest terms, and, if it proved to be mean, why then to get to the whole and genuine meanness of it, and publish its meanness to the world; or if it were sublime, to know it by experience,

and be able to give a true account of it in my next excursion.[67]

We have no way to suck out the marrow of life or to pursue life into a corner except through the intellect; no way to sample providence or savor sublimity apart from reason and emotion. Which is not to say that other avenues of experience do not exist, but that to "purposely" pursue any kind of experience is an act of reason, even if the objective is to empty the mind in meditation. Aristotle said, "Reason is a light that God has kindled in the soul." To reason is by its very nature an act of self-determination. Moreover, even as a means for being practical, there is no substitute for giving rein to the intellect. "A truly educated person is motivated by, and can find satisfaction in, a wide array of things that are not traded in markets or that cost very little."[68]

By addressing the intellect in this way I do not mean to imply that humans do not possess what might be called somatic, sensual, or tacit ways of knowing, nor do I wish to minimize the importance of those. On the contrary, I believe the visceral, sensual knowledge we absorb from our surroundings is vastly misunderstood and underutilized. Not until we place knowledge gleaned from our environment into the context of the intellect do we fully experience what it means to be human. We share the need for food with all other animals. When we are hungry we eat as they do, but once we have eaten, unlike the animal world, we not only have the physical satisfaction of being full, we have the intellectual understanding that we were hungry, we have eaten, and it has made us comfortable. (We will revisit this level of human awareness, as Dasein, in a later chapter.) True, the animal that eats its fill satisfies its hunger, but what it experiences is the cessation of a drive without the awareness to put the experience in context, derive further meaning, and enjoy being satisfied (or so we think). This predilection for context, this cunning ability to plan, is the basis with which we judge the worth of ourselves in relation to animals. Now consider this vivid bit of prose about a pack of dogs chasing rabbits, in light of our system of value:

> He was ranging at the head of the pack, running the wild thing down, the living meat, to kill with his own teeth and wash his muzzle to the eyes in warm blood.

There is an ecstasy that marks the summit of life, and beyond which life cannot rise. And such is the paradox of living, this ecstasy comes when one is most alive, and it comes as a complete forgetfulness that one is alive. This ecstasy, this forgetfulness of living, comes to the artist, caught up and out of himself in a sheet of flame; it comes to the soldier, war-mad on a stricken field and refusing quarter; and it came to Buck, leading the pack, sounding the old wolf cry that fled swiftly before him through the moonlight. He was sounding the deeps of his nature, and of the parts of his nature that were deeper than he, going back into the womb of time. He was mastered by the sheer surging of life, the tidal wave of being, the perfect joy of each separate muscle, joint, and sinew and that it was everything that was not death, that it was aglow and rampant, expressing itself in movement, flying exultantly under stars and over the face of dead matter that did not move.[69]

This is from Jack London's *Call of the Wild.* It is fiction, and it has little to do with the method with which we discern value. This isn't a dog's rendition of experience; it's an example imagined by a human. But isn't it just possible that other creatures could experience their lives with a sense of quality that may even surpass this human attempt to romanticize it? Read it over a few times. When you consider the substance of living, you may not be so sure that we humans have a lock on quality of life.

Our human superiority seems so apparent that most of us have little cause to think our way through an assessment of values within the biological world around us. And so we remain ignorant of the subtle but profound ways in which lower forms of life find articulation: how, for example, the oats in the Cheerios I ate for breakfast this morning wound up as ink stains of expression on this page in a book. A key to a better life for each of us as individuals and for the whole of the human race may lie in the realization that we are part of the animal kingdom and not separate from it. Our ideas are not superior patterns of existence if we don't work very hard to make them so. All life is related. We are, as the title of Jared Diamond's book implies, *The Third Chimpanzee.* We glorify the intellect and romanticize animal nature, but we seldom correlate the two with what has been discussed as embodiment.

When we truly seek knowledge, we can search for meaning and truth through the same gesture. In *The Fifth Discipline*, Peter M. Senge examines

> ...the power of the truth, seeing reality more and more as it is, cleaning the lens of perception, awakening from self-imposed distortions of reality—different expressions of a common principle in almost all of the world's great philosophic and religious systems. Buddhists strive to achieve the state of "pure observation," of seeing reality directly. Hindus speak of "witnessing," observing themselves and their lives with an attitude of spiritual detachment. The Koran ends with the phrase, "What a tragedy that man must die before he wakes up."[70]

Commitment to truth, Senge continues,

> does not mean seeking the "truth," the absolute final word or ultimate cause. Rather, it means a relentless willingness to root out the ways we limit or deceive ourselves from seeing what is, and to continually challenge our theories of why things are the way they are. It means continually broadening our awareness, just as the great athlete with extraordinary peripheral vision keeps trying to "see the playing field." It also means continually deepening our understanding of the structures underlying current events. Specifically, people with high levels of personal mastery see more of the structural conflicts underlying their own behavior.[71]

The intellect, then, can be regarded as the "drive-train" of our existence. Evolution may have equipped us with a brain designed to protect us from the harshness of reality, but surely it was a short-term measure. Once we understand this premise, we are far better prepared to act responsibly and compassionately in matters concerning humanity, whereas before, fear and superstition seemed the only recourse. It is crucial that we understand this because superstition and prejudice, as we will later observe, are cut of the same cloth. If we can develop a thirst for truth as understanding, we can continually move mind and body closer to reality. Motivation and meaning are inexorably knotted together.

Chapter Three

Culture and Questions of Value

In the morning when thou risest unwillingly, let this thought be present—I am rising to the work of a human being. Why then am I dissatisfied if I am going to do the things for which I exist and for which I was brought into the world?[1]

—*Marcus Aurelius*

Culture in Perspective

Imagine for a moment you are sitting in a darkened movie theater facing the screen. Behind you is a physical replica of our king-of-the-mountain model, fashioned small enough to fit inside the theater. About three-fourths of the way up the mountain, precisely at the same level as the movie projection window, a porthole opens and light from inside the mountain fills the screen. The name of this movie is *The American Dream*, and the producers of culture are running the projector. Eager for entertainment, we become the audience.

The king-of-the-mountain model embodies the message: society will define happiness for you; these are your reasons for living. It is authoritative by design. We believe in an American Dream based upon *having* because we are taught that if you move up the mountain, if you work hard enough, earn enough money, you will reach the ledge of perpetual happiness. Clearly, material success has significance, but it's not as important as the power to command your own dream.

81

When you draw an outline of the mountain, you have a pyramid, a hierarchy. Hierarchies are not bad by definition. They promote stability and enhance survival. Neither are institutions undesirable. Indeed, "We live in and through Institutions."[2] But we are infamous for creating institutions for purposes we do not long remember. It is therefore naturally crippling when we still look to them for external definitions of happiness long after they have atrophied into bureaucracies with little, if any, of the vision remaining that prompted their very existence. In this way, educational institutions produce able workers whose lack of knowledge with regard to other people makes them dysfunctional human beings. The myth of the efficiency of singular authority contributes to this problem. Philip Slater writes:

> Authoritarianism has an undeserved reputation for efficiency—based on the achievements of a handful of charismatic leaders. But these rare moments pale to insignificance beside the dreary norm—soldiers driven mechanically to their deaths by rule-bound generals following antiquated strategies, dictators chaining their people in misery and backwardness while the world passes them by, bureaucrats plodding through corridors swollen like clogged arteries with proliferating regulations.[3]

Democracy can be a recipe for stalemate if its constituents care more about winning than finding equitable solutions. But democracy also enables decisions to be made when and where they need to be made. Unfortunately the customary call for strong leadership with a simultaneous emphasis on individual freedom is a contradiction at best (this occurs regularly at election time). At worst it is an abdication of responsibility on the part of both citizens and their leaders.

Carl Jung spoke of the "collective unconscious," but postmodern culture projects a media screen full of cultural "shoulds" which amount to a "collective consciousness." The message projected on the screen by our culture says we can ignore the unconscious. For so long now we have watched this screen with its external messages about how to live that we fail to discover we have enough capacity for knowledge to effectively project our own images on the screen. We each have the power to define happiness for ourselves. Until we understand this fully and without question, what is already on the screen will continue to seem infinitely more important than we believe we are individually. Mrs. Oswald does not have to be in the public eye to be an important person, unless she pays attention to nothing but what is already on the screen. What she and most of the rest of us do not realize is that *value assumes the identity we assign it*. James R. Fisher Jr. captures this perfectly in *The Taboo Against Being Your Own Best Friend*:

> We are all authors of our own footprints in the sand, heroes of the novels inscribed in our hearts. Everyone's life, without exception, is sacred, unique, scripted high drama, played out before an audience of one, with but one actor on stage. The sooner we realize this the more quickly we overcome the bondage of loneliness and find true friendship with ourselves.[4]

What becomes valuable is what we learn to expect has value. Thus, genuine knowledge could be more important than possessions, if we could learn to regard it that way.

Our need to be heroic or feel important is closely related to Joseph Campbell's assertion that, instead of meaning, what we are really looking for is "the rapture of being alive."[5] Being a hero and being truly alive are part and parcel of the same aspiration, the desire to matter. How shortsighted it is to scramble for name-brand products instead of focusing attention on the things that are really worth having, like the "rapture of understanding." We matter, if we believe we do. Our lives are important, if we are active participants in them.

In his book *Coming to Our Senses*, Morris Berman writes:

> We have inherited a civilization in which the things that really matter in human life exist at the margin of our culture. What matters? How birthing takes place matters; how infants are raised matters; having a rich and active dream life matters. Animals matter, and so does ontological security and the magic of personal interaction and healthy and passionate sexual expression. Career and prestige and putting a good face on it and the newest fashion in art or science do not matter. Coming to our senses means sorting this out

once and for all. It also means becoming embodied. And the two ultimately amount to the same thing.[6]

Berman argues that we have become disembodied by failing to stay in touch with our bodies and their environments. He delves into history, philosophy, anthropology, and psychology to develop the hypothesis of disembodiment. In his view, we have lost touch with our senses because we deny the world of physicality. Berman uses the terms embodiment and disembodiment, in a way that is far more sophisticated than my own usage, to illustrate the history of ego consciousness. He also suggests that, as infants, we are whole beings, unable to separate ourselves from our experience. Growing up, we fracture into a self that recognizes objects. Thus we inhabit a self-object world in which the loss of wholeness haunts us for the rest of our lives.

Again, I point back to the screen in our theater as a rationale because, in focusing so hard on our culture's external cues, we deny our own experience and fail to feel our own feelings. Worse, we learn that emotion is something to be repressed and never displayed in public or on the page. If we become too far detached from our emotions, we mimic the cold, impersonal logic of our technology, or emulate artificial intelligence. Indeed, if we are successful in repressing our emotions deeply enough, we can walk right by the most unimaginable injustice without feeling or protest. We move further and further into abstraction—abstractions minus the emotional qualities which make us human beings. We confuse the symbol with what it is supposed to represent. Money is a prime example of this kind of objectification. We use money in an attempt to standardize value, but the process which works well in simplifying our economic transactions obliterates the need to continue making value judgments. "Money is not concerned with the unique qualities of experience."[7] In part, the power to *be* is found in the power not to buy.

If we were to observe a hunter-gatherer society whose members used rare seashells as currency and who spent more time looking for seashells than for food, we would likely view them as uncivilized. We, however, do exactly the same thing with money. Our currency, though, is one step removed from gold—rather like having tree bark represent seashells. Seashells and gold become valuable only when people believe they are valuable. An individual with a hut full of seashells but strapped for knowledge about how to live a good life appears as foolish as one hoarding a stash of gold with the same problem. It is easy for us to see that seashells are less important than people, but it is not so easy to see through our own cultural bias, if we use gold as the example. If tribal members were to suggest a human life is worth no more than 40 seashells, we would say they were mad; but, if the measure were 40 bars of gold, our own process for measuring worth might appear the more barbarous. There is something wholly unbelievable about the fact that a baseball card may have an economic value equivalent in worth to that of a hundred human lives, or that a rare stamp or a painting may represent the worth of tens of thousands of lives. But the message projected by our culture sanctions it, as long as there are people willing to pay any price for such objects.

Knowledge is an antidote to manufactured needs. Soft-drink manufactures reap the incomes of nation-states, yet nothing quenches thirst like water. Why is it so hard to imagine an economy in which "growth" stands for an increase in knowledge instead of an increase in goods? The amount of knowledge we can acquire is infinitely greater than the number of goods we can consume. In the final analysis, isn't knowledge worth more to us as individuals than seashells and gold? Net worth seems to me to have much more to do with having lived a full life, than with how much is left in one's savings account. Likewise, net loss represents the void felt by those who live on after a loved one's death.

When we are exposed to a system of economics from birth, without fully integrating our own experience in our assessments of worth, we make the mistake of confusing the means for the ends. Embodiment, as urged by Berman, requires us to *pay attention*, to compare our own experience with the messages our culture provides, and not to ignore, repress, or deny our own feelings in favor of the external abstractions on our theater screen. Embodiment requires the acknowledgment of principle. To become embodied is to learn the truth of Mary Parker Follet's assertion in 1924, "Integration is both the keel and the rudder of life: it supports all life's structure and guides every activity."[8] Or, as Philip Slater writes in *Earthwalk*, "No one who has become alienated from his own body is in control of his destiny, however much he may able to throw his dissociated weight around in the external environment." If we do not learn to feel and to think for ourselves, to define happiness and the fruits of a good life of our own volition, we keep our eyes on the screen, thus ensuring that we don't comprehend the first thing about the essence of being human. Our system of economics values a baseball card—which is but an image of an image—more than the worth of a human life, or it would forbid the circumstances which suffer such transactions.

Berman is right when he says we have moved most of what matters to the margins of our culture. But our history suggests that *work* is the most important thing humans can do. Certainly though, a career is not more important than raising children. "Putting a good face" on a career is a trivial pursuit, but how we spend the majority of our time matters a great deal. Moreover, we must understand that, if we are ever to rediscover a sense of embodiment and achieve the levels of competence necessary to discover equitable solutions to our most pressing problems, it will most likely occur through *right livelihood*. Finding right livelihood means finding work which suits our talents and temperament. And, in the Buddhist spirit where this term originates, it means work that also suits our planet.

Work both alienates and invigorates us. Work is the problem and the solution. Karl Marx's theory falls far short of his intention to define value, but Marx knew the danger work poses to society through alienation. The cure is found in making all work meaningful. This is not a mystical notion of adding intrigue to dull monotonous work. Rather, we must realize that a great deal of what is really meaningful is left undone. We need first to understand the nature of what we call work.

In his book *The Culture of Contentment*, John Kenneth Galbraith writes:

> There is no greater modern illusion, even fraud, than the use of the single term *work* to cover what for some is, as noted, dreary, painful or socially demeaning and what for others is enjoyable, socially reputable and economically rewarding.

Those who spend pleasant, well-compensated days say with emphasis that they have been "hard at work," thereby suppressing the notion that they are a favored class. They are, of course, allowed to say that they enjoy their work, but it is presumed that such enjoyment is shared by any *good* worker. In a brief moment of truth, we speak, when sentencing criminals, of years at "hard labor." Otherwise we place a common gloss over what is agreeable and what, to a greater or lesser extent, is endured or suffered.[9]

We make work meaningful through the respect and the reward we give to the worker. If a task is worth doing, it should be worthy of such meaning. The trouble is not that too few people are working (we may have too many people working), but not enough people are thinking and learning. If the opposite were true, bigotry and prejudice would disappear out of judicious mutual interest. Anthropologist Lionel Tiger tells us, "*The function of learning is to reduce social differentiation not to increase it*; the human being expresses gregariousness as much by sharing symbols as by sharing food, sharing children, sharing beds, and sharing space." (The italics are his.)[10]

Clearly, not enough people are thinking. Learning leads to understanding, and understanding helps bridge the gulf between the sensual self and the intellect. Both self and community are enriched. Achieving balance as individuals is critical to finding social balance. The social and environmental problems we have today are in part the result of millions of people working frantically, clinging to jobs that make them miserable, while having no idea what types of jobs they are best suited for, and little if any idea about what they would really like to do with their lives. How else could a nation (as we've done) reach the point of depending for its very survival on the perpetual consumption of goods its people *do not need?* This confusion prevents most everyone from learning enough to figure out for themselves what in this world really matters, what *needs* to be done and what *shouldn't* be done. Is it any wonder that a society in which the majority seldom engages in this sorting out is destined to produce problems greater than it is capable of solving? Precisely because we are disembodied, estranged from nature, we do not appreciate the value of nature and each other.

For years, I have been of the opinion that, whenever possible, menial tasks should be relegated to machines, but I am becoming increasingly less sure that is a good idea. Menial tasks bind us to nature—better that we maintain the link than live totally in abstraction. Burning 500 calories in a gym does not produce the kind of understanding that would result from expending 500 calories in one's garden. Moreover, if everyone participated in the menial tasks that must be done, we would be less likely to judge the worth of others by what they do for a living. It is a far greater tragedy for the majority of us to fail to pursue lifelong learning than for the poor to have menial work for this very reason. Emerson understood this thoroughly:

> Manual labor is the study of the external world. The advantage of riches remains with him who procured them, not with their heir. When I go into my garden with a spade, and dig a bed, I feel such an exhilaration and health that I discover that I have been defrauding myself all this time in letting others do for me what I should have done for myself with my own hands.[11]

People are necessarily different, no question. We have unique but similar personalities, distinct talents which represent natural and novel ways of adapting to our culture. Technology, however, favors only some of these natural human differences. The result is that only some personalities and talents are highly valued, causing economic power to fall only to those with the seemingly natural talents to specialize. In time such specialists prove to function well only at work, creating a situation where the people who are the least embodied are the most valued. The outcome of this maddening confusion is that technology increasingly develops products to make life more enjoyable while at the same time rewarding and encouraging the people who are least suited to benefiting from them. Executives use left-brained strategies to make products for right-brained users, and the reverse, while workaholics of either type have little time for leisure products. In *The Pursuit of Loneliness*, Philip Slater asks:

Must a powerful, wealthy nation keep people monotonously doing meaningless tasks in order to avoid starving to death, when those same people have severe needs of their own that go neglected? We seem unwilling to recognize and deal with the fact that our economy rests on a profound misdirection of energy. This timidity is catastrophic. All the economic BandAids in the world can't hide the fact that we've been spending our resources and labor stupidly for decades, and are beginning to pay the price....Money, after all, is symbolic, not real—an illusion that we agree to share for convenience. We've been staring at it for so long, listening to the hypnotic droning of professional economists, that we've forgotten it's just a mechanism for using our energies to meet our needs. Money is a way of matching needs and resources, but when we get caught up in it, and treat it as having value in its own right, it fails to perform even this rudimentary function.[12]

We cannot keep our own lives and dreams in perspective if we do not continually practice putting society itself in perspective. We must ask and re-ask the simple questions about what we are really trying to accomplish and what is really more important, the *form* or the *substance* of our efforts. It is seldom acknowledged, and even less well understood, that authority defines reality. How else do we explain why millions of us engage in mindless work and leisure activities while we ignore our real needs? Keeping our culture in perspective requires that we think as forcefully as those whose thinking has itself become culture.

Perhaps we can bring fresh perspective to the issue of work when we acknowledge that humans have always worked. Indeed, work is at core a human enterprise. James R. Fisher Jr. writes, "Without work, there is little self. Without work, it is an embarrassment to breathe."[13] Raising and educating children is work. Learning is work. Growing food is work. Caring for animals is work. Furthering human relations is work, which means politics is work. Creating institutions which nourish humanity is work. The grave error which leads the vacuity of contemporary society is that *jobs* are considered more important than *work*.

The first few years of life are critical to a child's intellectual development. There are finite windows of opportunity for the quality and capacity of cognitive development in logic, language, music, and spatial skills which, if ignored, are never fully recoverable. And yet, politicians garner votes by insisting that women without jobs cheat society by taking welfare, even if they would otherwise have to "warehouse" their children. So great is the confusion about the value of jobs versus work that both the rich and the poor—the former having time on their hands and the latter who can't get a good-paying job—are oblivious to the notion that there is still a lot of *work* which needs to be done. Henry David Thoreau took odd jobs all of his life so that he could attend to his work, which produced *Civil Disobedience* and *Walden Pond*. This was work worth doing.

Lessons of History

History provides clear evidence that cultures adopt behaviors because they are practical. These behaviors, in time, become sacralized as tradition. The record is also clear that if the people of any culture fail to think critically and reflect upon their traditions, they will not understand the fragile, temporary nature of practicality. Cultural diversity creates social conditions which bring to consciousness the temporary and arbitrary nature of traditions. Honoring tradition is a demonstration of loyalty and respect for one's culture, but blind obedience, the act of using tradition as an excuse for not thinking for oneself, is an abdication of responsibility. Blind obedience ensures that ethnocentrism will be a tool for manipulation by any power willing to use it. History often reveals obedience as cowardice.

Young people have always asked, "Why do I have to study history or government when I can't see any relevance in these subjects to the circumstances in my life?" There are many reasons: we have a barbaric past. Throughout recorded history millions of people have been oppressed and butchered for every conceivable reason with every conceivable justification. The record proves that power corrupts and absolute power corrupts absolutely.

We live in a dangerous world undergoing social and technological changes faster than ever before in the evolution of humankind. At any given time, at least a score of countries are at war, and, as long as they are, the danger exists that more countries will be drawn into the conflict. Thus, never has such a responsibility been thrust upon so many people to ensure that what we do is just and equitable for the nation as well as for each of us individually.

By understanding history we gain valuable information and insight for understanding ourselves. History discloses what our ancestors really cared about. What they said can be contrasted with what they actually did. History's real value does not lie in the exciting events we're expected to remember, but in the everyday problems of living that only a serious look at times past will reveal. There is much to be learned from a comparison of our own problems and strategies with the recorded experience of previous centuries. Recall that the early America described in Chapter One bears little resemblance to popular cinematic versions. When we reach beneath the crust of popular or textbook history we find that everyday life for our ancestors was not at all the way we have imagined it.[14] It is often startling to find that much of what we accept as tradition in the form of custom is based on accidental or arbitrary circumstances. For example, the ways in which we celebrate two of our most popular holidays, Thanksgiving and Christmas, have much more to do with manipulation by retailers than a purposeful effort to celebrate the occasions themselves. No one even knows if turkeys were eaten at what was supposed to be the first Thanksgiving; celebrating Christmas as anything more than a religious observance was suppressed until merchants began exploiting it with the idea of gift giving shortly after the Civil War.[15]

Conservative historian, Gertrude Himmelfarb refers to the history of ordinary people as "history from below."[16] Himmelfarb laments that the postmodern times we are living in have given rise to a multiculturalism, where history is so politicized that we now have a history of every man, every woman, race or group. I suspect what Himmelfarb really fears is the threat postmodernism brings to elitist historians who have attempted to professionalize history in a way that elevates and maintains their own status as guardians of culture. (Unless, of course Himmelfarb considers herself and her colleagues to be just ordinary citizens.) According to this line of thinking, if the history of the lives of ordinary people is not worthy of note, then obviously our lives are not worth living.

A few individuals in every culture in every age have claimed the spotlight, especially by performing momentous deeds, but that doesn't mean they held a franchise on quality of life or achievement. Todd Gitlin writes, "History from above rolls forward with seeming relentlessness. History from below is always stopping, retracing its steps, moving sideways, shifting back and forth, pausing to say 'meanwhile' and 'despite.'"[17] History is less the vapor trail of titans than a residue of the blood, sweat, tears, and cheers of the ordinary folks without whom life for any kind of society would not be possible. Attempts to understand history that do not include the points of view of those whose opinions were "marginalized" are worse than illusion.

The popular versions of history suggest that our past has unfolded neatly in storybook fashion, but nothing could be further from the truth. A related danger expresses itself in Stephen Jay Gould's assertion that "textbook dogma is self-perpetuating."[18] In other words, far too much license is taken with truth because it is easier to pass assertions forward than to check them or reason them out. If we dig below the surface, we find our ancestors often overcame (or succumbed to) unimaginable problems. Knowing what those were and how they solved them (or failed to) gives us the benefit of their experience, just as they would want us to have it. Thus, studying history is a way to narrow the generation gap. When we pay close attention to history, we learn that each generation's excess lays the foundation for what will be considered contemptible in the next.

A close reading of history reveals sharp contradistinctions between social convention and the intellectual plane of human existence. The American experience with prohibition in the 1920s, for example, offers insight into solving today's drug problems. The labor problems during the same period still suggest valuable lessons for today's students of management. A genuine appreciation for living conditions in the past helps us to realize how far we have come and how far we have yet to go in order to reach environmental equilibrium. Habits developed during the Great Depression could again serve us well in conserving resources and minimizing waste.

American history exemplifies vividly how intellectual patterns change social patterns. In the creation of our Constitution, intellectual patterns attained a superior standard which, once in place and taken for granted, have automatically reverted back to social convention. In other words, at the moment the Constitution was created it was an advance, but as soon as the ideals it represents were not lived up to, it became just another document amounting to little more than a prescription for social convention.

Our history shows a continuing rhythm of pendulum swings from liberal to conservative social postures. The era of the Puritans preceded the bawdy years from the 1790s through the 1820s. Then came the rise of Victorian values of the 1830s which were disjointed once again by the roaring 1920s. As was suggested earlier, Victorian values and manners were, to some extent, an effort by the prosperous middle class to set themselves apart from a booming influx of immigrants. The real impetus which betters society comes not from a desire to be superior to someone else but from the best thinking one can muster.

To adopt behavior through obedience for the sake of status is to willfully blind oneself to the best understanding of reality one can achieve. Such a response evolves not into a superior culture but into an ethnocentrism, oblivious to every injustice unacknowledged by authority. Life becomes automatic: stimulus, response. Rules assume the role of purpose. Experience becomes counterfeit expression. Witness the enormous historical record of societies who slaughtered their neighbors to satisfy the egos of tyrants.

We live in times today similar to those that prompted the rise of Victorian values. Many Victorians were socially repressed and excessively narrow, but they also considered themselves responsible for their own reasoning—and their emotions—and many were actively engaged in trying to create a better world. Today, because we have their experience as an example, we have the chance to have a much better go of it than they did. The same phenomenon that enhances individual life also betters society. To achieve an intellectual level which lays down a better pattern of society requires an attentive awareness, an aliveness, a direct involvement in the mastery of one's culture and as much knowledge of other cultures as one can obtain.

Individual Interpretations

History is written from perpetually changing points of view; these are easy to identify once you know what you are seeking. For example, the most commonly found perspectives are: authoritative (theological, divine, royal order, or aristocratic), geographical, economic, political, psychological, scientific, sociological, and environmental. Written history offers these "social" perspectives in varying degrees and proportions. When we learn to recognize and use them, they become keys for greater understanding.[19]

Each of these perspectives stems from an obvious posture of authority. If reality is a socially constructed process, then history, as Emerson suggested, is "only biography." Emerson slams the gauntlet at our feet asserting that "the sun shines today also." He attempts to startle us, to crack the armor of our external motivation and appeal to our intrinsic core by saying:

> Meek young men grow up in libraries, believing it their duty to accept the views which Cicero, which Locke, which Bacon have given; forgetful that Cicero, Locke, and Bacon were only young men in libraries when they wrote these books.[20]

Emerson asks that we develop our own sense of authority, that we make up our own minds about the past by the way in which we relate to the authority represented in books:

> Books are the best of things, well used; abused, among the worst. What is the right use? What is the one end which all means go to effect? They are for nothing but to inspire. I had better never seen a book than to be warped by its attraction clean out of my own orbit, and made a satellite instead of a system.[21]

The propensity to rely on authority, in lieu of realizing our own, explains why someone named Smith becomes a Jungian psychologist instead of a Smithian psychologist. Both Emerson and Nietzsche warned of the dangers of constructing a history that looms so large as to inhibit us from creating our own history. When we cling to authority we hold social patterns higher than intellectual patterns. Even the best of books afford only social patterns until their contents are acted upon through the intellect of the reader, not as recall or remembrance but through a deliberative dialog. In school, imagine what it would have been like not to have accepted the single authority of one textbook for class. What if instead, with the teacher's help, we had collectively searched for the knowledge most relevant to our own lives and had created our own books? What a difference in perspective it would have brought to learning. And what a joy it would be to read those books in later years.

There is a popular movement today in academic circles known as deconstruction.[22] Deconstructionists use the tools of perception, linguistics, and postmodernist ideas about the fragile nature of reality, to search for defects in written works, to identify contradictions, and inevitably to discover the bias of the author. In *Reflexivity,* Hilary Lawson writes,

> Deconstruction at its simplest, consists of reading a text so closely that the conceptual distinctions, on which the text relies, are shown to fail on account of the inconsistent and paradoxical employment of these very concepts within the text as a whole. Thus the text is seen to fail by its own criteria—the standards or definitions which the text sets up are used reflexively to unsettle and shatter the original distinctions.[23]

Deconstructionists lay open the work so that all may see its innards. This process is a little like letting the air out of tires, if books are to tradition as tires are to automobiles. Traditionalists are often dismayed to find revered works held to such ridicule, for it is implied that once a work has been deconstructed it is impotent. But nothing could be further from the truth. Deconstruction doesn't necessarily mean destruction. A vehicle can still move with flat tires, and its occupants will pay a lot more attention to the ride. Deconstruction by any means is as much of a tradition as the writing of books. A culture without a counterculture is incapable of genuine learning.

When we idealize the past, memory becomes a refuge to escape the present. I take issue with certain statements by Emerson and Kant, but I am not threatened by deconstruction of their works. I still trust that inspiration will dawn in the process of examining books with all the tools and techniques at my disposal. Concerned not only with what appears in the text but with what is left out, deconstruction is the heart, the soul, the very core of critical inquiry. Emerson says, "We as we read, must become Greeks, Romans, Turks, priest and king, martyr and executioner, must fasten the images to some reality in our secret experience, or we shall learn nothing rightly." Indeed, it's hard to read books assuming multiple points of view without employing a touch of deconstruction.

Perhaps the greatest difficulty with deconstruction is that it applies intellectual patterns which brandish little respect for social patterns. The mark of an intrinsic education is that, after deconstruction, one has the ability to reconstruct. After all, we do require social patterns. It is one of our greatest imperfections that we depend so heavily on our culture but remain estranged from all but a few generations of our own ancestors. We are, in effect, cut off from our collective history, as if the only important occurrences in human events are the ones we or a living relative of ours can remember. Millions of Americans have photo albums with pictures of family members no one can identify. This break with our past is so severe that our bones have to be in the ground only for a short time before the reverence for our passing is lost and we become artifacts.

History as Social Progress

In his book *The End of History and the Last Man*, Francis Fukuyama presents an intriguing view of history by resurrecting G. W. F. Hegel's interpretation of history as a progressive social struggle culminating in the elimination of social classes. Hegel's *Philosophy of History* (ca. 1835) provided the foundation upon which Karl Marx and Friedrich Engels produced the theory known as *dialectic materialism*, more commonly called *communism*. Fukuyama writes,

> Both Hegel and Marx believed that the evolution of human societies was not open-ended, but would end when mankind had achieved a form of society that satisfied its deepest and most fundamental longings. Both thinkers posited an "end of history": for Hegel this was the liberal state, while for Marx it was a communist society. This did not mean that the natural cycle of birth, life, and death would end, that important events would no longer happen, or that newspapers reporting them would cease to be published. It meant, rather, that there would be no further progress in the development of underlying principles and institutions, because all of the really big questions had been settled.[24]

Fukuyama's synthesis, albeit astute, doesn't ask the big questions. Fighting political oppression to achieve a more democratic way of life has been an ongoing campaign throughout human history, but it may pale in terms of difficulty when compared to the future challenge of reaching a stable human population while simultaneously affording those at the bottom of the social mountain a decent standard of living.

Fukuyama suggests that human history resembles a walk through time in which one step, based upon technological advance, is followed (not necessarily in lockstep fashion) by a thymotic step. Fukuymama's term *thymotic* is derived from Plato, who, in *The Republic,* described the soul as consisting of three parts: a desiring part, a reasoning part, and a "spiritedness" called thymos. Thymos is the substance of self-esteem from which grows the desire for recognition or pure prestige.

Fukuyama views history as a process driven by the innate need of human beings to be recognized by other human beings. We have already discussed in Chapter Two the human need to be a hero, which is but a manifestation of a need to matter. If the motor of history runs on the fuel of recognition, what will it mean if we reach a true state of equality? (Not to imply that we are anywhere near such a reality today.) When and if universal democracy is achieved, Fukuyama seems to be saying, the social struggle which provides the fuel for rising above adversity would be lost and all that would remain would be smoldering mediocrity. Significant events would still occur, but a progressive (dialectic) history in a social sense would cease to exist, having culminated with the triumph of Western ideology.

Courage and the nerve to risk one's life lie at the core of thymos. Fukuyama's most dramatic illustration sets forth the difference in temperament between that of the master and that of the slave. The master's willingness to wage war for the sheer prestige of recognition through victory contrasts vividly against the slave's willingness to remain a slave rather than risk death in a quest for freedom. Few slaves risked their lives for their freedom, just as few people in Third World countries put up a fight when faced with starvation. In comparison, when you tally the frequency of courageous acts found in a company of Marines or among a tribe of Zulu warriors, thymos begins to resemble a product of culture or, by extension, a product of learned behavior.

The vast majority of both slaves and masters, we must remember, owed their status to an accident of birth—it was not an expression of their thymotic worth. As Eric Hoffer observed in the *True Believer,* "The absolute equality among the slaves, and the intimate communal life in slave quarters, preclude individual frustration."[25] A slave born to slavery will act differently from a free individual who is abducted into slavery. Thymos, then, might very well emerge from frustration more than from an intrinsic form of moral superiority.

Our constant need for recognition derives from external motivation. If we get stuck in our personal growth, if we never move above the ridge of social convention, then we become mired in a rut where we gain our recognition mainly from "having." Thymos, it turns out, could have more to do with the engine of economics than with the motor of history. Today, *having* substitutes for *being.* Thus, we may never be successful in following our own path because our self-worth is bound to an economic ethos. Fukuyama appears to have confused a social convention for a biological one.

When one depends too much upon recognition, one ceases to exist. But thymos can be overridden through awareness and understanding. In the Maslovian model, thymos gets us only as far as the base camp for finding purpose and meaning. To Hegel, freedom was the point of history; to Maslow, freedom is merely the threshold of possibilities. Freedom is a means, not an end, as Fukuyama suggests. His book title has more to do with overemphasis on one ideal among human aspirations than with the literal end of anything. But then, that's my point.

In the past century the hierarchical and contingent nature of human needs and aspirations have played a primary role in our developmental history. Perhaps instead of reaching the end of history we'll find we can use this knowledge to bring forth a new beginning, and to start asking really big questions like, how can human beings achieve economic and ecological sustainability without butchering one another?

Few people manage to rise above their environmental circumstances. Those who do may actually create culture, but we can only imagine how many Galileos, da Vincis, and Einsteins have lived without escaping the bonds of poverty, thus never fully developing their natural abilities. The Hegelian idea, that wars brought about by the whims of kings and tyrants contribute more to human aspirations than does the pursuit of meaning in a just and peaceful world, seems patently absurd. Moreover, conquering disease, achieving environmental stability, and exploring space are sufficient and necessary conditions to challenge humanity.

German philosopher Johann Gottlieb Fichte asserts, "To be free is nothing; to become free is heavenly." Compare the shades of meaning: to *be* free; to *become* free. Being free is easily taken for granted. But *becoming* free involves an investment, a risk, a price beyond comfort. Only after we have fully understood our need for recognition are we able to change the locus of our motivation from being free to becoming free, from an external condition to an internal monitor, which satisfies our deepest and most fundamental longings to *know* and to *understand*.

People who have given us Dynamic Quality through the ages are those who have risen above desire or external motivation to thymos (or spiritedness). They sought truth for its own sake. They were people who did not need to win battles or to strut about like peacocks. Socrates died for principle, not prestige. What would be the effect if people were to find purpose and meaning through the mastery of culture and follow the same path as Socrates? If ideas were ubiquitously celebrated over social patterns, social convention would be upheld more by principle than by rules of social order. Fewer rules would be required for guiding behavior.

Historian John Lukacs offers another view of the driving force of history in his book *The End of the Twentieth Century*. Lukacs suggests, "the main political force in the twentieth century has been nationalism, not Communism." He argues that "communism is dead, but national self-determination is very much alive." Perhaps the vigor of nationalism stems in part from a greater need for power than for recognition. Lukacs has said,

> Near the end of...the so-called Modern Age—two dangerous circumstances threaten the world. One is the institutionalized pressure for material and economic "growth"—contrary to stability and threatening nature itself. The other is the existence of the populist inclinations of nationalism—contrary to a greater and better understanding among peoples, often debouching into barbarism. One is the thrust for increasing wealth; the other, for tribal power. One issues from the presumption that the principle human motive is greed; the other, that it is power. To think that the former is morally superior to the latter is at least questionable; but to think that the progress of history amounts to the triumph of money over force is stupid beyond belief.[26]

There are a multitude of ways to examine history for insight into the human condition. We could use fear, honor, lust, pride, curiosity, greed, pleasure, or any number of descriptive citations as the linchpins of our inquiry. They would be useful, but they would be more akin to the turns of a kaleidoscope than to a definitive view of history. The lesson here is that all historical perspectives are valuable, but none obliterate the need for further inquiry.

Now, before we leave perspectives of history, consider this. Humans severed ties with the wild species of the animal world at the onset of agrarian society. Ties with the cyclic nature of the earth were later disjointed by the industrial age. Today we move even deeper into an abstraction called cyberspace. Throughout this historical progression, traditionalists (those who valued things as they were) lamented a loss of genuine connection with the past, while rejectionists (people who thought things could be a lot better) sought change at any price. The cost has been that communal bonds were replaced by a cash economy which has become increasingly symbolic. True, human society is better off without slavery, and without feudal lord and serf associations fettered by oppression and ignorant superstition. But do we feel an appropriate kinship with nature? We are worse off if we don't, or if we are so insulated by the machinations of our culture that we no longer feel our own feelings or have any compassion for people who are in the least manner different from ourselves.

The major reason we are so ill-adjusted to life for the twenty-first century is that, as societies move through time, we do not bring enough of the past with us. The connections we have lost can be understood through Robert M. Pirsig's discussions about *hierarchy of patterns* and the concept of qualitative improvement via *static-latching*.

Humanity suffers because intellectual patterns are less suited for adaptation than are biological patterns. An idea reduced to social custom is no longer an idea. It remains an idea only as long as it is held and acted upon by human beings. But conservatives in every age attempt to reify "good ideas," and this leads to a closed-system culture. In the face of complexity, culture substitutes for thought. In this way, better ideas cannot supersede tradition because they threaten the system. Therefore, success is hard won; society more often than not winds up in a rut through the inability to make further adaptations without great conflict.

Biological organisms bring their learned adaptations with them as DNA, whereas humans must rely upon the knowledge of past generations in a form known as *education*. Indeed, "DNA is the source of meaning."[27] The DNA of education for human society is *wisdom*, and it is a scarce commodity. Since education is a means of sharing power, every society handles the concept of education differently. Pirsig suggests that cultures enrich themselves through a process of *static-latching* (which is sort of an elegant, abstract way to describe incremental and sporadic improvement, as innovation becomes tradition). But sustained improvement does not occur qualitatively because past improvements through static-latching are not captured, retained, and passed on through the process of education.

No one can be given wisdom. The achievement of wisdom requires the full attention, awareness, and skepticism of the student. Wisdom derives from understanding. Understanding emerges from the technical skill and psychological perception to deal with "what is," with reality. Most societies value wisdom far less than simple utility and obedience. As a result, human societies do not make sufficient use of history. New ideas threaten social status. So, without the benefit of wisdom as a truly prized force, human progress is herky-jerky and unstable at best.

Cash (symbolic) economies leave plenty of room for legitimate communal ties, when wisdom is valued more than material goods (desiring). But societies whose educational agendas are covert methods of perpetuating the *power* of the status quo elevate success (having) as a higher prize than wisdom. Moreover, the persistent misuse of power ensures that subsequent generations will re-experience the same baffling phenomenon. When citizens spend their lives striving to do what others claim is important without figuring out what is important for themselves, when recognition is more sought after than *understanding*, nationalism becomes a resourceful tool in the hands of the powerful to still questions of equity by those who wish to share power. Whatever is wrong with current arrangements must be someone else's fault, goes the thinking. Bigotry, projection, and prejudice become the smoke and mirrors of special interests. Thus, nationalism, which ultimately results in war, begins with the notion that some people are better than others. Virus-like we kill each other. Those who question the wisdom of this enterprise of war are called traitors. And so, what we learn from war reinforces Hegel's conclusion that "we never learn from war."[28]

Public Attention, Private Confusion

The cultural projection of the consummate American Dream comes to us as the media—radio, television, newspapers, books, magazines, and all of the apparatus through which we are bombarded with information, entertainment, and advertising. Media relationships increasingly substitute for human relations. Internet dialog stands in for conversation. Indeed, those who hold the worldview of the romanticist are easily seduced into the notion of self-realization through the consumption of images. In a real sense, we become what we think about. People who are off balance in their professional or personal lives, or who are somehow struggling to define themselves, are especially vulnerable to manipulation by media.

Advertising is a clear example of how intellectual patterns establish social patterns. It is a highly intellectual endeavor, playing to our biological predispositions. Advertising is music to human genes. Fashion is a social pattern, and labels are guides for behavior. Advertising specialists have created an illusionary world in which an unattainable perfection is deemed desirable and necessary for the sake of personal fulfillment. They have accomplished this by presenting airbrush-perfected versions of everything that we might wish, thus fostering unreal expectations. We can never look as good as the fashion models because their images are unreal celluloid representations. For anyone troubled by identity issues the result can be a treadmill existence. The strongly felt need to be better, or the identification of self-esteem with material rewards, is exacerbated by the growing revelation that one's efforts are not producing rewards quickly enough, or well enough. This in turn prompts one to run faster, to try harder to grasp something that can't be had.

Advertising is an emotional enterprise directed at people who are, for all practical purposes, emotionally illiterate. The ethos of advertising suggests that all problems have a commercial solution. It is profoundly important to understand that this is not true. The most meaningful external problems have internal solutions. We cannot find balance in our lives if we do not understand our emotions, and we can't master our emotions if we don't understand the mechanics of advertising and the nature of our own motivation. Getting a handle on these dynamics is equivalent to developing emotional intelligence.

One way to keep media in perspective is to borrow from Plato. Plato had the strange idea that the physical world we live in is but an illusion. The real world exists in the idealistic sense of Forms—Forms which as humans we barely have the capacity to comprehend, Forms that are the perfected blueprints for which all physical (material) bodies are but representations. For example, a Form exists for an apple, an orange, man, woman; all earthly examples are merely imperfect representations of the Forms themselves. The best example of an apple is still just an example; it derives its appleness from the Form. Plato's pupil, Aristotle, dismissed the theory of Forms as being unprovable (a clear example of the power of rational left-brain thinking winning out over what might have been the most preeminent right-brain idea ever expressed), but Plato's idea is a useful metaphor for relating to media.

Any goal we aim for, anything we set out to do or imitate, is but an aspiration measured against an ideal, an imaginary Form. For example, if I set out to run a foot race, I will imagine myself running. If I am determined to win, I will visualize myself running past the finish line before the other participants. For most everything that I might aspire to do there is a mental image, a desired state of action and competence, a blueprint with which to compare my progress. Aspiring to a form is what actors and actresses do. Simply put, idealistic forms are the stuff *dreams* are made of.

We can neither prove nor disprove Plato's theory of Forms, but we know from the start that media are drenched in idealistic representations. Comparisons of ourselves or our actions against those shown in the media should reveal that the media images are as far removed from our worth as individuals as Plato's Forms are from apples. (You can eat an apple but not a Form.) If we keep the perspective that media provide a source of inspirational images similar to the mental image of winning a foot race, we will realize that our self-worth does not depend upon success every time we are tested and that our self-esteem has nothing to do with the representations on the screen.

Plato's cave allegory, narrated by Socrates in *The Republic, Book VII*, has for centuries been used to demonstrate the fragile nature of knowledge and perception. Socrates describes a cave in which prisoners, whose necks are chained, can only observe shadows cast on the wall by a fire. He then points out the difference in the prisoners' perspective when they are unchained and released from the cave. The contrast between the images created by the shadows and the appearance of reality upon release from the cave is profound. Two millennia after Plato's careful analysis we have learned little. We act as if the shadows are more real than ever. We confuse the shadows cast by media with our own dreams.

It's hard to appreciate the depth of this phenomenon because it is so much a part of our culture. The very ethos of the rugged American heroic individual is a product manufactured by fiction writers and filmmakers. We celebrate a West that never was. Worse, even the Hollywood version of the West strains its own fantasy. What does it do to your cinematic sensibilities to learn that movie legend John Wayne hated horses? And although he appeared to win World War II single-handedly on the screen, in reality he avoided military service to enhance his acting career.[29] We fail to recognize that the shadows are not merely the misrepresentation of reality; they are, in effect, atoms of cultural power.

After the movie is over, after our televisions are turned off, the shadows linger. Thus, one of the most destructive effects of media is that they can serve as the boundaries or limits of our attention. In other words, what is not highlighted by media does not exist. Moreover, the very act of being part of an audience leads us to be more susceptible to suggestibility. An audience would not be an audience if not for receptivity. When we make a conscious or unconscious decision to be a part of an audience we give ourselves permission to listen, and to be influenced. If we allow no time for reflection, the media, in effect, substitute for consciousness itself.

Educator Neil Postman makes this point in his book *Amusing Ourselves to Death*. He writes:

> There is no murder so brutal, no earthquake so devastating, no political blunder so costly—for that matter, no ball score so tantalizing or weather report so threatening—that it

cannot be erased from our minds by a newscaster saying, "Now...this."[30]

Postman writes that George Orwell "feared the truth would be kept from us," while Aldous Huxley "feared the truth would be drowned in a sea of irrelevance." He continues:

> Everything in our background has prepared us to know and resist a prison when the gates begin to close around us. We are not likely, for example, to be indifferent to the voices of the Sakharovs and the Timmermans and the Walesas. We take arms against such a sea of troubles, buttressed by the spirit of Milton, Bacon, Voltaire, Goethe and Jefferson. But what if there are no cries of anguish to be heard? Who is prepared to take arms against a sea of amusements?[31]

In politics, advertising is infinitely more expedient than developing practical solutions to social problems. We elect representatives to public office based on their appeal to our emotions, knowing all along that they are not likely to keep their promises once they are in office. Political elections in America have become carefully stage-managed events orchestrated by political consultants, speech writers, film producers, and makeup artists. In a society drenched in symbols, with little time set aside for reflection, images replace ideas, and before long power falls to any person or group who can pay the price of a media campaign. Plato most certainly would voice strenuous objection to the paltry amount of time we allow for contemplation and reflection in today's society.

Media are potentially liberating and simultaneously threatening. Adolph Hitler mastered the art of imagery and captured the soul of Germany through the use of simple cliches, slogans, and symbols. His words vividly demonstrate how the ideals of patriotism and the human propensity for prejudice can be twisted into hatred. Hitler's propaganda minister Joseph Goebbels wrote, "Intellectual activity is a danger to the building of character." What he really meant, of course, was that it was a danger to his power and to the power of the Third Reich, a clear example of what happens when social convention suffocates intellectual patterns. Social custom is what happens when ideas atrophy and emerge as convention. When it becomes more important than ideas, society pays a tremendous price.

Media have the power to establish priorities that are out of all proportion with the everyday reality of most people. For example, thousands of children in Third World countries die each day from starvation; thousands of children in America are abused each day; hundreds die in automobile accidents unprotected by seat belts. Countless others die because of lack of medical treatment. But then a news story calls our attention to the drama of a single child who needs a heart or liver transplant. Then the public is impelled to respond with indignation and assistance. Remember the bombing of the federal building in Oklahoma City in the spring of 1995 and the photo of the fireman carrying a child from the carnage? Before long a cartoon appeared in the newspaper depicting a fireman holding a single child while standing in a sea of dead babies: with the word RWANDA stamped on his helmet.

It's ironic that most complaints about media today come not from people trying to learn more about issues, but from people striving to protect their own version of reality. By nature the media attempt to italicize and append parentheses to reality. The ability to focus, which the media can do so well, requires that a lot be excluded. Imagine what it would be like if the only way we were able to watch movies was to observe the whole movie set. In every scene we would be able to see the camera crews, the director, and all of the technical advisers. We would likely consider this wide angle panorama to be destructive to our sense of enjoyment, but which view is closer to being real? The idea that we must restrict perception in order to focus shows just how conditional our senses of perception are. It reveals that we can never take for granted knowledge gained in such manner. How ironic *and* instructive to realize the story that appears to occur is not on the screen but in our heads.

Viewing the world through the lens of our culture and the camera of media is a lot like looking at the world through venetian blinds. There are many narrow, slanted views available, but the window remains covered. The public has contempt for the shallowness of the media, but it objects even more to the raising of issues most people would rather not think about. Media networks are businesses, too, and are not that much different in their values and economic practices from the issues they attempt to cover. Even when they make exceptions, the economy of the sound byte ensures their subjects will not be probed deeply. The public's anger with media is most often about rattling the blinds, not about opening the window.

A public that avoids thinking critically is especially vulnerable to being told what to think about, even though little deliberation will occur. The media's greatest strength is society's greatest weakness, namely, the capacity to control perception by dominating the front pages of our awareness. The ability to wage war is now almost entirely dependent on anesthetizing public perception. During the Vietnam war, media coverage brought human suffering on a massive scale into the living rooms of noncombatants for the first time in history. In the more recent Persian Gulf war, the movements and reporting of media correspondents were highly restricted while the descriptions of battle became ever more impersonal. As the war progressed, references by pilots of the allied forces began to make the war sound like a colossal Nintendo game. Enemy convoys were described as cockroaches. "Now you see them. Now you don't." Imagine what it would be like, indeed what would happen, if the media were to capture in graphic detail groups of human beings being vaporized? What might this do to our notions about war? The power of media becomes especially vivid when you think how these real-life views of war could influence the power to wage war.

Our current predicament is truly incredible. We are the first culture in the history of civilization in which each member is exposed daily to hundreds of messages constructed by experts and specifically designed to cause us to act (or feel the worse for not doing so). Little wonder that we refer to ourselves less often as citizens and more often as consumers—consumers of products, images, symbols, icons, and manufactured reality itself. It's an open secret that the people who try their absolute best to influence us are attempting to contrive reality itself. And part of this open secret is the acknowledgment that merely being aware we are targets of such an enterprise is not an adequate defense against it. An equal defense requires diligence, conviction, and effort—a staggering proposition in light of our willingness to deceive ourselves. If we purposely shield ourselves from too much reality, is it any wonder that we substitute the interesting for the relevant, and let entertainment become a purposeful diversion, so that for millions of Americans "freedom" means "entertainment"? Is it any wonder that gossip magazines are successful because millions of people find actors and socialites to be more real and interesting than themselves? Or that this distraction has produced a society in which millions of people exhibit a nearly manic-depressive behavioral response to an assortment of balls kicked or carried past goalposts, thrown through hoops, or putted into small holes in the ground? Obsessions with the lives of the players of these games make sports just another business disguised as entertainment. People often know more about these celebrities than they do about members of their own families and derive their own self-esteem from the successes of those they admire.

What does such a pronounced affection for distraction suggest about our ideas of progress? Is a society progressive if significant numbers of its members are so adversely affected by stress that they must soak their psyches in entertainment at every available opportunity until their lives resemble an analog of pain versus pleasure? Would entertainment fare so well without such a profound need to look the other way? If all we want are goods and entertainment, then consumers and observers are all we can ever be.[32] But to blame television for our mindlessness is to criticize our eyes because we do not like what we see.

Should we want to master change, however, and build a future where work is congruent with our biological, sociological, and intellectual existence, we must not allow media to set the parameters of our attention. Otherwise, public opinion becomes public morality, observation substitutes for experience, and individuals who make the effort to truly distinguish themselves, to fully add to the culture, will be greeted with a passive resentment. This, in turn, leads to public mediocrity.

No, we must not let our culture's media projectors substitute for our own imaginations. We must learn instead to see what is important to us because it is meaningful and not simply because it is highlighted. We must become the makers of our own ideas, the producers and directors of our own dreams.

Chapter Four

Perception and Beliefs

Attachment is a manufacturer of illusions and whoever wants reality ought to be detached.[1]

—*Simone Weil*

Beliefs mold the bedrock of culture. If we are to have any hope of understanding ourselves and others, the nature of beliefs must hold our attention. Education without inquiry into why we believe as we do is little more than perpetuated illusion. Studying the types of thinking we most value can probe the very essence of the human psyche. The pronounced appearance of a duality of human consciousness (described as a split-brain architecture) has been observable for centuries in other cultures, especially in primitive cultures whose languages are more metaphoric and less reliant on a linear concept of time. It's been present in ours, too, except we were often too close to observe it.

Bob Samples, author of *The Metaphoric Mind*, offers a provocative argument suggesting that the left-brain "rational" thinking orientation that typifies Western thinking is destructive in its overpowering effect on the right-brain "metaphoric" mode:

Time is perceived in two ways...as a cycle or as a line. Cyclic time is the image that best applies to nature. Seasons, days, seeds, and birth-death cycles are all part of the rhythmic pulse of nature. Linear time is an abstraction. It is the invention of humans who arbitrarily divide up cycles into units. Unfortunately once the division is made, the units are often perceived as being more significant than the cycles. They are after all, more logical...that is, they are more addable, subtractable, and certainly more abstract. Cycles, on the

111

other hand, vary. None of the cycles of nature occur consistently in terms of linear time. Days, tides, seasons, and gestation periods are all different in terms of linear time. As a result they pose problems to those who measure them in linear time—the rational thinkers. They pose no problem to those who accept cyclic time, for these humans are closer to nature and to the metaphoric mind.[2]

About this propensity for applying (left-brain) rationalization at the expense of the (right-brain) metaphoric mode of knowing, Samples continues:

> The act of sorting out is vital to understanding the separation of the rational and metaphoric minds. Although it is not necessary to know the names of apples and oranges to know that they are edible, the names are necessary to separate them from each other and from grapes and tangerines. In fact the act of labeling any parcel of nature is to separate it from others. This act of semantic surgery quickly develops into a strategy of mind function that has at its core an act in opposition to holism and synthesis.[3]

In this context, it's easy to see how the adoption of a sophisticated language (which itself occupies one primary hemisphere) has allowed one mode of thinking to tower over the other. Traditional education in Western society virtually ignores the right-brain hemisphere as a way of knowing, even though, as we shall see, it is an element of deep understanding (wisdom) and is perhaps a critical component of genius. Once you begin to comprehend how a dual mode of consciousness apprehends and constructs its model of reality, all sorts of possibilities arise. In such territory the significance of symbols and beliefs begins to take on new meaning, as does the whole notion of embodiment.

In his book *The Dual Brain, Religion, and the Unconscious*, psychiatrist Sim C. Liddon uses the terms *objectification* and *adifferentiation* to examine this issue, arguing that psychology and psychiatry have spent precious little time in studying the nature of *believing*. Liddon defines objectification as "the phenomenon of experiencing symbols of subjective experience as 'real' and in the real world." Fear, for example, might be emotionalized into the symbol of a witch, and objectification occurs when the image of a witch would be interpreted not as an image, but as being real. Adifferentiation, on the other hand, Liddon describes as a variation of objectification that is "the inability to distinguish a symbol from that for which the symbol stands."[4] An example would be if one believed the American flag to be more important than the principals for which America stands.

Consider the implications of how we form beliefs and opinions when we perceive ourselves as having two independent but cooperative modes of consciousness, both organizing our experience, each with its own agenda. One seeks to separate, the other to assemble. The former is concerned with parts, the latter with wholes. Each is insensitive to the strength of the other. Like an animate pair of binoculars, each side scans the horizon, intent on its own presentation of reality. Each side discerns what it apprehends as real; one side furnishes a verbal explanation for what it beholds, the other doesn't need one.

German philosopher Immanuel Kant touched on this issue almost two centuries before the development of split-brain theory. He argued that the powers of *knowing* arrive from *understanding* and *sensibility*. Understanding (which best describes left-brain thinking) consists of concepts and judgment. Sensibility (which best describes right-brain thinking) consists principally of intuition. In his *Critique of Pure Reason*, Kant wrote:

Our nature is so constituted that intuition with us never can be other than sensuous, that is, it contains only the mode in which we are affected by objects. On the other hand, the faculty of thinking the object of sensuous intuition is the understanding. Neither of these faculties has a preference over the other. Without the sensuous faculty no object would be given to us, and without understanding no object would be thought. Thoughts without content are void; intuitions without conceptions, blind. Hence it is as necessary for the mind to make its conceptions sensuous (that is, to join to them the object in intuition), as to make its intuitions intelligible. Neither of these faculties can exchange its proper function. Understanding cannot intuite, and the sensuous faculty cannot think. In no other way than from the united operation of both, can knowledge arise.[5]

Immanuel Kant saw himself as bridging the gap between the feuding philosophic camps of his day, the rationalists (who believed that knowledge exists independently of experience), and the empiricists (who believed knowledge to be totally dependent upon experience). He maintained that synthesis is an act of unity—an act which sounds very much like what modern researchers call bimodal processing, or knowing through using both modes of consciousness.[6] Kant suggested that categories of the mind shape perception, and contemporary research in brain science bears him out.

With a dual consciousness we have two equally dynamic modes of apprehending reality. And, if our culture requires that we rely on one of them more than the other, this may have a significant effect on how we perceive and subsequently come to believe everything we hold in our consciousness. Both modes of consciousness have extraordinary qualities; each is capable of reaching for truth—one by analysis, the other by intuition. I ask whether one of these ways of knowing can interfere with the other, and if so, what are the consequences?

What can be learned from the phenomenon of people who simultaneously hold rational and irrational beliefs? What could objective pursuit in this line of inquiry tell us? Why do so many people believe in astrology, channeling, fortune tellers, tarot cards, and ghosts? Astrology has been totally discredited scientifically, but still most of our newspapers contain a horoscope column. Does the popularity of supermarket tabloids, with their bizarre, impossible headlines, reveal anything but a preference for the asylum of deep ignorance rather than a harsh reality? Why are humans universally superstitious? Why do so many people find the idea of a conspiracy more palatable than a thorough examination of the facts? Could it be that by shielding oneself from reality, one reserves the right to believe anything? Perhaps Bertrand Russell was correct when he said, "Men fear thought more than they fear anything else on earth—more than ruin, more even than death."[7] I suggest that insight into these questions through objective inquiry might lead to the greatest breakthrough in negotiating human differences in the history of humankind—not to mention a reduction of incidents like those orchestrated by Jim Jones at Jonestown, Guiana and Marshall Applewhite in San Diego, California, or David Koresh at Waco, Texas.

Albert Einstein used his intuition in the form of imagery to grasp flashes of insight—truths which held up when he subjected them to reason. Isn't it entirely possible, then, that a truth could be discovered in this way without the critical ability to explain it? I am not trying at this point to destroy the case made earlier. I am simply trying to demonstrate the validity and subsequent need for developing both modes of thinking, as Kant did. Intuition often amounts to little more than muddled perception. In his first book, *Zen and the Art of Motorcycle Maintenance*, Robert Pirsig made a similar, eloquent argument for the synthesis of reason and emotion into an order he referred to as *quality*. This concept of quality contained a critical preciseness coexistent with an intuitive feeling of rightness (my attempt at a definition, not his). If we gain nothing further from this inquiry, we need to realize that the pursuit of truth requires conviction, which, by definition, contains some ingredients of both modes of consciousness. But conviction must be linked to a genuine desire to understand and an eagerness to practice skepticism at all times. Any fool can have convictions, but it takes an agile mind to sustain doubt.

If it's true that for thousands of years our intuitive mode of consciousness has been gradually overpowered by our rational mode, is it any wonder that we become spellbound by the profundity of Eastern mysticism, or that we seem to be driven to find a deeper sense of meaning than life in a rational world seems to provide? Liddon suggests that "the integration of these two modes of processing gives rise to that restless urge in human beings to satisfy their religious needs."[8] Does overdependency on rationality (or, for that matter, on any mode that proves restrictive) have anything to do with the fact that millions of people appear to live for decades on automatic pilot, punctuated by brief moments of crisis when what really seems to matter to them is suddenly clear?

What of the young man or woman who, in order to support a family, becomes an executive and loses all sense of self to a world of rationality that renders participants estranged from their families—the very reason for beginning the effort in the first place? Does this reliance on rationality leave a person vulnerable to becoming so overwhelmed by a sudden encounter with the natural world that one abandons reason in order to defend nature (as seems to be the case with members of radical environmental groups)? For example, placing steel spikes in trees to protect them from lumberjacks is not a well-reasoned act, unless one values trees more than people. Does the person who is overly dependent on rationality and unable to find fulfillment suddenly load up on pop psychology or seek enlightenment from con artists, like the chocolate afficionado on a binge? What of the individual who shuns reason and tries to feel his or her way through life? Wouldn't a more balanced view be one that says dual modes of incompatible but cooperative consciousness are biologically calibrated to discern meaning in the same manner that sails are set to catch the wind?

John F. Schumaker, in his book *Wings of Illusion,* offers one of the most lucid arguments on this subject I have found. Schumaker submits the provocative thesis that our strongest drive, one we share with all other humans, is a "paranormal belief imperative" which shields us from the harshness of reality.[9] Indeed, a host of writers and philosophers have warned us of the inability of humans to gaze into the face of reality. Arthur Schopenhauer earned a reputation as a philosopher of pessimism for his penetrating prose about the horror and harshness of reality:

> The pleasure in this world, it has been said, outweighs the pain; or, at any rate, there is an even balance between the two. If the reader wishes to see shortly whether this statement is true, let him compare the respective feelings of two animals, one of which is engaged in eating the other.[10]

More recently Ernest Becker, in *The Denial of Death,* wrote that of all things that drive humans, a principle one is the terror of death: "a full apprehension of man's condition would drive him insane."[11] Schumaker argues that our propensity for self-deception is a biological adaptation, that pure intelligence would be incapable of standing up to and overcoming reality.[12]

"More than anything else," he says, "we are contradictions." Schumaker continues:

> What we have become, both physically and psychologically, was for a purpose. That purpose again was survival. It was no accident that we became a creature of apparent opposites. Coincidence was not responsible for our unique ability to combine genius-like yearnings for truth with a seemingly mindless willingness to accept the wholly unbelievable as fact. The delicate balance we maintain between truth and fiction is the hallmark of our species. One should not be too quick to dismiss our appetite for illusion as a mere idiosyncrasy of our species. We should also pause before jumping to the conclusion that we are "spiritual" beings that cannot be understood in an evolutionary context. Our unique species represents the end-product of an evolutionary "miracle" which endowed our species with the ability to deceive itself and to fashion a hybrid reality for itself.[13]

Schumaker posits that "paranormal believing became the antidote to pure intelligence" through the capacity of "suggestibility."[14] Without such capacity humans would not be capable of believing the unbelievable. Schumaker contends there is an urgent need to find out at what level of illusion we function best and what the consequences are for failing to find effective systems of self-deception. Even though reality-transcending paranormal beliefs have held a great survival value for our species, he concludes, our capacity for self-deception may prove to be a "biological checkmate" because of weapon technology (nuclear weapons in particular). The Cold War may be over, but nationalism looms as large as ever before.

This is not the most flattering light in which to view ourselves. Some readers might be offended by the implications of such inquiry, but, to my mind, that makes the effort all the more important. One can barely imagine the value and power to be derived from insights into why and how we believe as we do. Daniel J. Boorstin reminds us, "It is not skeptics or explorers but fanatics and ideologues who menace decency and progress. No agnostic ever burned anyone at the stake or tortured a pagan, a heretic, or an unbeliever."[15] At the very least there seems to be enough evidence to imagine that if we were detectives searching for culprits hiding the truth, we might find ourselves to be prime suspects.

We need desperately to understand why believers are respected more than nonbelievers. Why do religious followers accuse atheists of practicing a religion? Is it true? Is not believing still a belief? The bias for believing is not so obvious until it is put in perspective. For example, myriad religious believers of sharply contrasting ideologies join together to protest about social issues such as abortion in the name of their religion. Yet, each religion views the next not only as unbelievable but also as preposterous. Picture what would happen if large numbers of activists gathered outside of Christian churches during services carrying signs like: "Jesus is dead. Get a life!" The results would likely be violent, and infinitely worse if something similar occurred in an Islamic country (witness the predicament of Salman Rushdie). This is precisely why it is so important that we understand beliefs about believing. In America the freedom to believe is protected by law. The freedom to doubt, in theory at least, is afforded the same sanctity, except that in practice it doesn't fare so well. The skeptic is less well respected than those who are thought of as practicing a belief, even if it is viewed as a primitive belief. In the last quarter of the eighteenth century Thomas Paine became the architect of inspiration for the American Revolution. His essay *Common Sense,* published in 1776, catapulted him to a status of hero attained by few before or since. But when he attacked Christianity as "too absurd for belief" in 1794, he became one of the most reviled and demonized citizens in American history. He died a pauper, poor in status and purse.

In our own time, Timothy Ferris has examined the popular subject of near death experience in his book *The Mind's Sky.* Ferris notes, and evidence supports his claim, that the near death experience (what so many people report as a blissful movement through a tunnel toward a light) is actually a super dose of adrenaline as a reaction to extreme stress. For example, some individuals who have fallen great distances report having had this kind of experience before they hit the ground.[16] If these reports are true, we can begin to understand the explosion of religious impetus felt by our primitive ancestors who spent their nights huddled together in sheer terror on the Serengeti Plain.[17] Perhaps the greatest argument in favor of religion is not the suggestion of an afterlife, but the presence of a biological mechanism kind enough to make death a blissful event.[18]

Nobel Laureate Francis Crick published a book in 1994, titled *The Astonishing Hypothesis,* which offers the premise that the mind is what the brain does. That this idea would be viewed as astonishing near the third millennium is itself astonishing.

Religion and Reality

Thomas Carlyle once said, "Wonder is the basis of worship," but, I'm not so sure. Worship could very well be the antithesis of wonder. Although Albert Einstein suggested, "The cosmic religious feeling is the strongest and noblest motive for scientific research," and, "Science without religion is lame, religion without science is blind," he could not, and I cannot, comprehend or conceive of the existence of a God who would delve into the simple matters of human beings. At first, being agnostic made me a little hesitant to write about religion. But, if we really value truth, an agnostic approach to religion is the only approach one can take that is rational, ethical, moral, and emotionally intelligent. The history of the world is overburdened with evidence supporting Voltaire's assertion: "Anyone who has the power to make you believe absurdities has the power to make you commit injustices." Worship is embedded in social patterns more deeply than in intellectual ones, more dependent upon the bonds of loyalty than on the desire to know or to understand *anything.*

Beliefs form the substructure with which we fashion a worldview or a conception of reality. The evidence is irrefutable: cultures ritualize common practices and, in time, sacralize them. Cultures provide ready-to-believe worldviews and "ready-to-wear religions."[19] Thus, beliefs probe the epicenter of human existence; they provide the bedrock for all religions, which makes religiousness much too important to belong mainly to the realm of social convention.

Some scientists argue that science and religion are incompatible because science deals with empirical matters and religion does not. But the products of science continually hurl us into a stance where we must decide how meaning is to be defined. It would be as dangerous to let theologians chart the course for humanity by themselves (witness the Dark Ages) as it would be to let scientists do so alone.

Philosophy, the love of wisdom, is without doubt a religious quest. Thus, the really big questions pervading this text so far lead back to questions that appear to be religious. If Thomas Carlyle is right, if wonder is the basis of worship, then we dare not forget that worship also reifies authority. Many people use this relationship to gain security that, when taken to an extreme, leads to an abdication of responsibility. Moral dilemmas such as poverty and starvation, which require immediate attention, but which no one wants to deal with, are left to God. Thus, the end result of the belief in immortality is that the values that are so highly prized for the *next* life are ignored in *this one*. This bias for self-deceit makes the whole idea of religion and "spirituality" profoundly consequential.[20] Indeed, in *The True Believer*, Eric Hoffer has shown irrefutably that, for a certain kind of mind, religion is not an opium for the masses, but rather crack cocaine for zealots.

The essence of spirit can best be compared to Pirsig's Dynamic Quality, which arises from art, science, philosophy, and all of the similar endeavors that have the potential to add positively to life and to culture. But, as we enter upon the new millennium, beliefs are in collision. For millions of people, economic power has become a religion. For millions more, religion is used only as a shield, raised as a defensive tactic only when some aspect of the culture comes under attack. For many others, religion is a primary way of seeking recognition; they seek to convert and conquer doubt, especially their own. In *The Denial of Death*, Ernest Becker wrote:

Creation is a nightmare spectacular taking place on a planet that has been soaked for hundreds of millions of years in the blood of all its creatures. The soberest conclusion that we could make about what has actually been taking place on the planet for about three billion years is that it is being turned into a vast pit of fertilizer. But the sun distracts our attention, always baking the blood dry, making things grow over it, and with its warmth giving the hope that comes with the organism's comfort and expansiveness....Science and religion merge in a critique of the deadening of perception of this kind of truth, and science betrays us when it is willing to absorb lived truth all into itself....The problem with all the scientific manipulators is that somehow they don't take life seriously enough; in this sense, all science is "bourgeois," an affair of bureaucrats. I think that taking life seriously means something such as this: that whatever man does on this planet has to be done in the lived truth of the terror of creation, of the grotesque, of the rumble of panic underneath everything. Otherwise it is false.[21]

If we humans are hard-wired to insulate ourselves from too much reality, then, for many people, Becker's pit of despair is too much to bear without some sort of assistance. One can begin to understand why cultures around the world affirm the unbelievable in order to spare themselves from such a depressing view. Thus millions of people (who are aware of only a few generations of their own ancestors) choose to wholly embrace the beliefs of people who lived so long ago as to appear primitive and ignorant in our present-day culture, except for their belief in the supernatural. To make the wholly unbelievable convincing, supernatural beliefs must be borrowed from periods of time that are themselves shielded from too much reality. Countless followers believe God spoke to mortals in ancient times on a regular basis, but will not hesitate to point out that those today who say God speaks to them directly belong in mental hospitals. Miracles met the same credulity in ancient times that they do today: time makes miraculous claims more palatable.

Becker was right: we do not take life seriously enough. But I don't share Becker's fertilizer pit view of the earth. (Then again, I wasn't born in the slums of Rwanda, Delhi, Mexico City, Bangladesh, or the Mott Haven section of the South Bronx in New York.) Where beliefs are concerned, most people live as if there had never been an age called "the Enlightenment," not to mention Thomas Paine's *Age Of Reason*. We are, as Harold Bloom suggests, "a religion-mad country."[22] In *God's Laughter*, Gerhard Staguhn writes:

At the root of religion—to this day!—lies fear. More precisely, the fear of death, which is but a synonym for chaos. Religion is nothing but a heroic negation of chaos and death, man's attempt to oppose world-chaos by establishing a permanent center, and to define thereby a reference point for everything—in short, a meaning.[23]

If our religious nature is the result of a dual-brained neural architecture, is it also an evolutionary characteristic that we should outgrow? If this sounds like a reasonable expectation, then I have failed to make my most important point: simply that the propensity for human religiousness is also a part of, or is directly knotted to, the desire to know, and that the satisfaction found in understanding is even greater than that of believing, provided that desire can sustain the climb over our cultural mountains.

Recall John F. Schumaker's observation that the only attribute all cultures share is a paranormal belief imperative. Schumaker also points out the dark side of conventional religion in that it is "associated with general insensitivity, cruelty, overpunishment, intolerance, authoritarianism, child abuse, ethnocentrism, prejudice, and bigotry, dishonesty, inflexibility, lack of creativity, and diminished critical thinking ability."[24] His indictment is far from trivial. Still, to my mind, our religious nature can have an advantage. It can make us aware that we set the stage for providing and experiencing our own meaning. It can confirm that we have learned enough about our own human temperament to acknowledge the need for a "believer beware" apprehension, to understand that beliefs deep-seated in fear do not, will not, and cannot serve us well in the twenty-first century.

Postmodernism and Meaning

In July of 1994, space debris known as the comet Shoemaker-Levy 9 assaulted the planet Jupiter with a cosmic ferocity that forever shattered any notion that the cosmos is a peaceful, secure place. Scientists had never believed that it was, but now the proof was at hand for everyone to see. The psychic aftershocks from this celestial spectacle will reverberate through human consciousness until (and, we must hope, after) the earth shares a similar fate. It will happen. The only question is, when? Welcome to a postmodern world.

What is *postmodernism*? Postmodernism is culture shock writ large; pluralism in kaleidoscope. Postmodernism is a psychological parenthesis within which people simultaneously believe in everything and nothing; where the fundamentalist preacher shares media airwaves with psychic hotlines, political pundits, science magazines, and infomercials hawking products no one needs. Postmodernsim heralds the publication of books like *The End of Science* in the same year scientists announce the probability that there was once life on Mars and that a ubiquitious form of life known as archaea, or the third branch of life, has for all times (that is, until recently) escaped human detection. Postmodernism is an oxymoron incarnate: an open-closed system where everything is admitted entry but nothing changes as a result. Postmodernsim celebrates the end of imagination in the face of an exponential explosion in the growth of ideas. And—bizarre as it sounds—this incoherent, maddening uncertainty has the potential (as we will see in due course) to shine the brightest light ever on the human predicament. Once we see postmodernism up close, we realize that people of all cultures appear to be making up reality as they go along. This can be reassuring when, on reflection, we understand that it has *always* been that way. The difference is, now it's happening in plain sight.

What does it mean to be postmodern? Lots of thinkers in various disciplines are kicking this term around with dramatically divergent ideas about what it means, and that *is* the point. Philosophers, artists, and sociologists use the term in differing ways, even among their own colleagues, as each group focuses on unfamiliar riddles. But not until I heard Rush Limbaugh say he had never heard of the word postmodernism did I develop an affection for it. To me postmodernism is an epistemological abyss: reason turned inside out. Do we really know anything? Can we know? Is it likely that the only thing we know is that we don't know? Add the ferment of Shoemaker-Levy 9, and you can legitimately ask whether or not what we can know even matters. Is lifelong learning in a postmodern world a contradiction in terms? If we can't know anything, why bother trying to learn?

My answer is, yes, it does matter. Even if the only reason it matters is that we think it does, then that is good enough. From this plain, subjective exercise we call learning, we human beings can squeeze from life all we were ever designed to attain. The course we follow in a postmodern world is confusing and booby-trapped. If one travels through life without paying the price of attention, what appears practical becomes radical or the reverse. What we think and what we believe in a postmodern world may determine whether or not anyone is alive when the earth is visited next by space debris. But, before we move too far afield in the world of beliefs, let's tread for a while on the path we consider the most practical.

We'll start at the divisive question about whether truth is a given or whether it is a process of discovery. From a Western perspective we have moved historically from a prehuman (at least in a modern sense) world of "embodiment," through a primitive shadow world, to a classical Graeco-Roman world view, to the prominence of Christianity spanning thirteen centuries, to the Enlightenment and the rise of modern science, to a point in the mid-twentieth century which a few scholars have chosen to call Postmodernism. Postmodernism is sort of a scientific and philosophical consensus that we humans may not be equipped to *grasp* reality if, indeed, there *is* such a thing.[25] Postmodernism is seen as a diabolical threat to the very idea of an ordered universe of absolutes, even though theology began with, and in fact rests upon, the premise that God is unknowable.

I believe Huston Smith is correct when he writes, "Absence of evidence is not evidence of absence," but neither is it a stage for dogma.[26] The poet Rilke suggested that Reality or God may well be a *Direction* instead of an object or deity.[27] Smith himself writes, "The only thing that is unqualifiedly good is extended vision, the enlargement of one's understanding of the ultimate nature of things."[28] Think about this for a moment. If God or Reality is a Direction, then to learn is a deeply intellectual and spiritual experience. So, it is not surprising that the church destroys the best part of religion by defining what cannot be defined. Motivated by a desire to be necessary, it substitutes answers for questions. Genuine religious inquiry is lost to social convention.

Postmodernism derives from a lack of thirst for knowledge, and it may be worse than nihilism. Nihilism represents a loss of values, but postmodernism as a social direction is one in which *technique* takes over completely. Thus, the symbols and images produced by our highly technological blip culture become more real and more important than anything we ourselves can imagine; they become hyper-real. Cynics blame postmodernism on a breakdown of traditional values and argue that the move toward relativism is largely a result of the decline of religion. I disagree. We are moving in a postmodern trajectory not because of the demise of religion but because we have let ancient people think for us in the first place. In *A History of God*, Karen Armstrong clearly shows how the character of God has changed over a period of 4,000 years, and how we humans alone are responsible for it. The quality of human life is undeviatingly bound to the intellectual plane of existence and directly dependent on the amount of thinking going on at the time in which it is lived.

If reality evaporates before us as we near our limit of understanding, are we not still better off? Are we not hierarchically motivated beings even if the universe is not? If reality evades us, that doesn't mean our frail interpretation is meaningless. If I wear blue-tinted glasses and you wear green-tinted, neither of us will be affected by the objects we look at—only our perception will be influenced. To say that my blueness or your greenness is meaningless is like saying that Christians, Buddhists, Muslims, Hindus, Agnostics, and Atheists (the capital A's are intentional) can find no meaning. Yet, I should not propose to kill you because you cannot see blue. These colors represent our respective cultures, and if we could each rise above our culture through self-mastery we would be able to see in the same light.

In attempting to shield ourselves from too much reality, we fail to understand the religious nature of self-creation; we fail to seize the moment and the opportunity to create a life worth living. We are so haunted by the meddlesome idea that the only thing that matters is permanence, we fail to realize this bafflement would result in eternal confusion if we did live forever. Life may be absurd, "an idiot laughing," as Thornton Wilder suggested.[29] And, if astrophysicist Stephen Hawking is right, time may someday run backwards. But our dilemma as individuals need not be so complicated. Postmodernism itself may be enough to awaken the human race from the slumber of superstition. Walter Truett Anderson writes:

> In the collapse of belief, a thousand subcultures bloom, and new belief systems arrive as regularly as the daily mail....The fundamentalist lives in eternal fear that he or she may lose the faith; the freethinking liberal lives in eternal fear that he or she may tire of freedom and fall into the arms of some ancient, modern, or postmodern belief system—anything from Islam to Scientology—that has a solid structure and ready answers.[30]

People search hardest for what they grow up without. A few generations of people who are weaned in a chaotic society where meaning seems to be vanquished into a black hole of postmodernism may discover that they have the power—indeed, the will—to find their own meaning with an intelligence which honors a frame of reality like Pirsig's. The force of their efforts may produce a society so civilized that they will seem to be living in an "age of light" or an age of "genuine human progress."[31] Considering our history of superstition, it would be naïve to expect such an improvement in the exercise of human reason, except that in our current information age we're overcome daily with an army of realities which assault outdated beliefs on an unprecedented scale. High technology will undoubtedly lead to an infinite number of sophisticated forms of superstition, but science has for the past two centuries made it increasingly difficult for anyone genuinely interested in the truth to cling to ancient absurdities.

Science leads us to the kind of knowledge that yields a great deal of common sense about living, but it is barren of purpose because it only asks how and not why. Even though I am a skeptic and an agnostic, I believe the religious nature of human beings may equal or surpass science as a means of determining truth in values and ethics, but only when the inquiry is conducted with complete openness. The most tragic occurrence ever to befall human culture is acceptance of the notion that it is religiously wrong to "doubt." If it is wrong to doubt, then it is wrong to be human.

To study religion (which is really a study of culture) with anything resembling objectivity we must again consider the nature of belief itself and the history of such enterprise. In his book *Magic and Religion,* George B. Vetter wrote:

> Some 95% of us continue to believe throughout our entire lifetimes the religious ideas taught us when young, regardless of what that faith may have been. So it should be apparent to all but the willfully blind that factors other than a scientific logic determined the acceptance of those beliefs, or held sway when they were acquired. Most of the literature pretending to inquire into the nature of religion proves upon examination to be more or less subtly disguised attempts to justify varying portions of these early indoctrinations.[32]

There were many prophets who offered sage advice for living. The trouble began when "why" was closed off as a means of inquiry and the whole endeavor assumed an external authority for the purpose of establishing a base of power. Thereafter it was not enough merely to "believe"—now one had to demonstrate submissiveness *to* and support *for* authority. The televangelist pleads with his audience to accept Jesus, but what he really hopes, and in fact depends on, is that he himself will be accepted and financially supported. Inherent in his ideology are strings. Power goes to the group that can franchise faith and outlaw doubt. The result is inevitably corrupt because the advice offered by the prophets was never intended for such a purpose. Emerson wrote, "The faith that stands on authority is not faith. The reliance on authority measures the decline of religion, the withdrawal of the soul."[33] Faith without proof does not necessitate the subordination of inquiry. If it does, the greater part of religion is missed.

Genuine freedom is navigated by doubt. Understanding is our highest form of religious participation. If we leave all to social convention and simply follow rules prescribed by others, we miss religious inquiry and settle for dogma. History reveals beyond any doubt that power which rests upon ideological subordination will be abused as surely as gravity compels objects to fall. More people have been butchered in the name of religion than for any other cause.

In his book *Lila*, Robert Pirsig goes into great detail to show that what we have long viewed as a battle between science and religion is really a moral battle between reason and social convention. Leaving the argument to social convention is an abdication of responsibility—it denies the intellectual plane of existence in each of us and holds our ancestors responsible for current problems which we ourselves should own. It is like saying that all of the thinking that needs to be done has already been done. The problem is not that science is coming up with the wrong answers, but that the church has eternally sought to bolster its power by prohibiting questions.

Imagine what kind of society would result if the church were the place where one asked the most meaningful questions without regard to who might be offended by the inquiry. If truth really matters, science and religion could form a partnership of technique and principle; the church and the university could merge metaphorically, becoming one institution which serves to support the intellect of individuals instead of attempting to tower over them. If the church had sought to perpetually focus on what is truly important, human starvation never would have materialized, nor would opulent cathedrals have been built while many people remained poor and homeless.

Living is a constant struggle between the dual forces of intrinsic and extrinsic motivations, of deliberate learning and incidental learning. When truth is sought for its own sake by any individual, Immanuel Kant's "moral law within" is a greater force than Adam Smith's invisible hand in yielding accidental good[34] (see Chapter Seven). And when the search for truth is really a pretentious guise for acquiring power, it likewise yields harm in far greater proportions. The invisible hand becomes a fist. Truth—whether we think of it as being religious or secular in nature—is, at least in a metaphorical sense, as close as the seeker can come to the mind of God.

Belief and Ethnocentrism

There is nothing inherently wrong with following rules based upon sound religious principles, but when the overriding objective becomes obedience, the human attribute for developing a robust positive bias concerning oneself *redirects* attention toward others with an arrogance that is unmerciful. Thus, we excuse ourselves for infractions and blame others for every conceivable injustice under the sun. Belief itself is a form of obedience, and the observance of rules is a transfer of power. Although we desperately need rules for living, we must be very careful to use them with reflection. When the coercion of power is great enough, it burns its imprint into the corridors of the imagination; exploration is thwarted at every turn; curiosity is overshadowed by authority; and *association* becomes more important than truth. Thus, self-righteousness becomes the lifeblood of self-justification, and "ethnic cleansing" becomes a routine of custom. The war-torn religious history of human beings should prove this beyond doubt. Christianity was founded upon the principle of compassion; but, reduced to technique, it is compassionless.[35]

Considering the nature of belief, the human propensity for self-deception, and the presence of a robust positive personal bias, is it any wonder that billions of people cluster into small groups believing that truth has singled them out and settled upon their little congregation on Oak Street as selectively as a summer rain shower on *one* corn field, and that this simple truth has escaped every other poor fool on the planet? How fortunate it is for these groups with a lock on truth, and how sad this *miracle* is for the human race. How tragic it is, too, that millions of people who do come to question beliefs they acquired when they were very young suddenly give themselves license to believe anything.

During the past decade, books framing the past and future in the genre known as new-age have become popular. It is important to observe that new-ageism derives its authority from the imagination. Unlike Descartes who said, "I think, therefore I am," the new-agers seem to be saying, "I think, therefore it is." We will enter a new age if, and only if, we are lead by a sincere desire to know. A naturally self-deceptive species is easily fooled by design. When we do not develop a crisp sense of self-knowledge, we can become vulnerable to people who claim to be experts but are merely misinformed. This only exacerbates the problem. Gurus substitute for self. We become susceptible to the assertions and incantations of astrology, channeling, quasi-religions, and a myriad of oddities, often accepting them without ever really thinking deeply about them. Many beliefs systems, new-age and old, pose as foundations of truth, pedalling illusion under the guise of "faith" in exchange for economic support. Believing has become an excuse for not thinking, a way to avoid responsibility. Alan Watts made this suggestion:

> We must...make a clear distinction between belief and faith, because, in general practice, belief has come to mean a state of mind which is almost the opposite of faith. Belief, as I use the word here, is the insistence that the truth is what one would...wish it to be. The believer will open his mind to the truth on condition that it fits in with his preconceived ideas and wishes. Faith, on the other hand, is an unreserved opening of the mind to the truth, whatever it may turn out to be. Faith has no preconceptions; it is a plunge into the unknown. Belief clings, but faith lets go. In this sense of the word, faith is the essential virtue of science, and likewise of any religion that is not self-deception.[36]

What we believe about beliefs is most important of all. I respect every person's right to believe, but I do not respect purposeful self-delusion, especially when it results in ethnocentric behavior. A century from now I expect one of the greatest mistakes of our time will turn out to have been modern medicine's failure to study the placebo effect with as much enthusiasm as it's given to organ transplants. It is a tragedy almost beyond comprehension, and an embarrassment to our society and our ancestors, that we live in a country where telephone psychics can be sustained economically by a citizenry that believes total strangers know more about their own lives than they do.

When absurdities substitute for a well-reasoned sense of reality, tyrants thrive, fools serve, and ethnocentrism becomes the body of religion. Belief, in the conventional sense, has everything to do with selfish social inclusion and nothing to do with knowledge, rational judgment, or anything which promotes understanding of the human condition. Faith, as the term is most often used today, has become a euphemism for illusion.

Truth and Sacred Texts

Knowledge serves us as power, purpose, and principle. Whether truth is given or discovered, it still must be sorted out. Where is the truth to be found? *The Bible? The Koran? The Torah? The Talmud, Midrashim, Bhagavad-Gita, Bagavada Purana, Book of Li, Analects, Tao Te Ching, Upaanishads?* Dedicated scholars tell us that these books, though intended as prescriptions for living a good life, contain prudent advice but also many contradictions. Do we not have as much responsibility for determining what to believe as whom to believe? If we fail to develop our own reasoning ability, how can we judge whether the indiciduals we're asked to trust are using theirs? If truth is to be discovered through a continual process of reasoning, why should this not be the duty of all of us? A perennial succession of philosophers has demonstrated how hard it is to nail down simple truths. Nietzsche characterized truths as "mutually agreed upon fictions." If truth is evasive, who is to pursue it, if not you and I?

When knowledge of purpose and principle is provided for us, it is manifested through power and is handed down to us in the form of technique. When we share in the process of discovery, we share the principle, the power, and the responsibility for using it. To have found a purpose is an admission that purpose exists. To be without purpose is to be without power and principle. Most of us long to be a part of something greater than ourselves. And, in spite of the fact that most Americans profess a belief in God, few rely on such faith as a basis for discovering truth and for making moral decisions associated with everyday living. Paradoxically, people are choosing to rely more on their own judgment than on that of authority.[37] Ordinarily that would seem to be desirable, except that instead of discerning truth and morality through the power of their own experience and intellect, they simply compare themselves with the standards of others. Thus, unprovable matters that warrant a relativistic or fallibilist approach are treated as simple "either/or" problems, and matters on which one really needs to take a stand are left to popular opinion.

Inhabitants of most of the ridges on our king-of-the-mountain society defend themselves against the next with black-and-white thinking that inhibits exploration. Knowledge is not really welcome; being right and in the "right group" is the greatest value sought. Such value is based only on the power of technique. Purpose and principle are lost. And so it is that the truths in the sacred texts listed above are also lost. When the sage advice of these texts applies to ourselves, and only to ourselves, there is much to be learned from them. I believe strongly in the Christian values that are pertinent to how we should treat our fellow human beings. It is a noble effort to be a Christ-like or a Buddha-like person. But to use ancient scriptures to justify, to divide, to separate, and to judge and despise others is more than just an abuse of power; principle is abandoned, and purpose becomes perverted into an anthropomorphic evilness. People are killed in religious wars which have nothing to do with religion, but everything to do with domination. To avoid being dominated by the residue of unexamined beliefs, we must carefully scrutinize, over and again, the beliefs we have internalized through our culture.

In essence, the quest comes to this: We make our own meaning. This is not to imply that all beliefs are valid, only that the nature of beliefs must be understood. Meaning is measured in subjective degree; the greater the investment, the greater the return. Understanding—not obedience—is our greatest human achievement. Free inquiry is the capitalism of religion. And for this reason it should be religiously inconceivable that faith would be something to fight over.

Chapter Five

Biological Patterns Versus Social Patterns

*Two things fill the mind with ever-increasing wonder and awe ...
the starry heavens above and the moral law within.*[1]

—*Immanuel Kant*

From Self-Deception to Nationalism

Evidence is overwhelming that we human beings are masters of self-deception. A close reading of our history proves it beyond doubt. As we've observed, we're hard-wired for holding rational and irrational beliefs at the same time. The record clearly confirms that *we are automatically self-justifying creatures* who can adjust our perception of reality to suit ourselves. Self-delusion comes easily, especially when it's convenient. And we do it so well and so often that we remain unaware we are accomplices to our own self-deception.

The rapidly growing field of evolutionary psychology examines the human condition from the curious perspective of asking how behavior is influenced by environmental necessity. Researchers in this area have shown that evolution has equipped us to live in small groups, to become emotionally bound to those who are most like us, and to be suspicious of those who appear different from ourselves. When we find our group is no longer small, the natural tendency is to use bigotry and prejudice as a means of self-protection. None of this is a secret, but for millions of Americans it might as well be classified information.

133

In his book *The Moral Animal*, Robert Wright puts the subject in perspective:

> The way natural selection has worked its will is to make some things seem "obvious" and "right" and "desirable" and others "absurd" and "wrong" and "abhorrent." We should probe our common-sense reactions to evolutionary theories carefully before concluding that the common sense itself isn't a cognitive distortion created by evolution.... [T]he human brain is, in large part, a machine for winning arguments, a machine for convincing others that its owner is in the right—and thus a machine for convincing its owner of the same thing. The brain is like a good lawyer: given any set of interests to defend, it sets about convincing the world of their moral and logical worth, regardless of whether they in fact have any of either. Like a lawyer, the human brain wants victory, not truth; and, like a lawyer, it is sometimes more admirable for skill than for virtue.[2]

Thus defending our interests, our own brain mechanisms predispose us to nationalism. Worse, they predispose us to ethnocentrism, bigotry, prejudice, and racism. Social convention comes with a genetic bent, which is why we need such a strong dose of thinking to temper it. When, in *The Next American Nation*, Michael Lind says, "The very notion of a country based on an idea is absurd," he misses the point.[3] America as an idea may be absurd, but an America *of* ideas is not. The whole notion of the American Dream emerges from anticipation on the part individuals. Americans live by expectations based upon profound ideas—ideas reasoned by statesmen who not only shared Adam Smith's sympathy or concern for their countrymen (a subject we will examine later in more detail), but who also, with clear consensus, professed a heartfelt responsibility to act in the name of posterity.[4]

Since the quality of life in a democracy rests upon the quality of thinking that produced it, I'm not surprised Lind argues that Americans are strongly influenced by nationalism, especially those who are "less well educated."[5] He's right. Indeed, the less we are inclined to *think*, the more we are apt to act upon our biological predisposition—a predisposition which sugarcoats perception for our own kind, but tends to poison the well where *others* drink. The subtitle of Lind's book, *The New Nationalism and the Fourth Revolution*, sets the stage for a "call to nationalism or to common culture" and not the type of thinking which produces good culture. Lind writes:

> A nation may be *dedicated* to a proposition, but it cannot *be* a proposition—this is the central insight of American nationalism, the doctrine that is the major alternative to multiculturalism and democratic universalism.... A straightforward American nationalism, in one form or another, is the alternative to the fissioning that the multiculturalists celebrate as pluralism and the democratic universalists condemn as Balkanization....A real nation is a concrete historical community, defined primarily by a common language, common folkways, and a common vernacular culture.[6]

Lind's revolution champions a colorblind, equal opportunity society, based on economic nationalism and a checking of the power of influence from monied special interests by a strong government. Sounds good, but when he argues that, although his version of remedy is not the only path to a better future, "it is the only path... that can lead to an America in which you (and I) and your descendants would want to live," I take strong exception. We have gotten ourselves into a socio-economic mess the likes of which will not be solved without thinking our way out of it—you and I, all of us.

Make no mistake: nationalism *is* a uniting force. But to favor social patterns without an emphasis on the intellectual ideals upon which such culture is based, in other words, trying to solve these problems through loyalty without thinking, would be like trying to use a little hatred to stamp out bigotry. Offering nationalism as a solution to multiculturalism is to forget both are *isms*, which clearly makes them social patterns. The rapid rise of conspiracy theories, the abject paranoia of the growing militia movement, and the increasing number of hate-mongers on the media airways foretell the danger of appealing to base instincts, even in an attempt to harness them for noble causes. Nationalism is not all bad, but it is rife with seeds of hate—hate which, once brought to the surface, is nearly impossible to still. Nationalism is the ultimate expression of *us* versus *them*. In *The Stone Age Present,* William F. Allman makes it clear,

> ...racism is not part of our evolved psychology. Rather, our Stone Age mind is tripping over something that is more fundamental: "us" versus "them." Just as our propensity to eat fatty foods stems from the scarcity of fat in the past, our willingness to regard others as "them" has roots in the societies of our ancient ancestors. Early humans spent most of their lives interacting with very few people, all of whom looked and talked just as they did—and for whom strangers and members of neighboring groups were "scarce." When the "shadow of the future" is small—that is, when it is unlikely you will ever meet that person again—it is unlikely that cooperation will flourish. Thus our evolved psyches regard anyone who is not part of our intimate group as a "them."[7]

Bigotry and Racism

I grew up prejudiced, a product of the racist-imbred institutions of the South, and without the intellectual ability to know that my judgment was impaired. Today racism is even more significant than it was back then. Its effects are more subtle, difficult to prove, and every bit as insidious as when they were much easier to see. Can anything be harder to change than beliefs bound and bonded by trusted relationships? Prejudice is born of deeply embedded beliefs. "Hatred is the most accessible and comprehensive of all unifying agents."[8] Acts of prejudice affirm the relationships of bigots. To suddenly announce, "Yes, we now understand that discrimination based on race is wrong, so we won't do it anymore," is like saying, "Now that we know too many calories cause obesity, there will be no more fat people." Prejudice is diminished by understanding, but it takes resolve, conviction, and dedication to overcome it.

Conquering prejudice means changing perception by drawing on examples which defy stereotyping. True affirmative action is born of intrinsic affirmative effort. Only by studying human behavior do we realize the strength and value of differences among people. And only by learning to value those differences are we ever likely to find the basis for cooperation necessary to achieve a stable, prosperous society that is not dependent upon the growth of anything other than knowledge to sustain itself. Mutual respect is, after all, the bedrock of community, just as reciprocity is the lifeblood of justice. Only by knowing ourselves better do we have any hope of knowing others, and this knowledge forms the basis for an equity that favors human beings over human doings.

The most crippling attitude toward improvement in race relations is the absurd notion that time will eventually solve the problem by itself. This totally ignores the historical record of the activism necessary to change the status quo. In response to critics who suggested his activism was untimely, Martin Luther King Jr. wrote from his cell in the Birmingham jail, "Frankly, I have yet to engage in a direct action campaign that was 'well timed' in the view of those who have not suffered unduly from the disease of segregation." The appeal to wait for another time has always been another way of saying "never." This simple, but profound, realization changed my mind about the need for affirmative action several years ago; it suddenly dawned on me that waiting for the spontaneous dissolution of prejudice is like waiting for the next ice-age.

Using numbers as a display of power reduces human misery to an abstraction. A percentage point up or down in employment says nothing about the hundreds, thousands, or millions of people affected. On the other hand, if you attempt to use this abstraction as a direct means of redress, as in the case of affirmative action, the suggestion of a numeric quota will produce an outcry loud enough to return the problem back to human terms. Affirmative action carries a great deal of negative baggage, but it also changes perception. Even hard-core Caucasian bigots have to admit that African Americans can perform any job well; affirmative action has provided too many examples to dispute notions to the contrary.

If you ask people who do the hiring in large and small companies if discrimination exists they will say, yes. If you ask them if they discriminate against any groups of people they will say, no. If you attempt to show them proof, they will adamantly deny it. My point is that, if no one admits to discrimination in the first place, passing new laws to stop what no one will admit is happening cannot change behavior. People who are blind to their own prejudice won't take the kind of action needed to change statistics. (In point of fact, statistics illuminate the issue of emotional intelligence. Reactions to the misfortunes of others are stilled when they are reduced to numbers, because numbers are emotionally neutral. Thus, politicians who use nothing but statistics to explain the American Dream are hopelessly misguided.)

Others who do not understand the tenacity of prejudice claim to be for equality but against quotas. If we use numbers to define the problem, how can we ignore them when we attempt to correct it? It is a fundamental tenet of human behavior that we humans are inclined to take credit for actions simply because we intended that such actions be taken. Similarly, when we have no conscious negative feelings (but hold them subconsciously, as is the case with being prejudiced) we project a void of responsibility, which might better be characterized as "aggravated indifference." Aggravated indifference is the posture of people who think they have no deep feelings on the subject of prejudice, but have not examined their own consciences. I know from personal experience: When I was 23 years old, I became a police officer. At the time I held the conscious opinion that black people were inferior to white people. And yet, I sincerely believed that I was not prejudiced. Since then the process of my own self-education and the examination of my own conscience has taken me from agreeing with George Wallace to championing Mahatma Gandhi.[9]

We focus on numbers to justify every aspect of our lives. The same line of thinking that makes hiring quotas unpopular also renders us capable of viewing food stamps as a subsidy, but incapable of seeing a mortgage deduction or the right to use public grazing land for one's cattle as amounting to the same thing. Paying farmers not to grow crops represents a form of equity, but providing poor people with food is a give-away program in the eyes of many people. Psychologically we "invest" in programs we approve of and "throw money" at the ones we don't.

Please don't misunderstand my point. I am not trying to make a case for quotas and welfare. I am suggesting that these tiresome old-line distortions of reality so fog the issues that they keep us from discovering successful alternatives. But, until human beings have a right to employment and a right to health care—in short, a right to exist—we will never move beyond the consumer-driven version of the American Dream.

Political Correctness

For some time now various media have called our attention to "politically correct" language. The term is most often used to bring notice to discrimination based on ideology. For example, the charge is that college and university faculty members may not be given tenure if their views are not considered politically correct by those with the power to grant tenure. I would argue that a sense of what is politically correct has always existed, with its power stemming from its subtlety. The Victorians were a case in point. Political correctness is a major component of what we call culture or social convention. It is the kind of unspoken social approval that allows one who utters a racial slur to know that among peers it will incur no objection. In this sense it is perhaps more appropriate to use the term "socially correct." How ironic that our increasing ability to detect bias has prompted the issue of "free speech" to become a defense against political correctness. What is really at stake has more to do with protecting traditional bias than with the virtue of free speech.

I am not suggesting we should not allow people to be biased, bigoted and prejudiced, nor am I suggesting that a slip of the tongue, or a contrary opinion should prove that one is prejudiced and bigoted. I'm saying, look at the contradiction here. All my life I have witnessed a loud (though surely insincere) call to think for oneself by teachers who didn't mean it, a charge to develop one's own opinions by parents who didn't expect it to happen, and a summons to speak out on the issues by politicians who resent it when someone does. Now that more people are doing it, these acts are viewed as being somehow subversive. The '50s were the most "politically correct" years of the century with censure coming from the Right and complaints from the Left. Today the polarity seems momentarily reversed. I don't know whether it's more accurate to refer to this phenomenon as the "shoe being on the other foot," or as an example of people who profess to uphold principles but have only internalized rules.

In another context, political correctness is merely a postmodern awareness that our social sense of reality has always existed on a worm-eaten foundation of arbitrariness, ethnocentrism, and bias. We know enough today to be able to readily detect arbitrary bias, making political correctness nothing more than a call for representative reality. The current practice of purging words from the written and spoken language as a means of attacking prejudice has long surpassed silliness. We suffer prejudice because of a lack of understanding; stamping out words is like fighting a forest fire with blankets. Prejudice must be drowned with enough knowledge to alter perception.

America acts as a supercollider where values meet at high velocity. Fortunately, differences constitute the basis of and for democracy. Finding as many points of view as possible may be as close to reality as we will ever get; the fact that there is always another point of view to be considered is precisely why we cannot nail reality to the wall. Moreover, if we do not learn to value multiple realities, we cannot help but fail in our own search for meaning.

Multiculturalism is a loaded paradox. Multicultural roots constitute the foundational pilings of America, but so has the willingness of the immigrants to put aside their former identities and become Americans. In an ideal sense we might imagine this to be a trade, a compact, or a social contract in which one gives up an identity, "a social convention," and exchanges it for an intellectual plane of existence. This intellectual plane is, after all, the fuel of democracy. But, as we have observed, if this compact is not kept, if learning, understanding, and reunderstanding are not vigorous, the intellectual plane is quickly reduced once again to social convention. For as long as the American Dream seems a real possibility for some citizens, regardless of how long they have been in this country, then there is something to aspire to. When the dream turns to delusion, however, when the melting pot boils, multiculturalism is perceived as a threat. When people of noticeable differences *en masse* set out to conquer an economic mountain advertised throughout the world with the lure of intellectual ideals and wind up at the bottom of the mountain, it is our nature to focus on their differences as their reasons for failure, even though we held these differences against them in the first place.

Diversity has great value in allowing good ideas to surface quickly and vault to the forefront of what are viewed as positive changes. Robert Hughes writes, "Surprises crackle, like electric arcs, between the interfaces of culture."[10] But, if diversity is the source of our greatest strength, it is also a part of our greatest weakness. A multicultural society does not share the charitable attitude toward its various members that may be found in any "primitive" tribe. On the contrary, when differences are highlighted during tough economic times, like groups come together in fear that those "other" people may get something for nothing. We need to stop focusing negatively on our differences and set about the task of building on the ideals we have in common—those ideals which for two centuries have prompted immigrants from every conceivable background to want to call themselves Americans and which are drawn from the same intellectual plane that caused Socrates to proclaim that he was "a citizen of the world." These ideals, found on the other side of our mountain, offer rewards far greater than those which can simply be purchased.

At the heart of political correctness lies the hint of a cure. It is simply this: the attitude of a person who projects bias through the use of a racial slur is not likely to be changed by logical argument. One can seldom produce a series of facts compelling enough to change such an attitude. Whether we're conscious of it or not, many of us let such remarks slide for this very reason. However, if it were commonplace to take exception to such remarks, the perceptual change would eventually be total, and over time the bias would perish. Thus, conscience emerges. We've seen how the public attitude has changed toward cigarette smoke in recent decades. The tactic is the same. If enough of us are willing to risk accusations of being "politically correct" and lay bare our conscience, we can change perception. Eventually the new perception will come to be known as *traditional values*.

Don't misunderstand my point—I'm not suggesting we should assume an ethical posture in order to proselytize morality. I'm suggesting only that we stand up for our principles when it is of great importance that we do so. And, if we are careful, very careful, in reviewing this process we might realize the cure for political correctness lies in admitting that there is no cure. Dissent, or contrary opinion, is the heat source of democracy; the danger is in the cooling. Political correctness should not be something to gloss over in higher education, it should be the place for a learning dialogue to begin. Indeed, much of the fervor over political correctness is simply a thinly veiled effort to change the subject altogether. In *The Twilight of Common Dreams*, Todd Gitlin writes:

> Here is the unacknowledged truth of the nation's identity crisis. The publicists and scholars who obsess about political correctness, and the politicians who seize the opportunities they open up, are frozen into their own correctness. They are faction against factions. They feel victimized by those they accuse of cultivating victimization. Deploring hypersensitivity, they are hypersensitive to every slight directed at white men. Humorlessly, they decry the humorlessness of feminists and minorities. Those who charge distortion, distort.[11]

Political correctness is a clear example of a meme whose infection is kept virulent by powerful forces desperate for a scourge with which to preserve their own advantage.[12]

The Desire to Matter

To be recognized as equal, in democratic terms, is not the end of aspiration—it is a beginning. Once our need to matter is partially satiated, we can move to higher ground. Such an impetus lies at the heart of the confusion today over attempts by ethnic minority groups to "revise" history. The issue is not really that complicated. It is only during recent (postmodern) times that the arbitrary bias of our ancestors has become so easy to identify, simply because we are now aware of so many points of view. The real lesson here is that we shouldn't be critical of the bias of our ancestors without attempting to discover our own bias.

Protests by minority groups against cultural celebrations, such as the 500-year anniversary of Columbus coming to America, have emerged from a basic (thymotic) desire to matter. The protestors are simply asking that history honor their existence and their point of view. Obviously, if things had not happened exactly as they did, you and I would not be here, and you would not be reading this book. Still, to recognize the worth of others by observing the past in such a way that honors their existence is not an unreasonable request (unless it is made by unreasonable people).

The most often repeated maxim about history today says, "What we learn from history is that we do not learn from history." When we search through history with the best objectivity we can muster, it becomes apparent that almost any view is too narrow. To broaden our social perspective, an intuitive leap to anthropology becomes necessary.

Anthropologist Marvin Harris has made a persuasive case which suggests there are economic forces inherent in the ecological environment. In two books, *Cows, Pigs, Wars, and Witches* and *Cannibals and Kings*, Harris offers practical evidence and arguments providing rational solutions to riddles of culture such as: why the Hindus worship cows; why some people refuse to eat pork; why people during medieval and modern times believed in witches; and how the evolution of culture responds to changing ecological conditions. His assertions are deterministic. His own term is *soft determinism*, which I interpret to mean that, although there are strong reasons to act in certain ways which have for the most of history been beyond or hidden from human consciousness, these likely actions are in no way imperatives. "If we cannot know with reasonable certainty who did what, when, and where, we can scarcely hope to render a moral account of ourselves."[13] It is both an ignorant and an arrogant assumption to think we can live purposeful lives without the continual need to better understand ourselves.

Another way to demonstrate soft determinism is by looking at personality theory, with respect to marriage. When married couples take self-diagnostic tests designed to reveal thinking styles it becomes obvious that many have chosen mates who possess the very attributes they are lacking. None, however, appear to have made a conscious decision to choose that kind of person. Likewise, in a group setting, people unconsciously assume like physical positions in sitting or standing. Once you are aware of such behavior, it can be startling to notice that everyone in the room is sitting with legs crossed or arms folded in the same way. The point is that in most circumstances we are engaged in predictable behaviors of which we are totally unaware.

Awareness is an opportunity to take control instead of reacting unconsciously to external events. This is why it is so important to recognize and understand our own and other cultures. If we know that the pain in our foot is caused by a rock in our shoe, we can take action to remove the rock. If not, and we suffer long enough, we will eventually find a stranger to blame for the pain. Bigotry and racism are often products of the simple but frustrated and repressed desire to matter and the misperception that others are responsible for our pain. Understanding this propensity offers the greatest antidote.

Our Relationship with Authority

In the simplest sense, authority is born of culture. The reverse is also true. Culture may be thought of as predetermined solutions established on a large scale. Cultural rules were made before we were born, and since culture is essential for our very existence, we must obey those rules. But the proclivity to conform or be influenced must also be balanced if we are to be capable of making improvements. George Bernard Shaw put this in perspective when he said, "The reasonable man adapts to the world; the unreasonable man persists in trying to adapt the world to himself. Therefore, all progress depends on the unreasonable man." A bit overstated, perhaps, but not when you consider the enduring effects of blind obedience. [14]

The way we are educated influences the basis of our relation to authority. The customary student-teacher relationship is one in which the student is continually expected to see the point of view of the teacher. For the student, this is most often a passive experience without the opportunity for discussion or disagreement. The more structured the curriculum, the more passive the student's experience. Grouping students by age and perceived ability is a proven recipe for mediocrity; it destroys the intrinsic value of learning for millions of people. If, on the other hand, students were allowed the legitimacy of directing the inquiry, they would surely gain a sense of self-determination and intrinsic satisfaction from the activity.

After years spent as students, we become adjusted to accepting the views of others more often than having our own views prevail. Sometimes we lose the ability to form or recognize our own opinions. And, even though the motives of educators are noble, fostering passive acceptance can have a significant negative effect: we study democracy in the confines of a classroom dictatorship. We embrace the idea that each and every voice counts, but, in practice, we are prevented from speaking. Our teachers advocate free discussion, but, in practice, the packaged curriculum does not allow for it. By the time we are ready to leave school, many of us have consciously or subconsciously accepted the premise that learning is "behaving." We understand that conformity and agreement are more important than dissent, in spite of the fact that democracy is based on friction and is chaotic by nature. The balance of views and opinions produced in a democracy represents a truce born of disequilibrium and hammered into a state of tenuous harmony.

Consider those who tend to believe everything they read. On examination you will find, more often than not, that these are people who do not write. Of necessity, writing requires that what is written be more carefully thought out than general conversation—otherwise the writing does not make it into print. Therefore, people who are unaccustomed to thinking things through are unable to match well-reasoned written arguments, even those based on false premises. In *Educational Myths I Have Known and Loved*, Baird W. Whitlock wrote:

> There are two times at which we really discover what we think: when we speak and when we write. The advantage of the second is that we are forced to think even more clearly, precisely, and, we trust, coherently. This point can be made to students and can be made forcefully because the teacher can identify with the fact itself. If we cannot write clearly, it is probably true, as Montaigne pointed out centuries ago,

that we are not thinking clearly. If we fail to communicate clearly, it is likely that we do not know clearly what it is we wish to communicate.[15]

The ability to think clearly, to reason, and to communicate with precision forms the posture of how, and by what measure, we connect to authority. Our relation to authority is usually a good indicator of how much control we have over our lives. The more we defer to authority, the more personal power we give away. In time, our own actions legitimize our lack of control by default, the result of which is to view our limits as a perfectly natural phenomenon. History suggests that groups of people who have judged other groups as inferior have often established a social hierarchy by convincing the targeted group of its inferiority (the caste system in India is an example). When curiosity is overwhelmed by authority, the residue is indoctrination or internalized oppression. When it happens often and with force, the mind short-circuits to favor the who over the how and why. In this way, a person can be fitted for prejudice as easily as a computer with a new program. This is the program that produces rigid character.

During our teen years, most of us felt some need to rebel against parents, teachers, or society in general. In American culture this has come to be expected and is conditionally accepted as a way of establishing one's own identity. The experience of adolescence is in a sense the internal and external struggle of being catapulted from dependency toward responsibility. But rebelling as an emotional part of the process of growing up is not the same as taking part in the building of society based upon a reasoned effort. On the contrary, once we are past the age of youthful rebellion, we may compensate by *overconforming* as a means of making amends for our earlier conduct. By overconforming I mean we unquestioningly accept what we might otherwise intuitively reject (had we not gone though this phase), and we therefore miss an opportunity to enrich our culture. Some behavioral specialists refer to this period of wanting to do what is expected of us as an experience with the "shoulds."[16] Shoulds based upon the expectations of others gain such force that they become the software for automatic pilot: one's life goes on without one's intrinsic participation.

More important, however, is the fact that while we were growing up we continually formed opinions and values both consciously and subconsciously based on the assertions of others. Absent serious reflection, more often than not this amounts to living on borrowed opinion. The process works subtly over the years when family and friends make positive and negative comments about the president, a minority group, economics, personal values, or some aspect of politics. Although these were subjects we didn't care much about as young people, we couldn't help being exposed to the opinions of those who were important to us. We are literally overwhelmed by the opinions of others when we are young. Opinions adopted through passivity contain no basis for positive action except the need to agree or obey. If we are born into a long line of Republicans or Democrats we are likely to continue the tradition. In effect, when many of us reach the "shoulds," without benefit of the discourse and reflection associated with higher learning, we accept our borrowed opinions as absolute facts.

In this way, societies around the world pass their borrowed opinion (dressed up as culture) from one generation to the next, without ever examining their assertions of truth. In time, an earnest search for truth is viewed as subversive because beliefs passed through generations are wrapped in trust, held together by strong emotion. Beliefs deeply rooted in social bonds raise natural barriers to objectivity. The very process of believing precludes acknowledgment of contrary information. This, in turn, leads cultures to nationalism founded in the poverty of unawareness and bound by a resentment of dialogue.

A relationship with authority is thus established, the thrust of which is *whom* to believe rather than *what*. Borrowed opinion accepted on blind faith requires a sense of loyalty plagued by suspicion and mistrust of everyone who seems to be an outsider. The result is that one cannot be truly self-determining with any degree of objectivity because all acts of expression depend upon approval. Attacking someone's opinion that is rooted in friendship or family ties becomes an attack on the person and on the others who share in the belief. Truth subordinated to the need for loyalty leads to anti-intellectualism.

People who establish this type of relationship with authority give up thinking in favor of obeying their way through life. The American Dream as projected on the screen by the producers of culture is the only one they dare consider. Thinking, especially critical thinking, is a nuisance to people who wish to maintain a status quo based on association. Consider the implications of rapid change when a vast segment of our society clings to rigid beliefs based on loyalty instead of reason. It is easy to see how small disagreements could lead to armed conflict. A dramatic example of this is the history of religious conflict in the Middle East, where beliefs are so rigid as to have resisted attempts at negotiating differences for thousands of years.

Another example comes from my own past. During the late 1960s I was a police officer for the city of Dallas, Texas. I was working in a poverty-ridden area of West Dallas when Martin Luther King Jr. was assassinated. At the time, I accepted the character aspersions cast on Dr. King by the FBI, which were that he was a troublemaker without a legitimate platform. I was so sure that the FBI was right and so loyal to the ideology of law enforcement that I never seriously considered Dr. King's speeches. I didn't listen to him at all. Years later I read the now-famous letter written from his cell in the Birmingham jail.[17] It was one of the most profoundly stunning realizations of error I have ever experienced. The brilliance of his arguments made me wonder how I could ever have questioned his integrity. It's not the fact that I felt an allegiance to the FBI that bothers me today, but the fact that I let that association prevent me from looking at the evidence for myself.

If truth is not easy to come by, as the range of differences among cultures certainly suggests, it must follow that much of culture is false knowledge. The purpose of education, then, must be to give the student an opportunity to rise above culture. Indeed, educator Neil Postman, in his book *Conscientious Objections*, uses the term education to mean "a defense against culture."[18]

As a teacher, Socrates urged his followers to question. Granted, there is some debate whether Socrates was indeed a wise man or just an arrogant busybody, but we nevertheless celebrate his name as synonymous with wisdom. It was his assertion that the path to truth is best achieved by questioning our most cherished beliefs. Why, then, do we not do this out of habit instead of clinging to borrowed opinions which we have not reflected upon fully or subjected to critical scrutiny? "The history of intellectual progress reveals nothing more clearly than that every new truth must deeply wound the feelings of those with vested emotional, ideological or economic interests in outworn ideas."[19] Millions of Americans nevertheless hold pious views on a myriad of subjects about which, for all practical purposes, they know nothing. They believe capitalism, communism, or socialism to be inherently bad, without ever having examined in depth any of the fundamental assumptions on which these ideologies are based, or ever comparing one against the other. They "know" that Adam Smith or Karl Marx was a fundamentally flawed person without ever having read one word of the works these men spent a lifetime formulating.

American culture inspires a paradox in which the democratic notion of "one person one vote," combined with the pedagogical experience of education, perpetuates the idea that one opinion is as good as another, well-reasoned or not. We take a class, memorize a few of the finer points about the subject, and forget them promptly after the test. In time we construe this to be learning, but in reality it is only presentation. Since critical thinking is never emphasized, we continue the process even after we leave school. If we attend a seminar about a subject we are genuinely interested in, we resort to exposure as an equivalent to learning, failing to realize that, if we do not master the material, we will know no more about it in six weeks than we know about all the subjects we studied in the past that held no interest for us.

Such vague associations with subject matter lead millions of people to conclude that they are educated, when in reality they have only been exposed to information. This is like saying you know someone really well when you have only been introduced. Similarly, people with a little exposure often think of themselves as having expertise, and are likely to jump to conclusions based on very little knowledge. Small wonder that people resort so quickly to stereotyping others, because their judgment is often based on the confirmation of vague memories rather than on critical thinking. Ballot-box decisions are often made on the basis of familiarity with a candidate's name, with no thought given to the reason for voting in the first place.

Unless the focus of formal education is misplaced, how do we explain that, on the one hand, millions of people are easily influenced but, on the other, they hold adamant opinions on a myriad of subjects about which they know practically nothing? In time, they become comfortable with superficial notions about everything. A soldier unaware of the presence of land mines will eventually step on one. Similarly, a technological society unaware of its potential for destruction will likely poison itself or blow itself up.

The substance of loyalty is, in part, why we are so drawn to people who agree with us, even though—taking Socrates at his word—there is far more to learn by talking to people with whom we disagree. There is something instinctively social about shared views which leads to an affection for the familiar and a disdain for differences. In primitive times there must have been severe consequences for not conforming. Survival depended upon a high level of mental alertness. Hunting and gathering in a hostile environment required precise communication. How could a stranger be counted on to act appropriately in an emergency? Standing out from the group could easily draw attention to oneself, which could in turn amount to ringing the dinner bell for beasts. Besides, strangers would eat one's food. Thus, we have evolved suspicious and distrustful of those who are different from us; a trait we share with a multitude of animal species. Our discomfort with differences runs so deep we find relief in making fun of those who do not share our customs. The pronounced need to conform is with us still, even when doing so flies in the face of reason.

History offers vivid evidence of our inability to rise above arbitrary cultural prejudice and our failure to keep pace with learning and social responsibility. For centuries human beings have flayed, fried, hanged, dismembered, and impaled other human beings in the defense of beliefs that were eventually called into question, and ultimately proved to be wrong. Not long ago, people who today would be considered merely eccentric were routinely burned at the stake. Nowadays, if you make a convincing case that you are a witch, you might secure a book contract.

Those who obey their way through life often take their own measure by the perceived size or estimated strength of their enemies. Life becomes a contest of ideologies—between loyalties and associations with authorities—based more on the existence of differences than on the substance of those differences. When an enemy is fierce, each side demonstrates its potential strength through affirmations of loyalty. When an enemy is weakened, the platform of one's own side is diminished because there is little to rave about and no need for a system to support the platform. People who held the position that the Soviet military threat should be met with an unrelenting military buildup of our own reacted to the reduction in size of the Soviet military by switching to assertions about a conspiracy to establish a world government. We are no more headed toward world government than we are toward a world religion, but it's easier to embrace such notions than to acknowledge the real problems facing us. Indeed, for millions of people, the declaration of separation between church and state belies a deeply rooted notion that because the government is the *other* it is by design ungodly.

Evolutionary psychologists confirm that exaggeration of differences helps individuals and groups maintain their identity. Membership in clubs and associations conveys feelings of specialness among the members. If just anyone is allowed membership, the feeling that one is special is lost. People who see themselves as elite will go to extraordinary lengths to validate their eliteness. The need to think of oneself as being unique seems innocent enough were it not for the fact that, when we become too uncomfortable with ambiguity, drawing distinctions often leads to rigidity, and ultimately to bigotry and prejudice. Our excessive reliance upon authority causes us to try to see what is valued, and by whom, instead of discerning value for ourselves. Attempting a quantifiable comparison between self and others has become one of our greatest human pastimes and one that is utterly useless—except that it lays a foundation for nationalism. The result is that we closely scrutinize the activities of foreigners and ignore our own backyards.

Those who depend upon external authority, without ever developing a sense of their own authority, look for approval where they should find value and meaning. They possess a thirst that is by design unquenchable. If we are intrinsically aware, meaning is extracted bit by bit, piece by piece, from daily experience. The meaning we get from life derives from the meaning we add to life. We perceive value through context, but we become confused because we are predisposed to think context comes at the end: we are unable to fully judge a movie until we see the last scene, and we think we are unable to put our life in perspective until we are near its end. We get this predisposition from the external push of our culture, but it is an illusion; we have the capacity to discern context at most stages of life, if we maintain the power and will to think for ourselves. Context and meaning are shaped by purpose. If we can understand this, we might be a little more hesitant in judging what we perceive to be the relative worth of others. But whether we understand this or not, as we move through life we get glimpses of the last page of life; death casts a long shadow, and it brings to bear the need to throw out all of the rhetoric of culture and think for ourselves. It is a last chance to matter.

If philosophers are, as the definition implies, simply lovers of wisdom, why are we not all philosophers? What is any act of developing one's own opinion except a challenge to authority? And if we do not challenge authority, how do we make a contribution to our culture? Indeed how do we control our own lives? By whose authority do we stop burning witches, if not by our own?

The Environment

In every aspect of their lives, Native Americans express a wisdom that Anglos have never understood and may never understand with regard to their relationship with the earth.[20] Taming the frontier was supposed to bring progress. But what is progress? I grew up thinking that progress was development, the kind that meant turning vacant lots into buildings, rivers into hydroelectric plants, towns into cities, and cities into metropolises. In short, like millions of other people, I thought progress meant conquering nature instead of being a part of it. We fail to realize it is only by being a part of nature that we can put our human condition in global perspective.

Near the middle of the last century Henry David Thoreau wrote:

> If a man walks in the woods for love of them half of each day, he is in danger of being regarded as a loafer; but if he spends his whole day as a speculator, shearing off those woods and making earth bald before her time, he is esteemed an industrious and enterprising citizen. As if a town had no interest in forests but to cut them down.[21]

Our failure to see our tenuous relationship with the environment has led us to a position where it is painfully obvious, even to those still in the throes of denial, that something must be done to alter our present course of human activity. "Throughout our lifetimes, economic trends have shaped environmental trends, often altering the earth's natural resources and systems in ways not obvious at the time. Now...the reverse is also beginning to happen: environmental trends are beginning to shape economic trends."[22]

Our attitudes and opinions about environmental issues stem from our inability to be objective—to see things as they are, not as we wish them to be. Even those who point to environmental degradation often fail to see their own complicity. Everyone who drives a car, rides buses or planes, uses plastic, produces garbage, and participates in general in today's society is a part of the problem. Failure to think deeply about this subject is evidenced by the debris left at environmental protest rallies.

Standing near a small group of people at a local business I once overheard one man say to another, "I guess you heard that the greenhouse effect is bullshit." "No, I didn't," replied the other. "Yeah, it was on the news." This is a clear demonstration of opinion held with a casual, vague awareness of the issue. In a short time, I would bet, the individual quoting the news was arguing vehemently from this position without having learned any more about it.

The 1982 science fiction movie *Blade Runner* depicts the city of Los Angeles in a twenty-first century setting. The air is so thick that the city is always dark. When I first saw it, I thought the producers had lost their minds. Over the past few years, however, it has become obvious to me that, for the most part, we simply do not deal with our real problems. We just frame them in a different light so that we can continue to feel good about being Americans. When you look at Los Angeles today, the scenes in *Blade Runner* don't seem too far-fetched.

An economy in which success is measured by how much one consumes is antithetical to environmental congruence and individual well-being. My criticism of industrial waste procedures does not mean that I favor the abandonment of technology. It is even a frivolous notion to claim that one is for or against technology, since the present population of the earth cannot be sustained without it. Technology is not the enemy unless we fail to keep it in perspective. If everyone is frantically busy focusing on how, not enough people ask why. Technology is but another word for power. And what is power without purpose? What happens when power drives power? The indiscriminate disposal of industrial waste did not have to be a byproduct of industrialization. The fact that we can no longer eat fish from our major rivers was not an inevitable consequence. Sadly, intelligent disposal of waste was not, and did not, need careful consideration so long as streams to carry it away were abundant and people were so busy "doing their own thing" that no one felt inclined to protest.

I don't favor a return to a medieval state of agriculture any more than I want to live in a completely paved asphalt future. Nor do I wish to sound as if adopting an environmental stance automatically makes one morally superior. Environmentalism reduced to a blind religious fervor does more harm than good. Five billion-plus human beings engaged in any type of activity will produce consequences. The crux of seeing that these are minimally harmful lies first in awareness of what the consequences are, followed by the conviction to act responsibly. The greenhouse hypothesis may yet prove to be incorrect; after all, it was only a few years ago when scientists warned of a coming ice-age. Gaia-like thermostats may work in ways that we will never fully understand, but evidence in favor of global warming or cooling will not likely clear the haze over Los Angeles or bring back the ozone. Surely we don't have to be convinced that we are facing total environmental destruction before we are moved to act in the interest of clean air and water. Does the sky really have to be falling or can we act when it simply changes colors?

Psychologist Carl Jung observed that a large number of people live their whole lives divorced from the genuine use of their senses, while an equally large number of people make their way through life by feeling instead of thinking. Both ways of living seem to be harbingers of thick air.

Knowledge as a Resource

We've not yet scratched the surface of possibilities for using technology to fit into the natural world instead of conquering it. Consider the savings in energy resources if all of our electrical appliances—lights, televisions, radios, heating and cooling systems—had microchip thermostats to shut themselves off automatically when people were not using them. The savings would likely stagger the imagination. We have such technology today, but seem uninterested in applying it.

Resource savings are also possible through electronic media. Consider how many millions of trees are wasted for the sake of printing on paper daily stock prices, sports scores, and the myriad types of information that each newspaper reader skips over. Even if you follow the stock market closely, chances are you check only a few of the stock listings printed. Further, only a small portion of the unread newspapers will be recycled, while hundreds of millions of tons of them will find their way to landfills. We all know that the cutting of trees to make paper, the collection of information, the selling of advertising, and the printing and distribution of newspapers creates jobs, but imagine replacing these activities with electronic information on demand and replacing the use of resources with the creation of knowledge.[23] In other words, fill the economic void with knowledge itself as the resource. We know that advancing technology in all disciplines requires an increase of knowledge on the part of citizens to produce social equilibrium, yet we pretend education is something that can be attended to and gotten out of the way when people are still very young. We would be far, far better off as a nation, and as individuals, if we placed more importance on lifelong learning than we do on the need for low-paying, meaningless jobs. Electronic information on demand would eliminate minimum-wage newspaper delivery jobs, but the demand for skillful reporters would rise dramatically.

Is it unthinkable to replace the consumption of resources with learning as the driving force of the economy, thereby substituting the thing we need most for the things we must become accustomed to doing without? Lifelong learning becomes a sustained resource. Picture the economic explosion associated with *learning to earn* as opposed to paying to learn. Would graduate-level education for the majority be better utilized, better enjoyed by millions of citizens who now can afford big screen televisions to watch reruns, but who can barely read? We really could become a knowledge society. Imagine the possibilities of creating a positive value for thinking, in and of itself. Economic progress would mean real progress. Material goods would not be the "main point of life."[24] Growth in the GNP would mean that solutions arrived as quickly as problems. We would be taking up where the ancient philosophers left off. We would likely be the first real architects of civilization.

Economics based on the use of raw resources is the major impediment to widespread use of passive solar energy. Industry proponents disparage solar energy as being inefficient, but, as Hazel Henderson says, "Efficient for whom?"[25] The point of economic-based energy is not to produce energy so much as it is to create profit from having produced it. We are so accustomed to this arrangement that whenever we think of creating electric power we imagine monolithic power plants discharging electricity to millions of customers. But what if users created their own passive solar power? Can it be done? I don't think there is any question that it can, in spite of the dismal projections by industry. Would there be big bucks in it? Likely not, and it is this, not a lack of technological capability, that keeps us from becoming more serious about it.

Population Growth

Population growth is integral to any discussion about global economics and the well-being of the environment. In their book, *The Population Explosion*, Paul and Anne Ehrlich warn of the impending disaster we face if the global population is not stabilized. To illustrate the dynamics of exponential growth, they use the classic analogy of weeds expected to cover a pond in 30 days by doubling in growth each day. The big surprise comes when, on day 29, half the pond remains uncovered, and the next day all of it is covered. The Ehrlichs observe: "There is no question that the population explosion will end soon. What remains in doubt is whether the end will come humanely because birthrates have been lowered, or tragically through rises in death rates." The Ehrlichs point out that 80 percent of the world's population does not share our standard of living. About these disparities they have said:

> The plight of the underprivileged of Earth is probably the single most important barrier to keeping our planet habitable. Without the cooperation of the poor, the most important global environmental problems cannot be solved; and at the moment the poor have precious little reason to listen to appeals for cooperation. Many of them are well aware that the affluent are mindlessly using up humanity's common inheritance—even as they yearn to help us do it. And all poor people are aware that the rich have the ability to bear the suffering of the poverty-stricken with a stiff upper lip. To remove such attitudes and start helping the less fortunate (and themselves), the rich must understand the plight of the poor not just intellectually but emotionally.[26]

Perhaps the most confusing aspect of all this, according to the Ehrlichs, is our blind faith in what might be called "terminal growthism." They write, "Most people do not recognize that, at least in rich nations, economic growth is the disease, not the cure."[27] In fact, were it not for our human propensity for self-deception, it seems impossible that we could view the earth as it appears from outer space and not realize that our growing numbers threaten our very survival. It has taken several million years to reach our current level of population. Most people who read these words will likely live out their lives without witnessing the drama of the Ehrlichs' weeds-in-the-pond example, but if you think we aren't increasing our numbers at too high a rate, consider the words of the late Isaac Asimov:

> If the population of the earth were to continue to increase at the present rate indefinitely, by 3530 A.D. the total mass of human flesh and blood would equal the mass of the earth. By 6826 A.D., the total mass of human flesh and blood would equal the mass of the known universe.[28]

Now, this is not going to happen. The Ehrlichs are right, of course—the growth in population will end soon, either by intellectual design or by biological meltdown. Edward O. Wilson states the problem succinctly, "One planet, one experiment."[29] Unfortunately, optimists are heroes in the weeds-in-the-pond scenario, until the very last day, when it's too late to avoid catastrophe. So, how do we draw attention to humanity's greatest problem in a way that will cause ordinary people around the planet take human population seriously? We will revisit this issue in Chapter Seven.

Chapter Six

Social Patterns Versus Intellectual Patterns

The virtue in most request is conformity. Self-reliance is its aversion. It loves not realities and creators, but names and customs.[1]

—*Ralph Waldo Emerson*

The illusion of freedom is often far greater than the reality. A significant number of the philosophies we regard as great works were published posthumously. Daring ideas do not so readily produce bold behavior. We must never lose sight of the fact that authority defines reality. Or that the illusion of freedom of thought stops abruptly as one begins to tinker with the official version of reality. Diversity, by design, is a threat to centralized power. A community of one mind is far easier to influence than one of many.

Regardless of the era in our history, there is rarely a doubt about who really holds the reins of power. Power is highly concentrated at the top of our economic hierarchy, as much by design as through merit. There is also little doubt that what has posed as genuine education during these periods is for the most part the result of an indoctrination to ensure those in power remain in power. (If this were not true, democracy would be deemed unnecessary.) While a certain freedom of thought has always existed for us in one form or another, and while political debate is a norm, never have students of any society been encouraged to thirst for truth and quench it for themselves without elaborate political safeguards. The fate of Socrates is a case in point.

I am not suggesting it's desirable for societies to try to produce anarchists, or that we can live without the need for authority, but I am suggesting the only real opportunity for equity and equality is to be found by citizens who are their own best assessors of truth—citizens who readily understand that a high salary close to a center of power is the most subtle form of maintaining that power. (Thus, intellectuals can be the most identifiable cowards, the biggest sellouts, when they're willing to trade their silence for high salaries.) People educated to more clearly discern truth would be highly supportive of the phenomenon of self-interest, but they would understand that self-interest is balanced by public interest in the same way that freedom is balanced by responsibility.

Rights do not exist in a vacuum, nor simply because they are written on paper. Rights exist because there also exists a legion of people who are keenly aware of their responsibility as citizens. The problem with the agenda I propose is not so much that it would require a degree of economic equity, but that it would be a greater threat to hierarchical power than is a society where large numbers of people can be considered well-behaved but economically marginal. Bertrand Russell parodied this attitude when he said, "Better men should be stupid, slothful, and oppressive than that their thoughts should be free. For if their thoughts were free they might not think as we do."[2]

Quality of life depends in large part on the ability to live one's life through one's principles. If this is not possible, *form* will always become more important than *substance* because social convention will take precedence over thought. We might just as easily view progressive history as continuous disobedience. There is a lot we can do as individuals to create better lives for ourselves and a better world for others. Emerson said, "Do not seek yourself outside yourself." Kant said, "Determine yourself from within." We can live up to our responsibilities as citizens through continuous learning, and we can thoroughly develop our own conscience (Thoreau wondered why we should have one at all if it were not to use). We can conserve energy, discern the environmental results of our own individual actions, and eat lower on the food chain (which promotes better health). Further, we can remain beyond the reach of propagandists, both commercial and political, who try to influence us for their ends rather than our own. In short, we can learn to discover principles instead of just following rules.

Social Prophets and Biographical Life

Historical progress might result from people seeking recognition, and it might come simply from lovers of wisdom. Those whom we celebrate as the heroes of culture are the very people who have challenged the authority of social convention and upheld principle. Erich Fromm categorized people as prophets and priests to make this point. In *On Disobedience*, he wrote:

> Prophets appear only at intervals in the history of humanity. They die and leave their message. The message is accepted by millions, it becomes dear to them.... Let us call the men who make use of the idea the prophets.... The prophets live their ideas. The priests administer them to the people who are attached to the idea. The idea has lost its vitality. It has become a formula. The priests declare that it is very important how the idea is formulated; naturally the formulation becomes always important after the experience is dead; how else could one control people by controlling their thoughts unless there is the "correct" formulation?[3]

I'm not suggesting we become prophets in the literal sense—only that we develop the capacity to live in congruence with our principles, just like those heroes among us who have placed their principles ahead of their own self-interest. This is, after all, the embodiment of purpose. If we can't act in parallel with what we truly believe, then living itself is disingenuous.[4]

This seldom-acknowledged problem is deeply embedded in our culture: millions of people hold views which they cannot express at work for fear of losing their jobs. Many feel it necessary to act as if they share the views of their employers when nothing could be further from the truth. This is one reason why we derive so much pleasure from movies and shows where we can watch the guardians of the status quo register surprise when some heroic figure demolishes their worship of technique and brings the principle of purpose back into view, even if only for a moment.

This glimpse of purpose reveals the open secret of the power of hierarchies. Leon Festinger's theory of cognitive dissonance suggests that our thoughts, actions, and feelings must remain in consummate alignment, or we are compelled through dissonance to realign them. Thought, action, feeling is a description of a hierarchy. The privilege of thinking is afforded those at the top. It is in the interest of those at the top not too feel too much, for that will lead to dissonance; thus they appear cold and distant. Those in the lower ranks have plenty to feel about, but what keeps them busy with their noses to the grindstone is that they are led by their actions.

We are an action-based society. We are a nation of doers. When you consider dissonance theory and the psychology of commitment, it's easy to see that, if you can get people to lead with their actions instead of their thoughts, they will be forced to rationalize their thoughts and emotions into line with their actions. This is why well-meaning people will participate freely and with self-justification in activities (like insurance scams and tax fraud) for which they would support criminal prosecution, if they were to discover strangers doing the same thing. Through the process of their education, young people in our society don't decide what kind of a society they want and then proceed to build it. Instead, they find a small way of fitting in by finding a job. And in twenty or thirty years of employment—at a nuclear reactor, with an oil company, timber company, pharmaceutical lab, meat packing plant, or any one of a thousand different types of business—good, rational people with the best of intentions will be able to defend the industry that employs them, regardless of its effects on individuals or the environment.

People who act without giving thought to the consequences of their actions are led as effectively as the child who is grabbed by the collar and taken out of the room for misbehaving. One may voice views opposing those of the leaders, but this will work in the favor of only a few individual employees. Most people will not be able to hold substantially different views for long, and stay where they are, without rationalizing their continued actions.

Human brains use their pattern-matching skills extraordinarily well to ensure the stability of their hosts. Add a little robust positive bias, and the system becomes self-correcting and self-justifying. So, if workers knowingly leak a little radiation, spill some oil into the environment, help create a drug that kills or harms people unintentionally, or send meat out of their packing plant that is just a tiny bit contaminated, they must, even though their individual roles may have been small, either bring their thoughts and emotions into line with their continued actions, or be willing (and able) to quit. Granted, some of these infrequent accidents are acceptable trade-offs when weighed against the benefits the industries offer. Most people are willing to tolerate occasional oil spills in exchange for a dynamic transportation system. But we know intuitively what will happen if workers protest too loudly (they will become unemployable whistle-blowers) because we understand the power of hierarchies. Indeed, it is the nature of hierarchies to protect the hierarchy at all costs. And we know that the person who falls too far down the mountain might never make it back to his or her former level.

This fear of failure, combined with our need to reduce dissonance and complete with the dynamics of the power of hierarchies (where authority rises to the top of the pyramid as cream in a bottle), is so overwhelmingly prevalent that it is hard to comprehend. And yet, the power of hierarchy is the fulcrum of democracy itself. I submit that we can flatten the pyramid (at least to some degree), increase our quality of life, and still maintain enough cultural authority to bind our interests. John Rawls has suggested that political decisions should be made by people who don't know how they themselves will be affected by those decisions.[5] It would make sense for us to adapt this line of thinking and set aside our personal interests (or factions) to ensure that we can perpetually balance power, regardless of whose hands it might fall into. Just as pre-Civil War slave owners feared educating their slaves, so would those who hold the reins of power today fear a majority who were educated toward their own ends and who were unconcerned about the needs of the current hierarchy.

Prophets bring us quality, but it is priests who are in demand. Our schools are set up to mass manufacture priests; they have little tolerance for prophets. Indeed, our schools are better suited to warehouse the mentally impaired than to suffer the curiosity of an Edison or Einstein. What I am suggesting is that we know enough about human behavior to dramatically increase the number of prophets. Minus the formal externalization, education can be a synonym for meaningful life. Near the turn of the past century William James wrote, "The greatest discovery of my generation is that human beings, by changing the inner attitudes of their minds, can change the outer aspects of their lives." As one's level of intrinsic education goes up, one's dependence upon authority goes down. The result is an increase in the ability to discern value.

Erich Fromm characterized the difference in extrinsic versus intrinsic education as the difference between "having" and "being." In his book *To Have or To Be*, Fromm wrote,

> Students in the having mode of existence will listen to a lecture, hearing the words and understanding their logical structure and their meaning and, as best they can, will write down every word in their looseleaf notebooks—so that, later on, they can memorize their notes and thus pass an examination. But the content does not become part of their own individual system of thought, enriching and widening it. Instead, they transform the words they hear into fixed clusters of thought, or whole theories which they store up. The students and the content of the lectures remain strangers to each other, except that each student has become the owner of a collection of statements made by somebody else (who had either created them or taken them over from another source).[6]

Thus, an extrinsic-based education depends upon borrowed conviction. Millions of people become so anesthetized from the validity of their own experience that drugs and alcohol appear to offer a better reality than the one they inhabit. In sharp contrast, the students in the *being* mode do not come to the lecture as *tabulae rasae*. They have already thought about the subject being presented and have specific questions in mind. What they hear will spawn further inquiry. As Fromm suggests, "Their listening is an alive process."[7]

Intrinsic education provides the impetus for bottom-up instead of top-down authority. Bottom-up decision making was what Friedrich Nietzsche feared most. He argued it would produce nihilism by continually lowering standards. The rise to power of Adolph Hitler may have proved Nietzsche's point. Real tyranny emerges when there is no counterbalance to power. Society is not pulled down from below. Rather, as Pirsig suggests, society lurches forward in static-latching jerks when some individuals contribute genuine quality. Societies produce these individuals in direct proportion to the diversity and quality of life available in them. The more people there are living well above poverty level, the more genius shows itself.

In his book *Flow: The Psychology of Optimal Experience*, Mihaly Csikszentmihalyi wrote:

> To overcome the anxieties and depressions of contemporary life, individuals must become independent of the social environment to the degree that they no longer respond exclusively in terms of its rewards and punishments. To achieve such autonomy, a person has to learn to provide for herself. She has to develop the ability to find enjoyment and purpose regardless of external circumstances. This challenge is both easier and more difficult than it sounds: easier because the ability to do so is entirely within each person's hands; difficult because it requires a discipline and perseverance that are relatively rare in any era, and perhaps especially in the present. And before all else, achieving control over experience requires a drastic change in attitude about what is important and what is not.[8]

The reason we so rarely find people with the conviction to live independently of social convention has less to do with discipline and perseverance than with orientation. We have a multitude of disciplined people marching obediently to the beat of others' drums, while remaining totally alienated from hearing their own. This is because we have misunderstood the meaning of education at a fundamental level. Intrinsic-based education emphasizes the crux of human growth, which applies equally to the organic world: When we plant a vegetable garden, we perceive ourselves as "growing" vegetables; but we don't grow vegetables any more than we grow humans. Instead, we provide the conditions that enable growth; if any of these conditions are insufficient or overly harsh, growth is adversely affected.[9] Thus, intrinsic education can be the means by which we change biological life into biographical life.

If a person lacks fundamental knowledge and understanding, an inward journey is not possible. There is nowhere to go.[10] Those who depend too heavily upon authority copy biography. It's not that they have no lives, but that they respond to new stimuli with rented responses. Both money and education are necessary to sustain life; one can have too much of the former and still be unable to create a life, but the latter enables both production of and reduced dependence upon the former. Intrinsic education is vital for the creation of biography because it sparks the movement from the organic to the intellectual realm of life.

Composing a biographical life binds together the substance of principle and the fiber of conscience which give life purpose. Creating biography is a fine art disrespectful of mechanistic goals and obsessive possessiveness. A biographical life is worth living because it is worth dying for. So, it should come as no surprise that those who provide family members with unconditional love provide a living expression of wisdom. Unconditional love is a validation of self and is critical to the development of biography. A biographical life is a life rich in character—enough character to risk being different. Grandparents understand this intuitively, which is why they seem so wise in how they relate to their grandchildren.

We may sense that, without an education, our own lives would be of less value to ourselves. When we focus so forcefully on economic well-being—even though it is a precondition for further development—we often miss the point (and the shortcut), which is simply that, while economics can sustain biological life, it cannot of itself create biography. Biography is the result of the process of learning, which provides knowledge. This biography, in turn, provides the structure and the experience that not only make life worth living but make the dead worth remembering.

The majority of lives lived as copies become lost indistinguishably in a background of culture. It's the original biographies we long remember.

Francis Fukuyama argues that it is a consequence of the belief in the equality of all-of-nature (an example would be the point of view of animal rights activists) that leads to the "indifference to mass starvation in countries like Ethiopia."[11] But it seems to me that indifference to mass starvation was just as common an occurrence centuries ago when the Theistic belief in man's dominion over nature was the majority opinion. I find it an intriguing and a perpetually troubling issue that we humans (myself included) let so many other humans on this planet starve to death without making it a greater issue. I do know it is wrong that we allow this to happen, no matter how we try to frame it. If our indifference does not stem from prejudice, nationalistic bias, or the fact that we do not perceive those populations as having biographical lives, then where does it come from?

Suppose that tomorrow everyone now starving in Ethiopia woke up with the equivalent of an American college education. What would they do differently to eradicate poverty and starvation? It seems to me one of the first things they would realize is that their previous state of existence lacked any concept of human rights, much less recognition that they possessed such rights. Given proper tools for articulating arguments in their favor, these people could almost certainly pull together enough food for sustenance. Daniel C. Dennet poses this question: "Would you settle docilely for a life of meaningless poverty, knowing what you know today about the world?"[12] Not likely. And neither would the Ethiopians. With their new knowledge they would immediately see that they now had political power, simply because of their awareness. Wouldn't this awareness inevitably lead to the visible creation of biographical lives? Wouldn't this be an example of intellectual patterns' superiority over social patterns? Does it not follow, then, that education is at least equally important as, if not more important than, an economic assistance which barely supports a biological life?

In his book *Living Within Limits*, Garrett Hardin offers a compelling argument about the dire consequences of overpopulation and suggests that we fail to deal with the issue of political economics because "our brains are addled by compassion." [13] I think the reverse is true, however. The feeble efforts made by all the developed countries in the world to help those countries whose citizens are starving may have roots in compassion, but in reality their inadequacy implies indifference.

Aristotle's notion of actuality and potentiality suggests that one's value is represented by one's potential. If true, it clearly establishes the value of human life as greater than that of animals as a matter of rationality. And, if I have interpreted Robert Pirsig's metaphysics of quality correctly, I believe this view is confirmed. All this suggests to me that there is a rational basis for believing in the universality of human rights and that, although the idea of human superiority over other life forms has gotten us into a lot of trouble, it is nonetheless true. Moreover, because it is true, our level of responsibility is thus increased.

In the late summer of 1992, the arrival of hurricane Andrew on the Florida and Louisiana coasts coincided with massive starvation in Somalia. Media visuals of Americans sobbing over the loss of their material possessions contrasted eerily with the quiet tears of the Somalians who were dying from a political storm of indifference. I am unable to articulate the feelings I experienced from watching this, and yet I can't get these scenes out of my mind. I am still uncertain whether I have come closer to the reason we allow people to starve to death, but I can also find nothing of substance that absolves us from assuming responsibility for eliminating starvation.

There is another way to think about this problem which may offer some insight into why it is such a puzzling predicament. Imagine what would happen if, in each country where humans were dying from starvation, it were suddenly announced that wildlife would be slaughtered until such time as human starvation ceased. I believe the emotion brought forth by such an action would result in a wake-up call heard around the world. For once, the curtains covering our windows of cultural reality would be drawn open.

When governments commit atrocities like killing, raping, and pillaging their neighbors, many of us feel compelled to intervene, to commit troops if necessary to stop the killing. But why are the violent situations more urgent than slow starvation? Human slaughter is an abomination in any form, but slow starvation seems to be a greater tragedy precisely because so little effort is needed to stop it.

John F. Schumaker offers yet another way to look at culture, belief, and biography that illuminates the dark side of living and shows why understanding these territories is so important. Schumaker's provocative thesis suggests that, in a sense, anorexia nervosa is "a private religion," a defense mechanism adopted by young, upper-middle-class women to squeeze the harshness of reality down to something manageable. These individuals are so externally overwhelmed by "shoulds" that they fail to develop the means to cope with a chaotic world of external expectations.[14] In other words, they fail to develop their own sense of biography. They don't copy biography, they simply fail to develop it, and for this very reason they prove to be an exception to our rules about biography and remembrance: they are truly missed when they die. In large part, these young women have close relationships with loving parents. Mother and daughter become "psychologically enmeshed," and the daughter fails to develop a sense of self that is strong enough to cope with a harsh world. Thus, a simple world of "thinness" provides a trance-like escape: all problems are reduced to one. Schumaker writes, "The presence of the 'single ruling motivation' destroys all ability to concentrate on anything else."[15]

Recall the earlier analogy of an external definition of happiness projected onto a screen through cultural expectations, and then revisit the issue of starvation in Africa. When you realize that many economically well-off young women in America starve themselves each year, the abstraction of biographical life comes clear.[16] Africans die from an abuse of power in their culture; Americans from a fear of power in their culture. Something in our highly technical American society is missing—a sense of structure and an embodiment linked to purpose that would otherwise allow us to see and address the injustice of starvation in both cultures. That something is the highest use of intellectual patterns.

I am not trying to belittle the value of material wealth; it is extremely important. Money colors every aspect of living. To be able to respond independently of your social system means that you must be able to have a degree of economic independence so that you no longer have to choose between your principles and economic existence. Trying to create a life based upon the premise that existence is subordinate to gaining more and more wealth is like trying to put out a fire with gasoline. But, by focusing on the disparities of economic (or biological) life and not on education for living (biographical life), we are perpetuating the message of that premise. We are saying more gasoline is needed to fight fires—precisely the kind of philosophy that sustains a king-of-the-mountain ethos and keeps everyone busy juggling buckets and hoses instead of discovering purpose and principle. In our preoccupation we fail to pass on the most valuable lessons of our culture, namely, that learning reveals the true nature of interdependence and that knowledge has more to do with equality than it does with economic parity.

The ability to appreciate music is thwarted if one is only aware of a dozen melodies. And the ability to squeeze quality from life is similarly impaired if one has a very limited account of it. Indeed, the prophets who leave their biography as legacy go beyond exercising an ability to experience living to its fullest. They break through the barriers (genetic or cultural) that render the rest of us easily susceptible to self-deceit, bigotry, and prejudice. True biography represents a biological life stamped and imprinted for all time with the heart of one's ideas.

Socially Constructed Reality

The notion that reality is a social construction may have congealed into the dogma of postmoderist thought, as social critic Christopher Lasch has proposed, but that doesn't necessarily render the concept untrue.[17] What we believe predisposes us to act as if what we believe is real. This may sound ridiculously simple, but it has far-reaching implications. Cultural expectations create social reality. Most of us are so spellbound by culture as to be unaware of anything not delineated by some sort of social expectation. "The logic of reality creation is the following: if people believe this they will do that."[18] If reality is a product of social construction, then it follows that we are all architects, directors, actors, stage managers, and audience. We are all responsible "consumers of reality."[19] If reality is genuinely a constructive process, then a search for truth becomes a matter of finding a better seat in the theater. There are clear advantages for sitting up front, and all sorts of misconceptions born of not being able to see well. But, no matter where we sit, there is always a tall stranger sitting in front of us. In other words, there is no front row. Our delusions about reality are always with us.

In a very real sense we have a time machine between our ears. On any starry night we can look to the heavens and look back in time. What we do not realize is that we do something similar on a bright sunny day. When we look upon any scene, the perception that occurs is built of the residuum of past memories. All that we profess to understand is thus understood through a previous sense of understanding. We come to the play and bring our own mental props.

Through the constructs we provide, we are able to discern meaning. This is hardly a secret, but it is seldom acknowledged. It has a lot to do with how we experience life itself and how we relate to other people. Memory is, at least in an operational sense, the residue of emotion. Emotion is life's background music. Thus, when memory is joined with the intellect, the melody we experience amounts to leftover belief. Our props already contain instructions about what should be selected as verifications of reality. So, if one has narrow views, if one is obsessed with one's own interests, then one's perception will see to it that such views prevail over any and all obstacles. And, if similar views are shared with others, then the expression of such views affirms the relationship; and loyalty becomes the armor to fend off opposing views. Perception is more than a template for conscious attention. It is an *alive* process, which, when left to its own volition without reasoned concentration, becomes virtually autonomous.

Culture provides individuals with mental "highlighters" and "magic markers." Once highlighted, phenomena are subject only to confirmation and are rarely open to critical analysis. In similar fashion, we use cultural magic markers to blot out what our culture deems unimportant, and, unless we exert extraordinary personal effort, what is covered over ceases to exist. We use these tools with precise fashion to deal with environmental issues. We highlight excavated natural resources such as minerals and use magic markers to hide the ecological damage used in obtaining and refining them.

If our predisposition to rig perception were not enough, we are bound further to labor through the whole perplexing process with the trappings of language. In his book *I Am Right—You Are Wrong*, Edward De Bono aptly describes this problem:

> In a sense language is a museum of ignorance. Every word and concept has entered language at a stage of relative ignorance compared to the present greater experience. But the words and concepts are frozen into permanence by language and we must use these words and concepts to deal with present-day reality. This means we may be forced to look at things in a very inadequate way.[20]

If it were not for the experiential baggage we bring to the theater of reality there would be little use or need for art. Art is an external manifestation of internal reality, a solitary expression of social phenomena. Viewing art is a little like studying humanity through a two-way mirror. We see what the artist intends us to see, if we understand what we are expected to see. If we do not share the reality the artist intends, we turn the mirror inward for our own reality check. It's a little sad, though perhaps fortunate, that we are better at bridging the gap of culture with external representations of inner observations than we are at simply talking to our neighbors. Then, when we do put words together to communicate precisely as intended, we call it art. How odd that we admire the art of other cultures, but abhor their ideas.

We can "demand of art what life cannot give us," as André Maurois pointed out. "Why is artistic illusion just as respected as scientific truth?" he asks, and then reflects on his own question:

> If we give it some thought, nothing could be stranger. In life we are surrounded by houses, trees, fruit, human bodies, and yet we join the crush at the doors of an exhibition to gaze upon distorted reproductions of these very objects or beings. We are, daily, tormented or elated by desire,

jealousy, ambition and, instead of forgetting human suffering in our leisure hours, we go to watch, on stage or screen, dramas similar to our own. Again, why? Is life not rich enough, good enough or evil enough to satisfy us or to dishearten us?[21]

It is apparent that we need illusions desperately. Even more, we need to realize we do this. In our theater of reality, it's easy to see what appear to be flaws in the realities of other cultures and hard to see the frailties of our own. In an essay titled "The Concept of Freedom," the late A. J. Ayer wrote:

> In a completely planned society, the members of which were trained from birth for their respective functions and who were so thoroughly conditioned that they never conceived any desires but those that were appropriate to their station, the subjects would be perfectly happy; and since they would be granted the ability to satisfy their desires, they would seem themselves to be free. But we, surveying the whole system from the outside, would judge, without hesitation, that they were not really free.[22]

The more I study, the more I believe that the very essence of educating oneself lies in putting oneself, one's culture, and how it relates to other cultures, into perspective. An understanding of the complex nature of freedom (an idea commonly accepted as simple) can't be reached without it. *In Reality Isn't What It Used To Be,* author and social critic Walter Truett Anderson writes:

> You can only become truly tolerant of other people's realities by having found some new ways to inhabit your own. To develop tolerance is to develop a story about stories, a perspective on all our values and beliefs....Just as we develop an image of the world and the human species—as we create the world and create humanity—so do we develop an image of the human species as an indefatigable creator of stories, myths, values, beliefs, morals, laws, and religions. And to know that we create such things need not destroy our respect for the species nor our respect, even reverence, for the things created....Whatever freedom we are ultimately able to achieve will be gained not merely by shouting naughty words at social constructions of reality—not merely by

unlearning, but also by learning about why we think and be- have and believe as we do, and why and how we create reali- ties. Such learning is possible; much of it is being discov- ered, in many fields, and none of it is secret.[23]

Indeed, if we can move this kind of thinking from the status of an open secret to that of common knowledge, we will have the tools to lessen the effects on our society of the idiocies of bigotry, prejudice, and the narcissism of minor differences.

Personal Realities

In Plato's essay *Theatetus*, the title character is rebuked by Socrates for having made the mistaken assumption that knowl- edge and perception are the same thing. Even in our times, knowledge and opinion and the relationship between them have not received the kind of attention that would make their differ- ences self-evident. (Sadly, when we study Plato, we are judged by our ability to recall what Socrates said, but seldom required to demonstrate the ability to think as he did.) One could say that perception and opinion are the same thing, except that culture provides the blueprint for perception and fails to see the link with opinion. Without a Socratic effort at probing the essence of perception, truth appears to emerge when, in fact, our percep- tual processes have deceived us. Perception is the theater of art. Reality is Plato's guest, dressed as a Form who never shows up but is always treated as present. Thus, art is merely a flirtation with reality and belief is a condition for perception.

In recent years there have been many examples in textbooks to show how easily we are fooled by perceiving incorrectly. There is the picture of the faces of both an old and a young woman drawn in such a way that the viewer can perceive only one image at a time. There are drawings of objects that are all the same size, even though some appear larger or smaller than the others. Each of these examples shows how easily we can be fooled by appear- ances. If we observe two objects that appear to be the same size, but in reality one is larger than the other, it would be fair to say we are *of the opinion* that the two are the same size.

Our preoccupations determine the reality that dominates us. For example, the biologist looks at the world and sees genetic relationships; the behaviorist observes environmental stimuli; the clergyman sees a world of spirituality or of rule breakers. The salesman sees a multitude of opportunities; the subsistence hunter, the wage earner, and the street person observe the world in terms of survival. In the third century A.D., the neo-Platonist Plotinus said, "To any vision must be brought an eye adapted to what is to be seen." A mind made up with the expectation of what it is about to see is like a camera in which the light and distance meters are preset without regard for the object being photographed. A picture will still result, and what one hoped to see in the picture will be there, however distorted it may appear. Another camera, set differently, would produce a different picture.

An example demonstrating how easily this happens occurred in the late 1960s when I was a police officer in Dallas. One evening while working in a high crime area, I heard the dispatcher give a description of a suspect wanted for armed robbery of a convenience store near my location. The description went something like this: white male, late twenties to early thirties, 5' 9", wearing blue jeans and a red and black checkered shirt. A few minutes later, on a dark street, I spotted a suspect who perfectly matched the description. I questioned him, and he seemed so nervous I became convinced he was the culprit. When I arrived at the downtown jail about 45 minutes after the robbery, I found six other officers, all with suspects matching the dispatcher's description, each arrested within three miles of the robbery. Every officer including myself thought he had the right man. Moreover, each suspect, nervous at being found in such circumstances, had appeared to the investigator as someone with something to hide. So, if knowledge and perception were the same thing, six people who were unlucky enough to be wearing similar clothes would have gone to jail, perhaps even prison, though only one person (but not necessarily one of our suspects) had committed the crime.

Another less dramatic example of how we create our own sense of reality occurred to me not long ago through my observation of fall colors. Fall has always been my favorite time of year, and, although I have lived in Alaska for more than two decades, I still miss the fall colors of the Midwest. Alaska has its own special type of aesthetic beauty at any time of the year, but not the bright colors of hardwoods. After a time I began to convince myself that the fall colors were actually getting better. Then it occurred to me that what had really happened was that in my longing for fall in the Midwest, I was getting better at finding the smallest splash of color in the Alaska landscape. From such experiences and observations, I have come to believe one of the greatest impediments to human relations is our use of a frail sensory perception system to form strong opinions. We must learn to balance the process by probing the issues deeply enough to discover all of the relevant facts which we're more or less genetically bound to overlook.

Perhaps there is no better way to demonstrate the validity of personal realities than to describe the gender differences we experience daily but, for all practical purposes, remain unaware of. In her book *You Just Don't Understand*, author Deborah Tannen argues that "recognizing gender differences frees individuals from the burden of individual pathology." Tannen describes the male perspective as that of an individual in a hierarchical social order where he is either one-up or one-down, contrasted with the female approach which represents a network of connections where negotiations are for closeness, confirmation, and support. The fundamental difference in the way men and women perceive the world sets up a grid that perpetually inhibits communication—women discuss their problems with men in the hopes of finding a sympathetic ear and understanding, while men see this as a opportunity to solve women's problems for them. This interplay leads both to bewilderment. Theorists debate to what extent these differences are biological or learned, but the fact remains that most communication difficulties between the sexes stem from mismatched perceptions.

We live in a world of ever-increasing abstraction where it is easy to become lost in a dark corner, many times removed from "reality." The degree to which we protect ourselves from the harshness of reality is startling. Not long ago one of our local television news shows aired footage of pet euthanasia at the animal shelter. This was followed by a barrage of protests from viewers who claimed their sensibilities were offended. This was followed by a new round of protests from people who said it was about time others were aware of the needless suffering of animals. With all that is offensive in the world it's little wonder we're suspicious of what might unexpectedly be brought to our attention. But it is experiences like these which can serve to remind us that our reality is our own construct.

Self-Serving Perception

Our tendency to view ourselves with a distinct positive bias does more than protect us from bad news; it sugarcoats personal matters so that we view our own performance more favorably than is warranted.[24] Give this some thought, and you will likely be able to come up with examples of times when friends have described their own deeds (ones you witnessed) as far more praiseworthy than they actually were when you observed them.

In her book *Positive Illusions*, Shelly E. Taylor asserts that "normal human thought is distinguished by a robust positive bias."[25] Taylor suggests that we are so naturally self-serving that we are even likely to confuse good intentions with good results, even though the two are clearly not the same. Such propensity adds credence to the old saying, "Success has many fathers, but failure is an orphan." In *Positive Illusions*, Taylor writes:

> The tendency to take more than one's share of credit for a joint outcome would appear to be a maladaptive bias, inasmuch as it creates so many opportunities for misunderstandings. However, the bias may have benefits as well as potential liabilities. By perceiving one's share of a joint product to be larger than it is, people may feel more responsible for the outcome and work harder to make it a positive one.[26]

There seem to be clear advantages to being predisposed toward optimism and self-aggrandizing opinions where oneself is concerned. To me, however, these qualities seem to be a constant threat to a person's well-being, unless one is always aware that such forceful tendencies exist. Viewing ourselves more favorably than is warranted is a core issue in interpersonal conflicts. We minimize the consequences of our own mistakes and exaggerate those of others.

Upon reflection, we find we're endowed with a number of built-in reality buffers, many of which must be adaptive in nature. For example, we anesthetize ourselves from bad news through the process of denial. For a time, we simply refuse to accept painful information as being correct. Similarly, the second game animal the hunter shoots is easier to kill than the first, the third and fourth easier still. The same is true of the soldier in wartime. Even our sense of smell is muted by the continued presence of a foul or aromatic odor. But does buffered reality actually add quality to our lives?

Imagine what it would be like if, from the time of our birth, we knew the exact time and place of our death. For some this issue would likely loom so large that all else would seem unimportant. But, if we pretend to have only three months to live, we discover a courageous desire to live purposely, savoring each moment, each event, each emotion. What does this suggest? Does it mean that Earnest Becker was wrong about too much reality driving us insane? Does it mean that ignorance is bliss, or the reverse? Can knowledge of reality add meaning to life? Carl Sagan argues that we should be willing to look death in the eye. Depak Chopra has dared suggest that it's exciting to be stalked by death.[27] And, in his essay *The Conduct of Life*, Emerson warned, "No picture of life can have any veracity that does not admit the odious facts."[28] Why does it appear that, in the absence of quantitative time, qualitative time becomes of paramount importance? If ignorance is really bliss, does it follow that immaturity is preferable to maturity? And why, by not knowing the exact date of our death, are we predisposed to squander our time with so many activities devoid of meaning?

It is one of the greatest tragedies of our species that, in times of war, killing others brings us closer together; worse still that this contradictory social experience seems somehow related to our ability to hold the surgeon general's report on smoking in one hand, and a cigarette in the other—a clear example that one hemisphere of the brain knows something the other does not. These reality buffers diminish experience. If they work too well, they turn true living into mere existence because we depend upon contrasts for experience itself. For example, we understand hot in comparison to cold, pleasure to pain and sorrow to joy. Safety is more appreciated when danger is understood. Not until we have an enormous range of experiential criteria with which to make comparisons can we consider ourselves fully alert.

The Power of Mind-Sets

The propensity to see the world in terms of our preoccupations is as dangerous as it is useful. The late humanist psychologist Abraham Maslow once observed, "When the only tool you have is a hammer everything begins to look like a nail."[29] The great danger that accompanies our ability to focus on problems, like adjusting the lens on a camera, is precisely our capacity to do it so well. When we are not sensitively attuned to this strength, it becomes a crippling weakness, allowing us to see only a small part of a much larger picture. The camera itself taints the image. Our lives shrink to fit the narrow film of a contaminated imagination. We become fixed in opinion to the extent that our emotions wash away any attempt to use the powers of reason.

A simple preconception of what we are looking for, or about to see, can shift our attention from the whole to a fascination with parts and produce a willingness to accept almost any evidence as proof of what we thought we would find. "Nothing is simpler in understanding than dismissing what we are attempting to understand as having already been understood."[30] Prejudice and stereotyping of groups and individuals occur when we allow our internal cameras to default always to the same setting—a previous setting which, if the image is disagreeable, most likely occurred under negative circumstances, but will for the future be automatic and deprive us of the opportunity for reflection. If we focus on the Bermuda Triangle with the expectation that it is a place where bizarre things are bound to happen, then any unusual occurrence there will confirm our suspicion, regardless of the fact that just as many unusual incidents have occurred just as frequently in other areas of the ocean of similar size and human activity.[31]

Once we accept any premise as fact without the willingness to submit it to further critical inquiry, we become vulnerable to anyone with any cause, because our reaction, positive or negative, can be depended upon. Is it any wonder, when the vast majority of our experience in school is spent exercising our short-term memory, and so little time is devoted to critical thinking, that reality becomes equivalent to recall? We are predisposed toward selectivity and short-term orientation. In *New World New Mind*, Robert Ornstein and Paul Ehrlich observed:

> Our evolutionary history equipped us to live with a handful of compatriots, in a stable environment with many short-term challenges. Benefits had to be reaped fast if they were to be reaped at all. The lion had to be dodged before it ate you; the antelope speared before it escaped.
>
> Thus the human mind evolved to register short-term changes, from moment to moment, day to day, and season to season, and to overlook the "backdrop" against which those took place. That backdrop only changed significantly on a time scale of centuries or longer. Not only did our evolutionary background predispose us to live in a world of caricatures and physically equip us to draw only part of the picture, it also predisposed us to focus on certain parts of the "image" and ignore others.[32]

Our society is chock-full of unreasoning people who have preset mental templates ready to fix on individuals who have different skin color, speak a different language, are deaf, blind, or confined to a wheelchair, and on those who have been treated for a mental illness, been diagnosed with cancer, are over a certain age, are physically unattractive, or are just unfashionably dressed. Expectations allied with unreasoned opinion are so strong that teachers have been observed performing according to their own preconceptions, having been told in advance that certain students were either gifted or disabled. The teachers unconsciously set out to prove what they had been told. Their internal mental camera adjusted itself for either gifted or learning-disabled children and ignored any information that did not correspond to the adjustment. This whole process exposes the term *mind-set* as being exactly that. In another example, simply adding the word *assistant* to a worker's title has been shown to reduce that worker's performance.[33]

We are predisposed toward quickly adopting mind-sets through the nature of our experience and the way we are educated. Since we are accustomed to feigning expertise, having only vague familiarity with a subject, we tend to make up our minds based on very little information. A kernel of fact leads to a field of generalizations. We are easily prejudiced because we have an overwhelming bias toward generalizations with their simplifying effects on everyday living. It becomes much easier to categorize someone as a member of a group than it is to consider the person as an individual. This is exacerbated by our need for positive emotional attachments, thus laying the foundation for prejudice: the love or fondness for members of our own group causes us to overlook their faults. We refrain from being critical of those whom we care about while we become more critical than is warranted of people we know little about. In this way, little information is required to form a prejudicial view, yet when we review the salient characteristics of loyalty, we find that an overwhelming amount of evidence is necessary to overturn it. Mind-sets are reason-resistant.

Imagine buying a personal computer with 32 megabytes of random access memory (RAM) only to discover that your software is designed to make decisions with a mere 64 kilobytes of data. You would no doubt feel cheated. Why, then, do we cheat humanity by making 64-kilobyte decisions about our fellow man when we are hard-wired with a capacity so formidable as to make a 32-megabyte computer look like a toy?

An excellent example of how our sense of reality shades our actions was demonstrated several years ago when the architect Maya Lin designed the Vietnam Veterans Memorial. When her plan was first unveiled it unleashed a bitter protest from people, many of them veterans, who would not consider anything that did not fit their image of what a traditional monument should be. These same people today are reduced to tears at the sight of the memorial. Lin's genius of a monument to profoundly honor and focus on the sacrifice of individuals has contributed to a healing process for those who lost friends and family members in the Vietnam war. Yet, the design almost failed to be built because it did not match the perceptual reality of a monument.

In a similar sense, there have been many efforts to glorify history by selectively focusing on events which enhance a Western bias while ignoring any events that show our heritage in a bad light. For example, the heroic image of the taming of the West in America skips ever so lightly over countless broken treaties with Native Americans. Early American settlers made fun of Native Americans because of their seemingly strange ideas about property rights, by coining the term "Indian giver." Yet it was the U.S. government that would in time show what the term really meant.

If we were to observe a similar omission while studying another country, we would view it as a serious character flaw; we would be preoccupied with its gross injustice. We know that this happened in America, but what is represented as important is the idea that Western civilization prevailed. The injustice has been overshadowed by the implication that the accomplishment was so important its means didn't matter. Americans in positions of power at the time referred to their exploits as "manifest destiny," a concept that boils down to the premise that those in power are by the very nature of their superiority destined to be in power and that their triumph is inevitable. This mind-set resulted in the trampling of Native American cultures from which we have learned far more than we have ever acknowledged. As Robert Pirsig has shown us, American frontier values came from Native Americans.[34]

Though it is seldom noticed, being prejudiced is an impediment to one's own freedom. The act of hating requires more negative energy, and can have a far greater controlling aspect, than merely being hated. Taking oneself off the automatic pilot of mind-sets requires a deep sense of understanding of self and "others." Thus, moving beyond the American Dream requires that we always be attentive to the potential destructiveness of mind-sets.

Ethnocentrism and Interdependence

The profound way in which culture shapes perception manifests itself among the people living near borders who go to great lengths to distinguish themselves from those on the other side. As noted earlier, Freud called this phenomenon the narcissism of minor differences. An obsession with in-group/out-group is what we commonly call ethnocentrism. Ethnocentrism is the acknowledged certainty that one's culture has reality pegged correctly and therefore its behavior is more fitting than the behavior of other cultures. In *Our Kind,* Marvin Harris writes about cultural obsession with differences:

> Anyone who still doubts the power of culture to make and remake the world we live in might wish to ponder the following observation: while feminist women in the West have been struggling to liberate themselves by going bare-breasted in public, the women of India have been liberating themselves by refusing to go bare-breasted in public.[35]

It is ironic that differences are almost always exaggerated and that minor differences are viewed as major: one group insists on going bare-breasted the other refuses. One of the most liberating aspects of adult learning comes through the realization that all cultures bring some value to humankind. Moreover, if we are ever to achieve wisdom in the nature of human affairs, we must learn the value of Socrates' assertion, spoken in preparation for his death, "I am not an Athenian or a Greek, but a citizen of the world."

In 1936, Ralph Linton wrote a piece, titled *"100 Percent American,"* which was intended to challenge the ethnocentrism of the day. It is worth repeating:

> Our solid American citizen awakens in a bed built on a pattern which originated in the Near East.... He slips into his moccasins, invented by the Indians of the Eastern woodlands, and goes to the bathroom, whose fixtures are a mixture of European and American invention, both of recent date. He takes off his pajamas, a garment invented in India, and washes with soap invented by the ancient Gauls. He then shaves, a masochistic rite which seems to have been derived from either Sumer or ancient Egypt.
>
> Returning to the bedroom, he...puts on garments whose form originally derived from the skin clothing of the nomads of the Asiatic steppes, puts on shoes made from skins tanned

by a process invented in ancient Egypt and cut to a pattern derived from the classical civilizations of the Mediterranean, and ties around his neck a strip of bright-colored cloth which is a vestigial survival of the shoulder shawls worn by the seventeenth-century Croatians....

On his way to breakfast he stops to buy a paper, paying for it with coins, an ancient Lydian invention. At the restaurant a whole new series of borrowed elements confronts him. His plate is made of a form of pottery invented in China. His knife is of steel, an alloy first made in southern India, his fork a medieval Italian invention, and his spoon a derivative of a Roman original. He begins breakfast with an orange, from the eastern Mediterranean, a cantaloupe from Persia, or perhaps a piece of African watermelon. With this he has coffee, an Abyssinian plant, with cream and sugar. Both the domestication of cows and the idea of milking them originated in the Near East, while sugar was first made in India. After his fruit and coffee he goes on to waffles, cakes made by a Scandinavian technique from wheat domesticated in Asia Minor. Over these he pours maple syrup, invented by the Indians of the Eastern woodlands....

When our friend has finished eating, he ... reads the news of the day, imprinted in characters invented in Germany. As he absorbs the accounts of foreign troubles he will, if he is a good conservative citizen, thank a Hebrew deity in an Indo-European language that he is 100 percent American.

If this piece were rewritten today, it could expand into a book and still not sort out all of the interwoven relationships. Despite our valiant notions of American independence, we have always been and will always remain incredibly interdependent in relation to the rest of the world. How should we view this state of interdependence? Mahatma Gandhi wrote, "Interdependence is and ought to be as much the ideal of man as self-sufficiency. Man is a social being. Without interrelation with society he cannot realize his oneness with the universe or suppress his egotism."[36]

How can we acknowledge this need for interdependence and appreciate the differences of others without totally disregarding our own uniqueness? In *The Primal Mind*, Jamake Highwater writes:

That we are all related does not make us all the same. Relationship does not require conformity, and the fact that one orientation or viewpoint is valuable does not preclude that all contrasting attitudes and positions are therefore erroneous and useless. Pluralism is a significant state of affairs for those who have been neglected; it is extremely bitter and difficult for those who have been long dominant. That's something we are going to have to learn to live with. We must learn to stop using public relations when dealing with the human spirit. We must stop trying to help people by trying to make them the same as we are, *whatever* that may be and no matter how ideally we are served by our unique identities. *We must learn to praise dissimilarities just as we learned in the Renaissance to praise originality. We must learn to use our minds to discover meaning rather than truth, and we must come to recognize that a variety of meanings and interpretations is what ultimately makes life truthful.*[37]

Probing the core of human relationships adds meaning to life because it cuts to the quick of human reality. We are most alive when we are at risk. Soldiers returning from the battlefield find that, despite the horror of war, they miss the excitement, the accentuated feeling of being alive in the face of imminent death. The good news is, this sense of aliveness can also be found in learning, in trying to understand others—not learning based on taking in vast quantities of information, but learning which transforms information into the kind of knowledge that gives our lives purpose.

Chapter Seven

Economics Versus Quality of Life

Where justice is denied, where poverty is enforced, where igno-rance prevails, and where any one class is made to feel that society is in an organized conspiracy to oppress, rob, and degrade them, neither persons nor property will be safe.[1]

—*Frederick Douglass*

America has changed more in the past 50 years than in the previous 200. What's more, the only thing we can say with much assurance is that the change during the next 50 years will be even greater. America is headed toward a great economic reckoning. Social demographics and speed-of-light technology are moving us into an economic era for which we find ourselves totally un-prepared: a period of intense global competition for well-paying jobs; a time in which the financial interests of the young increas-ingly conflict with those of the old; an era when a massive flow of immigrants across borders and symbolic images over electronic airways portends drastic change. These conditions presage great social upheaval, since our economy is built upon the prom-ise of long-term employment, homes with 30-year mortgages, and the delirious assumption that jobs are more important than our *work* as human beings.

We live in truly paradoxical times. America has grown too large for big government, but is too small for meager commu-nity. Mario Cuomo simplifies it, "Without community, we can bid good-bye to the 'tradition' of American prosperity."[2] We need to turn the tide quickly to avoid a social meltdown. Francis Fu-kuyama tells us that in the past, "American democracy and the

187

American economy were successful not because of individualism or communitarianism alone but because of the interaction of these two opposing tendencies."[3] In his book *Trust: The Social Virtues and the Creation of Prosperity*, he writes:

> From the moment of its founding up through its rise at the time of World War I as the world's premier industrial power, the United States was anything but an individualistic society. It was, in fact, a society with a high propensity for spontaneous sociability, which enjoyed a widespread degree of generalized social trust and could therefore create large economic organizations in which nonkin could cooperate easily for common economic ends.[4]

The betterment of society, however, often runs counter to our need for economic security. Solving social problems is difficult if there are economic penalties for succeeding. "The quest for security debases the currency of whatever it seeks to ensure."[5] How low would the crime rate have to become before the police began enforcing archaic laws in order to rationalize the need for their existence in large numbers? How successful would fire departments have to become in preventing fires before a subconscious message suggested it was time to back off? This may sound like a fallacious argument, because we are obviously not near a point of solving crime or of adequately preventing fires, but there are thousands of such instances where we institute relationships that depend on limited success.

The establishment of a professional class of social workers is a subtle psychological guarantee that the social problems they're trained to address will never be solved, even though participants are sincere about their efforts. Status quo becomes a monolithic barrier to genuine improvement for individuals seeking career fulfillment, as much as it is a natural impediment to solving societal problems. Thus, the potency of our own economic self-interest blinds us to our environmental tax bill, which is long overdue and on the verge of exacting both penalties and interest.

Our recent economic history suggests that conservatives and libertarians are right: we don't need a monolithic armada of social service institutions with rigid levels of bureaucracy to sustain a high quality of life. But liberals are also right to argue for an economy which recognizes a need for something more than the popular meme of Adam Smith's invisible hand, and for a government which is equal to the task of dealing with big business. In 1995 Robert Lucas won the Nobel Prize for economics science for his theory of "Rational Expectations." The gist of rational expectations theory is that people are very adept at adjusting their behavior to benefit from economic policy—so good, in fact, that they outguess and outmaneuver attempts at fine-tuning the economy. But, if people can do this in a king-of-the-mountain economy, imagine what the results would be if rational expectations could be harnessed to move the individual-as-central sensibility to a communitarian effort. Then, the infantile cry that others are getting something for nothing would give way to a genuine concern that *everyone* should have enough. Consider the results of unleashing rational expectations on an assumption that meeting human needs is more important than wants, that the work humans do is far more important than their jobs.

Economics in Context

The inability to solve the problem of growing disparity of wealth in America is exacerbated by the very way we approach the issue. Instead of continually asking what our forefathers intended when they produced the documents that gave our nation status, we need to change the focus, engage in objective inquiry, and ask how we intend to redress today's problems. Arguments over the nature of equality and privilege in keeping with one's contribution will always be with us, just as the debate about the founding fathers' intentions about equality will never be settled. (What the founding fathers intended no longer matters. What *we* intend does.) The responsible thing to do is to reframe the original questions: What do we really mean by liberty? How do we define equality in a society where the greatest measurement of growth is the expanding distance between the poor and the rich? Are people really free if they're engaged in seemingly meaningless tasks and bound to the whims of a fickle economy?

A democratic government is a reciprocal bargain by design, a give-get scenario. We give up some freedom in order to receive the protection of government. From "we the people" we acknowledge a social obligation, a reason to pool our power and resources so that we may pursue public and private interests. This implied contract is not based on money, but on the crucial assumption that people are ends and not means. We trust that when our people are threatened we will "circle the wagons." But when power is held by special interests, the wagons circle only when those interests are threatened. If this social arrangement were likened to a balance between fire for heat and fire departments for protection, the bottom fifth of society would either freeze or be burned to a crisp. Nowhere is the need for balance in a democracy more obvious than when the honor of one group requires the death of another. Yes, it's easy to get caught up in patriotic ideals where one's abstract notion of honor is paid for with the life of another. But many of these abstractions do not stand the test of time. A case in point: Henry Kissinger's argument for a slow, "honorable" withdrawal in Vietnam. Kissinger's honor, someone else's sacrifice. How noble does the slow withdrawal seem today?[6]

The founding fathers were profoundly wise, but they did not, and could not, envision the complexity of the technological society we live in today. Thomas Jefferson was aware of his ignorance about the future. He asserted that the earth belongs not to the dead, but to the living, and that conventional laws should dissolve with each generation, placing squarely on the shoulders of each new generation the responsibility to think. Jefferson knew that if each fresh generation did not resolve the issue of the social compact (the reason for coming together to form a government in the first place) then citizens would forget and devalue the intellectual effort required of them to uphold such a contract. In 1776 his friend Thomas Paine had argued that "what we obtain too cheap, we esteem too lightly."

Jefferson knew the concept of freedom must be counterbalanced by intellectual responsibility. The actual cost of the freedom to do as one pleases must be recognized through the ability to see the actual cost of what is done. If you camp in a campground and stay long enough, you will run out of firewood. Moreover, the direct result of your effects on the environment are indisputable since there are no methods of flushing them out of awareness. On the other hand, if you use thousands of resources from all over the world, the only way to tell you are running out of them is to *care* enough to ascertain the results of your usage.

For decades it was believed that ending slavery would bring economic ruin to America. The actual cost of such human degradation seems unimaginable, but that was the dominant perceptual reality of the times. In his own era, Thomas Jefferson didn't put himself through the intellectual struggle necessary to acknowledge the injustice of slavery. Now, we can plainly see that slavery undermined the very existence of freedom.

Likewise today, the growth of poverty dishonors and threatens to undermine our economic system. The cost in human degradation is again unimaginable, but most of those who are not degraded by the poverty fail to see it, just as our forebears failed to see the injustice of slavery. Today, the growing disparity of wealth is as much a signal of impending crisis as the dead canary in the mine shaft. If we are to avert disaster, we have no alternative but to rethink some of our fundamental assumptions about economics.

Ideology

I am not a socialist—an accusation that often attaches to critics of capitalism. Having said that, I would add, in the spirit of reconciliation between reason and emotion, that a hybrid of the best of socialism with the best of capitalism is an obvious solution to many of our most pressing problems—the best of socialism being nothing more than the simple, yet noble, idea that everyone should have enough of what all people need most. To do any less is to entice a community's core motivation to oscillate between contempt and resentment. Caring, as we shall see, is a key ingredient for establishing and maintaining lasting community.

In a book whose title, *Post-Capitalist Society*, seems to suggest some movement in this direction, Peter Drucker observes, "The same forces which destroyed Marxism as an ideology and Communism as a social system are...also making Capitalism obsolescent."[7] As long as we live in a king-of-the-mountain society, we will never be able to achieve the equity intended in the original establishment of our form of government. Still, one of the greatest flaws of socialism is that it is based on egalitarianism. The ideal form of socialism, according to Mortimer Adler, is "nonegalitarian socialism." In *Haves Without Have-Nots*, Adler writes:

> To try to eliminate such inequality between the have-mores and the have-lesses would be an act of injustice. Hence in a justly constituted society, one class distinction must remain. It would not be a perfectly classless society, for while all would be haves, some would have more than others.[98]

Adler's message is simple: those who work harder should have more, but everyone should have *enough*. Modern day politics turn any effort aimed toward equity into a "conspiracy to soak the rich." We needn't eliminate the rich, but, while the bottom fifth of society is drowning, the rich could at least stand to get wet. The greatest disadvantage of capitalism is that power increasingly is the province of fewer people—not by virtue of harder work, but by the sheer formidability of capital itself. The steep incline that props power up keeps others from climbing. Communism ended with a whimper, and global capitalism in its current form will also end. But, if the masses of people on this planet cannot relate to other human beings as human beings with an acknowledgment of the equity required for their very existence, the result will be written in blood.

Franklin D. Roosevelt coined the term "economic royalists" to call attention to this great disparity. Not that Roosevelt disapproved of rich people, but he thought a small group of idle individuals living lavishly off the "interest" of their fortunes, while a large group of hard-working people failed to have their basic needs met, was antithetical to democracy. To Roosevelt the contract, compact, or association that prompts us to change the characterization of ourselves from "us" to "we" is the same power that enables the wagons to circle in case of an emergency. If only the rich can do this, the original need that brought us together to form a "we" remains unmet: poor people become means while the rich are treated as ends. Roosevelt's New Deal was in large measure an attempt to set right what he thought the old deal (the United States Constitution) did not address: economic rights. He knew that the political power inbred in big business undermines democracy in an overtly oppressive sense.

I am not advocating a mushy form of altruism here, but a means to strengthen the rational self-interest of the many against the protected advantage of the few. Capitalism needs safeguards to ensure that the minimum levels of equity originally sought for forming a government are not lost. I believe strongly in the virtue of hard work, but how does one person *earn* a billion dollars? One can certainly *acquire* that much, but it takes a lot of people to earn that amount of money. How much virtue do we find in the billions "earned" through insider trading on Wall Street in the 1980s? It is a dishonor to the ideal of capitalism to equate a telephone call to a broker, based on inside information and resulting in millions of dollars of "earnings," with years of hard work by men and women who barely scrape together a living wage. The early Victorians categorized wealth into two classes: one from honest labor and the other from shrewd speculation. The former was honorable, and the latter was evidence of a character flaw.[9] Indeed, Andrew Carnegie, the great nineteenth-century captain of the steel industry, said, "The man who dies rich, dies disgraced."[10]

For perspective, consider that all the money spent for welfare entitlements in America since inception of the concept does not equal the debt incurred by the great savings and loan robbery of the 1980s.[11] The scandal was an embezzlement of colossal measure, pulled off and magic markered away by the producers of economic reality. Whenever Adam Smith's invisible hand is backed by enough wealth, it is as capable of becoming a pickpocket as it is of tendering unintended benefits. Indeed, is there any product with characteristics so harmful that legions of sales people would not sell it to an unsuspecting public, if there were money to be made and no safeguards to prevent it?

To balance the monopolistic advantage of great wealth requires not the redistribution of wealth, but the continual redistribution of opportunity. Though all governments redistribute wealth in some form or fashion, it's when money is redistributed to poor people that protests reach screaming decibels. But, unless the Constitution is for sale, the power of money from any source must be checked by a power equal to the task. As long as our economic interests dominate our sense of reality so that each of us views the world only through the eyes of our *own* occupations, there is little chance of achieving what might be considered real social advancement. Again, in *Haves Without Have-Nots*, Mortimer Adler continues:

> The principle we have learned is that the tyranny, or injustice, that is the almost inevitable result of factional conflict cannot be remedied by shifts in power from one faction to the other, but only by eliminating conflicting factions from society, as they are eliminated in two important respects by the establishment of political and economic equality for all.[12]

Perhaps we have made the mistake that Emerson warned us about: We have let history loom so large as to smother our imaginations. It may be time, as Hazel Henderson suggests, to give Karl Marx and Adam Smith a "decent burial."[13]

One of our problems, though, may spring from never having taken a close look at Smith in the first place. In *The Age of Paradox*, Charles Handy points out that Adam Smith was first and foremost a professor of "moral philosophy" not economics. Smith's foundational premise for a stable society was that it be based on sympathy. But sympathy meant something different in 1759 than it does today. Charles Taylor captures the essence of the earlier definition with this characterization: "The substitute for grace is the inner impulse of nature."[14] Sympathy was a plain, unspoken assumption of universal concern, an *active* empathetic concern widespread enough and sincere enough that most everyone understood at a visceral level that community, which is an extension of family, depended upon caring for one's fellow citizens.

In Smith's day even the word patriotism combined the love of country with love of one's countrymen. In other words, sympathy was in part a product of principle; it was practical evidence of the moral law within. Smith further advocated that we should hold ourselves to an awareness of such principles by imagining we have the counsel of an impartial spectator.[15] To Smith this meant using your imagination to judge your own actions with the same criteria you use for judging the actions of others. Combine Smith's impartial spectator with Kant's moral compass, and the notion of human relatedness changes dramatically. It was Smith's clear intent that society should be habituated to stretching the beneficent feelings people have for their families to the community at large.

All of my adult life, I have been aware of Adam Smith's popular notion of the invisible hand: that each of us, in an effort to see to our own interests, cannot help but positively affect the interests of others. But there are few, if any, references to the fact that Adam Smith also believed that at the center of any community is a *visible heart*. Today, Smith is celebrated as the most famous architect of the meme of laissez-faire capitalism (a term he never used) by millions of people who haven't a clue as to what this philosophy was really about. Adam Smith had a deep, abiding concern for the common good. He believed that compassion is a sympathetic consciousness of the suffering and distress of others and that there is a prevailing human desire for communal goodness which can be called on to alleviate it. "For Smith the motor of history is the inner struggle between self-interest and impartial sympathy and reason."[16]

Adam Smith saw "good" as a noun. He wanted to appeal to the better nature of human beings in such a manner as to reinforce an empathetic concern for others and to pass the attributes of community on through benevolent institutions. History professor Jerry Z. Muller writes about Adam Smith's intentions:

> This is the thread that runs through all his works: how the market can be structured to make the pursuit of self-interest benefit consumers; how the passion for the approval of

others can make us act more selflessly; how public institutions can be structured to ensure that they deliver the services they are mandated to provide; how our desires for sex and for progeny can be structured by the law to create family institutions that foster self-control; how institutions concerned with defense and taxation can be structured to avoid unnecessary wars, while averting military defeat which had so often destroyed civilized societies in the past.[17]

The meme of self-interest has proved itself to be one of the most virulent ideas ever to mutate into the province of social convention. It rendered Christianity's meme of brotherly love impotent so long ago that (in spite of all of the lip service) few take the idea of brotherly love seriously. Because of the Cold War crusade against Communism, altruism and all reminders that there might indeed be anything like beneficent tendencies in human nature were stomped out of America like sparks in a dry forest. From psychologist and economist, to salesperson and consumer—all became suspicious of a sincere offer to help anyone do anything at any time, without strings. The last thing anyone wants to be accused of being is a "do gooder."

Self-interest as an explain-all, be-all meme, often referred to as psychological egoism, is considered by most philosophers to be a simple-minded fallacy, yet our king-of-the-mountain society worships at the temple of self-interest as if it were the supreme good of life. We hear ad nauseam in sports that "winning is not everything, it's the only thing." Alfie Kohn writes, "We act selfish because we believe we are, and we believe we are because we see ourselves acting that way."[18] Whether altruism is an inherent human trait or a perversion is a philosophical debate which may never be solved, but one can make a fair argument that *good will* toward others is, in fact, an effective way of enhancing the probability of passing one's genes on to future generations.

Self-reliance in the twenty-first century calls for a re-alliance of community in the sense that Adam Smith had in mind all along. We can make progress as a community of human beings only if we learn the value differences between *jobs* and *work*. "American values" and feelings about work so muddy our perception that we have little opportunity to discover anything approaching objectivity.

For generations "factions" (or conflicting occupations) have fought over livelihood without regard to community or anyone or anything except their own interests. Jobs produce positive and negative value. Working hard at jobs produces both faster. But much of what is done in the name of hard work is really only a job, and would be better left undone. So, how do we apply an equation about negative value to the moral virtue we attribute to jobs and to work? Does anything matter more than working hard? Jobs provide money, but money is an abstract idea, a cultural meme so imbued with politics that many say the two are interchangeable. The virtue of work is important, but is it more important than the reasons we do it? Do we work to live, or do we live to work? Is work more important than the reasons we come together to form a government? Is money more valuable than people? Surely, we behave as if it is.

Our culture encourages a myriad of irrational ideas about the value of jobs versus work. If a woman works for a family as a live-in governess and, in effect, raises that family's children in exchange for pay, she is seen as a valuable worker, a contributor to society. Likewise, if she is married. But if she is poor and single (regardless of the reason) and stays home and accepts assistance to raise her own children, she is thought to be cheating society.[19] In an interview on National Public Radio, British business writer Charles Handy put our predicament in perspective in describing the way capitalism is practiced in the United Kingdom and America. He said:

> We may have mistaken a requirement for a purpose. The requirement is to make a profit, but to turn a requirement into a purpose is not right. We have to eat to live, but if you live to eat you become a distorted human being in more than one sense. We have to make a profit to survive, but that's not enough. The major task of leadership in both countries is to say what's the purpose beyond the requirement.

Millions of us frantically pursue money at a cost greater than it is worth. This daily grind is confusing enough by itself, but it becomes alien and pathological when we begin attributing worth to other people. To value only those people who are pathologically "busy" is foolish. There must be enough time in the lives of average citizens to think about and participate in the process of democracy. Making democracy work *is* work. "The first rule of totalitarianism is silence, and the isolation it implies," says Earl Shorris.[20] Action without reflection is a recipe for totalitarianism. Autonomy is the seedbed of democracy. Shorris continues:

> Morality depends upon the ability of men to initiate the actions for which they are responsible. Without that basic justice, moral systems are farcical. A world of responsibility without autonomy can only lead to nihilistic despair: everything is permitted them and nothing is permitted me, nothing I do makes any difference, I may do anything.[21]

Moreover, if the only recourse differing cultures have for resolving conflict depends upon what they have been taught by previous generations, if they cannot rise to their own cultural mountain tops and breathe the air of all cultures, if they cannot reason for themselves, then war will seem to be their only available avenue of resolution. It is indeed ironic that as well-paying jobs leave the United States and raise the standard of living of the citizens of Third World countries (jobs that only a "qualified middle class" were allowed to perform, and which are now being done well by people who are barely literate), the champions of capitalism who have preached its virtues the loudest are now crying foul.

All cultures do not respond in the exact same way in discerning and attributing value. Some judge wealth not by how much one can hoard, but by who can give the most goods away. In judging value in America most of us are so attuned to the ethos of capitalism that we confuse it with human nature. Most of us readily assume that capitalism is self-justifying and exists solely by intuitive consensus. But such is not the case. In his book *The Land of Desire*, William Leach writes,

> ...the culture of consumer capitalism may have been among the most nonconsensual public cultures ever created, and it was nonconsensual for two reasons. First, it was not produced by "the people" but by commercial groups in

cooperation with other elites comfortable with and committed to making profits and to accumulating capital on an ever-ascending scale. Second it was nonconsensual because, in its mere day-to-day conduct (but not in any conspiratorial way), it raised to the fore only one vision of the good life and pushed out all others. In this way, it diminished American public life, denying the American people access to insight into other ways of organizing and conceiving life, insight that might have endowed their consent to the dominant culture (if such consent were to be given at all) with real democracy.[22]

At the heart of liberal democratic philosophy is an unarticulated belief that the contract that gives rise to government acts in a similar way to the franchise for a commercial business. For example, if you buy a franchise to sell hardware you expect that the parent company will provide all kinds of support to help you help yourself succeed. Liberal Democrats believe that the blood, sweat, and tears of past and present generations make each and every citizen a franchisee, for without such support there would be no government. Moreover, if there are no advantages to having a government, there is no reason to band together and form one. Although poorly articulated, at a very deep level this philosophy acknowledges that citizens represent intellectual patterns, that they share more with ends than means, and that economics at best is a clumsy social convention originally intended as a means and not an end in itself. The African-American family farming 40 acres in the Deep South and who lost a son to the Vietnam war are citizens as surely as the nurse in the veterans hospital, or the Wall Street banker who invests in military industrial stocks.

Conservative Republicans believe that hard work and personal responsibility are of paramount importance and that effort is a virtue. So do I. Libertarians believe that security comes at the price of freedom, and I concur. Liberals have left a clear record of carelessness with other people's money. While conservatives have a like history of self-deception and amnesia with regard to programs which *subtly* subsidize their own efforts (farm supports, corporate and educational subsidies are examples), they're indignant about *obvious* efforts to help others with less advantage. Libertarians are champions of freedom and responsibility, but are demonstrably naïve about the results of total deregulation. Libertarian Thomas S. Szasz writes, "There is only one political sin: independence; and only one political virtue: obedience. To put it differently, there is only one offense against authority: self-control; and only one obedience to it: submission to control by authority."[23]

Now, clearly, this is a gross exaggeration, if only on the premise of the number of political sins and virtues. But Libertarians have a point. No doubt about it, people feel less personally responsible when it is up to someone else to decide *anything*.

It is not accidental that family values began to hemorrhage when parents increasingly began to leave education of their children to the school system. So, it should not surprise us that the Victorian ethos of virtue and responsibility occurred during an era with very little regulation. If a massive bureaucracy stands between a franchisee and the franchisor, then the loss of autonomy afforded the franchisee cannot help but destroy the initiative for what is clearly needed. One doesn't need to decide upon rules for behavior if they are already written for every conceivable situation. And, if one looks to rules for resolution, the rules cannot help but become more important than the original intended behavior.

Capitalism by nature is investment driven. Large amounts of capital must be allowed to accumulate before investment is made. Investment is driven by the opportunity for profit, but, before profit can be achieved, the wages for labor must be held down. In business, then, the king-of-the-mountain scenario is a hierarchy based on economic necessity. The ledges on the mountain delineate degrees of money, power, and prestige, and these elements tend to have a way of attracting one another. The important thing to realize is that, even though there may be a compelling ideology of equality and an impetus for social improvement in our rhetoric, there is little basis in economic reality to expect equality to happen spontaneously without political effort.

The distribution of wealth in a capitalistic society is inexorably tied to the equality of opportunity. Conservatives play king of the mountain with a focus on fair play. Liberals insist on fair shares first, before fair play can begin. I prefer to simplify it to a question of equity versus efficiency, with a prejudice for the former. The game can't last if America is sharply divided into distinct classes with a shrinking group of "haves" and a rapidly growing number of "have nots." But the concept of community is of far greater importance than a *game*. Community is to society as soil is to agriculture, which means there is no more reason to expect a dynamic society without a strong community than to expect a great harvest from planting crops in impoverished earth.

Conservatism is the politics of advantage with a philosophy based on "shoulds." Liberalism is the politics of indecisiveness, with a philosophy based on "could be." Capitalism has improved more lives than any political system in history, but it remains fundamentally flawed because of its tendencies toward frequent, and extensive destruction. Indeed, capitalism is by design a short-term illusion with long-term devastation built in. If you don't believe it, do the math: work out the current rates of interest over the next few centuries with today's investments, and observe how the exponential growth reaches insane proportions.

Liberals ask the right questions with regard to the well-being of all citizens, but do not follow through with fiscal responsibility through accountability. Conservatives are as fiscally close-fisted with their money as they are with their narrow views about who is worthy enough to receive assistance (recipients somehow end up being identified as people who are very much like themselves). But a sound government in a democracy requires that its participants understand the problems faced by their group as a whole. Mihaly Csikszentmihalyi makes this point in *The Evolving Self*, saying, "The larger the group with which one identifies, the closer to ultimate reality one gets. Only the person who sees the entire planet as her world can recognize a toxic substance as poison no matter where it is dumped."[24] Similarly, the core of any social contract worthy of the respect and allegiance of its participants must have some benefit which can be experienced as equity.

Self-Interest and Free Markets

The driving force of our king-of-the-mountain economic ethos stems directly from self-interest in the sense Adam Smith originally intended. But blatant self-interest, without regard to the consequences of one's actions, is much more than just being irresponsible; it represents a virulent malfeasance. Self-interest taken to extreme leaves no room for community or any larger purpose than one's self, let alone common cause. If there is nothing but self-interest, then fighting for one's country in wartime is foolish—it is each person's self-interest to let others do the fighting. If self-interest is the overriding value, then productive people, by definition, are too busy and too successful to serve on juries. The very idea of economic self-interest (the individual-as-central sensibility) has become reified to such degree that most people assume virtue is the core property of self-interest.

In *The Virtue of Selfishness,* social critic Ayn Rand wrote, "Altruism declares that any action taken for the benefit of others is good, and any action taken for one's own benefit is evil. Thus the *beneficiary* of an action is the only criterion of moral value—and so long as that beneficiary is anybody other than oneself, anything goes."[25] Balderdash! If self-interest had not long ago reached a state in the consciousness and subconsciousness of the majority of Americans higher than that ever held by religion, people who made such statements would more readily stand out as kooks. Having a concern for others does not mean anything goes. Concern for others comes built in with our genetic makeup. So is our tendency for selfishness and self-deception. But the incremental and sporadic improvements necessary to create a community requires that these predispositions are harnessed in a manner which enhances community. Total self-absorption is the criterion for anything goes. Consider this:

> The wise and virtuous man is at all times willing that his own private interest should be sacrificed to the public interest of his own particular order or society. He is at all times willing, too, that the interest of this order or society should be sacrificed to a greater interest of the state or sovereignty, of which it is only a subordinate part. He should, therefore, be equally willing that all those inferior interests should be

sacrificed to the greater interest of the universe, to the interest of that great society of all sensible and intelligent beings, of which God himself is the immediate administrator and director.[26]

Karl Marx? No, this is Adam Smith in *The Theory of Moral Sentiments*, the book he considered to be his most important contribution.

In his more famous volume, *The Wealth of Nations*, Adam Smith writes, "It is not from the benevolence of the butcher, the brewer, or the baker, that we expect our dinner, but from their regard to their own interest."[27] In *Adam Smith's Mistake: How A Moral Philosopher Invented Economics and Ended Morality*, Kenneth Lux writes:

> Smith, by an intellectual sleight of hand, but no doubt unwittingly, collapsed two very different principles into one. If we say,"I get my dinner through my own self-interest," there is nothing wrong with this statement per se, as long as we understand self-interest as the natural pursuit of one's livelihood. *But*, Smith says something quite different in his butcher-baker statement. There he says, "I get my dinner out of *your* self-interest." Economists following Smith, have taken these two different kinds of statements as equivalent. My self is nothing different than your self. My self-interest is identical to your self-interest. But this is nonsense.[28]

The subtitle of Lux's book does not mean that he has little respect for Smith. On the contrary, "Adam Smith may have made a mistake, but he was not all wrong."[29] Lux writes, "What Adam Smith ought to have said was, It is not *only* from the benevolence of the butcher, the brewer, or the baker, that we expect our dinner, but from their regard to their own interest." Adding the word *only* makes a world of difference.[30]

In *The Theory of Moral Sentiments*, Smith said:

> Though the ruin of our neighbor may affect us much less than a very small misfortune of our own, we must not ruin him to prevent that small misfortune, nor even to prevent our own ruin. We must, here, as in all other cases, view ourselves not so much according to that light in which we may naturally appear to ourselves, as according to that in which

we naturally appear to others. Though every man may, according to the proverb, be the whole world to himself, to the rest of mankind he is a most insignificant part of it.[31]

It is not Adam Smith's mistake but our own if we conclude that free markets are solely the virtuous result of self-interest. Moreover, there is a huge gap between what we imagine our self-interest to be and what it actually is. If the marketplace drives all major decisions, then those at the corporate helm rule, and democracy becomes just another term for employee relations. In *The Work of Nations*, Robert B. Reich observes:

> The idea of a "free market" apart from the laws and political decisions that create it is pure fantasy anyway. The market was not created by God on any of the first six days (at least not directly), nor is it maintained by divine will. It is a human artifact, the shifting sum of a set of judgments about individual rights and responsibilities. What is mine? What is yours? What is ours? And how do we define and deal with actions that threaten these borders—theft, force, fraud, extortion, or carelessness? What should we trade, and what should we not? (Drugs? Sex? Votes? Babies?) How should we enforce these decisions, and what penalties should apply to transgressions? As a nation formulates and accumulates answers to these questions, it creates its version of the market.[32]

Assuming personal responsibility for making these kinds of decisions is what American citizenship is about. Leaving them to the social convention of our ancestors amounts to more than just an abdication of responsibility—it is a clear acknowledgment that we favor social patterns over ideas, which will keep us from moving beyond the American Dream. I'm not suggesting we adopt a more communitarian society simply because Adam Smith said we should. I'm just pointing out that many of the people who invoke his name to conjure the meme of laissez-faire self-interest don't know what they are talking about. Adam Smith did advocate limited government, but he assumed that individual character was something very different from postmodern individuality. He would have found the individual-as-central notion incomprehensible. To assume people in America and throughout the world can simply live their lives *unfettered* by anything other than free enterprise is ridiculous, and the notion that economic virtue is inherent in capitalism is a meme advertised and paid for by the people who benefit most because of it.

The salient message in the study of our economic system is "efficiency," supported by the notion that a free market is a rational market. We hold these assumptions to be true at such a visceral level, it never occurs to us to question them. *Free* in an economic sense means without cost, any cost. We know beyond a doubt that many of our business practices exact an environmental tax that totally destroys the notion of no cost. I grew up thinking the American agricultural system was the most efficient method of farming in the world, but in-depth analysis suggests differently. It takes 10 calories of energy to produce one calorie of corn, and 100 calories of energy to produce one calorie of beef, while cattle feed upon grain.[34] A sixth grader can deduce that this equation means we are losing more than we gain. If this were not bad enough, these agricultural practices lead to an annual loss of billions of tons of topsoil, threatening the very form of agriculture.

This gross inefficiency is a direct result of the idea that a free market is a rational market. The current state of the global environment (smog alerts, depleted ozone, poisoned ground water, shrinking water tables, loss of topsoil, acid lakes, nondisposable hazardous waste, fishless flammable rivers, the accumulation of pesticides in the food chain, and toxic garbage piling up faster than we can dispose of it) leaves little doubt as to the irrationality of unchecked "free" markets. The sands of the Middle East were once the agricultural breadbasket of the world. The mighty Mississippi river has become a mighty sewer, referred to occasionally as America's colon. All over America (and the world) songbirds and amphibious creature populations are declining at alarming rates. The earth's ocean fisheries are being decimated and the rainforests of the southern hemisphere are disappearing at a catastrophic *free market* pace.

Saying uncategorically that a free market is a rational market is like saying that appetite is driven by its responsibility to feast. The American system of agriculture has long been held up as the global model of efficiency. We propose to teach our methods around the world so that others will be able to prosper as we have. But if this were actually to occur, many of the world's raw resources such as petroleum would last less than a decade.

Models for the New Millennium

The basic tenets of capitalism make the best foundation for a free society, *as long as that society understands the mechanics of personal responsibility with respect to society and the environment*. In America we come up short on both counts. A large part of the contempt directed toward welfare recipients comes from people who may be considered fortunate according to economic standards, but their scorn and lack of compassion stems from the fact that they simultaneously hate their jobs and are afraid of losing them. People who care about what they are doing feel sympathy for those who are not able to find right livelihood. In primitive societies, every activity members engaged in had an obvious, meaningful purpose. Except among those who deemed slavery necessary, the issue of laziness did not appear until, in the name of specialization, people began to engage in mindless activities, many of which should have been left undone. People did not become lazy until "jobs" became more important than work. It is sad but true that a great deal of the worth we attribute to "adults" has to do with their willingness to do what their hearts tell them not to.

Many people live their whole lives insulated from the good and bad fortune befalling others, but they become irate at the thought that others might prosper with less effort than themselves—especially since the greatest social danger comes from inequality. In other words, as long as everyone prospers, social stability is attainable, regardless of the cause. Only when large numbers of people are left out, is there something to fight about.

In his book *The End of Equality*, Mickey Kaus suggests a new Civic Liberalism alternative to our current inequality. Kaus writes, "Instead of trying to suppress inequality of money, this strategy would try to *restrict the sphere of life in which money matters*, and enlarge the sphere in which money *doesn't* matter."[34] He suggests the "great unfinished business of Liberalism is not to equalize money, but to put money in its place."[35] Kaus reminds us that, "cultures don't fall from the sky. They come from institutions."[36] Thus we should try to "democratize life instead of the tax tables."[37] Kaus suggests that the obvious place to begin this effort is in the public sphere through a draft, a national service, the ballot, health care, day care, education, and a new WPA work program. By seeing that all people are treated as equals within these institutions, we move a long way toward living up to the social contract that initially brought us together.

There is another concept offered by Edgar Cahn and Jonathan Rowe in their book *Time Dollars*. They suggest "people time" is more important than money, and that, in fact, two economies exist: a market economy and a household economy. The latter economy is often hidden by the first but is just as important. Cahn and Rowe contend that people need a form of currency that enables them to respond to values which are more important than money. Time dollars allow participants to earn credits by helping others in need. A central time bank keeps track of credits and coordinates services. Services depend entirely upon community needs. They can range from babysitting to adult day care, from gardening to English literacy classes. All time is valued equally. "It is liberating to the retired housewife to know that her time is as valued as that of the retired executive."[38]

In her book *Interest and Inflation Free Money*, professor of ecological building techniques Margrit Kennedy writes,

> The communist attempt to create freedom from exploitation failed because, in order to secure a minimum existence for everybody, communism eliminated personal freedom. The capitalist tendency, on the other hand, by letting land and capital be exploited in an unrestricted practice of personal freedom has endangered the minimum existence of the majority of people. Both systems have gone too far in their respective directions. One has set the priority of freedom from hunger above freedom to choose one's own life style. The other has set the top priority on personal freedom which, in the present monetary system, can only be achieved by very few people. Both are partially right, but both have failed to create the preconditions for a genuinely human existence including genuine freedom.[39]

Professor Kennedy proposes to transcend capitalism and socialism, following the advice of Silvo Gessel, a merchant of Germany and Argentina, who, in 1890, argued that you could move far more goods by reversing the practice of interest payment on capital principal. Gessel suggested that, instead of paying interest to those who held onto money, citizens should instead pay a circulation fee for hanging onto it thus changing private gain to public profit. Kennedy claims, "It would go farther in providing social justice than any aid program."[40] Kennedy writes that in the early 1930s, Worgl, a small town in Austria, experimented with Gessel's idea. They printed money on which a one percent per month fee was attached. The person who held the note at the end of the month paid the fee through the purchase of a stamp which was then placed on the back of the note. Without the stamp the money was worthless. The results: people paid their taxes early to avoid the fee, the experimental money circulated through their economy 463 times per year versus the 21 times for an ordinary shilling, and unemployment was reduced 25 percent, while the 12 percent fee went for public works.

In *The Age of Unreason*, a book which *Business Week* magazine (hardly a socialist publication) touted as one of the best business books of the year when it was published, English business writer Charles Handy described the economic dilemma for rich nations with poor citizens this way:

> A free and rich society in comparative terms, ought to be able to guarantee its people enough money to pay for food, clothes, and heating, as well as free education and free health care which many societies already give them....Instead of paying cash to the needy few, we should pay it to everyone and then claw it back progressively from those that *don't* need it.
>
> Put more idealistically, the argument is that as citizens we are both entitled to an income from our collective property, our society, as well as obligated to pay a portion of our individual earnings for the maintenance of that society. *All* of us have the entitlement and the obligation.[41]

Further, in his book *The New Realities*, Peter Drucker (no anti-capitalist) discusses a current shift to a post-business society and quotes Old Testament prophets who preached that governments should be a shepherd unto their people.[42]

Indeed, the very idea of a post-business era embodies what could be the greatest social improvement in a millennium: the simple notion of raising the issue of human needs out of the socio-biological realm of *us versus them* to the intellectual realization that we're all in this world together and that meeting minimum humans needs—without the need for playing the blame game about who is deserving, and who is not—is an entirely *sane* thing to do.

In *Economic Insanity: How Growth-Driven Capitalism Is Devouring the American Dream*, Roger Terry argues that we confuse speed with growth, that "escalating productivity simply creates a convincing illusion of greater wealth, to say nothing of a more hectic lifestyle."[43] Terry advocates designing an economic system which reconsiders allowing the unlimited ownership of private capital in favor of a method which would permit ownership of only what a person or organization can utilize. He writes, "Instead of fixing the score by redistributing income, the fruit of capitalism, we should instead consider leveling the playing field by redistributing capital, the source of income and the only factor that inspires motivation and creates genuine opportunity."[44]

Bill Shore, founder of Share Our Strength and author of *Revolution of the Heart*, writes, "Poverty is so prevalent it has lost its drama."[45] He argues, we should realize the need for a new language and vocabulary for fighting poverty: a new type of association—a for-profit nonprofit organization. Shore calls this a Community Wealth Enterprise, which "creates wealth by providing a product or service of value, by selling something that people want to buy for reasons independent of their charitable intentions."[46]

Indeed, insanity is again appropriate terminology when one examines the current welfare bureaucracy. In *Tyranny of Kindness*, an excoriating indictment of the welfare system and also the best book I've ever read on the subject, Theresa Funiciello makes a compelling case for revolutionary reform. She shows how a veritable "poverty industry" has come into being which has a conflict of interest with poor people, and how, even though nonprofit organizations have noble intentions, they have a way siphoning funds intended for the poor to greater causes such as "larger budgets, career advancement and political power."[47] Funiciello writes, "Politicians who chatter incessantly about the growth in welfare spending *aren't* talking cash assistance through Aid to Families with Dependent Children (AFDC) unless they're serious dunces....AFDC is *less than one percent* of the federal budget and has fallen.[48] Funiciello shows how the whole notion of assistance to women and children is based on their past relationship with a man, that a widow of any age can receive social security benefits until she dies without anyone being obsessively concerned whether or not she has a job, and that it will often be an assumption that a woman is a better mother if she is at home taking care of her small children.[49]

Theresa Funiciello's solution to the welfare bureaucracy is simple: provide a guaranteed income—a solution which has also been offered by Milton Friedman and Richard Nixon. In a 1970 White House Conference on Children, Nixon said, "The welfare system has become a consuming, monstrous, inhuman outrage against the community, against the family, against the individual—and most of all against the very children whom it was supposed to help." Again, Funiciello writes,

> For some reason, as a nation we upset ourselves when we think about giving to our own poor people. Giving to older, even wealthier citizens in the form of social security, or to dairy farmers in price supports is no sweat. Do we stop giving to foreign nations or U.S. seniors or young widows with small children "for their own good"? Do we really even question it? Not on your life....Let's face it, one of the reasons the United States introduced the Marshall Plan to rebuild parts of Europe and its counterpart in Japan was to create markets for U.S. goods, services, and technology. For a long time it worked—for all the countries involved. In any event, a socially responsible culture does not cause economic disaster.[50]

Today inner cities all across America resemble the devastating bombed-out conditions which prompted the Marshall Plan—a plan whose purpose was, in many cases, to help those who had been our enemies in war. Yet we do little more to help our own citizens living in similar environments than to play a perpetual finger-pointing game with the enduring torture of a Kafkaesque bureaucratic hell.

Democratic solutions must address the fact that all humans have both needs and wants. What makes sense is to focus on co-operation at the needs level and competition at the wants level. Needs bring us together. Wants allow the celebration of our differences. Needs acknowledge our common relatedness. They provide the substructure for community—not as an idealized, pastoral figment of our imagination that politicians ask us to recall, but as a foundation for building a society with a future. The goal of fulfilling one's needs provides the impetus for seeking security through a pact or social contract by forming tribes, associations, communities, and nations.

Fortunately, we have compelling evidence that Adam Smith's inherently human sympathetic basis for community is still alive and is very much a part of our nature in spite of the current cry that "the only interest worthy of discussion is self-interest."[51] But, if left unabated, the social consequences of our current economic trajectory are going to turn the notion of the American Dream into an unmitigated social nightmare where community strongholds of the well-to-do are fenced off from the exponential growth of prisoners who are fenced in. And, in a few years, both of these types of enclaves will be surrounded by sprawling conditions of poverty. Cross-country travel may soon feel reminiscent of a Mad Max adventure.

We have listened to the economists for too long, acting as if the free market is virtuous by nature. The absurdity of perpetual economic growth needs to discarded.[52] Perpetual growth is bound to the meme of "productivity," which essentially means doing more with less. But isn't appropriateness more important than efficiency? Cicero said that all a person really needs is a garden and a library. Does it follow, then, that to improve one's life planting and harvesting must increase in efficiency until the labors of gardening are no longer enjoyable?

It is long past time to re-apply intellectual patterns to the notion of markets and community. As James Lincoln Collier puts it,

"A people who will not sacrifice for the common good cannot expect to have any common good."[53] To create a greater sense of community when it is so popular to criticize government requires radical measures—what James Adams called *conceptual blockbusting.*[54]

Mary Catherine Bateson writes, "We will not learn to live responsibly on this planet without basic changes in the ways we organize human relationships, particularly inside the family, for family life provides the metaphors with which we think about broader ethical relations."[55] So, to inspire some ethical blockbusting it takes but a small twist of imagination to combine the ideas of Mickey Kaus, Edgar Cahn, Jonathan Rowe, Margrit Kennedy, Charles Handy, Peter Drucker, Roger Terry, Bill Shore, and Theresa Funiciello and start an avalanche in our king-of-the-mountain society, with pretentiousness crumbling and intellectual patterns subsequently rising, to forge a community of equity and purpose.

The ideas of these thoughtful writers need to be hammered out democratically in alliance with the following premises: that everyone has a right to live; that the work humans do is more important than their jobs; and that the qualitative survival of humanity requires a massive dose of attention, acceptance of responsibility, and a fundamental rethinking of the notion of relatedness. The pages that follow contain some proposals for the radical actions necessary to move us beyond the traditional, economic American Dream. These suggestions are based upon a dramatic rethinking in seven principal areas. I offer them not as an economist, but as a self-educated philosopher. They may seem radical, but time and hindsight could make many of them seem obvious and inevitable:

What if we had direct-access government?

What if we abolished the government's bureaucratic institutional hierarchies which have lost sight of their original objectives? The massive welfare and education departments have become self-serving obstacles to education and welfare. Marvin Olasky wrote *The Tragedy of American Compassion* about the welfare dilemma, as if compassion had anything, whatsoever, to do with the bureaucratic mess we call welfare. Compassion is the DNA of a healthy community; a community, by definition, requires an active concern by the members of the community for its members. The American welfare system, however, is not a demonstration of compassion, even though many of its advocates are compassionate people.

Immanuel Kant recognized the intellectual difficulty required for compassion to amount to something more socially beneficent than pity. In 1788, he said, "This very feeling of compassion and tender sympathy, if it precedes the deliberation on the question of duty and becomes a determining principle, is even annoying to right thinking persons, brings their deliberate maxims into confusion, and makes them wish to be delivered from it and to be subject to law giving reason alone."[56] In our time, compassion means leaving such matters to the courts and to those willing enough to think their way through the maze. Understanding as an element of compassion has all but disappeared. As Mary Catherine Bateson writes, "Compassion is a more complex idea than equality, but the very word is distorted in Western usage into something like the faintly scornful pity felt by the strong for the weak."[57] No doubt about it, compassion can be unfamiliar, even unfriendly territory for timid explorers. Perhaps we should remind ourselves that the word *compass* is present in the term.

Christopher Lasch has observed, "The ideology of compassion, however agreeable to our ears, is one of the principle influences, in its own right, on the subversion of civic life, which depends not so much on compassion as on mutual respect....Compassion has become the human face for contempt."[58] This is true only if the term is too narrowly defined and fails to acknowledge that authentic compassion is a deep *feeling for* and *understanding of* the plight and misery of others. Responsibility is an essential component of genuine compassion, regardless of whether one is a politician or a welfare recipient. Compassion without an intellectual element of awareness is a destructive concept because, absent understanding, it moves abruptly from pity to contempt. William James hit the nail on the head when he said, "Real culture lives by sympathies and admirations, not by dislikes and disdains." [59] Admirations require understanding, and that level of comprehension is an outcome of accountable effort.

If we were truly compassionate *and* responsible we would cut out the multi-leveled bureaucracy by providing an informational infrastructure that allows citizens direct access to government services, regardless of whether that be access to information or direct economic assistance. Consider the possibility of splitting the difference between Margrit Kennedy's and Charles Handy's proposals. Instead of replacing all currency with fee-bearing notes or putting everyone on assistance, try using separate currencies for *needs* and for *wants*. We would immediately rid ourselves of the compulsion to stigmatize needy people for needing what *everyone* requires. It would still the constant blather from nonthinking haves about "no free lunch" for have nots, and indignation over the idea of others getting something for nothing. That there is no such thing as a free lunch does not have to obliterate a willingness to pay for lunch. A free lunch makes a lot more sense than war over who gets lunch, or an unwarranted long-term destruction of the environment to provide *temporary* jobs. Indeed, a free lunch which eases social entropy and environmental degradation is an investment—especially when you realize that Americans throw enough food away every year to sustain 50 million people.[60]

If the end run of American increases in technological productivity renders us incapable of meeting human needs unabashedly, without regard for making judgments of moral worth, then surely we are unworthy of calling ourselves a great nation. The challenge of moving beyond the American Dream is simple: Aspire to do the work of human beings in ways which suggest such work really matters, with as few jobs as possible.

Establishing needs- and wants-based currencies could be accomplished easily by using electronic credits for needs-based goods and the currency we already have for wants-based goods. In other words, our economic system would acknowledge three sector realities: a public sector of government, a private sector as the business domain, and a community service or nonprofit sector. Peter Drucker writes, "The nonprofits have the potential to become America's social sector—equal in importance to the public sector of government and the private sector of business." The delivery system is already in place."[61] But, if we heed

Theresa Funiciello's warning about the private agenda tendencies of all organizations, we might also conclude that, with a guaranteed income, the nonprofits could be better utilized filling the needs identified by a citizenry with enough equity to have their *own* opinions about value.

Government cannot provide meaningful work unless people really are the government. The very idea of a guaranteed income may sound absurd in an era often described as a rising tide of conservatism (at least in appearance), but guaranteed economic security is not just a left-over idea from the New Deal. In 1796, two decades after he had written *Common Sense*, and after tirelessly championing the doctrine of free markets with the power of his pen, Thomas Paine came to the conclusion that direct payments to citizens was the only way to compensate for the oppression systemic in capitalistic economics.[62] The subject of a guaranteed subsistence will return with a vengeance when future economic downturns reveal the extreme dependency of millions of middle-class workers left in the wake of the employment restructuring of the '90s. Erich Fromm put it this way:

> Guaranteed income would not only establish freedom as a reality rather than a slogan, it would also establish a principle deeply rooted in western religious and humanist traditions; man has a right to live, regardless! This right to live, to have food, shelter, medical care, education, etc., is an intrinsic human right that cannot be restricted by any condition, not even the one that he must be socially "useful."[63]

Creating a strong community is not predicated on something for nothing; if it were, too much valuable work would be left undone. I'm not advocating a welfare state but a full-employment state where the real work of human beings is a genuine priority. For years the strategy of the Federal Reserve System has depended upon a high unemployment rate in the name of staving off inflation. An energized and subsidized nonprofit sector might allow that any able-bodied adult could receive an income from the government (administered through an agency like the Social Security Administration) in the form of electronic (credit card) currency in exchange for community work in the nonprofit sector. Through a democratically determined number hours of community work per week, a person could receive a beneficent subsistence level income which could be augmented through additional hours in any work sector. A percentage of these funds could be automatically withdrawn each month as a community appropriation if they were not used by the recipient. This electronic currency could not be exchanged for hard currency, but hard currency could be used for any goods. The real difference would be that the funds would be paid directly to the person doing the work and not to the organization. Moreover, the Federal Reserve could bind the value of the currencies together and maintain them in such a way as to prevent commercial banks from borrowing money into existence.[64] In other words, the Federal Reserve would better control the money supply in both spheres, with the power to creatively stimulate either sector of the economy.

Now, I am fully sympathetic with the notion that extrinsic rewards diminish intrinsic motivation. But, even though critics might suggest that paying people to do community work will lessen their desire to do so, I think the opposite would occur: the possibility to do meaningful work—work that really makes a difference in people's lives—coupled with the ability to donate one's time, talents, and unneeded electronic subsistence currency would redefine and recreate community. Such efforts would be dramatic: the demand for community based work—*real work*—would take off like a rocket. What has long been neglected would become a major focus of attention. The sudden availability of a reasonable subsistence through work in areas such as childcare, eldercare, teaching, the maintenance of neighborhoods, and all issues deemed community service by local communities, plus a bonus of subsistence credit for lifelong learning, would have the simultaneous effect of creating exponential growth in community relatedness while dramatically increasing the leverage of those who chose to work in the business sector. Nothing is more empowering to workers than making workers relatively scarce. No need for unions if corporations have to woo employees.

Under this type of community-based arrangement, all monies for needs-based credits could be taxed automatically each month. Hard currency purchases could be subject to a value-added tax, and interest could accrue to the holder of hard currency with a tax on capital gains. There would be an obvious incentive benefit from earning needs credits through community service work in order to avoid using interest-bearing currency. The tax percentages required to structure a needs-based economic community could be determined through myriad incentives and adjustments to fuel the nonprofit sector, but the criteria for the percentage would be plain and simple: however much is required is what is required. Thus, a balanced budget is really a balanced society.

Sounds crazy? Not when you consider the alternative of doing nothing. Imagine how much would be saved by dismantling the current bureaucracies of the departments of agriculture, commerce, education, and welfare. In time, social security as we know it could be phased out (except for people who can neither work nor continue learning because of health problems). With the potential for continual growth and development in the spheres of community work and individual learning, there would be little need to reach a point in life where one would want to stop learning or to stop working altogether.

What if we decredentialed education and the professions?

In a society where occupational choice is the focus of education, critical analysis of business never occurs. The personal imperative is not, should I engage in this kind of business activity because it is good for society, or for the environment? The overriding issue is, how do I fit in and how much money will I make? College should be a place to learn about living, a place where one is able to discover values for living that will dictate the rules that business will have to follow. In other words, college should be a bastion of self-education, and everyone should be able to attend. Business school should be about business.

Millions of Americans have been so jaded by traditional education (as I was for many years) they fail to comprehend that learning and quality of life are interdependent. Traditional education has duped us into believing, or at least behaving as if we believed, that learning to earn a living is hard and that learning to live well is easy. But the evidence—divorce, child abuse, suicide, mental illness, midlife crisis, burn-out, and a multibillion-dollar stress industry—suggests the reverse: we are good at earning a living, but not good at living a living. How did we stray so far from the wisdom of the ancient philosophers who warned against underestimating the amount of contemplation required to live a good life? Squandering an education solely for credentials is analogous to eating for the sole purpose of gaining weight. Both efforts are likely to lead to malnourishment.

The velocity of technological change in the business marketplace and in community-based enterprises increasingly makes current knowledge obsolete. Indeed, where learning is concerned, we are witnessing the rise of the self-educated individual simultaneously with the unraveling of the expert. Self-taught computer gurus in organizations all over America have demonstrated this beyond question. What individuals can learn and demonstrate is becoming more important than how and where they learned it, or whom they know. For decades we have misused our institutions of higher learning by having a few people pay enormous tuitions for tickets to high-paying jobs. It would make a lot more sense to have millions of people enrolled out of a genuine concern for knowledge, and engaged in study for the greater part of their lives, while lower tuition fees reflected their large numbers.

Moving beyond the American Dream requires that we remove all barriers from learning. This means decredentialing educational bureaucracies and the professions. To inspire an authentic learning revolution *all learning* must be respected, acknowledged, and rewarded, regardless of how it is acquired. New hires in the workplace and promotions trace to actual performance instead of paper credentials. Such a shift in emphasis would greatly reduce the time required for, and therefore the cost of, formal education. Economic, ethnic, and gender barriers would thus be diminished. The costs of career preparation would be much less because training positions would become paying positions. In other words, one could *earn* one's way into a profession. In a system where everyone understands the problems and concerns at each level of training, a more equitable pay structure would obtain. Even if a substantial number of people elected to remain at the middle or lower levels of a profession, the chances for an equitable salary would be enhanced.

In *The Road to Serfdom*, F. A. Hayek wrote, "Every restriction on the freedom of entry into a trade reduces the security of all those outside it."[66] Decredentialing would lead to increased quality of service in myriad ways. The environmental conditions for teamwork would be dramatically improved. There would be no reason to hoard knowledge at any level. The public would view working people with much more respect, leading to greater self-esteem among those workers. For example, any hospital orderly or staff law clerk would be viewed as a potential doctor or lawyer. Apprenticed work would receive greater supervision than present systems allow—especially in medicine. Decredentialing could greatly enhance the role for colleges and universities. Without the need to act as employment screening agencies, colleges and universities could bring cutting-edge knowledge to all subjects while simultaneously promoting the intrinsic value of education. And, with an infusion of community support, learning institutions could shift from grade-driven curricula to student-centered, knowledge-centered agendas. If they failed to provide students with valuable knowledge, they would cease to exist, as they should. With student-centered curricula, colleges and universities could compete to provide students with meaningful learning—they could achieve what Abraham Maslow called the ideal college, a place of essential self-discovery. Once such value existed, society would understand the need for these institutions, not just for our early years, but throughout our whole lives.

These efforts would result in perpetual redistribution of opportunity which would lead to greater equality among all elements of society. Having fewer people trapped in jobs they hate would significantly reduce our multibillion-dollar stress industry. The cost of goods and services would drop as the inflated cost of education decreased. There would be no need for add-on service charges to pay for the high cost of becoming a professional, which is precisely what we pay for each time visit a doctor's office. Finding one's right livelihood would be much easier. Having more people using their strengths in the right place would reduce frustration and increase efficiency and effectiveness.

The tyranny of a "professional elite" over the lives of free people is at least as oppressive as that of one determined by capital. What I propose is not the end of education but the beginning: if a country is to be great, an affiliation with educational institutions should be a lifelong engagement for all of its citizens.

What if we provided universal access to information?

In today's world, we are deluged with information in long streams of data. But we don't have to scan the social or environmental horizon very far to determine that we are starved for knowledge. In every sphere—physical, biological, social, and intellectual—the need for greater understanding is critical. Questions prevail in every branch of scientific endeavor and human knowledge. Dilemmas beg for our attention: how does one function day-to-day within a marriage, a family, a corporation, a city, state, a nation and as a citizen of the world?

One surefire way to give Americans a dividend in the productivity revolution is to provide universal access to information. Better yet, replace economic growth with growth of knowledge as the yardstick for measuring societal well-being, regardless of whether the increase in knowledge concerns hard science, the humanities, or the curiosity of an individual. In other words, organize community as a fully functioning celebration of higher learning; act as if the *life of the mind* is important to every human being. Kill once and for all the notion that only a few citizens are worthy of entering into the "great conversation" of humankind, that education is something one can finish. All citizens should be encouraged, even helped, to learn all they are capable of learning and to understand that this work—this learning—is many times more important than the creation of insignificant jobs.

But, if knowledge is power, then responsibility follows. Being responsible requires literacy about the biological and social world and the realm of ideas, participation in the great conversation about the meaning of value. Being responsible means developing one's own opinion instead of living on the thinking of others. Being responsible depends upon a willingness to face life and death without illusion. Being responsible means being accountable for oneself and one's children. It means learning and understanding the obligations of parenthood before one has children, and it requires the numeracy to comprehend the problems of exponential growth in human population.

The wiring of the world into a global infrastructure is one of the most exciting promises of the new millennium. The possibilities stagger the imagination. The great danger, however, is that information inequality may further and radically widen the distance between the world's haves and have nots. Democracy demands universal access. Anything less is a recipe for disaster.

What if we really reformed taxes?

In *Federalist Paper Number 10,* James Madison wrote:

> The apportionment of taxes on the various descriptions of property is an act which seems to require the most exact impartiality; yet there is, perhaps, no legislative act in which greater opportunity and temptation are given to a predominant party to trample on the rules of justice. Every shilling with which they overburden the inferior number is a shilling saved to their own pockets.

Now I'm sure, if you've stayed with me this long, I don't have to go into great detail about the growing influence of special interests to convince you that in the 1950s corporations paid a far, far greater share of the federal tax burden than they do today.[66] Corporate welfare should be abolished, and corporations' fair share of taxes should provide much of the seed money for stimulating community service. Technological advances have been increasing productivity for decades, while real wages for workers have declined. It's time to turn the tables and allow American workers a share of their innovational labor. Corporate taxes should reflect real productivity gains from automation and employee ingenuity. Corporations deserve to benefit from such gains, but so does the community at large.

We must also explore new ways to assign value to natural resources. For example, all product and service taxes should capture an amount equal to coping with their use. If drilling for oil and gas, however, or cutting timber in a particular forest, is found to produce net negative environmental effects, then these resources should be worth more to society where they are and their positive value should still be available as income for people in those industries. In other words, if utilizing a resource creates $1 billion worth of economic activity but $2 billion worth of environmental damage, then it's not too farfetched to use an accounting methodology in which we write ourselves a $3 billion deposit slip and leave the resource where it is, as it is.

We should use the tax system to provide a strong incentive for organizations to bind the salaries of those at the top echelons to wages in the lower ranks, so that if you raise one you raise the other. Assess environmental taxes for all products which have costs associated with their disposal. And finally, enact zero-based budgeting: make government organizations and agencies justify their existence each year to eliminate the malignancy of bureaucracy which is inherent in the genes of all organizations public and private.

What if we exchanged bureaucratic rules for common sense?

In *The Death of Common Sense: How Law Is Suffocating America*, Philip K. Howard shows how the quest for a risk-free society, through the creation of a rule of law to cover every predicament, has robbed citizens of their responsibility to themselves and their communities. In an attempt to perfect the law, federal statutes have grown to 100 million words.[67] Howard writes, "The drive for certainty has destroyed, not enhanced, law's ability to act as a guide.... We made slums illegal and then, with our building codes, made it impossible to build low-cost housing."[68] The founding fathers often referred to America as a nation of laws, which is a very good thing to be, but it would have been appropriate to have added that America should be a nation of principled awareness.

Principle as an intensified form of awareness is hopelessly dissipated if we all have to look for a rule instead of what is called for to solve every problem. In the noble quest for fairness, the appearance of fairness has become more important than the reality of fairness. The more copious and complicated the rules, the greater the opportunities for hidden corruption. But, in the absence of rules, responsibility looms large, and principle leaves room for judgment. Howard writes, "Principles are like trees in open fields. We can know where we are and where to go. But the path we take is our own."[69]

The most significant ingredient missing today is accountability. Subjective decisions have to be made in the public, private, and community sectors by individuals who are held accountable to citizens who themselves understand that on-the-spot judgment is sometimes superior to the constraints of rules (a clear illustration of the ascendancy of intellectual patterns over social patterns). Following the letter of the law inspires indecision and passivity while one awaits the "looking up" of the regulation meant to cover one's every predicament, instead of responsibly exercising the judgment the occasion calls for. "The fears that keep us quivering in law's shadows are, in fact, the rudiments of a strong society. Constant exposure to uncertainty and disagreement is critical to everything we value, like responsibility, individualism, and community."[70] Thus, democracy—however messy and imperfect—is still superior to bureaucracy.

A further way to enable a genuine democracy to use access to information as the fulcrum for responsibility is to run all information up the flagpole for public scrutiny. Failure and success rates in all areas of the public, private, and nonprofit sectors should be available to anyone who wants to know. Democracy is based upon choice, and choice depends upon informed judgment. To hire a doctor, or lawyer, or to use any service public or private in any way for pleasure or profit, one should be able to access the kind of information that would hold the providers accountable. If one is to undergo surgery, the success rate of the attending physician should be readily accessible. Again, knowledge is power.

Indeed, public scrutiny and access to information are often the greatest protection against the abuse of power. The popular call for states' rights and for block grants is, in part, a call for the ability to make local decisions at the local level. If we examine recent history, though, we find local political machines, big city bosses, and a multitude of civil rights violations which were the reason discretion moved to the federal level to begin with. I offer this caveat: The only way to reach a balance is through democratic access to information with the ability to focus attention on injustice. The U.S. Constitution and the Bill of Rights offer standards from which it is unacceptable to deviate. If states' rights turns out to be a euphemism for "This is how we do it in Mississippi," then the movement must be exposed as such.

What if everyone's health really mattered?

The next radical measure we must take to move our society toward an embodied community is to eliminate the massive bureaucracy called private health insurance. There are no worse trials of bureaucratic hell than those experienced by the average citizen who tries to fight a major corporation over a health insurance claim. In fact, there may be no idea more hair-brained than to expect that the medical well-being of people can be tied directly to businesses which are designed to profit by not paying for services. Making public health totally dependent upon the "free market" is as ludicrous as trying to make war a profitable enterprise. Legions of health insurance executives make a wonderful living by denying health care benefits to the maximum number of people that the letter of the law will allow. American medical technology is unsurpassed, and yet a growing portion of our population receives about the equivalent of Third World health care.

How can any group of citizens call themselves a responsible community, if the largest outlay for medical expenses occurs in the last years of life, while growing numbers of children lack proper care? There is also the glaring issue of personal responsibility in relation to one's health care. Should a person who has smoked for 30 years be a candidate for a lung transplant? We need a new framework in our approach to health care. Establishing a board of judges fashioned after the Supreme Court might be worth considering: decisions have to be made and someone must make them.

What if we stopped the war on inner city youth?

It is a cultural disgrace to use the metaphor of a war to eradicate drug problems, unless of course winning wars is unimportant. The American effort to fight a war on drugs is really a war against poor people, especially African-American, inner-city youth. Madison Avenue values project a "win at any cost" ethos throughout our culture from the Wall Street boardroom to the ghetto barroom. To expect that young people with zero economic prospects in a king-of-the-mountain, "greed is good" society, where tobacco executives eagerly testify that cigarettes are not addictive, will *just say no* to drug money is an imbecilic illusion.[71]

American tobacco companies openly export slow death products to Third World countries, while America uses military patrols to intercept drug shipments from foreign shores. And yet, no drug kills as effectively as tobacco. The major crime of the drug user is a blatant disrespect for the reality of the status quo.

According to FBI crime statistics, African Americans make up 12 percent of the population, and yet there are more African-American men in prison than white men. African Americans make up 13 percent of the drug user population, but they are convicted for drug possession at the rate of 55 percent and serve 74 percent of the prison sentences. Indeed, one in three young African-American men is in some way subject to the rigors of the criminal justice system. Moreover, crack cocaine is the drug of inner-city youth, while white powder cocaine is the drug of choice of middle class whites. It takes possession of 5 grams of the former to win 5 years in prison and 500 grams of the latter.[72] One can hardly find a greater demonstration or example of political power than in the disparity between these penalties.

The solution to this problem is deceptively simple: legalize drug use. Legalizing drugs will not make the problem go away; it may, in fact, increase drug use. But, if done correctly, it will put an immediate end to the war on the poor and the exponential growth of prison populations. Legalized drugs do not have be advertised in laissez-faire fashion as is the case with tobacco and alcohol. If every effort were made to discourage drug use and to build character in every individual, the numbers of users would eventually subside. But no matter what we do, people will never give up drug use completely, and it is insane to pretend otherwise.

From Kings of the Mountain to Citizens of the World

In *A Nation of Salesmen,* Earl Shorris hints at what a more equitable community, which truly values ideas, might be like:

> Man the customer, the thing the salesman puts to use, can not be made suddenly to disappear, replaced overnight by enlightenment's daring thinker. The cost of such a revolution would be too high. The tutelage of the market must continue. But for how long and to what extent?...Thinking will create difficulties, discomforts, dislocations. The free man, the person who refuses to rule himself according to the tutelage of the market may choose different satisfactions: time instead of things, happiness instead of wealth. If so, the productive capacity of nations will have to be diminished or production will have to be described in a different way, revalued, like something brought out of a long sojourn in darkness and suddenly exposed to light. Wisdom could become more valuable than widgets. Professors and poets would become the wealth of nations. It is not a mad scheme I propose; even now, there are wise men saying that knowledge is in many ways more valuable than things. I have even heard them say so in the great suites of great corporations. They are not merely asking the question. It is the system of valuation that impedes them now. And they are neither fools nor revolutionaries. They have won Nobel Prizes and made fortunes.[73]

Indeed, Shorris suggests, "Under the autonomy of human reason a rich man might be one who had enough, and poverty would describe the lonely."[74] If we Americans are not seriously confused about "values" how do we explain the fact that there is so much work to be done and so few jobs? By combining the best of capitalism with the simple idea that everyone should have their basic needs met, we are assured a strong, healthy, educated citizenry fully capable of competing and cooperating in a global economy. We are then certain that enough time is available for families to pass principled culture from one generation to the next.

Our failure to achieve this simple equity is the basis for the nagging sense of guilt that even the most ardent defenders of capitalism feel when they are confronted with abject poverty and find themselves without a rationale to explain it. The only way to empower each and every citizen to be free of factional interests is to ensure that none fall far enough down the economic mountain to lose their voice in the affairs of democracy. If average citizens cannot affect the decisions of their employers in matters which concern quality, safety, and the environment, then only employers have power. Real power *of, by, and for* the people, requires a safety net high enough above the bottom of the mountain to accommodate basic human needs.

The political spin on free markets is that the emphasis on *free* pertains to individuals, but in reality free market is a euphemism for "increasing returns." Slaves made the ancient Greeks and Romans independent, the buffalo made the Plains Indians independent, rich farm land made the settlers independent. But our technologies are moving us further and further into a world of increasing abstraction. And although we have always been more interdependent than has been acknowledged, the concept of people being practically independent is becoming more and more abstract. If the power of moneyed interests is left unchecked, greater manipulation of a growing number of *dependent* citizens is a certainty. The slaves, the buffalo, and the abundant available farm land are gone. We need to develop an equity that lessens the effect of a fall off our mountain. We need to worry less about creating inconsequential jobs and a lot more about seeing to the *real work* that needs to be done, about thinking our way into the future or meeting a fate similar to that of the ancient Greeks and the Plains Indians.

For decades economists have prattled about gains in productivity, and yet as productivity increases, as machines free us of labor, as the mass production of goods becomes easier and cheaper, the ability of more and more families to meet their basic economic needs is ever more problematic. The only way to check the power of moneyed interests is to see that money is not bestowed a greater value than our ideas. The power at the top of our mountain must not be so great as to drown the voices at the bottom. The essence of freedom requires balanced measures of independence and interdependence.

Economics and Global Prosperity

There has never been a time in history when there was a greater need for cooperation worldwide, yet almost everyone who pretends be a leader rises to the podium to shout about the need to compete. We have developed a national obsession about competition, even though economic competition, when pushed to extreme, results in the ultimate form of competition: war. Where are the leaders who will recognize the need for cooperation locally and globally?

I take no personal pride in our claim of having won the Cold War. Had either side entered the Cold War with leaders who were more serious about peace than about gaining a temporary advantage, we could have ended the arms race before it began.[75] Black-and-white thinking on both sides prevented the exploration of genuine peace.

Millions of us (myself included) grew up during the Cold War era with little idea about what we were *for*, but there was no doubt about what we were *against*: Communists. When what you are against is clearer than what you are for, rationality flies out the window, and you become a tool for any special interest group that has a clear vision of what *it* is trying to do. In the case of the Cold War, we all became tools of the military-industrial complex, as Eisenhower warned. If we have enemies, we should need the ability to defeat them but once or twice; when we prepare weapons enough to destroy them several thousand times over, as evidenced by our Cold War nuclear arsenal, the injury is done to ourselves.

The nuclear build-up between the U.S. and the former Soviet Union was an exercise in mutual madness. The resources wasted could have stabilized the earth's population by wiping human hunger from the face of the earth. Only arrogant fools would congratulate themselves upon squandering enough resources to revolutionize the world, simply to reach a point where they could destroy their efforts through disarmament. The nuclear arms race created defense department millionaires and a workforce so dependent that they would prefer to continue making weapons which are no longer needed rather than apply their skills to the more pressing problems of their communities. Why are we not outraged by this waste? At the very least, we might ponder the stupidity of it all with as much enthusiasm as those who would celebrate a victory of winning the Cold War without regard to its cost.

There is, however, a great lesson to be learned from this waste of effort and resources. It is simply that an economy can be built upon any premise (even arbitrary ones—perhaps *only* arbitrary ones) under which people are willing to assign value. We champion efficiency and effectiveness in creating valuable jobs, but if we decided tomorrow to rearrange the asteroids in the asteroid belt, we could use it as a basis for expanding the economy. (In light of the spectacle of the Shoemaker-Levy 9 comet in 1994, it might even be a good idea.) We could also achieve the same effect with something as arbitrary as investing heavily in community, as I've suggested, by eliminating poverty, improving the lives of the world's children and elderly, and ensuring that everyone has affordable health care. We might even decide to replace the former Strategic Defense Initiative (SDI) with a new SDI called Self-Directed Inquiry.

In *The Trap*, Sir James Goldsmith writes:

> Global free trade will shatter the way in which value-added is shared between capital and labor. Value-added is the increase of value obtained when you convert raw materials into a manufactured product. In mature societies, we have been able to develop a general agreement as to how it should be shared. That agreement has been reached through generations of political debate, elections, strikes, lockouts and other conflicts. Overnight that agreement will be destroyed by the arrival of huge populations willing to undercut radically the salaries earned by our workforces. The social divisions that this will cause will be deeper than anything ever envisaged by Marx.[76]

It is indeed a trap to conclude that isolationism is the way for developed countries to respond to the problems of global population and human starvation. Millions of Americans wail continuously about giving too much money away in foreign aid, even though our foreign aid expenditures are barely one percent of our GNP. If the citizens of the world's rich nations were truly to think their way through this proposition, five to ten percent of their GNP for aid to developing countries would be more just, especially if such assistance came with absolute strings requiring recipient countries to meet the basic human needs of their citizens—one sure way of arresting population growth.

In addition, if we really think this issue through, there is a way to help developing countries and ourselves at the same time: Simply provide most foreign aid in the form of needs-based goods and then subsidize the American labor. That way, Americans would have many more opportunities for meaningful employment and far less reason to make weapons of mass destruction simply out of the requirement to hold onto a job. Then, as developing countries began to meet their own needs, they could be allowed some leverage for trading American needs-based goods to lesser able neighbors.

If we truly believe that competition contains natural forces for optimum achievement among human beings, then we cannot rise to the occasion of our culture unless we are assured of the ability to compete with the very best of all cultures. If responsible foreign aid became the norm, we could change immigration policy to allow entry to the United States only after we have reached a sustained, negative growth population and then only by citizens from countries who have done likewise. This is not an isolationist posture, but an ever sobering realization that as a price for doing nothing about this issue, the catastrophe that awaits will be a socio-biological holocaust of Biblical proportion.

It seems impossible to overstate the case that we human beings are inexcusably reckless and irresponsible when it comes to our own procreation. So, if my earlier examples of exponential population growth have failed to convey a sense of urgency to this matter, think about it this way: Had the world's current population existed in the year 1310, and had it grown at the modest annual rate of 1.7 percent, today there would be standing room only on earth.[77] Human population is the problem that, left unresolved, negates the solutions to all other problems.

Human Rights

Our history suggests we Americans are politically preoccupied with the idea of freedom. This focus was for decades exacerbated by our continual ideological debate with the former Soviet Union over the implied freedom of capitalism versus the responsibility supposedly inherent in socialism. We are so attuned to this argument, the issue is so important to us, that its residue still shapes economic reality. We continually beseech other nations, insisting that if they wish to stand in good favor with America they will see our reality and promote freedom through the enactment of human rights. But the evidence indicates that we have adopted a very narrow, self-centered view of reality. Starvation is the ultimate infringement of human rights, but because it is not *real* to us, we ignore the political corruption in developing countries that allows starvation to occur. We continue to clamor about human rights but only with respect to the way people are treated in a political sense. Perhaps the loss of the Soviet Union as an arch rival (although this could still prove temporary, or China could take its place) will cause us to rethink the issue of human rights. We may come to realize how our rivalry has kept us from examining Leslie W. Dunbar's assertion that, "The right to live is the most radical of all political values. But one that ought to be."[78]

A right exists only if it is honored. That is, it must be acknowledged as a right by others. But, viewed in this way, how can the right to act, to demonstrate one's political freedom, be more important than one's right to exist? How can the right to *do* be more important than the right to *be*? Why does the right to have a lawyer take precedence over the right to have a doctor?[79] Prisoners have a right to food, even if the *free* man does not. This is socially manufactured reality like memes boiled in a kiln, and poured into molds to cure. The case for humanity can be neither made nor understood without a full appreciation of inorganic, biological, social, and intellectual patterns. Like it or not, we are all in this world together; what some do affects all.

We rationalize our posture by arguing that scarce resources are the reasons for starvation, but the evidence clearly shows there is, at least for now, enough food to feed the world. There is only a lack of political fortitude to see that food is available for everyone. Another rationalization says the world is simply over-populated. No one can argue otherwise, but most fail to recognize that when countries reach a high level of prosperity, birth rates fall dramatically (the U.S. is a case in point). In Third World countries a high birthrate is often a desperate effort to survive: the people need families large enough to produce enough to eat.[80] As a further insult, our immigration policy favors the wealthy and the technically literate, the very people lesser able nations cannot afford to lose. If the opportunity to live a good life were ubiquitous, regardless of geography, immigration would cease to be an issue.

Our views of economic reality are so confused regarding the values of well-being and the ideals of individual freedom that we can't tell they are integrally related. This is demonstrated by the fact that we allow immigration on the basis of ideology. That is, if the immigrants cherish our ideals of freedom we will allow them entry. We disqualify them as potential citizens—even if staying where they are means they will perish from starvation—if they don't have the "right" ideology, as though living were not somehow connected with freedom. When asked, we will unequivocally say that people are more important than money. Our actions, however, at least in terms of immigration policy, suggest otherwise.

This failure to see that the equity required for human survival on this planet is indeed a part of the fundamental ideology of freedom flies in the face of every religion and every concept of democracy or just government that has ever been conceived. The arrogance of the well-to-do in society to speak of progress and the greatness of their economic systems measured by such indices as GNP, while millions starve to death, would likely bar us from membership in a galaxy of civilized beings. We allow American citizens to die because they lack the money for a simple medical procedure, and yet we refuse to disconnect a brain-dead patient from life-support systems because of the ideological implications associated with the freedom of choice and human rights.

Our ideals and attitudes about human rights issues are influenced by a repressed but pervasive certainty of our own mortality. Overwhelming fear of this impending consequence is all the worse because most of us refuse to deal with it. Instead, we become caught up in the conflicting core values of American culture: activism, achievement, efficiency, materialism, progress, freedom, individualism, equality, morality, conformity, and humanitarianism.[81] These socially constructed issues become outposts where we can see each of the other issues clearly, but not all of those in between.

Activism and achievement are, at least in part, residue from the value of Manifest Destiny. Common sense tells us that efficiency is a great value, even though many of the things that add the greatest quality to our lives have absolutely nothing to do with efficiency. Economic materialism as a core value prompts us to say, "The one who dies with the most toys wins." Progress as a core value is probably the most confusing—few of us go to much trouble to figure out what true progress is, even though we are determined to see that it occurs. Exemption from restraint so colors the values of freedom and individualism, that it overshadows individual responsibility. To most of us, equality means equal opportunity, morality defines black and white issues of right and wrong, and conformity symbolizes loyalty to the status quo. Humanitarianism is a value too often constricted by terms of the just world hypothesis, i.e., we are willing to help only those who appear to deserve it.

In *The State of Humanity*, Julian L. Simon dares to predict, "The material conditions of life will continue to get better for most people, in most countries, most of the time, indefinitely. Within a century or two, all nations and most of humanity will be at or above today's Western living standards."[82] Simon and a host of hopeful associates postulate a technological future which will overpower all obstacles, social and environmental, as if solutions to humanity's problems are inevitable. This view reminds me of a passage in *My Dinner With André*, where André Gregory describes a physician's pleasure in examining the improving condition of an arm attached to a dying patient. Such optimism about resources in the face of exponential population growth are possible today precisely because of barbarian inequality. Twenty percent of the earth's population have reason to be optimistic while the other eighty percent own their misery outright.

We Americans take pride in a cultural heritage which celebrates a war over high tea taxes, but which will tolerate little commotion from people who press for something as simple as enough equity to exist. With our own population stabilizing we have learned to need immigrant labor to keep "growing," so that we always have more people working to support those who have retired. But, if we were to embrace the future without this kind of growth, we would confront the problem faced by those whose future is already desperate. Let's be clear about this: A consumer-driven, laissez-faire, global marketplace, in which billions of neurotic people, ignorant enough to want what they don't need, lacking the emotional intelligence to know what they do need, and possessed of little regard for their fellow man, represents in sum the terminal stage of human malignancy for planet earth.

Combine the human need for specialness with the search for meaning, a pathological fear of death, and the need to be connected to something larger than ourselves, and you begin to sense the magnitude of the contemplative inquiry necessary to put ourselves and others into perspective. To find purpose worth pursuing requires a greater assessment of the big picture; it requires that consumers become working citizens—citizens of a global community.

Chapter Eight

Rising to the Role of Citizen

Live as if you were living already for the second time and as if you had acted the first time as wrongly as you are about to act now![1]

—Viktor E. Frankl

We fulfill many roles during our lives. We are sons or daughters, students, husbands, wives, breadwinners, fathers, mothers, grandparents or retirees, and we acquire one job title after another. Through education and socialization we learn to perform and appreciate these roles, but during the whole of our lives we also have the role of being citizens. This role of citizenship requires further examination. Because we live in a democracy, we have an obligation to *think and act* and to apply intellectual patterns equal to the problems we encounter. If we escape or shirk the responsibility that goes with the role of citizenship, we do so at the peril of leaving our interests unrepresented and our values depreciated. We do not, cannot, and will not have a democracy until such time as each citizen is the possessor of his or her own opinions.

Democracy, as defined and discussed when I was in school, appeared to me and to countless others to be a profoundly stable condition, established by the Constitution and the Bill of Rights, protected by three branches of government. My teachers painted a vision so focused on the greatness of our forefathers that the documents establising our government seemed powerful enough to sustain it by themselves. But democracy depends upon *process* and is antithetical to giving the appearance of

235

order. Process depends on content, and content means ideas. Too much order can be evidence that democracy is not working. How ironic that we learned about democracy in an atmosphere that put a greater premium on order than it did on learning. If we accept the assertion that "knowledge is power," it should be obvious that democracy depends on an educated citizenry, just as the protection of our own individual rights depends on our standing up for them. In this context it's easy to see that education is as necessary to our personal lives as citizens as it is to our economic success. The sorry state of the global environment suggests that we citizens are born into the world with a tremendous responsibility few of us acknowledge.

Paul Johnson concluded his book *Intellectuals* with the assertion that "a dozen people picked at random on the street are at least as likely to offer sensible views on political matters as a cross-section of the intelligentsia."[2] On more than one occasion I have heard columnist William F. Buckley Jr. make similar statements. It is hardly surprising that intellectuals develop contempt for one another. Who can antagonize, infuriate, and thus neutralize an intellectual better than another intellectual? But the fact remains that America was founded by intellectuals and will not likely be sustained without them. When people stand for nothing, nothing exists to lean on. Carrying out a constitutional government is more than an equal challenge to starting one. In the field of economics the term "level playing field" represents fairness. In a democracy, a level playing field is one where citizens recognize that the principles upon which the democracy is founded are harvested from ideas. They must understand and nourish the intellect thoroughly in order to replant. If we are indeed a government by the people, we will either attain knowledge equal to our predicaments or cease to be such a government. People who do not think for themselves allow ideas to be discredited not on their merit, but by attacking the individuals who propose them. The very term merit is increasingly becoming a synonym for those who are "like us." So it is not surprising that many of our political elections more closely resemble popularity contests than exercises of thoughtful democracy in action.

Democracy requires that intellectual patterns take precedence over social patterns.

The ancient Greeks, notably Plato, and Aristotle, had a special contempt for democracy, arguing that uneducated, uninformed citizens have little but their own narrow interests to consider and should therefore be excluded from the governmental process. They argued that only an educated aristocracy should take part in government. Even though we hold the ancient Greeks in high esteem because of their wisdom, we question their judgment philosophically on this one point. We believe that everyone in America should have a say in government: one person, one vote. But could anyone successfully argue that ignorant people routinely exercise good judgment? Indeed, the frequent assertion by politicians that the majority of the American people, though admittedly poorly educated, have a deep abiding wisdom when it comes to voting is itself a product of anti-intellectualism.

We operate on the principle that we have a representative form of government, but our society has grown so complex, and there are so many issues affecting so many different people, representative democracy is no longer an adequate means of ensuring that everyone is treated fairly. In today's society, representative democracy without participation is an illusion. Participation means taking a vigilant, active role in the public affairs that influence private ones. Increased participation in the *process* of democracy is necessary to provide a just government. Voting is simply a mustard or mayonnaise selection that has little, if anything to do with what's for dinner. So, if we are to uphold our ideal of democracy and maintain the balance necessary for democracy in a highly technical society, we must educate ourselves to meet our responsibility as citizens. Otherwise, we must admit that Plato was right: democracy is a bad idea.

More than eighty years ago, in a book called *The New State*, Mary Parker Follett wrote:

A crude view of democracy says that when the working-people realize their power they can have what they want, since their numbers being so great, they can out-vote other classes. But the reason the working-people have not already learned something so very obvious is because it is not true—*we are never ruled by numbers alone.*

Moreover, a fatal defect in majority rule is that by its very nature it abolishes itself. Majority rule must inevitably become minority rule: the majority is too big to handle itself; it organizes itself into committees—committees of fifty, fifteen, three—which in their turn resolve themselves into a committee of one, and behold—the full-fledged era of bosses is at hand, with the "consent of the governed" simply because the governed are physically helpless to govern themselves. Many men want majority rule so they can be this committee of one; some of our most worthy citizens are incipient Greek tyrants longing to give us their best tyranny.[3]

To participate, to assume one's role as a responsible citizen, to stand up for one's rights, embracing the core American value of activism, has practical limits. For example, it is practical to call, write, or send wires to our representatives to let them know our wishes about specific legislation, but we can't all sit in on or be engaged in the actual legislative process. We can't really be sure that our interests are served.

In his book *The New Realities*, Peter Drucker writes about citizenship emerging through the "third sector."[4] This term identifies a counterculture with an emphasis on values, intended to bridge the gap between representation and participation. The third sector defies our king-of-the-mountain mentality and the economic ethos which says people will not act unless there are economic incentives to do so. People in the third sector act from their own definitions of purpose and meaning. What matters to them matters simply because it does. This third sector comprises thousands of nonprofit, nongovernmental institutions, such as private hospitals, colleges, universities, and a myriad of philanthropic and volunteer organizations. Drucker characterizes the matter-of-course design of these organizations as being human-change institutions. In effect they envision an agenda of change for betterment, from better health to better individual and societal growth and development. Drucker writes:

> Now that the size and complexity of government make direct participation all but impossible, it is the human-change

institution of the third sector that is offering its volunteers a sphere of personal achievement in which the individual exercises influence, discharges responsibility, and makes decisions. And increasingly executives in business, especially people in middle management, are expected to serve in decision-making positions as board members of non-profit institutions. In the political culture of mainstream society, individuals, no matter how well educated, how successful, how achieving, or how wealthy, can only vote and pay taxes. They can only react, can only be passive. In the counterculture of the third sector, they are active citizens.[5]

There is a great paradox in the contempt we shower on those who today aspire to public office or public service. We accuse them of lacking vision and objectivity, but overlook that some of this contempt is a thinly veiled effort to excuse ourselves for having failed to conjure our own vision of the future. In other words, some of our disgust for our leaders is simply another way of showing that we are also annoyed and fed up with ourselves.

Public outcry is growing increasingly shrill about politicians who look out only for their own self-interest. Ironically, that is what most of the rest of us do. How can we expect politicians to live by higher principles than we do? Politicians are people too, and in a democracy where so many people hold differing views, a politician can at best hope to please only a few constituents. If politicians can't be trusted, then neither can democracy, because that's all we have. E. J. Dionne Jr. is right, "A nation that hates politics will not long thrive as a democracy."[6] We can improve the system by eliminating political action committees (PACS) and the influence of big money, but we can't maintain a political system without politicians. A large part of the public outrage stems from a public's being torn away from its self-interestedness and being forced to think about issues that it would prefer just went away.

The popularity of billionaire Ross Perot as a presidential candidate has derived largely from the notion that here is someone who will just take care of things. Many of his supporters, though sincere, are politically naïve. They want a strong leader who will allow them to return to their own interests while he attends to those of the government. This is the kind of thinking that got us into the social and economic trouble we are in today.

Pity the nation that needs *powerful* leaders. The penalty for inattention to government affairs that affect us directly expresses itself in the *surprise* exhibited by the thousands of workers who have lost their jobs through corporate downsizing. Some of the jobs lost because of downsizing are attributable to structural changes in the global economy, but a significant number have been lost through the runaway greed of investment bankers, junk bonders and arbitragers, to whom many of our elected officials had connections. Scores of companies were virtually looted in the name of business efficiency; lifelong employees found themselves in unemployment lines. Many have only now begun to realize their unemployment is the price they have paid for immersing themselves in entertainment while leaving someone else to look out for their interests. Others have yet to make sense of it all. They are confused and bitter, wondering what went wrong and why their representatives betrayed them.

In 1831 Alexis de Tocqueville, a young Frenchman, visited America. His observations are as relevant today as if he'd traveled here last year instead of last century. Five years after his nine-month stay, he wrote:

> I think, then, that the species of oppression by which democratic nations are menaced is unlike anything which ever existed in the world: our contemporaries will find no prototype of it in their memories. I seek in vain for an expression which will accurately convey the whole idea I have formed of it; the old words despotism and tyranny are inappropriate: the thing itself is new, and since I cannot name, I must attempt to define it.
>
> I seek to trace the novel features under which despotism may appear in the world. The first thing that strikes the observation is an innumerable multitude of men, all equal and alike, incessantly endeavoring to procure the petty and paltry pleasures with which they glut their lives. Each of them, living apart, is as a stranger to the fate of all the rest—his children and his private friends constitute to him the whole of mankind; as for the rest of his fellow-citizens, he is close to them, but he sees them not; he touches them, but he feels them not; he exists but in himself and for himself alone; and if his

kindred still remain to him, he may be said at any rate to have lost his country.[7]

Contrast our view of life in America in 1831 with our way of life today, and imagine what he would say if he could return.

What is so striking is that our idea of freedom, which is the only way of life most of us have ever known, was so new and so uncommon to de Tocqueville that he had great difficulty characterizing its weakness. But, even then, the sinister face of an over-focus on self-interest, with so little attention to felt responsibility, was obvious. If freedom is that uncommon in light of human history, perhaps it is also uncommonly fragile—so much so that it's rather silly to postulate an end of history simply because the ideological battle between the U.S. and the former U.S.S.R. appears to have ended. Moreover, the "reality" we observe about government reflects something of the principles we care most about. The English novelist Charles Dickens visited America eleven years after de Tocqueville, and he was so concerned with the atrocities of slavery that he remained unmoved by America's democracy. If he could return today, what would he say about the sprawling slums in America's cities, which in so many ways are similar to Dickens' London? In 1842, the majority of people in America ignored the issue of slavery, just as the majority today ignore the rapid rise of the "estranged poor."[8]

We have been taught to revere the greatness of the vision of our forebears, who, we are told, put into place constitutional documents of such perfection that for all practical purposes they cannot be improved. Today it appears that our system fails to produce Washingtons, Jeffersons, Franklins, and Lincolns, though many citizens long for such leadership. But this is a misconception about the nature of our own history. Washington, Jefferson, Franklin, and Lincoln were not awarded hero status in their own time. Without a painstaking understanding of history we wouldn't recognize a George Washington or a Thomas Jefferson if we heard such a person address the nation. And herein lies part of the problem. If ours is a government of the people and by the people, but we are not yet scholars or even interested students of government, doesn't this suggest we have what Plato would have argued is a government by amateurs? An insufficient supply of strong leaders is not the problem. Needing them is. History has a habit of making statesmen out of scoundrels.

One of our biggest obstacles to achieving the creation of a better future is our propensity for optimism. It may sound like a ludicrous idea to caution against optimism, but when you combine optimism with a lifestyle of relative comfort, for millions of people it leads to the conclusion that things are okay as they are. From this viewpoint, no action is required to live happily ever after.

Personal responsibility as the driving force of society is always preferable to a centralized authority, but the values of personal responsibility are not born spontaneously. They have to be taught, learned, and internalized in the same way that all of us come to form our beliefs about the world. Ashley Montagu said this best, "Freedom is the most demanding of all responsibilities, and like every responsibility it is something that must be learned."[9] Beliefs that grow into us as a result of our culture crystallize our expectations about life. Personal expectations of our ability to have an effect on the world take form over the whole range of our childhood development.

Asian immigrants are a case in point: Arriving in America penniless but filled with expectancy, they put forth extraordinary efforts. The result is that they prosper. Such examples exacerbate the disfavor with which the middle class views third-generation welfare recipients, but the simple fact escaping such critics is that a strong ethic of responsibility is a product of learned behavior. Responsibility requires apprenticeship. Those of us who follow a work ethic forget that we did not come by it accidently. We either learned it because we were taught that hard work is expected of us, or we learned by the examples set for us by family, friends, and teachers.

There will always be individuals who rise above what seem to be insurmountable obstacles, but success, nevertheless, is a product of generations of learning. Large families ensure survival in primitive cultures, and in a similar way successive generations do so in hierarchical societies.[10] Being backed by a long line of antecedents ensures that if one makes a serious economic error (which at one time or another most of us do) one does not fall all the way down the mountain. Some family member will likely help the unfortunate one become reestablished. The importance of this kind of support is profound. The middle class takes it for granted, failing to realize what it means to live without it.

Belief precedes action. People without a strong work ethic cannot teach it to others. A key to understanding the phenomenon of responsibility lies in the seemingly impossible task of remembering what it is like not to know. Those of us with a strong work ethic cannot remember acquiring it as we acquired a coat or a car, but we act as if we expect other people to take on the value of hard work as easily as one dons a new outfit. If children are not taught the need to develop a solid sense of responsibility, and if they have no examples to follow, the next hope is through teachers. But if the teachers believe the children lack fundamental ability, the children are doomed.

Our current (controlling) welfare system would not exist if we had thought deeply about the problem in the first place. Had we concentrated on education and employment assurance instead of a monthly dole, we would not be in our current predicament. We have millions of children who need guidance, while millions of older people with a great deal of practical experience are unemployed. We have tens of thousands of people who need home medical care, while thousands of lonely people sit idle. Employment assurance could go along way in establishing an ethic of caring in our society. Why do we pay welfare recipients to do *nothing* when some of the most necessary human tasks are left undone? I'll tell you why. It is because we haven't mined wisdom from the great cultures of our world to understand the differences in value between work and jobs. Second, third, and fourth generation welfare families suffer the jaundice of a fractured culture. Values and skills not learned cannot be passed on. But the greatest tragedy is that in seeking remedies for themselves, people strive for status instead of knowledge. Status is as easily lost as gained, but knowledge lays a permanent foundation upon which to build a better life and a better culture.

If the populace is to learn a work ethic through education and in jobs that are ever increasing in complexity, such jobs *must exist* and they must be accessible to individuals who are *different* in many ways from what is considered by the majority to be customary. And if those who hire for these positions do not understand their own cultural bias, then the people who need these jobs *will not* get them. It is not sufficient only to try to be fair in this regard. We can be incredibly creative at screening out people whose company we'd rather not keep. We can give a multitude of reasons that sound like common sense but have nothing to do with anything pertinent to the job at hand. People receive positive feedback about themselves from others who are most like them. That is why "birds of a feather flock together." We can try to be fair with a vengeance, but if we don't thoroughly understand how much it is a part of our nature to surround ourselves with people who are similar to us, then we have little hope of being fair to those who are different.

Social Ideology and Personal Reality

A disquieting, yet potentially liberating, effect of higher learning is to realize just how little we know. Knowledge makes us conscious of our ignorance; what remains to be learned looms larger than ever. As we've seen, science continually offers evidence that reality is a constructual experience based in part upon biological predispositions. In other words, as we grow, we build internal models of reality with such care that the models we construct act as templates, allowing us to form opinions without our awareness, or fooling us into concluding we have open minds.

For example, during the American Civil War soldiers on both sides thought they were fighting for the principles of freedom. Their preoccupations set the boundaries for their versions of reality. The same is true for us. I am not suggesting that a factual version of reality does not exist outside our individual experience (although I have doubts), but rather that the versions we regard as real, no matter how we've constructed them, permeate our lives and our thinking. In his book *Voluntary Simplicity*, Duane Elgin put it very elegantly, "We live almost completely immersed in a socially constructed reality that so fully absorbs our energy and attention that virtually none remains to experience the wonder of our existence."[11]

The knowledge that reality is a constructual process should render us highly suspicious, since we tend to shade conditions to our advantage, add a twist of cultural bias, and thereafter call it common sense. Similarly, it is insufficient to study politics only where one system is examined relative to another. In order to remain objective, we must continually contemplate what kind of a system we would want if there were no government at all.

Life Beyond Symbols

Formal education is but one chapter in a person's learning life. If it is treated as the last chapter, something crucial is missing. I speak from my own experience. I was past 35 before I made a serious effort at self-education. It is especially disturbing to me today to realize that the period before my adventures with self-education was when I was most adamant and sure of the correctness of my opinions. In actuality, all I knew was borrowed opinion, most of which I had not reflected upon with any serious degree of critical thinking. I simply held these opinions because I thought they were the right thing—a living example of the old saying, "The fewer the facts, the stronger the opinion."

Based on my own observations, then, I believe many undereducated people try to compensate for their lack of knowledge by demonstrating their willingness to protect and defend the symbols we identify with and hold dear. A constitutional amendment to prevent people from desecrating the American flag is one case in point. Before I began a careful study of the principles upon which democracy is founded, I would have voted unhesitatingly for such an amendment, but, after serious study and reflection, I have come to see the issue in a completely different light. I now view the flag as a symbol that is merely a representation of ideas—ideas which, by the very nature of the Constitution, each of us is free to interpret on our own. Consider the Confederate flag. For many southerners it simply represents their home, but for others it is clearly a symbol of oppression. In short, I can't tell you how you should feel or act in regard to national symbols; you have the complete right of ownership of your own ideas. Even though I am offended by the burning of the flag, I believe, paradoxically, that it is the freedom to do so which is the source of a democracy's greatest strength.

To see what happens when critical thinking is deferred in favor of a national symbol, one need only review the Nazi propaganda films from World War II, in which thousands of troops marched about with banners emblazoned with the Nazi swastika—a symbol capable of producing loyalty among Hitler's followers. Imagine what would have happened to anyone who dared to burn one of Hitler's symbols. When a country's leaders can wave a symbol and get a dependable response—positive or negative—which serves as a substitute for thinking, I would argue that its citizens have been reduced to simple-mindedness. I don't mean to imply we shouldn't feel a strong sense of loyalty or a sense of pride when the American flag passes by, but its presence should never produce an emotional response that blinds us to the ideals and principles for which it stands. Otherwise we are again reduced to a posture where behaving is substituted for learning and thinking.

The propagandist becomes the matador, secure in the knowledge that, if needed, flag-waving will produce rage and the masses will charge on cue. Loyalty, emotion, song, and symbol can coalesce into one convention of all-encompassing reality, so strongly felt it is almost indestructible—a hold so binding that it is not diminished but reinforced by the spilling of blood. When legislators call for punishment for those who burn the flag, in essence they are calling for obedience without discussion. The strength of the U.S. Constitution is born of the principle in the First Amendment which affirms that ideas are a higher value than social convention. Thus, freedom of thought makes each of us the owner of our ideas; no one can force us to hold someone else's views at a higher value than our own.

Symbols, rites, and rituals provide psychological structure for cultures to build on. Psychologist Carl Jung held that symbols mirror our unconscious and are profoundly important to our mental health. Certainly, ritual understood honors tradition, but ritual reduced to behavioral response honors no one. If it predisposes people to blind obedience, ritual becomes deadly. Caring about symbols is not nearly as important as seeing through them. Earlier periods of civilization (e.g., the Middle Ages) during which symbols were held in the greatest esteem, in fact, were some of the most repressive times in our history.

Educator Neil Postman laments "the great symbol drain," as our national symbols lose their power to provide meaning.[12] To me, however, the symbols are at least partly to blame for our current state of incoherence because they substitute for substance. We are awash in and are consumers of a never-ending barrage of symbols which move us further and further into abstraction, disembodying us from our own physical awareness. Symbols and icons repress reflection. We need to equilibrate thoughtful action with the emotion-laden. Reflection stimulates participation, which gives ownership to meaning instead of simply calling for acts of obedience. Compare a "search for meaning" with "living a meaningful life." Both require the authority of one's culture, but the latter requires participation. Without participation, tangible meaning is never realized. Indeed, postmodernism is itself an oppressive, forceful collision of symbols, images, and icons in an electronic blip culture with an unbelievable amount of trivia and silliness thrown in.

Money is one of our most venerated symbols. Money itself is not real, but our faith in it is. The designer labels and status symbols that delineate the path toward kingship of the mountain have no value except the value we assign them. If we regard ourselves as less than successful because these representations of value are not within our reach, it is because we have deemed it so. The effects of symbols on our thinking emerge when we perceive the workings of the economy. For example, today we talk about spending or consuming our way out of recessions, even though we are already dominated by our material goods. There is something diabolical and disingenuous about arguing that the government spends too much while at the same time promoting a cultural imperative that individuals should spend their way out of a recession. What would be the result if, instead, we made a more personal investment in our economy by substantially adding to our knowledge through our own learning? Genuine knowledge can save individuals a fortune from the services of doctors, lawyers, and a multitude of technicians. Knowledge of self-worth can enable individuals to resist the need for hundreds of seductive, but utterly useless products. Through such learning we can increase the quality of our public and private decisions.

The economy is, in large part, an act of faith. When faith is lost, our symbols of wealth lose their meaning; the economy collapses, and the money vanishes. Where does it go? And why is it so hard to get back? Social economies require faith in their systems to exist, but when they depend too much on faith and substitute faith for knowledge (by letting money do the thinking), a state of dependence grows exponentially. It is easy to lose faith in your economy, but you do not lose knowledge unless you simply fail to add to it.

When nourished, the desire to know is more powerful than belief. When we bring genuine interest to any subject, we are capable of finding meaning without cue cards. Culture then becomes a guide and not a palace guard; we provide our own symbols of meaning whenever and wherever they are needed. The symbols waved before us by advertisers and politicians are intended to move us toward extrinsic ends which seldom have our own interests at heart. The symbols which we co-create through meaningful experience with family and friends provide us with intrinsic meaning to be used for our own ends.

Quality of Life through Self-Restraint

Quality of life in a democracy depends directly upon the quality of that democracy's decisions, which depends, in turn, upon the quality of education of its citizens. A close look at American history reveals a continual struggle, both religious and secular, which champions the importance of "simple living and high thinking" as opposed to unrestrained material success.[13] This contention amounts to a battle of principle versus technique because, even though we desire that money represent a universal standard for making decisions, it falls short. Thus, if technique is treated as superior to principle, it means that appetite is more important than intellect. Simply stated, it means that lizards rule.

The Puritan ethic and its idea of virtue came to be regarded as repressive, not because abstinence and self-restraint were wrong, but because the precepts were not arrived at by deliberative individuals. The motivation for virtuous behavior became a pose because its external thrust took on the characteristics of a possession. These attributes became a way of having instead of a way of being for its own sake. Victorianism turned artificial when having became more important than being. For most people the rules of behavior were formulas prescribed by authority. Thus, today, it is ironic to see intrinsically self-educated individuals arrive *en masse* at the conclusion that simple living and high thinking are the pinnacle of human existence (as the Puritans and Pirsig's model would bear out), while the poor and uneducated, who are forced into simple living without the craving for high thinking, view themselves as prisoners of circumstance. Until they cross the fence, they will always think the grass on the other side is greener. But when the impetus of an individual's posture changes from authority to inquiry, repressiveness is replaced with enthusiasm, and obedience gives way to understanding.

I grew up with scorn for the notion of self-denial (witness the uptight '50s), failing to understand the nature of control it affords. I have always believed that Karl Marx's theory of economic value is an error of epic proportions, but surely it is also an error to design a system for geometric progression of massive consumption, dependent on an ever-increasing bubble of debt and based upon our environment's destruction. At the very heart of capitalism lies a malignancy most of us take for granted as the bed-rock of economic reality: the idea that economic principle produces interest. This notion suggests that value produces value, as a perpetual motion machine produces energy—an assessment of value that denies entropy.

We laugh at the inventor who proposes to produce something from nothing, but we swear at the banker who fails to pay us "interest." Our economic system of interest is inexorably bound to denial that our growing population is a problem. Indeed, buried in the psychology of interest lie the reasons we are eating away at the principle of our planet. The notion that principle automatically bears interest has not only created the exponential growth of a privileged class, which lives off an increasingly larger share of a pie it does not help create, but it also is the greatest worldly manifestation of getting something for nothing. Thus, we humans reproduce without regard to the consequences. Doctors and nurses minister care, farmers grow food, mechanics make repairs, teachers teach, carpenters build, janitors clean, cooks cook, engineers design, laborors toil, painters paint, and sales people sell, but money grows without doing *any* of these things. It's an emperor without clothes enigma, the missing piece in the puzzle of equality. We don't call the rich man lazy who sits on his capital and earns interest. Why not? Isn't a working poor person more industrious that an idle rich one? If not, why not?

Abraham Lincoln observed that "labor is prior to, and independent of capital. Capital is only the fruit of labor, and could never have existed if labor had not first existed. Labor is the superior of capital, and deserves much the higher consideration."[14] But we give labor little consideration at all when compared with monied interests. The interest-bearing capacity of capital is the residue of the power of monarchs, feudal lords, and slave masters couched in more a more egalitarian arrangement: anyone who accumulates enough money can have such power. Why do we allow an advantage to remain an advantage with no other added value other than the fact that it is an advantage? A stack of wood doesn't grow lumber, why should a heap of money do so? Answering these questions depends, in part, on understanding how we have been conditioned to perceive value.

Suppose the thirty pieces of silver (worth about two ounces of gold) Judas received for the betrayal of Jesus had been placed in a perpetually stable bank for the past two thousand years at five percent compounded interest. If this deposit were to be divided among all of the people on earth today, how much would each person receive? One hundred dollars? One thousand? Ten thousand? More? The answer, based upon the round number of five billion citizens is, that each would receive 160,000 earth-masses of solid gold.[15] Seeing this issue clearly requires learning to differentiate between wants versus genuine needs.

Capitalism without interest loses its "-ism," but it demands principle defined as awareness and demonstrated as responsibility. Capitalism without interest pulls the big rocks out from under a king-of-the-mountain economy. If one's capital does not earn interest, then one's actions are required to stand for what one's capital once did. That is what responsibility is about.

Self-restraint is the throttle of self-control. The wisdom and virtue of self-denial and self-restraint, and all the freedom and control they represent, are fully demonstrable in the ability to truly understand one's own needs, to be oblivious to "manufactured needs," and to put off the purchase of nonessential material goods until one has the money to pay for them or, better still, to forgo their acquisition altogether. As affection for ideas increases, the value of material goods diminishes. Equity at the bottom of the mountain restrains the power of those at the top. Those whom we celebrate as having been the greatest prophets are the ones who managed their own needs so well that the power it afforded them was startling. By economic standards we Americans lead rich lives, but we cannot with any confidence argue that we lead the most meaningful lives. Chasing fleeting material rewards, measuring our success by over-consumption may at some time in a future history qualify us as having been some of the biggest fools the world has ever known. Travelers from space, on an archaeological dig far in the future, may someday regard the humans of earth as having had the crazy notion that value held in place by faith could increase everlastingly while at the same time growing numbers of their kind were alienated from any such value. Perhaps, they would be even more puzzled at how the idea of conservatism could become associated with an ideology as change-driven as capitalism.

If we could change from a culture of acquisitiveness to one of inquisitiveness, we would realize that even those who view themselves as being poor by the old standards have great wealth of a different sort. Socrates was not much better off than a street person, but he was rich in quality of experience. Look at it this way: the idea that one is poor is itself partially the result of a lack of ideas.

The Los Angeles riots set off by the not-guilty verdict for the police officers accused of beating Rodney King in 1992 showed us the frightening power of an angry mob. Imagine the impact if the poor from America's slums and ghettos suddenly took to the streets, crying out in search of knowledge and wisdom. For those who hold the reins of power, it would be one of the most psychologically and politically threatening events that has ever occurred. Steven Goldberg writes, "The most lovable thing about truth is that it is true. But a close second is that it is subversive; no authority system, and certainly no political administration, loves truth for its own sake, because truth by its nature fails to ratify the values that give an authority system power."[16] H. L. Mencken makes the point specific to education:

> Education in the true sense—education directed toward awakening a capacity to differentiate between fact and appearance—is and always will be a more or less furtive and illicit thing, for its chief purpose is the controversion and destruction of the very ideas that the majority of men—and particularly the majority of official and powerful men—regard as incontrovertibly true. To the extent that I am genuinely educated, I am suspicious of all the things the average citizen believes and the average pedagogue teaches. Progress consists precisely in attacking and disposing of these ordinary beliefs. It is thus opposed to education, as the thing is usually understood, and so there should be no surprise in the fact that the generality of pedagogues, like the generality of politicians and super politicians, are bitter enemies to all new ideas.[17]

Similar reasoning reveals that the use of drugs threatens our society, not so much because of the crime, violence, and deaths that accompany it, but more because drug users openly and blatantly reject or cannot cope with our commonly held views of reality.[18] Drug users and homosexuals defy traditional authority because they defy the reality of people who are uncomfortable with the idea that there might be more than one version of reality.[19] We can stop the drug war tomorrow by legalizing drugs (but not marketing them), thus saving billions of dollars and an enormous human toll of suffering exacted by both victims and criminals. The reason we don't has much more to do with our view of social reality than it does with saving lives. In her book *Fear of Falling*, Barbara Ehrenreich says:

> The indiscriminate hysteria over drugs reflects that old anxiety at the heart of the middle class: *the fear of falling*, of losing control, of growing soft. "Drugs," as an undifferentiated category, symbolize the larger and thoroughly legal consumer culture, with its addictive appeal and harsh consequences for those who cannot keep up or default on their debts. It has become a cliche to say that this is an "addictive society," but the addiction most of us have most to fear is not promoted by a street-corner dealer. The entire market, the expanding spectacle of consumer possibilities, has us in its grip, and because that is too large and nameless, we turn our outrage toward something that is both less powerful and more concrete.[20] [Italics mine.]

The fear is that our view of reality may further hemorrhage. The powerful might lose some of their authority, and we might have to face our worst fears, which would involve raising the veil of postmodern reality and seeing ourselves as we are. Milton Friedman writes, "The case for prohibiting drugs is exactly as strong and as weak as the case for prohibiting people from over-eating. We all know that overeating causes more deaths than drugs do."[21] Why the fuss then? Thomas S. Szasz, quoted earlier as saying independence is the only political sin, provides a Libertarian answer:

> Why is self-control, autonomy, such a threat to authority? Because the person who controls himself, who is his own master, has no need for an authority to be his master. This, then, renders authority unemployed. What is he to do if he cannot control others? To be sure, he could mind his own business. But this is a fatuous answer, for those who are satisfied to mind their own business do not aspire to become authorities. In short, authority needs subjects, persons not in command of themselves—just as parents need children and physicians need patients.[22]

What better example of placing social convention on a higher level than the intellectual plane of living? It has taken many years for me to reach this conclusion about drugs, and I write as a former police officer. I have never in my life used illicit drugs, but I have jailed many people who did, so it is with a great deal of careful reflection that I now construe American drug policy as being far more destructive than the drugs themselves.

If we are ever to resolve this issue, the idea of individual responsibility must prevail over those whose positions in life depend upon their capacity to moralize. It is fortunate that as human beings we are hard-wired to reap more from ideas than from consumer goods. Not only would it be easier to adopt a lower impact on the tangible environment through the elevation of intangible ideas, it would also be an intrinsically enjoyable thing to do.

Intellect Is Higher Than Culture

It is conditionally true that we satisfy our base needs before we reach the level from which we are able to make the most of our personal contributions to our culture. Yes, a few acorns always seem to fall from the oak and find the right depth, just as those whom we celebrate for making a genuine contribution to our society (not the celebrities, but the real heroes who give us Dynamic Quality) also find the right conditions for their own development. The greatest gift a culture can bestow, however, is to prepare all its members to access and assimilate knowledge. Basic human needs must be satisfied as an elemental feature of association, but if a culture's need for knowledge is stifled, the culture itself starves. Culture should be a support, not a straightjacket. If basic human needs are unmet, then fundamental human talents remain undiscovered.

Karl Marx, Friedrich Engels, and Charles Dickens were right to call attention to society's deplorable conditions of poverty, but I think their proposed solutions to the problem put emphasis in the wrong place. What we do not so easily realize is that focusing on eliminating poverty through the redistribution of wealth (by doling out just enough money or opportunity to sustain life, as we have done with the working poor) amounts to little more than seeing that all acorns reach the ground.[23] Contrast this with purposely planting all the acorns at the right depth and adding the right amount of water and sunlight.

For humans this kind of purposeful treatment would be equivalent to a genuine intrinsic-based education. No more pre-packaged formulas to indoctrinate students, rank them, and prepare them for the workplace (sort of an inept form of educational Darwinism). Instead, a more effective educational approach would treat each student as an individual (an end) whose personal development was as important an agenda as could be found.[24] The major objective would be an intrinsic education for each student as if no other student existed.

We need a system totally dedicated to truth, intent on replacing the empty container philosophy of education with the goal of enabling students—each working at his or her own pace—to fill their intellectual cups to capacity. We need a strategy to help students discover and develop their own natural talents. Let them follow their own curiosity as far and wide in any direction as they are able to go, and damn any bureaucracy that dares to get in the way. We need to act as if each student is a Plato, and our task is to produce the environmental equivalent of a Socrates. All children need to be treated as if they are gifted. Knowledge as its own reward has been suffocated by a thymotic notion of measuring achievement. Students seek not knowledge, but societal approval through good grades. Success in school takes precedence over learning itself. Remove the negative judgment that binds a student's "observable measurable progress" to feelings of self-worth, and the attitude of the student toward education will change radically.

In light of the turmoil in the American educational system, this approach may seem incredibly naïve. Nevertheless, the change from an extrinsic to an intrinsic core curriculum (not a "feel good" course, but a genuine "Outward Bound" for the mind) is so radical a change that it would no longer assure social stratification, an achievement that a national testing system guarantees. Teaching "to the test" is the embodiment of technique.[25] Teaching for genuine learning is the embodiment of principle. It's the way we learn to be animated participants in our own lives. Benjamin R. Barber may be right when he says, "Education is unlikely ever to win an 'open market' competition with entertainment because 'easy' and 'hard' can never compete on equal ground, and for those not yet disciplined in the rites of learning, 'freedom' will always mean easy."[26] But once students of any age reach a genuine level of expertise, their internal motivation assumes mastery. For example, when one masters the art of reading, reading becomes its own reward.

Another immediate objection to this line of reasoning is, don't we really need to educate people with specific skills in mind so that they can perform specific jobs? My precise point is that intrinsically educated individuals would decide to do different things than we are doing. They would understand the value difference between *jobs* and *work*. In a king-of-the-mountain society the real value of community service appears to have little value in actual practice because it has no economic or hierarchical value. The kind of education system I have in mind might not produce specific answers to specific problems, but the process would produce individuals who would think, hear, and see through their own senses instead of thinking, hearing, and seeing as popular culture dictates.

Public education is supposed to be the vehicle that promotes equality, but in its present form it does precisely the opposite. James Fallows said it best, "Whatever damage today's welfare system may do to the work ethic, today's urban public schools do more grievous harm. Education has a greater importance than ever; bad schools mean that children not only have no second chance in life but have no chance at all."[27] Many of our public schools have shockingly low standards.

A low-level economic existence sustains biological life, but little more: people need ideas even more than they need cash. Moreover, once we are raised to the intellectual realm, sensible self-interest should make us intuitively aware of how important it is to protect the biological patterns of our existence. Focusing so forcefully on the education of the individual is not antithetical to community as critics argue. It has the opposite effect: fully developed individuals offer communities vitality.

Had Marx and Engels, and all who followed with similar interests, focused more on reform in education, I seriously doubt that the idea of Communism would ever have existed.[28] Marx made the same mistake that the Libertarians and Objectivists (the philosophy of Ayn Rand) made later, which was to ignore the importance of human behavior. To Marx, sociology and economics were the same phenomenon. He didn't focus on education. He expected that economics would solve all social problems (which is really a claim that social patterns are higher than intellectual patterns). Marx used Hegel's dialectical view of history to postulate that civilization had begun with primitive (communistic) tribes and had proceeded through slavery, feudalism, and capitalism to inevitably result in a sophisticated form of true Communism. This progression is most easily observed as a continual transfer of authority from shamans, tribal chiefs, monarchs, religious leaders, nobility, slave owners, and tyrants to captains of industry. Now, you could certainly make the case that "American democracy" has usurped arbitrary authority, but on closer examination, you would find it does so only marginally.

The lesson here is profound but simple: ideas empower citizens more quickly than do growing economies. People who are intellectually empowered improve commerce, but they also know the difference between real work and jobs. They know how to distinguish wants from needs. And they expect to share power. Marx argued, "It is not the consciousness of human beings which determines their being. But on the contrary, their social being which determines their consciousness."[29] To some degree this may be so, but as Pirsig has pointed out, intellectual patterns still drive social patterns (via static-latching), making education profoundly more important than Marx and Engels allowed. Two thousand years ago, Epictetus warned that "we should...believe the philosophers, who say that the educated only are free." He would know—he was a slave who later became a teacher.[30]

Morality and the Human Family

Perhaps, if it were not for our experience with traditional education's focus on weakness, we would more readily value the strengths of others. The way we become whole, Jung suggested, is through expanded awareness. We become whole human beings through understanding that, even though each of us is different in terms of our temperament, personality, and talents, we all contain the potential for wholeness through better appreciating the strengths of others in areas where we fall short. By sounding all human attributes as a common chord, all people can be acknowledged as having value.

We are but small beings on a ball of organic matter accelerating through space at an unimaginable speed. There is precious little time to hate and kill our fellow human beings over matters that will seem trivial to those who follow us. What would Confucius, Lao Tzu, Muhammed, Jesus, or the Buddha have said about giving priority to GNP over poverty, or to starvation over the state of the global environment? What the prophets shared in common (at least as they are celebrated) was that they cut through culture to the bone of existence; they defined the other side of the mountain. This is what we all must do to gain a genuine sense of our interconnectedess with life on this planet. The Quaker idea that the family of human beings should be thought of as the children of one father may be the only way to reconcile the human race with a sustainable future. Were it not for the ethnocentric buffering effects of our respective cultures, we would know this intuitively.

We cannot find our meaningful place on the other side of our metaphorical mountain, nor can we build newer, higher ranges of cultural mountains, without the illumination of exploration. If the nature of the universe is hierarchical ontologically, as theologians suggest, or metaphysically, as Pirsig suggests, if both or either are true, then we each share the attributes of a hierarchical mountain range of knowledge and experience within ourselves. In a metaphorical sense, "the Kingdom of God is within us." And if this is so, perhaps we should spell *Conscience* with a capital C. Conscience is, after all, the essence of the inner-self and the social-self. Moreover, we must act as if this is true, even if—and especially if—cognitive scientists are right who claim that consciousness is only a useful illusion or hallucination.[31]

German philosopher Martin Heidegger (1889-1984) used the term *Dasein* to capture attentiveness at the highest level of Conscience. Heidegger was attempting to cut to the quick of the question of Being. Dasein is the ultimate expression of being—a level of awareness in which one utilizes one's senses to be and to see without regard for custom or tradition. Dasein represents the cosmic core of existence, the precise juncture of being where the concept of wholeness and interconnectedness becomes manifest. Dasein represents being as a verb.[32] It literally means *being there*. Western culture overshadows this level of existence. To Heidegger, Dasein is an avenue of understanding and social awareness. Dasein is an element of conscience. He explains it this way in *Being and Time*:

> In understanding as an existential, the thing we are to do is not a what, but being as existing. The mode of being of Dasein as a potentiality of being lies existentially in understanding. Dasein is not something objectively present which then has as an addition the ability to do something, but is rather primarily being-possible. Dasein is always what it can be and how it is its possibility. The essential possibility of Dasein concerns the ways of taking care of the 'world'...of *concern for others* and, always already present in all of this, the potentiality of being itself, for its own sake. [33] [Italics mine.]

The concept of understanding as an existential is a slippery one. It's another way of saying that understanding is so deeply rooted in the essence of human beings that it amounts to a bootstrap dynamic at the core of human existence. Simply put: the hole in a doughnut amounts to nothing, but without it the doughnut ceases to exist. Understanding is to humanity as a hole is to a doughnut, although the gist of the connection is bound together at a level below everyday consciousness. Consciousness, probed in depth, gives rise to Conscience, a genuine concern for others. Thus, understanding becomes the marrow of embodiment, the biological-sociological-intellectual adhesive which holds the human race together.

Only in the worst of times do we even acknowledge that a human conscience derived from emotional intelligence is superior to human culture (i.e., that the intellectual plane is higher than the social plane). It often takes something as unlikely as the war criminal to show us what responsible Conscience is supposed to look like: that we do in fact hold ourselves accountable for our actions regardless of who orders us to act wrongfully for any reason. The core of Conscience is not a repository to store guilt; the essence of Conscience is to "know," to crash the cultural barriers of perception, to see for oneself what must or must not be done, not because it is good or bad, but because it is or is not the right thing to do.

Central to such a view of Conscience is the long-waged, weary battle of Eastern versus Western philosophy in which "being" itself is contrasted with "knowing"—the East having placed a greater value on the former, and the West on the latter. As I see it, both views are too narrow. The two states are really one: the individual cannot *be* without a sense of *knowing*. Much of what we call knowledge is really the residue of culture, and it must be let go before we can *be* and *know*.

To achieve Dasein one must pay the price of understanding. And paying such a price requires a sense of heightened awareness: a *being here*. That we have a sense of not actually *being* in the present can be revealed in stories about time travel. They give us a glimpse of times past when we did not fully appreciate the quality of experience which was available to us. Having a chance to visit with deceased friends or relatives would demonstrate this beyond question. What would we say? What would we do differently, if there were one more chance to visit? How much time would pass before the perceived quality of the experience gave way to ordinary memory? How long before memories of this special visit would be like any other?

Immanuel Kant held us accountable for creating social values and not simply bowing down before them. The meaning we get corresponds to the meaning we give, and the same applies to morals. Kant's categorical imperative makes this point precisely: "Act only according to that maxim by which you can at the same time will that it should become a universal law."[34] In the *Critique of Practical Reason*, Kant writes, "Morality is not properly the doctrine of how we make ourselves happy, but how we may make ourselves worthy of happiness."[35] If the moral law does not exist within, then it does not exist anywhere, because legislated morality becomes reduced to rules, which are further reduced to technique.

Kant's critics accuse him of reasoning a prescription for moral behavior, as if there were no need for each and every one of us to do the same thing to our very best ability. Indeed, whether any of us believe in Kant's position or not, the United States of America is founded upon a premise very similar: that each of us will reason for ourselves.

Kant's categorical imperative is an abstract guide for moral behavior. A compass for a moral north, a Platonic Form, it will not work for paranoid-schizophrenics, homicidal maniacs, or anyone bent on being immoral, but then, nothing will. A compass is of no use near magnetic north, but works well almost everywhere else. Similarly Kant's categorical imperative may break down before a myriad of principled choices, but even then, it is still a better guide than most people use for making moral judgments, and it habitually points to an ethical north. Expecting a precise formula for making moral judgments misses the point. What counts is knowing one needs to exercise judgment in order to make up for one's normal human frailties.

So, what I propose is not an imperative or even a rule, but what should be thought of as a bookmark on the front page of awareness. Think of it as "Kant's Moral Reminder," which goes something like this:

> "Act only according to that maxim by which you can at the same time will that it should become a universal law *with full knowledge and awareness of the self-deceptive nature of human beings. Always consider that anyone affected by your actions may in good faith totally disagree with your notion of what should become universal law.* Think this prescription anew each and every time circumstances require that you make judgments about matters of morality."

In *The New Golden Rule*, Amitai Etzioni states it this way, "Respect and uphold society's moral order as you would have society respect and uphold your autonomy."[36]

Wonder vs. Boredom

When people accept religion solely on the basis of authority, arrogance substitutes for reflection. Whenever the genuine desire to know is subordinated to authority, it's as if that authority becomes the radius of one's awareness. Authority has the power to blind us to the exploration of truth; inquiry becomes subordinate to an enforced sense of limited awareness. Aldous Huxley once observed:

> Truth can be defined in many ways. But if you define it as understanding (and this is how all the masters of the spiritual life have defined it), then it is clear that "Truth must be lived and there is nothing to argue about in this teaching; any arguing is sure to go against the intent of it."[37]

Organized religions have, in the name of God (but really for the sake of their institutions and those who run them), effectively killed the spirit of genuine wonder associated with learning—a spirit that could place religion in partnership with science. Far too often organized religion becomes a euphemism for politically orchestrated illusion. Here's Huxley again:

> Professional moralists have confidence in the surface will, believe in punishments and rewards, and are adrenaline addicts who like nothing better than a good orgy of righteous indignation. The masters of the spiritual life have little faith in the surface will or the utility, for their particular purposes, of rewards or punishments, and do not indulge in righteous indignation. Experience has taught them that the highest good can never, in the very nature of things, be achieved by moralizing. "Judge not that ye be not judged" is their watchword and total awareness is their method.[38]

Social convention restricts our awareness. Natural wonder is subordinate to approved interests, and thus we become jaded. Our curiosity and sense of wonder are restrained; at an early age we lose our ability to see the miraculous in the common. Our culture bids that we get busy at tasks which may begin to seem superficial and unimportant as we near life's end. Thus we fail to understand that the unfolding of the inner world is discovered through an expanded awareness of the outer world. That's how we gain perspective. In his essay *Nature*, Emerson wrote:

> If the stars should appear one night in a thousand years, how would men believe and adore; and preserve for many generations the remembrance of the city of God which had

been shown! But every night come out these envoys of beauty, and light the universe with their admonishing smile.[39]

It is truly unfortunate that so many of us have become insulated from this admonishing smile. If science and religion were partners they would tell us that we are stellar beings: made of the same primordial carbon soup that we see in every evening sky. Indeed, were it not for centuries of superstition and contempt for human inquiry, we *might* be traveling freely among the stars today.

When faith is "an unreserved opening of the mind," as Alan Watts suggested, then matters of profound human importance can be called both religious and scientific because both are subordinate to the truth, regardless of where it is found.[40] When we, as ordinary people, begin to live our lives with such regard for truth, all of the cultural and hierarchical models in this text are turned upside down. Instead of moving upward through an ever-increasing bottleneck of socially approved dogma, we move from knowledge our culture can build on to healthy understanding of what it means to be a living human being. How dull life would be without some kind of adversity or challenge, and yet how easily we seem to give up and complain that life has treated us unfairly. Why do so many people go through life as if every act of living is drudgery? Why are there so many people who seem to have little to live for but who remain cheerful? Why isn't rising to do the work of a human being a sufficient calling?

In fairy tales, when a magic wand turns a piece of wood or a rock into a human, the new creature finds the opportunity for exploration completely wondrous. The whole world is a celebration of interest and awe. "Can anyone deny—unless they resort to some very special pleading—that human mental life seems to be simply too good to be true?"[41] "The pleasure of life is according to the man that lives it...Life is an ecstasy." [42] And yet, all too many of us sleepwalk through life. In the movie *Joe versus the Volcano*, actress Meg Ryan makes this point vividly when she explains, "My father says that almost the whole world is asleep. Everybody you know, everybody you see, everybody you talk to.

He says that only a few people are awake and they live in a state of constant, total amazement."

Similarly, in *Walden Pond*, Henry David Thoreau wrote:

The millions are awake enough for physical labor; but only one in a million is awake enough for effective intellectual exertion, only one in a hundred millions to a poetic or divine life. To be awake is to be alive. I have never yet met a man who was quite awake. How could I have Looked him in the face?

We must learn to rewaken and keep ourselves awake, not by mechanical aids, but by an infinite expectation of the dawn, which does not forsake us in our soundest sleep. I know of no more encouraging fact than the unquestionable ability of man to elevate his life by a conscious endeavor.[43]

We are not truly awake if we can't see through, above, and beyond our culture. For example, when we say something like, "Today doesn't seem like Sunday," what we're really saying is that our experience seems out of ritual order. But, you see, that's the whole problem—you can't truly *experience* until the concept of social order itself is bridged. No two Sundays are ever truly alike. Ever.

In the spring of 1992, scientists working on the Cosmic Background Exploration project (COBE) discovered cosmic clouds which may come close to being the very signature of creation. It may be one of the most significant cosmological discoveries of the century. University of California astrophysicist George Smoot, the project leader, said it was like seeing "the face of God."[44] Why, then, are so few of us amazed? Why is there so little excitement about the mysteries continuously revealed and examined by the Hubble telescope? How can we probe deep space, observing a universe earlier humans could not even imagine, and still be plagued with boredom in our schools? What is to become of a society whose time for reflection is overwhelmed by reruns?

Social convention increasingly smothers the spirit of wonder, but science and religion both should add to the human spirit of wonder. Science tells us how, and, even if religious inquiry cannot tell us why, we can still frame our questions to focus on what is really important in a religious sense. The scientific and religious nature of human beings should be wed in an eternal bliss of how's and why's.

Both money and religion can insulate us from reality; both can become excuses for not thinking. As Jacob Needleman explains, in his book *Money and the Meaning of Life,* "Authentic human existence requires the co-presence of two worlds, the inner and the outer. To exist in one alone is not to exist at all." Meaning, he says, is what we find in the middle where these two opposing forces meet.[45]

When we look again at our king-of-the-mountain economic model, Needleman seems correct when he claims, "Avarice is the process of being devoured by material needs and desires, and an individual can be just as avaricious about 'salvation' as about wealth or money."[46] If we really think this problem through, balancing the inner and outer forces is the triumph. To turn our backs on either force is a recipe for the diminishment of experience or responsibility. Needleman argues that "money is intrinsically a contradiction because man is intrinsically a contradiction."[47] He suggests we escape the thrall of money, not by turning our backs to it, but by taking it even more seriously that we do now, studying ourselves and our relationship with money until "the very act of self-study becomes as vivid and intense as the desires and fears we study."[48] He says that, when we do this, we will experience the "unbelievable contradiction" within ourselves through our conscience:

> When a man discovers something for himself, he truly understands it. Nothing can take it away from him. It means that he has discovered a part of himself—or, rather, he has been, as it were, "discovered" *by* a part *of* himself! And this was the whole entire meaning of the money question in modern life. Money enters so deeply into our personality and into our psychophysical organism that the personal exploration of money is necessary for the discovery of oneself, the discovery of those hidden parts of human nature that hold prisoner energies that need to be in relationship to our consciousness.[49]

People who have internalized economics as the standard of all standards view themselves as being very practical. They often claim to live in the real world, but it is real for them precisely because they have manufactured it. At times money has a great deal to do with value, and at other times it has nothing whatsoever to do with value. In a very real sense a liberal education is the process through which one learns definitively what money will and will not buy. It is the duty of adults to decide what role economics ought to play in the inner and outer realm of the real world, and it is a challenge and provocation to adults that, tangled up in this struggle, is the enigma of technique and principle. A liberal education may seem to be a paltry compensation in comparison with the acquisition of material riches, but the greatest power an individual can obtain is the power to define quality and success in one's own terms. A liberal education is no small ambition.

Early on the path of my own self-education I found my sense of reality was simply overwhelmed with conflicting information. The ability to process these conflicts came gradually and spontaneously. Once the walls of perceptual reality began to crumble, there was a domino effect, followed by a hesitancy, a not wanting to rebuild what might quickly be torn down, unable to stand up to further inquiry. This was followed once again by a period when I looked forward to challenging my newly constructed beliefs. Thus, through exploration, I developed a sense of security in the knowledge that the world does not end when one's sense of reality is shattered. On the contrary, this feeling of confidence gets better. The thrill of understanding replaces the fear of the unknown. Sadly, this stimulation and sense of enjoyment remain distant and unknown to those who cannot break the painful barrier of uncertainty.

Throughout my life, I believe I have met at least as many people who were suffering from boredom as were genuinely interested in what they were doing. Boredom is a sort of metaphysical time-out. In an essay titled "Studies in Pessimism," Arthur Schopenhauer wrote:

No little part of the torment of existence lies in this, that Time is continually pressing upon us, never letting us take breath, but always coming after us, like a taskmaster with a whip. If at any moment Time stays his hand, it is only when we are delivered over to the misery of boredom.[50]

Countless times I've heard the familiar refrain, "I just don't know what to do with myself when I'm not working," only to find out that the person who said it, actually performs boring work. Boredom is something you don't cure by distraction, you either deal with it head-on, or live with it. It's that simple and that profound.

I remember boredom. I know what it's like to live without the thrill of understanding. I remember what it was like to live on borrowed opinion, to mistrust people of different cultures for reasons that were accepted as common sense but in reality were bathed deeply in ignorance and arrogance. And I remember what it was like to have so internalized the economic ethos of capitalism that I thought every human problem had an economic answer. Little more than a decade ago I would have been one of Rush Limbaugh's "ditto heads," letting popular opinion substitute for my own thinking.[51] Today my views are decidedly different. I believe it is of critical importance to understand how the worldview one holds can change through the process of one's own inquiry.

Temporary amusements won't lead us to the source of our discontent. But boredom itself may be the very place to begin to develop self-knowledge, to find out how our large brain has become muted and stupefied, even as science tells us that the brain is capable of rewarding itself with opiates so powerful that external possession of them would lead to arrest.[52] It seems to me the greatest open secret in the history of education has to be that we can solve the problems of humankind (including the drug problem) by triggering the natural drugs we carry in our own bodies and produce naturally with the right stimulation. You have only to experience the thrill of understanding to know how powerful they are.

Eternal Return: Wanting To Be the Person You Are

There is an ancient idea that provides a profound lesson for living a purposeful life today. Nietzsche, who may deserve being called the "Van Gogh of thought," was thunderstruck with the

Stoic idea of *Eternal Reoccurrence* (the idea that everything that happens will reoccur for eternity exactly as it happened the first time).[53] As bizarre as it sounds today, Nietzsche thought eternal reoccurrence was the most scientific idea (in a metaphoric sense) ever conceived. (But surely it is no more bizarre than the notion that only a select few humans will be resurrected from the dead because of a shared idea, then biologically reassemble and live forever in a Disneyland-like eternity.) Nietzsche asks each of us this question:

How, if some day or night a demon were to sneak after you into your loneliest loneliness and say to you, This life as you now live it and have lived it, you will have to live once more and innumerable times more; and there will be nothing new in it, but every pain and every joy and every thought and sigh and everything immeasurably small or great in your life must return to you—all in the same succession and se-quence—even this spider and this moonlight between the trees, and even this moment and I myself. The eternal hour-glass of existence is turned over and over, and you with it, a dust grain of dust. Would you not throw yourself down and gnash your teeth and curse the demon who spoke thus? Or did you once experience a tremendous moment when you would have answered him, You are a god, and never have I heard anything more godly.[54]

No better example exists to show what is meant by rising to the occasion of one's culture through the creation of a better cul-ture by going beyond the American Dream: creating a life wor-thy of emulation, a life with enough meaning so that one would want to live that life over again for all of eternity.

In the movie *Groundhog Day*, actor Bill Murray plays the part of a sullen, mediocre weatherman locked into Nietzsche's pre-dicament by having to live Groundhog Day over and over again, except that he has the power to change the details of each day. At first he uses his freedom to indulge his every whim; then he re-sorts to technique using manipulation to get what he wants. Fi-nally, out of a sense of boredom, which evolves into a growing spirit of wisdom, he begins to act upon principle and creates a life that is genuinely worthy of living over again. In short, he begins to act as if *good* were a noun.

Life's greatest tragedy, to paraphrase George Bernard Shaw, is to live your life for the selfish reasons of others which you determine ultimately to be base. [55] Each of us has a record of eternal return inside our heads. We call it memory. And a better life through the principle of active awareness leads us to better memories. Principle and Dasein are related. Authenticity amounts to a lucid awareness of one's predicament and the ability to see beyond the forces that influence your everyday behavior. There may be may be no greater measure of meaning in a religious sense, than to completely desire to be the person you already are.[56] This is only possible when you know and *understand* who that person is.

Chapter Nine

Self-Reliance in a Postmodern World

We think our civilization near its meridian, but we are yet only at the cock-crowing and the morning star. In our barbarous society the influence of character is in its infancy.[1]

—Ralph Waldo Emerson

Thoreau's words, "Dreams are the touchstones of our character," bring us to a fresh appreciation of the notion of responsibility. Thoreau's mentor, Ralph Waldo Emerson, authored the famous nineteenth-century essay *Self-Reliance*, which for many people became the nucleus of the sentiment of self-reliance in his day and in ours. (For a reality check, however, Nel Noddings of Stanford University has pointed out that when Emerson wrote *Self-Reliance*, he was, in fact, waited on hand and foot by his wife.) Emerson's philosophy lies at the very heart of American individualism, but the self-evident connection has been lost. He would never have settled for what in these times we call the American Dream.

Today individualism is increasingly associated with antisocial conduct—an all-out getting ahead at the expense of others. Sociologist Charles Derber characterizes this behavior as wilding. "Wilding is individualism run amok."[2] Indeed, wilding is a virulent strain of bottom-level mountain fever, a disease among those who don't seem to matter unless they can prove otherwise through sheer terror. But wilding and mountain fever are not examples of Emersonian individualism.[3] At the core of Emerson's concept of self-reliance is the notion that learning and the cultivation of one's intellect are crucial for achieving a responsible

271

level of citizenship, where each of us is accountable for the development and use of our own conscience. To Emerson, individualism was expanded awareness, and a way of standing up to authority through his own willingness to accept responsibility for himself and the society he lived in. He argued against injustice all of his life and he spoke out about the disgrace of slavery long before it was a popular thing to do. Representing the best thinking of the Victorian era, Emerson's ideas about self-reliance embodied the principle of compassion as understanding, as a form of expanded awareness, achievable through the willingness to embrace a life of learning. His definition of compassion included responsibility.

Most all of the improved living conditions which earlier generations of America dreamed about have come into being. Yet America's inner cities foster a savagery which makes the early Western frontier seem tame by comparison. (Indeed, media increasingly use words such as "feral" to refer, not to animals, but to inner-city adolescents; juvenile authorities speak of a new breed of young males whom they describe as "super predators.")[4] Today women and minorities can vote and hold public office, and yet voter turn-out is embarrassingly low. Black men are no longer lynched by white mobs, yet their chances of being murdered at the hands of other black men are unbelievably high. Black children are no longer thought to be returns on investment, but are thought by many to be an overly indulged expense, some say the greatest single problem America faces. And, where it was once a crime to live by oneself, millions of Americans now live alone and die in obscurity.

Americans spend $5 billion a year on pizza, and ten to twenty times that for beer to wash it down, $30 billion a year to lose weight, $700 billion in tax compliance, and $350 billion advertising products that most would be better off without. Twenty percent of the food we produce in America is wasted or thrown away. This should come as no surprise, though, since conspicuous consumption is how we measure our success. It's not enough that we consume; our waste must be obvious and wanton. Not surprising, too, is the fact that child abuse is the leading cause of death for children under the age of four, and that domestic violence is the leading cause of injury for women. Nor should it amaze us that, in an effort to display worthiness in a society which judges worth by one's material possessions, Americans have incurred more than one trillion dollars in personal debt. None of this resembles Emersonian individualism.

Emerson believed that positive change depended upon individuals, not institutions, and that personal responsibility is the cornerstone of character. Victorians readily welcomed this ethos. Conservatives are right to lament the best of this bygone legacy. The Victorians may have been guilty of living a pose, as is true in any culture including ours, but substance lay beneath their façade. Their sense of responsibility was not a pose—it was heartfelt and it went deep enough to include a general concern for posterity. The way they lived their lives has much to teach us about the sentiment of responsibility.

My grandfather was a Victorian. Born in 1889, he reached the age of 21 just as the era ended. But he would exemplify Victorian values until his death in 1981, at the age of 92. He was strait-laced, as they used to say, honest to a fault. He took pride in everything he did, from drilling oil wells to building his grandson a wooden sled. His core philosophy of life was inexorably bound to his sense of personal responsibility. He had clear ideas about right and wrong. He paid his bills on time and in person. He never bought anything on credit until he was over 80, and only then at his children's insistence so as to establish credit—something he thought he didn't need, and in fact he didn't. His generation of Americans made their share of mistakes, but they were as solid a group of citizens as have ever lived in this country.

My grandfather's service in World War I was to him a badge of honor, so much so that he insisted upon medical treatment in veterans hospitals. The most anger and embarrassment that I have ever felt as an American was when I accompanied him on a trip to a V.A. hospital. After sitting in a waiting room for several hours with a group of very old veterans, I discovered that the sole reason these men were kept waiting was a clerk, on the phone with personal matters, who had not taken the time to rubber-stamp their medical forms. It appears to me in retrospect that if this clerk and the rest of the inattentive hospital staff had been cognizant of the history of these old men's contribution during the war, and had they been in better touch with their own emotions, they would have utilized Adam Smith's brand of sympathy as a principle concern in performing their jobs. Would a Victorian hospital clerk near the turn of the last century have let old Civil War veterans sit for hours while attending to personal business? In the rarest of circumstances, possibly, but I don't think so.

We're still capable of sharing Adam Smith's concern when it comes to a sick child in the media spotlight needing a transplant. And Peter Drucker's Third Sector is clear evidence that we still maintain an interest-bearing concern for others. What we lack is the thinking necessary to bridge our social patterns with our intellectual efforts—to put the full weight of our concern into our own communities and the world at large. During World War I, Mary Parker Follett saw very clearly an emerging global reality in which emotional intelligence would become the responsibility both of nations and of individuals:

> Sympathy is a whole feeling; it is a recognition of oneness....Sympathy is not pity, it is not benevolence, it is one of the goals of the future, it cannot be actualized until we can think and feel together. At present we confuse it with altruism...but sympathy is always a group product...Kant's categorical imperative is empty; it is only a blank check. But through the life of the group we learn the content of the universal law.[5]

My characterization of sympathy is not a plea for bleeding-heart activism any more than Follett's is an endorsement of socialism. It's simply a call for an emotionally intelligent, well-reasoned acknowledgment that *all* human beings have the right to a level of equity which supports their very existence. This doesn't sound like much, but it's light-years away from the reality of our ethnocentric world. There is a great difference between granting others the right to exist and deciding what's best for others for their own good. Moreover, granting others the right to exist, by acknowledging their need to take appropriate measures to ensure their own survival, is an enormous step in leveling the field among factions because it makes everyone a legitimate player. When we can relate to others at a level of common experience, sympathy creates the dynamic which gives rise to community and provides meaning to the concept of morality.

Accepting Responsibility

Accepting responsibility involves the profound realization that 260 million-plus Americans making rugged individual decisions en masse may ultimately result in irrational behavior. For example, if everyone continues making the rational decision to drive to work, soon no one will be able to do so. Even if there is enough fuel, there won't be enough traffic lanes to handle all of the vehicles. Moving beyond the American Dream requires us to acknowledge that the twenty-first century will see biological, social, and intellectual patterns forged into relationships so fragile, interdependent and increasingly stressed that, without the broad acceptance of responsibility, the latter two will not survive. Everything I've said about organizing society in a way that ensures we value work over jobs is possible now. Today. While we may not be able to change the socio-economic system we live in, we do have the power to define *value* for ourselves. And, if enough of us do so, we will tilt the balance of power in favor of human *responsibility*.

Was Plato right? Is democracy a predestined failure? If the majority of Americans are far more interested in entertainment than in the affairs of their own government, if justice depends upon the size of one's pocketbook, if most citizens have little regard for their fellow countrymen, if I-got-mine-too-bad-about-yours becomes the order of the day, then, perhaps so. And, to the degree that public opinion can be dramatically swayed by simple advertising slogans and political cliches, then perhaps we are becoming a nation of idiots or, worse, ditto heads. To the degree that we are overwhelmed and marginalized by the very technology which was supposed to set us free, or that people doubt their very existence because they have not yet signed onto the Internet, we may have already become a nation of imbeciles.

In a technological society responsibility escalates with utility. Consider the history of war and the progressive rise in responsibility associated with weapons. As we went from club and spear to bow, gun, cannon, jet fighter, bomber, aircraft carrier, and nuclear arms, the dramatic increase in the responsibility to fellow humans became obvious. More disturbing is to realize that, in the creation of weaponry, we have undergone incredible leaps of technological understanding, but, in human relations, we are not much better off than when we began. The increased responsibility resulting from the replacement of the horse and buggy by the automobile becomes clear when you consider the subsequent increase in pollutants into the atmosphere, or when you learn that we lose more people each decade in automobile accidents than we have in all the wars we've ever participated in.

The abridged "be a winner" version of the American Dream has focused on individual freedom in a "do your own thing" fashion for so long that to insist on discussing today's real problems will ensure that you are accused of being a prophet of gloom and doom. Consider the savings and loan scandal of the late 1980s, the disrepair of the nation's bridges and highways, traffic gridlock, drug abuse, child abuse, cancer, heart disease, AIDS, mental illness, water pollution, air pollution, acid rain, landfill exhaustion, unemployment, crime, welfare, poverty, divorce, illiteracy, stress, nuclear waste, and the myriad economic predicaments associated with inequality. These problems are very real; some are critical to our immediate future. Millions of Americans, however, hooked on feeling good to the exclusion of reality, deny such troubles exist. To insist that we must face up to these issues and start to deal with them is viewed as being somehow subversive.[6]

The ability to live as if these problems are not relevant to our own lives is a part of the same condition which allows us to be duped into believing that inequality is a just state for human affairs. Even a cursory review of science and history suggests that the strength of "haves" is diminished by "have nots." When we enhance the security of those at the bottom of our society, the result is an increase in value for everyone. Progress in all human endeavors requires that we substitute knowledge for blame and accept full responsibility for the present by facing our problems directly. It means we must embrace the future with a commitment to lifelong learning.

Most all of the things we really need are things most everyone did for themselves just a few generations ago: growing vegetables, cooking, designing and making clothes, walking to work, conversing for entertainment, and deliberately learning through meaningful dialog. We now take fast food in our cars because we devalue our time. To gain approval we buy brand names which have no worth apart from the value we assign. Posterity demands more of us.

Posterity in 2046

In 2046, I will be dead, but my granddaughter will be exactly the same age that I am today. Her world and her grandchildren's world will be the residue of our cultural values. What Americans do during the next five decades will heavily influence whether the following questions will still be pertinent in 2046:

Do we really know the cost of everything and the value of nothing? Why is there so much talk about human values in a world where so few humans are valued? Why do politicians continually posture about a decline of values while demonstrating their own lack of them? Why do doctors perform unnecessary surgeries? Why do mechanics charge for parts they do not install? Why do stockbrokers trade on inside information? Why do adults sell drugs to children? Why do manufacturers sell products they know are unsafe? Why do health insurance companies cancel policies of people who need them most? Why do bankers who won't make loans to people without collateral give themselves large signature loans? Why do industrial waste polluters minimize the negative environmental consequences of their actions? Why do companies avoid paying pensions by firing employees who are about to retire? Why do home repair contractors take advantage of old people? Why do arms dealers sell guns to tyrants? Why do attorneys care more about winning cases than about guilt or innocence? Why do auto makers place profits ahead of safe cars? Why do students cheat on exams? Why do people cheat on their tax returns? Why do absentee fathers refuse to pay child support?

These are all questions about value and values. The more you ask such questions, the longer your list grows and the more troubling the subject of values becomes. Most of us have pole-vaulted over the question of ultimate value all of our lives without ever having thought it through. Now the problem looms ever larger for succeeding generations.

What values do those of us who are grandparents today pass on to those who will be grandparents in 2046? What kind of a society have we become? How do we explain to our grandchildren that we have built a society in which the virtue of frugality and simple living, so cherished two generations ago, is subordinate to an economy that would totally collapse if people simply stopped buying what they do not really need?

What kind of future will our grandchildren face? Will there be wars ahead? Certainly, if the future in any way resembles the past. Will our heirs have to decide the morality of another Vietnam experience? The odds favor it. Will there be recessions ahead? No doubt about it. Depressions? Again, if the past is any kind of a guide, a depression is a very likely occurrence before 2046. So, what are the lessons we have learned from the last half-century that will help in the next? Will obedience and conformity be as important as they were to our generation or should thinking for oneself be more important? Should society define value in the future, or should individuals learn to define value for themselves? What responsibilities do individuals owe to society, to each other, to democracy? Will there be any values worth dying for, worth killing for? Where will the boundaries of freedoms and rights be placed? Have we learned anything from the past? What are we doing today that will look as appalling in fifty years as the institution of slavery does today?

In 2046, all memory that my grandfather ever walked upon this earth will be gone—a fate which awaits us one and all, no matter what we do, or how famous we become. And yet, to suppose that impermanence makes these events less important to us is to miss the point entirely.

The Key to the Future

The founding fathers of America had a passion for learning, and their decisions reflect it. Had the Marxist movement concentrated as fervently on the need for student-centered education as it did for economic parity, and had we done the same in our feeble attempts at social engineering, abject poverty and the need for social welfare would have long since abated. Attempting to solve poverty in America by doling out a monthly economic subsistence is like trying to heal the sick by sending get-well cards.

We operate on the assumption that only a small percentage of the population is academically inclined, even though all humans have huge brains and are capable of incredible mental feats. Moreover, as demonstrated in different cultures all over the world, similarities among people cluster into noticeable categories where related strengths are easy to observe. If we value only a few of these strengths, we have little chance of achieving anything resembling social balance. Scarcely a day goes by without media coverage by a critic with a political agenda crying about how American students compare with those of Japan, Germany, or some other country. If we would help each student reach his or her maximum potential, it wouldn't matter whom we compared ourselves with.

Is our objective to mass-produce manic consumers whose major purpose in life is to qualify for a job that exists solely to turn up the heat of consumption? Or is it just as important to turn out people who are able to define quality of life, experience it for themselves, and help make it possible for others? What are we going to do with an underclass that is growing exponentially? If we applied what we know about the dynamics of botany to our educational system, we could change the center of the educational experience from external to internal and treat each student as an individual. If we applied the right nutrients at the right time, we could produce adults who, instead of shuddering in disgust every time someone mentions the prospect of going back to school, eagerly want to continue with their own education (both formally and informally) for the rest of their lives.

If we truly value people, we are bound to value the relative distribution of individual strengths and not just the few that hold our economic attention at the moment. We may wish for a nation where everyone is a technician, but we are not (and it's a good thing) going to produce one.[7] The externalization of education, the overfocus on learning to earn, inhibits; worse, it squelches the drive for intrinsic learning, the kind of learning which brings quality and enrichment to human life. What we desperately need to learn is how to respect the general distribution of the strengths that we have, so that each citizen can develop in a way that honors us all. I love music but have little aptitude for it. Is it fair to say that Mozart had a natural talent for music? Would it be proper to say that Einstein had a flair for physics? Was Edison creative? Does it make sense then, to maintain an educational system which will unintentionally do more to judge Mozart's worth by his grade in physics class and Einstein's grade in music than to give each a genuine appreciation for the other? Sadly, our traditional educational system, through its prepackaged requirements, has no room for, nor will it tolerate, an Einstein or an Edison.

If we were to adopt an intrinsic posture toward education, what kind of a curriculum should we use? Educator Neil Postman suggests that schools use a curriculum in which each teacher is a teacher of semantics and where each subject is taught with its own history.[8] Postman does not advocate a curriculum that is student-centered, as I have suggested, but one that is "idea-centered and coherence-centered."[9] But student-centered or idea-centered philosophies may not be nearly as important as promoting the notion that an education should be thought of *not as something you get, but as something you take*. John Stuart Mill warned that "next to selfishness, the principle cause which makes life unsatisfactory is want of mental cultivation."[10] The aggregate demand for a search for knowledge by the sum of citizens within a society is a clear indication of the caliber of life they will experience in the future. Culture and authority both are necessary to human life.

Culture is to humans as genetic instruction is to lower animals. If all human knowledge were suddenly lost, we would perish in a fortnight. But the character of a culture depends upon the contribution of its citizens. Those who add quality, enrich culture; those who do not, diminish both their culture and their own ability to experience the rapture of living. This failure to rise to the intellectual occasion of one's culture is evident in the enormous degree of bigotry, hate, and prejudice that passes from one generation to the next. Too little culture results in the inability to adapt. Too much culture amounts to the same thing. Overadaptation, like overfertilization, leads to stunted growth.

Today's welfare recipients have more physical comforts than did many kings and feudal lords. Many have the leisure to pursue enlightenment for any purpose, but lack the knowledge and confidence necessary to begin. Their poverty stems from a lack of culture, a lack of awareness about who they are and why they are who they are. Yet countless stories in news and fiction tell of individuals whose great wealth leaves them emotionally depressed. It is ironic that welfare recipients are culturally impoverished, while many of those whom we consider economically successful are correspondingly poor of spirit. Culture is sustained by ordinary people, but it is ordinary people with a sense of purpose who become extraordinary people and light the way. Without them we live in darkness. Wisdom is, in part, the ability *to want what we need*.

A dynamic culture is one whose highest priority is to pass *principle—a* form of awareness that expands beyond the influence of culture—from one generation to the next without suffocating the quest for knowledge. A resplendent culture's literature plumbs the depths of human experience and depends upon diversity. Indeed, a rich culture is one which is capable of discerning the truth of George Lakoff's assertion that "morality is empathy."[11] A strong community which understands morality as empathy knows instinctively that Immanuel Kant and Adam Smith were right when they said true goodwill requires more of a commitment than that of the simple golden rule: it requires not only that we feel what others feel, but that we be willing to base our actions toward them, at least in part, on "their values" as an expression of sympathy, tolerance, and trust.[12] The meme of brotherly love has been right all along, but only as a step in the right direction. The problem is, until we embrace the intellectual case for compassion, brotherly love on a grand or global scale is unrealistic. We humans are genetically predisposed to use love sparingly for kin and close associates.[13] In centuries past this kind of behavior increased the odds that one's genes would be passed on. But humanity has reached a stage of existence that, while it's still extremely important that we love those who are close to us, it's clearly not enough. The answer is not to pretend to love people, whom we really don't, but to increase our respect, appreciation, and regard for others through learning more about them. If we attempt this enterprise, even minimally, it will grant others the right to exist, at least in our own minds.

This simple effort, in a nutshell, is the whole point of this book. When we share experience, our needs bring us together emotionally and intellectually. The dark side of human temperament is forever scorched into the pages our history books, but our better nature keeps us from total self-destruction. We have to be very much aware of the human predicament at the biological level before we can compensate for it in the intellectual sphere. Robert Wright states it succinctly, "To be moral animals, we must realize how thoroughly we aren't."[14] Using a little common experience and interrelatedness to jumpstart our better character in a global context seems the least we can do for our fellow human beings. How fortunate we are that this effort adds quality to our very existence.

Nietzsche railed against compassion as a corrupt component of Christian morality, partially because he thought religion subordinates efforts to understand anything to those ideological authorities who claim to already have the answers to all of life's questions. To Nietzsche, religious authority prevents authentic existence. But real corruption manifests itself in a species whose members are unwilling to use the reasoning capacity of their large brains to better their society. Compassion is a means to understanding, just as principle is a measure of expanded awareness. It is a responsible expression of biological, social, and intellectual patterns of being and a social barometer for measuring quality of life. Life without compassion, life without brotherly love beyond the level of everyday familiarity, is inhuman. Period.

Moving Beyond the Dream

The chapters in this book are intended as an introduction to the many areas which need to be studied thoroughly by adults. If you've stayed with me this long, you no doubt take issue with many of the assertions I've made. These are precisely the junctures to begin pursuing your own inquiry. Once we learn to tear away the veneer of limited awareness that causes us to cling to only what is familiar, we are liberated to the delightful pursuit of truth, regardless of where the pieces fall. Thus, understanding becomes a greater value than the fleeting illusion of ownership. As impossible as it sounds, knowing is more important than knowledge. The nature of perception should render us perpetually skeptical and appreciative of George Santayana's observation that "skepticism is the chastity of the intellect."

The very structure of American society is built on the premise that effort will be rewarded. It is a noble idea. But this assumption about merit runs so deep that millions of us form an internal template of reality that suffers the over-influence of this principle. Self-worth, and ultimately the worth of other human beings, is judged in terms of economic worth. Combined with natural and normal human feelings of frustration and inadequacy, this prospect causes us to begin a frenzy of activities aimed at achieving worth but totally misdirected. We mistake means with ends, quality with quantity, and *doing* becomes more important than *being* itself. The situation worsens when people allow themselves to feel threatened by those who are less fortunate. Individuals and organizations who understand this human folly transpose it into political power. The propagandist becomes the matador, the poor his red cape, and those who fail to understand their own worth respond as the bull is expected to.

This book began with the idea that Americans dream and that, individually and collectively, these dreams shape our future. What we dream is valuable because our psychic investment in dreaming deems it so. Much of what our predecessors dreamed of has come to pass, and yet, because we do not readily understand the history of their struggle, we can't fully appreciate it as they would have. In what I've described as a search for the other side of the mountain, we opened a discussion about external versus internal values, the postures of dependence, independence, and interdependence, and the concept of rules versus principles. Many thinkers have tackled these matters with differing, but somewhat similar, points of view. The similarities become obvious when we compare their models. Yet their slight differences continue to fog the picture. It is not until we can put them all in perspective within a simple but far-reaching framework that we can probe the core issues with the hope of developing insight.

Pirsig's model enables us to see that at the very heart of our existence lies the interplay of culture versus biology (us against nature) and culture versus the free pursuit of ideas. These conflicts cloud the really important point that only through the faculty of ideas can we make our finest contribution to our society by rising above our culture. Rising above one's culture doesn't mean abandoning it; rather it means developing one's intellectual capacity to levels which enable one to add to it or better it. Through our ideas we have the potential to live off the interest of our biological world instead of eating away at the principle. Either we improve society through our ideas or we participate in its deterioration through a lack of them.

The quality of any society rests on the synergy of its individuals, just as the quality of any building depends on the caliber of the materials with which it is built. What we build with principles we are able to maintain only temporally through the use of rules, which means our future will largely reflect our character. The building of character and the maintenance of society depend on learning, enabling creativity, and producing quality. Taken together, Maslow's hierarchy of needs and Kohlberg's theory of moral development strongly suggest that, once one's lower-level needs are met and understood intellectually, there is a spontaneous tendency to consider the needs of others. Why, then, do we not take full advantage of this fact? The future of society is inexorably tied to the sorting out of what is really important in life by as many individuals as possible. Unless some find the other side of the mountain, all will perish.

If we are to rise each morning enthusiastically to do the work for which we were made, then we require all of the history we can gather to help us determine what that work might be and how we might best pursue it. We must understand, at a visceral level, the value distinction between *jobs* and *work*. Even if we have a hard time defining "progress," we must proceed as though making progress is possible. If the study of history yields lessons or directions, we have an enormous need to be capable of learning from them. In a word, if we are to sustain our culture, we must rise above it.

Our education process must emphasize the importance of the role of citizenship by establishing such a clear advantage for being an active citizen that everyone will want to accept the responsibility. It must become self-evident that individual interest and the public interest are represented by a process which requires participation in both spheres. We must realize that understanding the past offers hope for the present and the future. How can we let ourselves argue over the political ideologies and biases of our ancestors and still be foolish enough not to try to discover our own?

For Thoreau, "Time is but the stream I go a-fishing in." But today our concept of time—the very lifeblood of change (and reality itself) as we perceive it—is, by the thrust of technology, reconfiguring the stream we fish in. Clock time is being replaced by computer time. It has taken experience with the computer to show us that we cut and paste our own reality, and that awareness and editing are similar propositions. We are moving further from the world of nature into a world of abstracted cyberspace. Structural changes alter the way we live and the very nature of work. Thoreau wrote:

> In short, I am convinced, both by faith and experience, that to maintain one's self on this earth is not a hardship but a pastime, if we will live simply and wisely; as the pursuits of the simpler nations are still the sports of the more artificial. It is not necessary that a man should earn his living by the sweat of his brow, unless he sweats easier than I do.[15]

Structural changes have profoundly altered Thoreau's assertion about perspiration and labor. It is becoming increasingly more likely that one will not earn a very good living by the sweat of one's brow. In the 1890s working with one's hands was accepted as the sign of an honest man. Today it is viewed by many as the mark of a loser.

Jobs provide most of us with the economic leverage to live what we hope are meaningful lives, but, if we fail to balance jobs with human work activities that are genuinely meaningful, we can easily succumb to the notion that we are not working hard enough. Thus, we work harder at jobs, let our *real* work go, and try to quench our thirst for meaning with entertainment. When jobs that are dissatisfying are punctuated by empty entertainment, meaning becomes ever more distant, and the work people really need to do not only never gets done, it isn't even defined as having value. Nothing is more important to the qualitative character of any society than the thoughtful raising of its youth, and yet most people seem more concerned that welfare mothers have menial jobs than the cognitive wherewithal to raise their children effectively. It is a far greater tragedy that educated middle-class working people will increasingly do anything to get ahead than it is that the poor "uneducated" classes do not follow similar pursuits, or that too many poor women are having children. It's a greater disaster because poverty is more easily cured than greed.

If we do not understand the nature of change and how it affects our jobs and our work, or how these conditions are tempered by media, then we will have progressively less and less influence in our own lives. Indeed, we will more closely resemble the caged animal whose response to certain stimuli is to press a lever for a pellet of food. But if we pay close attention to the history of change, we cannot help but recognize that a livable future requires that we stand at the helm of responsibility.

If democracy depends upon balance, as I've suggested, and if balance is achieved through discussing differences, then we surely have the possibility of living in democratic times. The most crucial issue is whether or not this discourse will result in wise actions. The problems we identify as having to do with human rights, economics, and the environment are so interrelated and interdependent that they are almost inseparable, but they are not commonly understood that way. When we look closely, we see how each of them depends upon the others.

The fact that we are investigating social and environmental problems with such vigor today would normally be cause for celebration. Unfortunately, we don't probe deeply enough, and each side rarely communicates effectively with the other. Most people regard these matters with little more familiarity than their vague, distant memories of academic courses—a mental stance far short of the knowledge required to solve them. Imagine what it would be like today if, during the last three centuries, the love of wisdom had kept pace with technological developments. Most likely people from all nations would think for themselves to such an extent that no one would put conscience aside and attack someone else on command. Such a condition would announce the arrival of civilization, and a civilized world is what is needed to resolve today's most pressing issues. This would be a world where all human types are valued, not because they are similar, but because they are different. This form of justice or equality would be the principle providing the very substructure of morality. It is more tragic than sad that, in an effort to shield themselves from the reality of human mortality, cultures around the world remain oblivious to injustices all about them—injustices which they would have the power to alleviate, if only they could *see* them, and if only they had the will.

Suffice to say, our priorities are backwards: the time needed to find the truth necessary to conduct a meaningful, purposeful life far exceeds the amount of time our society allocates for reflection. In ages past, reflection was a product of leisure, and *leisure* stood for a great deal more than entertainment. Leisure in ancient Grecian society was the arena where all serious matters of human conduct were administered. Democracy itself grew out of the earlier Greek definition of leisure, which is now what is most needed to sustain it. It's ironic but fortunate that the qualities which uphold the concept of democracy are the same that add purpose and meaning to individual lives, for it takes a lifetime of reflection to experience a commendable life.

Still, in spite of the fact that more Americans are craving more leisure, the consume-and-spend cycle that drives us will not permit it.[16] We desperately need more time for our personal well-being and to shore up democracy; yet many of the people who have jobs are spending too much time working at them, even as many others have no jobs at all. Meanwhile the *real work* which needs to be done is ignored. The solution is startlingly obvious: shorten the hours, share the jobs, and don't make them more important than the real work of human beings.

Adam Smith said people who spend their lives performing simple tasks often become stupid themselves as a result.[17] It's undoubtedly true, but it doesn't have to be. The paths of learning to which popular culture directs our attention rarely have much to do with the quality of existence, and the majority of us would never have been duped had we not been taught to associate learning exclusively with *earning*. To reshape an American Dream worthy of a great nation, we must all choose to grow as anthropologists, historians, sociologists, scientists, politicians, philosophers, and lifelong learners. We must understand the truth of Ronald Gross' assertion that "any significant improvement in life—from a more rewarding job to more enjoyable leisure time—is based on learning."[18]

Rapidly changing times bring tidal waves of dissonance that can inspire us to rediscover what is really important. As we look for ways to cope with today's uncertainties, Emerson reminds us that we turn to philosophy in times of crisis. Such reflection offers great opportunity to reexamine our reasons for living. In the very near future we will be able to take a walk in the woods in the manner of Emerson and Thoreau but carrying a small reader which contains 10,000 books. We will read the books in our choice of size and fonts, or if we prefer, they can be read to us with our choice of background music. The entire contents of the Library of Congress will soon fit in a cube the size of a child's toy block. That's progress.

We are on the brink of a digital future. In *Being Digital*, Nicholas Negroponte writes, "Like a force of nature, the digital age cannot be denied or stopped. It has four very powerful qualities that will result in its ultimate triumph: decentralizing, globalizing, harmonizing, and empowering."[19] Indeed, the big bang of computer technology has given us an unrelenting expansion of cyberspace, a power for human expression unequaled in our history. Only by accepting responsibility for scientific innovation, and by rekindling the fires of curiosity in people of all ages, are we likely to add the kind of quality to our culture that might afford us a chance to live in the most humanitarian age ever recorded. Walter Truett Anderson is right when he says, "Today we have possibilities that put the Renaissance to shame."[20]

Individuals may not need to seek knowledge as voraciously as the scientist or the philosopher, but the amount of learning necessary to realize one's highest quality of experience is far, far greater than we are commonly led to believe. In short, principle-based self-directed inquiry enables individuals a clearer, uncontaminated view of reality that greatly improves a person's chance of moving closer to what is meaningful, regardless of the path chosen. Understanding increasingly fosters a better prospect of coming closer to reality; we become able to see the backdrop. What's really important stands out clearly when we have enough information. Then we have a why.

Raising the Final Curtain

One last time, imagine you are in a darkened movie theater. This time Pirsig's four-sided model, made of inorganic, biological, social, and intellectual patterns, acts as the frame for your movie; all four elements must be considered with regard to your own production. Ancient and popular culture furnishes the light which fills the screen. But, in the postmodern present, the projector is operated by a cultural-corporate Wizard of Oz. Now, *turn it off.* Shut down this power which mesmerizes the masses. Observe that you face a dark void, a postmodern abyss. At the core of this black hole we encounter death—eternal nothingness. Jean-Paul Sartre characterized it as a void between ourselves and the world, and the title of his book reveals our predicament: *Being and Nothingness.* Like a child's sparkler on the Fourth of July, our lives flame and then fizzle into burnt-out cinders of spent material. Nietzsche writes:

> In some remote corner of the universe, poured out and glittering in innumerable solar systems, there once was a star on which clever animals invented knowledge. That was the

haughtiest and most mendacious minute of "world history"—yet only a minute. After nature had drawn a few
breaths the star grew cold, and the clever animals had to
die.[21]

Throughout our lives we tread near the abyss, measuring the
breach between polarities: science and religion, reason and
emotion, masculine and feminine, love and hate, the idealist and
the materialist, light and dark. Addicts try to fill this emptiness
with drugs; zealots with religious dogma. The uninspired hide
their terror through the distraction of entertainment; many
spend their whole lives looking the other way. Yet nothing is
more powerful in summoning creativity and ingenuity than the
face of emptiness. Nietzsche tells us that if we look long into the
abyss it will look back at us. Postmodernism is a clarion call for
responsibility, a reason for rising above culture, a compelling
case to settle for nothing less than a meaningful existence. In the
absence of absolute culture, if culture is made up, if diverse notions about good and evil are subjective, shouldn't you and I
participate?

As we stand on the threshold of a new millennium, legions of
new-age gurus make a living pedaling myriad forms of mystical
mumbo-jumbo, talking about subjects they know nothing
about, pretending to know what no one knows, acting as if they
can do what no one can do. We would be better served by vivid
reminders that we are all going to die soon and by compelling
appeals to discover what really matters in this life—an enterprise that neither requires nor tolerates gurus. If, on tomorrow's
evening news, we were to learn that a very large asteroid was on
a direct collision course with the earth, that it would happen in
exactly 13 months and that absolutely nothing we might do
could prevent it, there would be denial, anger, guilt, and resigna-
tion. But there would also be a greater outpouring of sympathy
and brotherly love than all the world's religions have produced
in the history of humankind. Simultaneous extinction is unequivocally democratic.

For thousands of years the best and brightest of our kind have
enriched our lives in attempting to traverse the question of death
as the eternal abyss. Through their intellectual efforts they have

tried to fill this void with understanding. Emerson sought to bridge this chasm with curiosity, imagination, and sympathy for his fellow man; to use his intellect to fill the cleft between the romanticist and the modernist. Emerson's was a mind on fire.[22] That's the point of Transcendentalism: transcending. Not in a literal sense, but in a metaphorical sense, which is the best humans can do. Nietzsche claimed that man is a rope across an abyss. His metaphoric scaffold of the Eternal Return—wanting to be the person you are—is a bold attempt to fill this dark space with the light of your *own* purpose. The Eternal Return portrays one's life as the ultimate project. The brighter the spark in the void, the more likely you would want to experience it over again, and the greater the likelihood that your light would add quality to the lives of others.

Both Emerson and Nietzsche attempted to rise above their culture. That's what filling the empty space is about. The effort we use to fill this void is the primary way we experience quality of life, and were it not for the fact that social convention has perverted the process, we could still call it education. Nevertheless, it's mistaken to think of this learning as a possession. Knowledge builds, but understanding bridges. Understanding grants purpose. Understanding shines the light of history on current actions through the realization that any attempt to answer the question of who we are is inexorably bound to the history of who we have been. When understanding is our objective, we pull together reason and emotion. That's what understanding is. It enables us to perceive that our differences are minor compared to our common needs. Tyrants use social convention to assume power by hiding similarity through the manufacture of differences. Understanding sees through such differences.

The truly high ground of human experience exists where the desire to know is strong enough to encroach upon the sanctuary of cultural perception and to continually seek a better view of reality. From this posture, the cognitive effects of self-directed inquiry can win out over nurture and classical conditioning. On this acclivity we are likely to find the treasures of accumulated life experience and significant emotional events, plus a willingness to embrace the unknown and to continuously prick the bubble of limited perception in an effort to learn more about living. By stoking the Promethean fires of our own curiosity we can move closer to Reality. We can encounter Maslow's being-values, comprehend self-actualization, embrace Csikszentmihalyi's Flow, convert thymos into Dasein, and become capable of creating Dynamic Quality in our own lives and in our culture. Emerson had this figured out a century before anyone uttered the term postmodern. In his essay titled "Fate" in *The Conduct of Life*, he wrote:

> He who sees through the design, presides over it, and must will that which must be....Thought dissolves the material universe, by carrying the mind up into a sphere where all is plastic. Of two men, each obeying his own thought, he whose thought is deepest will be the strongest character....Every jet of chaos which threatens to exterminate us, is convertable by intellect into wholesome force....The water drowns ship and sailor, like a grain of dust. But learn to swim, trim your bark, and the wave which drowned it, will be cloven by it, and carry it, like its own foam, a plume and a power. The cold is inconsiderate of persons, tingles your blood, freezes a man like a dew drop. But learn to skate, and the ice will give you a graceful, sweet, and poetic motion....A man's fortunes are the fruit of his character....Why should we be afraid of nature, which is no other than "philosophy and theology embodied"? Why should we fear to be crushed by savage elements, *we who are made up of the same elements?*[23]

Thus the intellectual plane provides aspiration for the social plane, and the knowledge gained gives rise to respect for the biological sphere of existence. Both Emerson and Nietzsche asserted profusely that, when one is willing to pay the price of existence, this life in and of itself is enough. The profound question each of us should ask ourselves is: If we can't make a short life meaningful, what would be the point of an eternal existence?

We learn a great deal from books, and from teachers, but our reasons for living cannot be given to us any more than truth can be discovered for us. Wisdom is a product of autonomy. Emerson cautioned us that "the riddle of the age has for each a private solution." Krishnamurti tells us, "We must open the door ourselves."[24] Through this process of disclosure we discover the essence of our essence: we create a better world.

It is through apprehension and comprehension that we sense quality of life, and it is in the pursuit of dreams that we leave behind a better culture than the one we inherited. Filling the gap which separates us from the material world and from each other is the primary project of each life. That's what it means to live. The degree to which each of us succeeds at this is the quality we wrest from existence.

Even an attempt to confront reality without the support of culture produces a nothingness so vacuous that we soon realize whatever we choose to project onto the screen will, for better or worse, become the overriding thesis of our existence. This vast plane of emptiness is the barren battleground where humans have fought the great cultural wars, where the traditionalists were rendered obsolete by the rejectionists, who realized that by erasing tradition they had also severed their own ties with meaning. As we enter the third millennium, postmodernism makes us increasingly apprehensive by reminding us of the abyss. Yet these times are also rife with seeds of hope because, in an environment where we cannot prove absolutes, where language fails us, where chaos confronts us at every turn, where life represents endless choice, then at some point each of us must choose. The age-old dilemma comes clear: either put your own spin on reality or, rest assured, others will do it for you.

Postmodernism is evidence of too much culture, not a lack of it. We have internalized at a very deep level the economic ethos of our culture. The model of the business organization has overwhelmed the ideal of community, and is a damned poor substitute. It's not that we no longer have values; the dilemma of postmodernism is simply that what we value at an intellectual level is different from what we value at an emotional level. Many of the people we deem most successful harp about a loss of family values and then promptly abandon their families to pursue careers, leaving the care of their children to the *cheapest* (sometimes illegal) nannies they can find. Lacking "principled awareness," they fail to see the contradiction.

Any modern-day philosopher can, with quick dispatch, deconstruct and render meaningless all of the terms I have used to draw your attention to a higher level of conscious awareness. So, if we accept that language is a roadblock to reality, then we must acknowledge that Dasein, Conscience, Dynamic Quality, and terms like "essence of essence" can, in a technical sense, be reduced to meaningless gibberish. In other words, postmodernism can be viewed as a philosophical dead-end. But, just because efforts fail to capture meaning in an absolute sense, the meaning we derive from living does not necessarily lose its significance. What matters to us, matters—when it does, because it does. No more, no less. And that's quite enough. We may not be able to get from an ought to an is, but we can still perceive that "good is a noun." Good is a noun because kindness is a noun—it's in our genes, our literature, and our highest ideals. In a very real sense, life is metaphor: comparison is all we have. Moreover, we are biologically hard-wired to comprehend that it is impossible to precisely bridge the divide which separates us from one another. We can never know exactly what it is really like to be another person, but we are bound together through our capacities for sympathy and empathy. Nicholas Humphrey summarizes these certainties:

> That all of our intercourse, our words, our loves and hates are directed only towards other transiently existing packages of flesh and blood, and that we receive love only from the same. That we are totally debarred by our and their embodiedness from communicating with our fellow human beings directly, mind-to-mind. That not even in the deepest crisis will our needs be known to absent friends. That, since the inner qualities of our experiences have no surface translation into speech or bodily behavior, we are unable to share crucial aspects of our consciousness even in the closest of encounters.[25]

We're both blessedly charmed and doomed to experience life through the limits and capacities of being biological, social, and intellectual human beings. Ideas represent the apex of human achievement, and yet, because we emphasize only the intellectual sphere, and disregard the importance of biological, emotional and social aspects that contribute to genuine intelligence, nothing we do is as worthwhile as it could be. Still there's a chance artificial intelligence may someday bring humans much closer to ultimate Reality. In *The Evolution of Progress*, C. Owen Paepke writes, "Just as human muscles now seem a poor substitute for machines, future generations will likely consider twentieth-century brains to have been shockingly feeble instruments of thought."[26] But it seems more likely to me that artificial intelligence will produce a virtual reality so abstract and so profoundly devoid of humanity that we may begin to appreciate the wholeness of existence, just as we comprehended the fragility of planet earth when we first viewed it from deep space.

You and I face an empty frame of Reality which we will never fully fathom, even though we may get progressively closer near the end of our lives. Approaching Reality is like unraveling pi. Each new random number expressed by the powers of long division moves us (in theory) nearer to a closure we never experience. And yet, the approximation may be the greatest measure and experience of human quality that we can achieve. Just because we can't reconcile the circumference of a circle mathematically doesn't mean that "round" has no meaning.

We humans, by design, are forged to live side by side with a ponderous barrier between ourselves and the ultimate notion of value. Each of us is born hard-wired to easily attribute value to any tangible or intangible act, deed, transaction, or edict which furthers our own ends and affords our genes the chance to live for another generation—often with little regard as to how others may be affected by those acts. Such is the way we are wired to perceive value. If *I* must cut a tree, drill a well, pollute a river, clear a rain forest, drain a swamp, or build a city to sustain my own life and that of my immediate family or clan, the justification for doing so will be automatically forthcoming. But, if *you* proceed as naturally as I to pursue such ends, there may be trouble. It is much more difficult for me to ascribe justification to your efforts, even though your actions are as critical to your survival as mine are to mine. My human qualities cause me (consciously or unconsciously) to assume my experiences are more important to me than yours are to you. Moreover, as I make my way through life, I must of necessity be more forgiving of my own transgressions than I am toward those of others. Were this not possible, I might reach the point where my self-recriminations would become too heavy to bear.

Without a herculean effort to better understand social reality, we humans are condemned to distorted perceptions of value and concepts of worth. *My* acts are automatically self-justifying. But in my eyes *yours* are not (unless my conscience and consciousness inhabit the intellectual plane actively enough to figure this out). Nothing that you or I can do will ever remove this barrier to discerning value, nor should most of us wish to remove entirely this aspect of living, which also enables us to enjoy life so much. But, in these days of exponential population growth, it is imperative to humanity that this barrier to value be intellectually bridged by as many of our species as possible.

This simple but confounding perception of value is the root of bigotry, prejudice, and ethnocentrism, as well as the origin of all human wars. Nationalism itself is the epitome of narrow perspective. Recall Adam Smith's argument that we should bridge our cultural abyss with sympathy which, when thoughtfully applied, acts as the endowment for community. The good news is that sympathy and empathy are an integral part of our genetic makeup. All we have to do is add intellectual substance to our biological predisposition and think our way around our outdated need for self-deception. Then we can extend to the human family at large the concern we have for our individual families and stop ignoring global starvation and overlooking our responsibility for population growth. The ultimate success of our species depends upon the discovery of "good" as a noun.

A New Ethic: Lifelong Learning

In many ways we are a far more moral society than we have ever been. We no longer own slaves or burn witches; it's no longer acceptable for men to beat their wives. Women and minorities can vote, and (on paper at least) they have equal rights. We don't allow people to brutalize their children, and we don't allow youngsters to work in sweat shops. We won't tolerate cruelty to animals. And yet, a preponderance of evidence suggests that too many people at every level of our king-of-the-mountain society are oblivious to all but their own self-interests. Self-interest is a profoundly important motivation, but, all by itself, it leaves little room for community. On a sparsely populated planet, obsessive self-interest might be enough; it might even embody some of the virtue Ayn Rand attributed to it. But in a world of exponential population growth, with a base line already in the billions, abject self-interest is little more than biological malignancy.

To move beyond what we have traditionally called the American Dream we must move beyond culture, beyond good and evil, beyond morality. Only then can we stop making judgments about the shortcomings of others and start striving to understand the human predicament. In his book *Beyond Morality*, Richard Garner makes this crucial point:

> If an accurate version of reality is important, then we should trust our natural information processing devices when we can, and stop trying to force beliefs on ourselves and others. We do not need noble fictions and inspired myths to make sense of the world, which they never really do, or to guide us in our choices, which they usually do with unfortunate effect. Skeptics say that nothing is knowable, metaphysicians that everything is unreal, priests that magic works, and moralists that morality is objectively prescriptive; but when we "command a clear view" of our words and the world, we can begin to see these pronouncements for what they are, and to see beyond them to the ordinary world that words were designed in and for, a world of trees and truths, of conventions and useful standards, and of explanations that make sense.[27]

The heart of moving beyond the American Dream rests in commanding a better view, in being present in one's own consciousness, in being not there, but here. NOW! Raise your interest in life to levels sufficient to break the barriers of popular culture. This doesn't imply a loss of ability to find value or to act morally. To the contrary, the results of focusing on compassion and responsibility with critical awareness will accomplish more than a generation of moralizing. Determining right and wrong in this context is more important than it ever was before, especially since all of the hype about relativism during the past decade has created the illusion that only more tolerance is needed. Unfortunately, moralizing leads to rules, which are poor substitutes for the thinking each of us has to do to be present in our own experience. Garner continues:

> Morality turns out to be based on mistaken assumptions, confused concepts, self-deception, duplicity, fear, and a sometimes well-meant desire to control the way others act. No rule, principle, right, value, or virtue could be both objective and prescriptive, but moral rules, principles, rights, values, and virtues have no chance of doing their work unless they are thought to be both.

Moralists have doomed themselves to endless arguments, to idle and imaginative fantasying about future consequences, and to conflicts of interest dressed as conflicts of principle. When people complain about the lack of values, they are usually complaining about the fact that other people fail to value the things *they* value; they're presupposing that the things they value are the things that are *truly* valuable.[28]

Robert Pirsig argues that Quality and morality are identical. "The world is primarily a moral order."[29] Thus, morality is but another word for responsibility. The void or abyss which separates us from one another should render it infeasible to impose our own power or brand of morality on another by force. A person cannot experience the Quality of another. Your greatest means of persuading others is to live the example you advocate.

Recall the global awareness that surfaced when Mother Teresa died in 1997. And, glamour and celebrity aside, the same can be said of Princess Diana, who was killed the week before. Compassion was the trait for which they were most revered. Compassionate understanding and charitable giving gained prominence in the eyes of millions—maybe for the first time—because of the work of these women. On a more personal level, I've always aspired to emulate my grandfather's example—not because of what he said, but because of who he was and what he did. It was easy to tell what he cared about. He lived his values.

Compassion and responsibility used in tandem produce results comparable to the non-violent protest rallies of Martin Luther King Jr. and Mahatma Gandhi; they invite sympathy, empathy, and emulation. Thus, a commanding view through understanding is a much greater avenue to finding purpose and meaning in this life than letting others decide for us. Compassion, understanding, and responsibility can take us beyond the American Dream to the possibility of having a life worth living more than once. These intellectual qualities give rise to the operative reality that what needs to be taught is best taught by example. Each of us can find purpose and meaning by leaving the world a better place than we found it. It's that simple and that hard.

By moving one piece of Pirsig's four-component screen we can reframe our postmodern dilemma with an eternal reminder of the posture required to have a positive effect on the future. Simply take the vertical piece on the right and place it horizontally in the middle. Now, instead of a square, we have the letter E. It stands for ETHICS with a built-in structural awareness that any question about ethics requires acknowledgment and consideration of inorganic, biological, social, and intellectual patterns. In other words, moving beyond the American Dream means going past the poverty of "being a winner" mentality. It means that the goal of enabling citizens to live the kind of lives they would wish to repeat must include continuous efforts to understand how our actions affect biological, social, and intellectual patterns. Peter Singer explains how we might do this in his book *How Are We To Live*:

> A better life is open to us—in every sense of the term, *except* the sense made dominant by a consumer society that promotes acquisition as the standard of what is good. Once we get rid of that dominant conception of the good life, we can again bring to the centre of the stage questions about the preservation of the planet's ecology, and about global justice. Only then can we hope to see a renewal of the will to deal with the root causes of poverty, crime, and the short-term destruction of our planet's resources. A politics based on ethics could be radical, in the original sense of the term: that is, it could change from the roots. [30]

Ideas represent the apex of human existence, and persuading others of this notion can best be accomplished through the power of compassion and responsibility. Do we need great teachers to further this enterprise? Absolutely! If ideas are important, then teaching is at the summit of professions. But those whom we consider great teachers in the past have taught us that moralizing has little to do with morals. Great teachers teach by example. Hypocrites teach hypocrisy. But when those who profess to teach demonstrate compassion and responsibility, they supply us the only force powerful enough to forge communities inclusive of humanity.

Since the birth of modern civilization, knowledge in thousands of disciplines has grown exponentially. Still, the really big questions remain. And now postmodernists remind us that the big questions themselves rest upon foundations so disjointed as to render them moot. So, in the absence of absolutes, we are compelled to return to the Stoic question of how we should live? We are once again forced to use our conceptions of knowledge to the best of our abilities. The fact that we can't know everything doesn't render all learning meaningless. As human beings we are both privileged and condemned to find meaning and purpose. Emerson reminds us that "intellect annuls Fate." And yet, it is a mistake to think of knowledge as a possession. [31]

We do not come into the world, but out of it. We bring with us no possessions when we are born and we take none with us when we die. Thus, it is a serious error to measure success through the possession of knowledge or material goods. Humans experience quality through intellectual patterns, through understanding, for as long as our biological body permits. It is through *understanding* and *not possession* that we improve society and that we experience the greatest quality of life as individuals. But to do this we have to project dreams of our own. We can't live on other people's purpose without striking a pose; we can't fully experience this life by copying someone else's. If we practice attentiveness with the expectation of being rewarded through understanding, we can easily achieve—through our own thoughts—an enriched zest for living. Once we reach this level of understanding, it becomes clear that America's greatest treasures are not in our shopping malls but in our libraries. Moreover, if this realization could be passed on to future generations, it would render absurd the assertion that today's youth will not live as well as their parents.

When we are aware of our pervasive tendency to see what we expect to see, we are forearmed with a much better chance of achieving objectivity with regard to our relations with other cultures. We eliminate simple mind-sets, realizing that nothing is quite so powerful as the genuine desire to know, and nothing is quite so destructive as people who think they know and don't. We realize further that a life without interests cannot experience quality in the truly human sense and that we likewise diminish our human distinction when we deny our biological link to the animal world.

Learning is an act of becoming, and lifelong learning yields the richest dimension of human experience available to us. Learning of our own volition throughout our lives is the key to a meaningful future. Purpose and meaning are born of sophistication, comprehension, and clarification. Learning, understanding, and re-understanding provide the impetus for moving beyond the American Dream. The quality of the future is the legacy of today's applied intelligence. The times we are living in call for a great investment in intellectual patterns, a psychic investment of *faith* in our better nature demonstrated by our willingness to learn, and a greater sense of awareness and embodiment through the mastery of culture. Carl Sagan was right when he said, "Our species needs, and deserves, a citizenry with minds wide awake and a basic understanding of how the world works."[32] It is the only way to perceive the monumental responsibility which rests on our shoulders. We, you and I, have an opportunity to open the door to riches far greater than those experienced by the royalty of centuries past or the wealthiest of today's elite. The key is already in our hands.

Notes

Preface

1. Ashley Montagu. *Growing Young* (Granby, MA: Bergin & Garvey, 1989*)*, p. 120.
2. David W. Stewart. *Adult Learning in America: Eduard Lindeman and His Agenda for Lifelong Education* (Malabar, FL: Robert E. Krieger,1987), pp. 171-187.

Introduction

1. Henry David Thoreau. *The Selected Works of Thoreau* (New York: Houghton Mifflin, 1975), p. 190.

Chapter One

1. J. Krishnamurti. *You Are the World* (New York: Harper & Row, 1972), p. 135.
2. James Lincoln Collier. *The Rise of Selfishness in America* (New York: Oxford University Press, 1991), p. 5.
3. Jack Larkin. *The Reshaping of Everyday Life 1790-1840* (New York: Harper & Row, 1988), p. xv.
4. Ibid., p. 112.
5. Ibid., p. 158.
6. Ibid., p. 185.
7. Ibid., p. 172.
8. Ibid., p. 25.
9. Ibid., p. 27.
10. Ibid., p. 22.
11. Ibid., p. 14.
12. Ibid., p. 193.

13. Ibid., p. 74.

14. Ibid., pp. 172, 296.

15. Collier, p. 5.

16. Larkin, p. 35.

17. Ibid., p. 302.

18. Collier, p. 5.

19. Larkin, p. 6.

20. Ibid., p. 48.

21. Robert M. Pirsig. *Lila* (New York: Bantam Books, 1991), p. 95.

22. Collier, p. 9.

23. Sigmund Freud. "Civilization and its Discontents," vol. 54 of *Great Books of the Western World* (Chicago, IL: Encyclopaedia Britannica, 1952), p. 788.

24. Collier, p. 17.

25. Larkin, p. 296.

26. Ibid., p. 302.

27. Ibid., p. 53.

28. Collier, p. 24.

29. Ibid., p. 24.

30. Ibid., p. 47.

31. Ibid., p. 149.

32. William Leach. *Land of Desire* (New York: Pantheon Books, 1993), p. 27.

33. Collier, p. 40.

34. Leach, p. 40.

35. Ibid., p. 66.

36. Ibid., p. 84.

37. Ibid., p. 124.

38. W. Fitzhugh Brundage. *Lynching in the New South* (Chicago: University of Illinois Press, 1993), p. 1.

39. Richard Weiss. *The American Myth of Success* (New York: Basic Books, 1969), p. 140.

40. Kenneth J. Gergen. *The Saturated Self* (New York: Basic Books, 1991), pp. 6, 7, 229.

41. It is ironic that, as James Fallows points out in *The Atlantic Monthly*, February 1980, "The Tests and the Brightest" (p. 43), the term "meritocracy" was first used with satirical intent by Michael Young in *The Rise of Meritocracy*, 1958. Young meant that such a premise would not likely be better than any of the other earlier methods for establishing a fair system. In *Between Past and Future*, Hannah Arendt wrote, "Meritocracy contradicts the principle of equality, of an equalitarian democracy, no less than any other oligarchy."

42. In 1978 the Stanford Research Institute introduced theVALS typology profiling nine demographic groups that fit well in this scenario. Beginning at the bottom of the mountain and progressing upward there are survivors, sustainers, belongers, emulators, I Am Me's, experientials, achievers, societally conscious, and integrateds. Most people who are asked to visualize society as a hierarchy will draw a model of the mountain based strictly on income. But SRI'S example does not derive strictly from economics. The integrateds on top are not the super-rich, but rather have attained their status because of their ability to find balance.

43. Rebecca Piirto. *Beyond Mind Games* (New York: American Demographics, 1991), pp. 77, 80. In 1989 the VALS typology was revised in an effort to provide advertisers with a better marketing tool. The nine categories were reduced to eight. The VALS 2 model is a hierarchy that moves from minimal resources to abundant resources with three postures of motivation: the principle oriented, the status oriented, and the action oriented.

44. Alfie Kohn. *No Contest* (Boston: Houghton Mifflin, 1986), pp. 3-4.

45. Ibid., pp. 96-131.

46. The idea that the terms "struggle" and "competition" are synonymous is at the very heart of the issue that causes people to presuppose a just world attitude.

47. Loren Baritz. *The Good Life* (New York: Alfred A. Knopf, 1989), p. 308.

48. Ernest Becker. *The Denial of Death* (New York: The Free Press, 1973), p. 4.

49. Walter Truett Anderson. *Reality Isn't What It Used To Be* (San Francisco: Harper & Row, 1990), p. 122.

50. Ibid., p. 125.

51. Melvyn Kinder. *Going Nowhere Fast* (New York: Prentice-Hall, 1990), p. 5.

52. Ibid., p. 12.

53. John Dewey. *Human Nature and Conduct* (New York: The Modern Library, 1922), p. 110.

54. Marvin Harris. *Our Kind* (New York: HarperCollins, 1989), p. 375-376.

55. Eric Hoffer. *The True Believer* (New York: Harper & Row, 1951), p. 29.

56. Richard Stivers. *The Culture of Cynicism* (Cambridge, MA: Blackwell Publishers, 1994), p. 54.

57. Ibid., p. 54.

58. M. J. Lerner. *The Belief in a Just World: A Fundamental Delusion* (New York: Plenum Press, 1980).

59. Lewis H. Lapham. *Money and Class in America* (New York: Weidenfield & Nicolson, 1988).

60. Referring to man as existing in "a state of nature" has long been at the heart of a line of reasoning dividing philosophers such as Thomas Hobbes and David Hume. Hobbes argued that man in a state of nature is, in fact, in a state of war, making a good case for the need to form a government. Hume argued the opposite, saying that man is naturally a social animal. Either argument suggests to me that abject poverty should not exist within any system organized for the betterment of its members.

61. Philip Slater. *A Dream Deferred* (Boston, MA: Beacon Press, 1991), p. 185.

62. Arthur G. Miller, ed. *In the Eye of the Beholder* (New York: Praeger, 1982), p. 448.

63. Slater, *A Dream Deferred*, p. 110.

64. Michael Lewis. *The Culture of Inequality* (Amherst, MA: University of Massachusetts Press, 1978), pp. 86-87.

Chapter Two

1. Carl Sagan. *Broca's Brain* (New York: Ballantine, 1974), p. 17.

2. Benedict de Spinoza. "Ethics," trans. W.H. White, vol. 31 of *Great Books of the Western World* (Chicago, IL: Encyclopaedia Britannica, 1952), p. 458.

3. Emerson actually made this statement in reference to Thoreau. He said, "He chose to be rich by making his wants few, and supplying them himself."

4. Stephen R. Covey. *The Seven Habits of Highly Effective People* (New York: Simon & Schuster, 1989), pp. 18-19.

5. Abraham H. Maslow. *Religions, Values, and Peak Experiences* (New York: Penguin Books, 1987), p. 92.

6. Covey, p. 18.

7. Ibid., p. 51.

8. Ibid., p. 35.

9. Robert D. Richardson Jr. *Emerson: The Mind on Fire* (Berkeley, CA: University of California Press, 1995), p. 155. Richardson writes that, to Emerson, "The eye was always more than a metaphor," and that Emerson wrote in his journal in the fall of 1883, "To an instructed eye the universe is transparent." Indeed, throughout Emerson's works there is an unrelenting effort to enhance awareness in the manner of an all-seeing nature.

10. Peter Jarvis. *Paradoxes of Learning* (San Francisco, CA: Jossey-Bass, 1992), p. 9.

11. Sim C. Liddon. *The Dual Brain, Religion, and the Unconscious* (Buffalo, NY: Prometheus Books, 1989), p. 185.

12. These theories have encountered considerable criticism from the feminist perspective. There is little doubt that most of these models have a masculine bias that diminishes the role of women with respect to human behavior in general. This footnote, unfortunately, may appear to have the same effect, but it is a far more ambitious task than the one I have undertaken to set these models right by gender. It is incumbent on us all to realize that these biases are present and to discover and deal with them as they occur. Feminist author Carol Gilligan doesn't refute Kohlberg's hierarchical theory of moral development in total as is often claimed. She argues that the weight given to logic is inadequate. What I interpret from her contention is that she made a case for emotional intelligence long before it became a popular idea.

13. Mihaly Csikszentmihalyi. *The Evolving Self* (New York: Harper-Collins, 1993), p 82.

14. One can certainly take issue with me for listing these particular names and for omitting others. Any attempt to evaluate the contribution of others involves difficult decisions. In her book

In a Different Voice, p. 103, Carol Gilligan points out that Erik Erikson was almost persuaded to stop writing his book *Gandhi's Truth* when he discovered how disrespectfully Gandhi had treated his own family.

15. Pirsig, *Lila*, p. 163. Pirsig suggests this is untrue and instead that morality amounts to a "complex struggle of conflicting patterns of value" representing "the residue of evolution."

16. This is most easily observed in the popular development theory known as transactional analysis, in which each of us retains multiple identities as adult, parent, and child as a result of our childhood experiences.

17. James Davison Hunter. *Culture Wars* (New York: Basic Books, 1991). Hunter traces this great cultural divide of competing moral visions from early American history to our most divisive contemporary issues, couching it as a polarization between the orthodox and the progressive.

18. Rick Roderick. *The Philosophy of Human Values*, audio cassette series (Kearnysville, WV: The Teaching Company, 1991).

19. John Stuart Mill. "On Liberty," in vol. 43 of *Great Books of the Western World* (Chicago, IL: Encyclopaedia Britannica, 1952), p. 284.

20. Friedrich Nietzsche. *The Portable Nietzsche*, ed. Walter Kaufman (New York: Viking Penguin, 1954), pp. 46-47.

21. Arthur Schlesinger Jr., in *The Truth About the Truth*, ed. Walter Truett Anderson (New York: Tarcher/Putnam, 1995), p. 229.

22. Roderick. *Philosophy of Human Values*, Lecture One.

23. Irving Singer. *Meaning in Life* (New York: Macmillan, 1992), p. 113.

24. John Stuart Mill. "On Liberty," p. 282.

25. Edward De Bono. *I Am Right—You Are Wrong* (New York: Viking Penguin, 1990), p. 259.

26. George Bernard Shaw. *Man and Superman* (New York: Brentano's, 1903), p. xxxi.

27. Immanuel Kant. "The Critique of Practical Reason," trans. J. M. D. Meiklejohn, in vol. 42 of *Great Books of the Western World* (Chicago, IL: Encyclopaedia Britannica, 1952), p. 360.

28. Spinoza, "Ethics," Part Two and Three, pp. 373-422.

29. Pirsig. *Lila*, p. 149.

30. Andrew Nikiforuk. *The Fourth Horseman* (London: Phoenix, 1991), pp. 6, 5, 3, 12.

31. Richard Preston. *The Hot Zone* (New York: Random House, 1994), p. 289.

32. Pirsig, *Lila*, pp. 160-161.

33. Csikszentmihalyi, *The Evolving Self*, p. 72.

34. William F. Allman. *The Stone Age Present* (New York: Simon & Schuster, 1994), p. 140.

35. William A. Henry III. *In Defense of Elitism* (New York: Doubleday, 1994), p. 59.

36. Ibid., p. 3.

37. Ibid., p. 19. I know my comments about Henry's assertions sound harsh. They are not intended as personal criticism. I simply take issue with what I perceive is his contempt for the valuation of others which neither he, nor you, nor I can be in a position to judge. Of all human sentiments, contempt is the easiest to evoke and the hardest to extinguish. Because someone does not appear to be aspiring toward what we think are laudable goals does not mean that person's actions are unworthy. Anger may be warranted, but contempt is not. Nothing shores up self-righteousness more quickly than judging others who have problems which we don't perceive ourselves as having.

38. Anderson, *Reality Isn't What It Used To Be*, p. 156.

39. Attributed to Alfred Lord Tennyson in response to Charles Darwin's *The Descent of Man*.

40. W. Feller. *An Introduction to Probability Theory and Its Applications* (New York: Wiley, 1967).

41. Richard Dawkins. *The Selfish Gene* (New York: Oxford University Press, 1976), p. 206.

42. Daniel C. Dennett. *Darwin's Dangerous Idea* (New York: Simon & Schuster, 1995), pp. 364-365.

43. Ibid., p. 365.

44. Dawkins, p. 215.

45. Gerald E. Stearn. *McLuhan Hot and Cool* (New York: Dial Press, 1967), p. 85.

46. Alan Watts. *The Wisdom of Insecurity* (New York: Vintage Books, 1968), p. 149.

47. Stephanie Coontz. *The Way We Never Were* (New York: Basic Books, 1992), pp. 23-41. Coontz shows how the media-constructed myths of the Ozzie and Harriet, '50s did not square with the reality of the times.

48. William James. *Pragmatism* (New York: Longsman, Green, 1910), p. 19.

49. William James. "What Pragmatism Means," in *The Writings of William James*, ed. John J. McDermott (Chicago: University of Chicago Press, 1967), pp. 376-377.

50. Csikszentmihalyi, *The Evolving Self*, pp. 28-29.

51. George J. Stack. *Nietzsche and Emerson* (Athens, OH: Ohio University Press, 1992), p. 123.

52. Immanuel Kant. "The Critique of Pure Reason," trans. J. M. D. Meiklejohn, in vol. 42 of *Great Books of the Western World* (Chicago, IL: Encyclopaedia Britannica, 1952), p. 34.

53. William James. *The Letters of William James (n.p. 1920)*.

54. Richard Hofstadter. *Anti-Intellectualism in America* (New York: Vantage Books, 1962), p. 25.

55. Ibid., p. 27.

56. In his book *The Moral Sense* (New York: The Free Press, 1993), James Q. Wilson argues that we have a core self, a conscience "not wholly the product of culture," which is sort of a reflection of the care given each of us as we grow from childhood to adulthood. He writes, "The feelings on which people act are often superior to the arguments that they employ." I agree, but Wilson also argues that Kant's commitment to truth would have kept him from lying to a homicidal manic about the whereabouts of a child. Kant did make this argument, but he went on to say that the truth was due only to one worthy of the truth. This most assuredly would not have included murderers. If Kant himself had had a granddaughter, I've no doubt he would have lied to a homicidal manic asking about her whereabouts. The facts about the child's location would be instrumental, a means; a child is an end. What's truly moral in this instance (according to one's conscience) is easy to discern through feeling. But reason also plays a role in this example. Reason is the system of truth we use to limit the number of homicidal maniacs roaming the streets. Knowledge in the form of education enables us to observe and understand and pass on to children through nurture the kind of actions which will foster the formation of a social conscience, and to see that such a conscience is receptive to both feeling and reason. If this is not

true, if conscience has nothing to do with learning, then there would be no reason for anyone to write books about morals.

Even as Wilson argues that a conscience is innate, in part, independent of culture, he complains about cultural relativism in the same breath. If all human beings had a conscience independent of culture, if the core of humanity rested upon an internal sense of right and wrong, cultural relativism could not exist. Everyone would intuitively reach the same conclusions.

57. Robert C. Solomon and Kathleen M. Higgins. *A Short History of Philosophy* (New York: Oxford University Press, 1996), p. 189.

58. John McCrone. *The Myth of Irrationality* (New York: Carroll & Graf), p. 251.

59. Daniel Goleman. *Emotional Intelligence* (New York: Bantam Book, 1995), p. 28.

60. Steven Pinker. *How the Mind Works* (New York: W.W. Norton, 1997), pp. 373, 370.

61. Hofstadter, p. 51.

62. Viktor E. Frankl. *Man's Search for Meaning* (New York: Pocket Books, 1984), p 131.

63. Ibid., pp. 133-138. The very notion of truth in Eastern religions is that truth is a person-centered phenomenon. Thus, one's attitude toward suffering will, without doubt, assure meaning and perspective.

64. Monica Furlong. *Genuine Fake* (London: Unwin Hyman Ltd., 1986).

65. Watts, *The Wisdom of Insecurity*, pp.107-109.

66. David Cernic and Linda Longmire, eds. *Know Thyself* (Mahwah, NJ: Paulist Press, 1987), p. 5.

67. Henry David Thoreau. *The Portable Thoreau*, ed. Carl Bode (New York: penguin Books, 1947), pp. 343-344.

68. Robert B. Reich. *The Resurgent Liberal* (New York: Times Books, 1989), p. 96.

69. Jack London. *Call of the Wild*, (New York: Scholastic Book Services, 1963), pp. 61-62.

70. Peter M. Senge. *The Fifth Discipline* (New York: Doubleday/Currency, 1990), p. 161.

71. Ibid., p. 159.

Chapter Three

1. Marcus Aurelius. "Meditations," vol. 12 of *Great Books of the Western World* (Chicago, IL: Encyclopaedia Britannica, 1952), p. 268.

2. Robert N. Bellah et al., eds. *The Good Society* (New York: Alfred A. Knopf, 1991), p. 256.

3. Slater, *A Dream Deferred*, p. 17.

4. James R. Fisher Jr. *The Taboo Against Being Your Own Best Friend* (Tampa, FL: The Delta Group, 1996), p. 7.

5. Joseph Campbell et al. *The Power of Myth* (New York: Doubleday, 1988), p. 5.

6. Morris Berman. *Coming to Our Senses* (New York: Bantam Books, 1989), pp. 341-342.

7. Philip Slater. *Wealth Addiction* (New York: E. P. Dutton, 1980), p. 7.

8. Mary Parker Follett. *Creative Experience* (New York: Longmans, Green, 1924), p. 302.

9. John Kenneth Galbraith. *The Culture of Contentment* (New York: Houghton Mifflin, 1992), p. 33.

10. Lionel Tiger. *Optimism* (New York: Kodansha International, 1979), p. 70.

11. Ralph Waldo Emerson. *Ralph Waldo Emerson: Selected Essays* (New York: Penguin Books, 1982), p. 135.

12. Philip Slater. *The Pursuit of Loneliness* 3rd ed. (Boston, MA: Beacon Press Books, 1990), p. 152.

13. James R. Fisher Jr. *The Worker Alone* (Tampa, FL: The Delta Group, 1995), p. 24.

14. Howard Zinn. *A People's History of the United States* (New York: Basic Books, 1995). If your knowledge of history rests exclusively on what you learned from public school textbooks, then you know nothing of history. Nothing. Zinn's book makes this clear. Everyone should read it.

15. Richard Shenkman. *Legends, Lies and Cherished Myths of American History* (New York: William Morrow, 1988), p. 141.

16. Gertrude Himmelfarb. *On Looking into the Abyss* (New York: Vintage Books, 1994), p. 18.

17. Todd Gitlin. *The Twilight of Common Dreams* (New York: Metropolitan Books, 1995), p. 20.

18. Stephen Jay Gould. *Ever Since Darwin* (New York: W. W. Norton, 1977), p. 85.

19. Charles D. Hayes. *Self-University* (Wasilla, AK: Autodidactic Press, 1989), pp. 102-103.

20. Emerson. *Selected Essays*, p. 88.

21. Ralph Waldo Emerson. *Emerson Essays and Lectures* (New York: The Library of America, 1983), p. 57.

22. Deconstruction is most often associated with the work of Jacques Derrida. In the '60s, Derrida began new approaches to literary criticism that challenged the ability of language to convey meaning in a literal sense. He is called a genius by some and a charlatan by others. Deconstruction is a tool of criticism like formalism and semiotics, but definitions of it differ radically. The most common criticism of deconstruction theory is that it is irrational and nihilistic. I have used the term deconstruction in a more simplistic way.

23. Hilary Lawson. *Reflexivity* (LaSalle, IL: Open Court, 1985), p. 93.

24. Francis Fukuyama. *The End of History and the Last Man* (New York: The Free Press, 1992), p. xii.

25. Hoffer, pp. 31-32.

26. John Lukacs. *The End of the Twentieth Century* (New York: Ticknor & Fields, 1993), p. 289.

27. Robert Wright. *Three Scientists and Their Gods* (New York: Perennial Library, 1989), p. 110.

28. Georg Wilhelm Friedrich Hegel. "Philosophy of History," in vol. 46 of *Great Books of the Western World* (Chicago, IL: Encyclopaedia Britannica, 1952), p. 155.

29. Gary Wills. *John Wayne's America* (New York: Simon & Schuster, 1997), p. 116.

30. Neil Postman. *Amusing Ourselves to Death* (New York: Viking Penguin, 1985), p. 99.

31. Ibid., p. vii.

32. Perhaps our affinity for spectator sports is not such a mystery. Zoologist Desmond Morris points out that all of our sports contain two prime ingredients of the hunt: aiming and chasing. If this is indeed part of our fascination with sports, we need to understand how this abstract attention squares with our actual estrangement from the natural world. In other words, if we engage in the chase by proxy without the kill, and

instead all of our food appears in the supermarket magically wrapped, does it mean that sports media further add to our disembodiment and estrangement from the world of nature?

Chapter Four

1. Simone Weil. *Gravity and Grace* (London: Routledge and Kegan Paul, 1947), p. 14.

2. Bob Samples. *The Metaphoric Mind* (Reading, MA: Addison-Wesley, 1976), p. 32.

3. Ibid., p. 37.

4. Liddon, p. 69-73.

5. Kant. "The Critique of Pure Reason," p. 34.

6. In Ned Herrmann's whole-brain (four quadrant) model, the term *synthesis* appears as a function of the upper right quadrant or as Level Four (see *The Creative Brain*). This is not how Kant uses the term. His view of synthesis is itself a whole-brain concept.

7. Bertrand Russell. *Principles of Social Reconstruction* (London: George Allen & Unwin, 1916), p. 115.

8. Liddon, pp. 188-190.

9. John F. Schumaker. *Wings of Illusion* (New York: Prometheus Books, 1990), p. vii.

10. Arthur Schopenhauer. *Essays of Arthur Schopenhauer* (New York: A. L. Bert, 1949), p. 381.

11. Becker, p. 27.

12. In *Ever Since Darwin*, Stephen Jay Gould takes sociobiologist Edward O. Wilson to task for asserting that human beings seek indoctrination, which is simply another way of saying we are purposefully self-deceptive. Gould says such a finding does not meet with his own experience, but it certainly meets with mine. Gould is probably the best natural science essayist in America today, but he may be too generous in believing that natural curiosity like his own is more widespread than it really is. There are some other theories about our propensity for self-deception to consider: the ability to deceive ourselves may help us deceive others or help us spot those who are trying to deceive us (see *The Adapted Mind*, Jerome H. Barkow, Leda Cosmides, and John Tooby, p. 603).

13. Schumaker. *Wings of Illusion.* pp. 3, 15.

14. Ibid., p. 40.

15. Daniel J. Boorstin. "The Amature Spirit," in *Living Philosophies* (New York: Doubleday, 1990), p. 24.

16. Timothy Ferris. *The Mind's Sky* (New York: Bantam Books, 1992), p. 138.

17. In *Blood Rites* (New York: Metropolitan Books, 1997), Ehrenreich offers the fascinating theory that the human propensity for war may be the residue of the primeval fear from the time when human beings were prey.

18. Daniel Goleman. *Vital Lies, Simple Truths* (New York: Simon & Schuster, 1985), pp. 30-43. Goleman offers the provocative thesis that our capacity for self-deception may in part be the result of an evolutionary adaptation designed to spare us mental pain in the same way that we are protected from extreme physical pain through an overdose of brain chemicals.

19. Walter Truett Anderson. This term appears in the extended subtitle to *Reality Isn't What It Used To Be.*

20. Mortimer J. Adler. *Intellect* (New York: Macmillan, 1990), p. 192. Adler suggests that, if we should ever reach the point where we are compelled to accept a completely materialistic view of human nature, we should then expunge the term "spirituality" from our vocabulary. As much as I respect Dr. Adler's reasoned opinion, I heartily disagree. I can find no reason whatever to disparage the human spirit simply because I can't attach it to an immortal soul.

21. Becker, pp. 283-284.

22. Harold Bloom. *The American Religion* (New York: Simon & Schuster, 1992), p. 37.

23. Gerhard Staguhn. *God's Laughter* (New York: HarperCollins, 1992), p. 14.

24. John F. Schumaker. "The Mental Health of Atheists," *Free Inquiry*, summer 1993, p. 13.

25. Huston Smith. *Beyond the Post-Modern Mind* (New York: Crossroads Publishing, 1989), p. 7.

26. Huston Smith. *Huston Smith: Essays on World Religion* (New York: Paragon House, 1992), p. 240.

27. Ibid., p. x.

28. Huston Smith. *The World's Religions* (New York: HarperCollins, 1991), p. 8.

29. Thornton Wilder. *The Eighth Day* (New York: Harper & Row, 1967), p. 134.

30. Anderson, *Reality Isn't What It Used To Be*, pp. 8-10.

31. Hazel Henderson. *Paradigms in Progress* (Indianapolis, IN: Knowledge Systems, 1991), pp. 261-272. Henderson writes of an age of light that lies beyond the information age in the same manner that C. Owen Paepke writes of the evolution of human progress demonstrated by the title and subtitle of his book *The Evolution of Progress: The End of Economic Growth and the Beginning of Human Transformation*.

32. George B. Vetter. *Magic and Religion* (New York: The Philosophical Library, 1958), preface to the first edition.

33. Emerson, *Selected Essays*, p. 223.

34. Adam Smith, "The Wealth of Nations," vol. 39 of *Great Books of the Western World* (Chicago, IL: Encyclopaedia Britannica, 1952), p. 194.

35. Friedrich Nietzsche offers a provocative argument to the contrary. In *On the Genealogy of Morals*, he suggests that the roots of morality are themselves tainted with immorality. The origins of Christianity, he maintains, are born not of compassion, but of resentment and revenge.

36. Watts, *The Wisdom of Insecurity*, p. 24.

37. James Patterson and Peter Kim. *The Day America Told the Truth* (New York: Plume, 1991), p. 199-206.

Chapter Five

1. Kant, "Critique of Practical Reason," p. 360.

2. Robert Wright. *The Moral Animal* (New York: Pantheon Books, 1994), pp. 175, 280.

3. Michael Lind. *The Next American Nation* (New York: The Free Press, 1995), p. 5.

4. Pinker, p. 404. In contrast, cognitive scientist Steven Pinker speculates that sympathy, as we define it today, may be an emotion for earning gratitude.

5. Lind, p. 7.

6. Ibid., 5.

7. Allman, pp. 250-251.

8. Hoffer, p. 91.

9. During the 1960s George Wallace preached a subtle racism based, in my opinion, more on ignorance than on hate. Later, I believe he came to understand this himself. He was never a David Duke.

10. Robert Hughes. *Culture of Complaint* (New York: Oxford University Press, 1993), p. 121.

11. Gitlin, pp. 198, 199.

12. A cursory review of Dinesh D'Souza's *Illiberal Education* contains enough errors about political correctness to invalidate the whole concept.

13. Marvin Harris. *Cows, Pigs, Wars and Witches* (New York: Vintage Books, 1974), p. 215.

14. Shaw, p. 288.

15. Baird W. Whitlock. *Educational Myths I Have Known and Loved* (New York: Schocken Books, 1986), p. 20.

16. Marsha Sinetar. *Do What You Love, the Money Will Follow* (New York: Paulist Press, 1987), pp. 94-95.

17. The aspersions cast on Martin Luther King Jr. continue to the present day. As I was writing these notes, he was being accused of plagiarism in his doctoral dissertation. Even if I were to discover that Dr. King did not write his "Birmingham letter" while in jail, even if I were to find that he had employed a dozen writers in a fully staffed office, it would not distract me from the truth of what he said.

18. Neil Postman. *Conscientious Objections* (New York: Alfred A. Knopf, 1988), p. 22.

19. Corliss Lamont. *The Illusion of Immortality* (New York: Continuum, 1990), p. 20.

20. Jack Weatherford. *Savages and Civilization* (New York: Crown, 1994), p. 210. Weatherford writes, "People see what they want to see in native cultures. They can see vicious barbarism and pagan idolatry, or they can see wise, understanding, noble savages living in harmony with animals and plants as well as other humans....Our vision of native people, no matter whether positive or negative, often reveals more about ourselves than it does about them." He's right. I'm not suggesting otherwise, only that Native Americans did not destroy the resources they depended on.

21. Thoreau. *The Portable Thoreau*, p. 633.

22. Lester R. Brown et al. *State of the World* (New York: W. W. Norton, 1990), p. 3.

23. In the very near future books will be available on a computer disk which will be readable through the use of a book reader about the size of the books we use today. The reader will be able to select size and style of type, get instant word definitions, make notes in the margins, and read in the dark, as a minimum of features.

24. David Bohm and Mark Edwards. *Changing Consciousness* (San Francisco: HarperCollins, 1991), p. 51.

25. Hazel Henderson. *The Politics of the Solar Age* (Indianapolis, IN: Knowledge Systems, 1991), p. xv.

26. Paul R. Ehrlich and Anne H. Ehrlich. *The Population Explosion* (New York: Simon & Schuster, 1990), p. 42. Critics of Ehrlich call attention to his earlier prediction of catastrophe from overpopulation in *The Population Bomb* in 1968. That we are all not yet visibly affected by overpopulation is indeed fortunate, but what about the millions today who are affected? Try telling them it's not a catastrophe. The February 8, 1993, issue of *U.S. News & World Report* contained an article titled "Defusing the Bomb" with the subtitle, "Population experts are no longer panicking about global crowding." There may be some hope based upon population demographics, but the article is misleading. There are still a multitude of experts who are extremely worried about the growth of world population. Who wouldn't be, if they understood that a population growth rate of 2.5 percent would produce a trillion people per square mile in a thousand years (a point made by David Bohm and Mark Edwards in *Changing Consciousness*)?

27. Ibid., p. 162.

28. Isaac Asimov. *Isaac Asimov's Book of Facts* (New York; Wings Books, 1979), p. 294.

29. Edward O. Wilson. *The Diversity of Life* (Cambridge, MA: The Belnap Press of Harvard University Press, 1992), p. 182.

Chapter Six

1. Emerson. *Selected Essays*, p. 178.

2. Bertrand Russell. *Principles of Social Construction* (London: G. Allen & Unwin, 1916).

3. Erich Fromm. *On Disobedience* (New York: The Seabury Press, 1981), p. 43.

4. Many people will say, "But I do live by my principles," and they may be correct. Still, even those whom we most admire for standing their ground often compromise their principles for the sake of saving their jobs. Such is the real world we live in, and it will not substantially improve until more people refuse to "go along" for the sake of "getting along." In his book *Man's Search for Meaning*, Auschwitz survivor Viktor Frankl observed that, though few in number, there were always people in the concentration camps "comforting others, giving away their last piece of bread." I believe the reason so few of us reach this level of living by our principles is that we have yet to discover for ourselves what they really are. People who have developed the intrinsic ability to define what is really important have something to be courageous about.

5. John Rawls' notion of justice as fairness requires that those who cut the pie will do so not knowing which piece they will get. One could reach similar conclusions about using this method for obtaining justice from studying Plato's *Dialogs*. In his book *The Moral Sense*, p. 73, James Q. Wilson writes, "As I understand him, everybody in Rawls's universe is adverse to risk; each wants to make certain that, if he winds up on the bottom of the heap, the bottom is as attractive as possible." I would argue that Wilson doesn't understand Rawls at all. The point of Rawls' philosophy is not risk adversity—rather, it involves means versus ends. Rawls understands that we do not grow beautiful flowers by saying, "Hold back the water, take a chance." In Rawls' prescription for blind justice—justice is fairness as it applies to human needs—risk adversity is another matter which applies to human wants. Hundreds of thousands of young American students are taking a chance for an education in ghetto schools, which are clearly at the bottom of the heap in facilities and resources, while the majority of those who reside at higher levels in our king-of-the-mountain society are blind to the injustice of it.

6. Erich Fromm. *To Have or To Be* (New York: Harper & Row, 1976), p. 28-29.

7. Ibid., p. 29.

8. Mihaly Csikszentmihalyi. *Flow* (New York: Harper & Row, 1990), p.16.

9. Miles D. Storfer. *Intelligence and Giftedness* (San Francisco: Jossey-Bass, 1990). Storfer adds to the nature/nurture debate by suggesting that intelligence is 70 percent attributable to heredity and 30 percent attributable to environmental conditions.

Storfer cites numerous studies which indicate the 30 percent of intelligence subject to influence is only open to stimulus during individual-specific windows of developmental opportunity.

10. James Rachels. *The End of Life* (New York: Oxford University Press, 1986), p. 26.

11. Fukuyama, *The End of History and the Last Man*, p. 298.

12. Dennett, p. 517.

13. Garrett Hardin, *Living Within Limits* (New York: Oxford University Press, 1993), p. 242

14. Schumaker, *Wings of Illusion* pp. 111-147.

15. Ibid., p. 114.

16. Naomi Wolf. *The Beauty Myth* (New York: William and Morrow, 1991), p. 182. Wolf's statistics have been refuted as a gross exaggeration by a number of critics. That such starvation occurs at all is worthy of much reflection.

17. Christopher Lasch. *The Revolt of the Elites* (New York: W. W. Norton, 1995), p. 20.

18. Anderson, *Reality Isn't What It Used To Be*, p. 10.

19. Ibid., p. 9.

20. De Bono. *I Am Right—You Are Wrong*, p. 20.

21. André Maurois. *Illusions* (New York: Columbia University Press, 1968), p. 73.

22. A. J. Ayer. *The Meaning of Life* (New York: Charles Scribner's Sons, 1990), p. 138.

23. Anderson, *Reality Isn't What It Used To Be*, pp. 267, 268, 52.

24. Shelly E. Taylor. *Positive Illusions* (New York: Basic Books, 1989), p. 7.

25. Ibid., p. 7.

26. Ibid., p. 19.

27. I'm fortunate to have attended lectures by both of these gentlemen. Carl Sagan could be called an archetypal scientist; Depak Chopra, a popular metaphysician. Their messages are very different but both are profoundly life affirming. Chopra's authority for explaining the cosmos, however, comes from his imagination. Sagan who died while this manuscript was being written, derived his scientific authority from a profound desire to know. If I understand anything about the notion of spirituality

(and I'm not at all sure that I do), Carl Sagan had greater claim to use it than Chopra.

28. Emerson. *Essays and Lectures*, p. 952.

29. Abraham Maslow. *The Psychology of Science* (New York: Harper & Row, 1966), p. 15-16.

30. Roger Schank and Peter Childers. *The Creative Attitude* (New York: Macmillan, 1988), p. 14.

31. Michael Shermer. *Why People Believe Weird Things* (New York: W. H. Freeman, 1997), p. 55.

32. Robert Ornstein and Paul Ehrlich. *New World New Mind* (New York: Doubleday, 1989), p. 29.

33. Ellen J. Langer. *Mindfulness* (Reading, MA: Addison-Wesley, 1989), p. 74.

34. Pirsig, *Lila*, p. 70.

35. Marvin Harris. *Our Kind*, p. 374.

36. Mohandas K. Gandhi. *The Words of Gandhi*, selected by Richard Attenborough, (New York: New Market Press, 1982), p. 87.

37. Jamake Highwater. *The Primal Mind* (New York: Harper & Row, 1981), pp. 205-206.

Chapter Seven

1. Frederick Douglass. A speech titled, "What to the Slave is the Fourth of July?" given July, 4, 1852.

2. Mario Cuomo. *Reason To Believe* (New York: Simon & Schuster, 1995), pp. 80-81.

3. Francis Fukuyama. *Trust* (New York: The Free Press, 1995), p. 273.

4. Ibid., p. 281.

5. Philip Slater. *Earthwalk* (New York: Anchor Press, 1974), p. 13.

6. H.R. Haldeman. *The Haldeman Diaries* (New York: Berkley Books, 1994), p. 264. This turned out worse than I expected. Haldeman revealed that Kissinger favored a Vietnam withdrawal policy choreographed in 1970 to affect the 1972 presidential election. The welfare of the men and women in the armed services was never a consideration.

7. Peter Drucker. *Post-Capitalist Society* (New York: HarperCollins, 1993), p. 7.

8. Mortimer Adler. *Haves Without Have-Nots* (New York: Macmillan, 1991), p. 49.

9. Weiss, p. 37.

10. H. W. Brands. The *Reckless Decade* (New York: St. Martin's Press, 1995), p. 65.

11. Irwin Garfinkel (Columbia University) in an interview aired on "All Things Considered," National Public Radio, Washington, D.C., September 2, 1992. In *The War Against the Poor*, Herbert J. Gans writes, "Past experience has shown that welfare grants or their equivalents are cheap. Federal welfare expenditures have never exceeded one percent of the federal budget; the total cost of welfare and food stamps in 1992 came to $47 billion; and in 1991, the census bureau determined that it would have to cost another $37 billion to raise the incomes of all poor families with children to the poverty line, then set at $13,900 for a family of four" (p. 117). In *The Return of Thrift*, Phillip Longman puts poverty and welfare in perspective, "Of the trillion-plus the United States spends each year on direct and indirect entitlements, only a small fraction actually goes to the poor" (p. 5).

12. Adler. *Haves Without Have-Nots*, p. 98.

13. Henderson, *The Politics of the Solar Age*, p. xxii.

14. Charles Taylor. *Sources of the Self* (Cambridge, MA: Harvard University Press, 1989), p. 411.

15. Adam Smith. *The Theory of Moral Sentiments* (New York: Oxford University Press, 1976), p. 16.

16. David L. Hall. *Richard Rorty: Prophet and Poet of the New Pragmatism* (Albany, NY: State University of New York Press, 1994), p. 43.

17. Jerry Z. Muller. *Adam Smith: In His Time and Ours* (Princeton, NJ: Princeton University Press, 1993), pp. 6-7.

18. Alfie Kohn. *The Brighter Side of Human Nature* (New York: Basic Books, 1990), p. 197.

19. Theresa Funiciello. *Tyranny of Kindness* (New York: The Atlantic Monthly Press, 1993), p. 297.

20. Earl Shorris. *The Oppressed Middle* (New York: Anchor Press, 1981), p. 10.

21. Ibid., p. 261.

22. Leach, p. xv.

23. Milton S. Friedman and Thomas Szasz. *On Liberty and Drugs* (Washington, DC: The Drug Policy Foundation, 1992), p. 83.

24. Csikszentmihalyi. *The Evolving Self*, p. 59.

25. Ayn Rand. *The Virtue of Selfishness* (New York: Signet Books, 1961), p. vii.

26. Adam Smith, *The Theory of Moral Sentiments*, p. 235.

27. Adam Smith. "The Wealth of Nations," p. 7.

28. Kenneth Lux. *Adam Smith's Mistake* (Boston, MA: Shambhala, 1990), p. 106.

29. Ibid., p. 97

30. Ibid., p. 87.

31. Adam Smith, *The Theory of Moral Sentiments*, p. 83.

32. Robert B. Reich. *The Work of Nations* (New York: Alfred A. Knopf, 1991), p. 186.

33. David Pimentel. "Expert Says Only Hope To Feed World Is with Food Production Unlike That in U.S." *New York Times*, December 8, 1976.

34. Mickey Kaus. *The End of Equality* (New York: Basic Books, 1992), p. 18.

35. Ibid., p. 181.

36. Ibid., p. 78.

37. Ibid., p. 154.

38. Edgar Cahn and Jonathan Rowe. *Time Dollars* (Emmaus, PA: Rodale Press, 1992), p. 38.

39. Margrit Kennedy. *Interest and Inflation Free Money* (Philadelphia: New Society Publishers, 1995), pp. 98-99.

40. Ibid., p. 76.

41. Charles Handy. *The Age of Unreason* (Boston, MA: Harvard University Press, 1989), p. 243.

42. Peter F. Drucker. *The New Realities* (New York: Harper & Row, 1989), pp. 69-174.

43. Roger Terry. *Economic Insanity* (San Francisco: Berrett-Koehler, 1995), p. 69.

44. Ibid., p. 91.

45. Bill Shore. *Revolution of the Heart* (New York: Riverhead Books, 1995), p. 2.

46. Ibid., p. 83.

47. Funiciello, p. xiv.

48. Ibid., p. 267.

49. Ibid., p. 269.

50. Ibid., pp. 314-315.

51. Drucker, *The New Realities*, pp. 204-206.

52. Hardin, p. 193.

53. Collier, p. 262.

54. James Adams. *Conceptual Blockbusting* (Reading, MA: Addison-Wesley, 1986), p. 13.

55. Mary Catherine Bateson. *Composing a Life* (New York: Penguin Books, 1989), p. 114.

56. Kant. "Critique of Practical Reason," p. 342.

57. Bateson, p. 115.

58. Lasch, *The Revolt of the Elites*, p. 105.

59. William James. "The Social Value of the College Bred," in *The Academy Classics Book of Modern Essays* (New York: Allyn and Bacon, 1924), p. 12.

60. This conclusion is based upon remarks made in public on several occasions by Secretary of Agriculture Dan Glickman. He estimates 20 percent of the food in America is thrown away.

61. Peter F. Drucker. *Managing in a Time of Great Change* (New York: Dutton, 1995), p. 275.

62. Eric Foner. *Tom Paine and Revolutionary America* (New York: Oxford University Press, 1976), p. 94.

63. Fromm, *On Disobedience*, p. 92.

64. Terry, *Economic Insanity*, pp. 54, 162.

65. F.A. Hayek. *The Road to Serfdom* (Chicago, IL: University of Chicago Press, 1944), p. 142.

66. Donald L. Barlett and James B. Steele. *America What Went Wrong?* (Kansas City, MO: Andrews & McMeel, 1992), p. ix.

67. Philip K. Howard. *The Death of Common Sense* (New York: Random House, 1994), p. 26.

68. Ibid., pp. 30,41.

69. Ibid., p. 177.

70. Ibid., p. 178.

71. In April of 1994, seven major tobacco company executives testified before Congress that tobacco is not an addictive sub-

stance. Never mind that nicotine, a known narcotic, is one of the chief properties of tobacco.

72. Arnold S. Trebach, ed. "The Drug Policy Letter," no. 28, (winter 1996).

73. Earl Shorris. *A Nation of Salesmen* (New York: W. W. Norton, 1994), p. 335.

74. Ibid., p. 335.

75. Peter M. Senge. *The Fifth Discipline* (New York: Doubleday/Currency, 1990). Senge offers clear examples of the lunacy that drives military buildup.

76. James Goldsmith. *The Trap* (New York: Carroll & Graf, 1994), p. 35.

77. Hardin, p. 121.

78. Leslie W. Dunbar. *Reclaiming Liberalism* (New York: W. W. Norton, 1991), p. 57.

79. In 1991 Democratic senator Harris Wofford of Pennsylvania used this argument to come from behind and win his election. In 1994 the issue was overwhelmed in an advertising blitz by the health insurance industry.

80. Having large families as a survival strategy is an oversimplification of the complexity of human population, but it still rings true in many parts of the world, despite the other dynamics at play.

81. Jonathan H. Turner and David Musick. *American Dilemmas* (New York: Columbia University Press, 1985), pp. 14-21.

82. Julian L. Simon. *The State of Humanity* (Cambridge, MA: Blackwell, 1995), p. 642.

Chapter Eight

1. Frankl, pp. 131-132.

2. Paul Johnson. *Intellectuals* (New York: Harper & Row, 1988).

3. Mary Parker Follett. *The New State* (New York: Longmans, Green, 1918), pp. 142-143

4. Drucker, *The New Realities*, p. 195.

5. Ibid., p. 205.

6. E.J. Dionne Jr. *Why Americans Hate Politics* (New York: Simon & Schuster, 1991), p. 355.

7. Alexis de Tocqueville. *Democracy in America* (New York: Mentor Books, 1956), pp. 302-303.

8. Jennifer L. Hochschild. *Facing Up to the American Dream* (Princeton, NJ: Princeton University Press, 1995), p. 6. "Estranged poor" seems a much better term than "underclass."

9. Montagu, *Growing Young*, p. 138.

10. If you have any doubts about the validity of the assumption that successive generations improve the success rates of individuals, I suggest you read *The Promised Land* by Nicholas Lemann.

11. Duane Elgin. *Voluntary Simplicity* (New York: Quill, 1993), p. 116.

12. Neil Postman. *Technopoly* (New York: Alfred A. Knopf, 1992), p. 164.

13. Shi, David. *The Simple Life* (New York: Oxford University Press, 1985). Simple living and high thinking is the principle thesis of this book.

14. Abraham Lincoln. First Annual Message to Congress, December 3, 1861.

15. Hardin, p. 63.

16. Steven Goldberg. *When Wish Replaces Thought* (Buffalo, NY: Prometheus Books, 1991), p. 17.

17. H. L. Mencken. *H. L Mencken's Smart Set Criticism* (Washington, DC: Regnery Gateway, 1987), pp. 221-222.

18. It is erroneous to think that the typical drug user is a disenfranchised person at the lowest economic rung of society. Numerous studies have shown that drug users are often people of above average "intelligence" who crave novelty and sensation. Indeed, since we create our own drugs (endorphins) by thinking, could it be another indictment of our educational system that such people are bored stiff in a world that should produce as much intellectual stimulation as one's nervous system could handle? On the other hand, could it be true, as some who study behavior suggest, that altering one's consciousness is a drive as fundamental and normal as sleeping? The coffee and tobacco industries act as if they believe it is true.

   In his book *The Third Chimpanzee* (New York: HarperCollins, 1992), pp. 192-204. Jared Diamond offers an intriguing and provocative thesis that our predilection for drugs amounts to a once-useful instinct in which we rise to the challenges of our culture and demonstrate that we have achieved mastery by the continued ability to function *even* while under the influence of drugs.

19. People who are critical of homosexuals often suggest that homosexuality is aberrant behavior and the result of individual choice. But, even a cursory review of human history suggests that homosexuality has always been with us. Although it may be uncommon, it is not aberrant. It is, in fact, a norm throughout the animal kingdom. Moreover, from all the personal stories I have heard over the years, I cannot help but believe it is more a genetic predisposition than a personal decision. It's illogical that such a significant portion of the population would consistently choose any alternative which would lead to so much ridicule and torment. Anyone who has ever become sexually aroused and thought about it carefully will realize how little conscious effort was required and how much of a role biology played in the process. To say that homosexuality is only a matter of lifestyle preference is clearly a simple-minded assertion. Indeed, given our population predicament, we should be overjoyed to have more, not fewer, homosexuals.

20. Barbara Ehrenreich. *Fear of Falling* (New York: Harper Perennial, 1989), p. 247.

21. Friedman and Szasz, p. 70.

22. Ibid., p. 83.

23. This oak/acorn analogy places us precisely within the realm of the Darwinian or Spencerian notion of survival of the fittest. But, we do not set out to educate only those whom we consider strong. We are trying to assist all human beings so that they may become capable of reaching their maximum potential. The quality of our society depends upon education. The advantage of ensuring a Darwinian struggle in education is illusionary because the result is that the only advance is to secure an advantage one has already attained; further value is stifled.

24. Traditional pedagogy places its greatest emphasis on the external sphere of social convention. Intrinsic education changes the locus of control to the intellectual sphere. The influence of traditional education is so pervasive and so formidable that people may find the idea of intrinsic education difficult to comprehend. Intrinsic education is something all of us have experienced in bits and pieces, but rarely in a formal educational context. Intrinsic education is the quality of learning experience that Socrates afforded Plato and that Plato offered Aristotle. It had everything to do with learning the truth for one-

self and nothing whatsoever to do with grade point averages or SAT scores.

25. F. Allan Hanson. *Testing Testing: Social Consequences of the Examined Life* (Berkeley, CA: University of California Press, 1993), p. 6. Hanson argues that even though standard intelligence tests are designed to promote equality, what they really measure is the level of income of the parents of the students.

26. Benjamin R. Barber. *Jihad vs. McWorld* (New York: Times Books, 1995), p. 117.

27. James Fallows. *More Like Us* (Boston, MA: Houghton Mifflin, 1989), p. 193.

28. This may sound like a contradiction, since many communist school systems have often proved superior in educating people—especially when the criteria for judging success is how well students acquire skills. But this type of education is rather a form of indoctrination and has little to do with learning to think for oneself.

29. Richard Osborne. *Philosophy for Beginners* (New York: Writers and Readers, 1992), p. 124.

30. Epictetus. in "Discourses," vol. 12 of *Great Books of the Western World* (Chicago, IL: Encyclopaedia Britannica, 1952), p. 139.

31. This is the conclusion I draw from reading Daniel C. Dennett's book *Darwin's Dangerous Idea*.

32. Thomas Ellis Katen. *Doing Philosophy* (Englewood Cliffs, NJ: Prentice-Hall, 1973), p. 209. Heidegger's work, though considered profound, would have likely gained much more prominence had he not been at one time a Nazi sympathizer.

33. Martin Heidegger. *Being and Time*, trans. Joan Stambuagh (New York: State University of New York Press, 1996), p. 134.

34. Immanuel Kant. "The Metaphysic of Morals," vol. 42 of *Great Books of the Western World* (Chicago, IL: Encyclopaedia Britannica, 1952), p. 268.

35. Kant. "Critique of Practical Reason," p. 347.

36. Amitai Etzioni. *The New Golden Rule* (New York: Basic Books, 1996), p. xviii.

37. Aldous Huxley. *Huxley and God*, ed. Jacqueline Hazard Bridgeman (New York: HarperCollins, 1992), p. 197.

38. Ibid., p. 211.

39. Emerson. *Ralph Waldo Emerson:Selected Essays*, p. 37.

40. Watts, *The Wisdom of Insecurity* p. 24.

41. Nicholas Humphrey. *Leaps of Faith* (New York: Basic Books, 1996), p. 192.

42. Emerson, *Essays and Lectures*, p. 963.

43. Thoreau. *The Portable Thoreau*, p. 343.

44. Dennis Overbye. "Cosmologies in Conflict," *Omni*, October 1992, p. 93.

45. Jacob Needleman. *Money and the Meaning of Life* (New York: Doubleday/Currency, 1991), p. 166.

46. Ibid., p. 65.

47. Ibid., p. 161.

48. Ibid., p. 171.

49. Ibid., p. 206.

50. Schopenhauer, *Studies in Pessimism*, p. 12.

51. Rush Limbaugh has gained a large audience by appealing to popular ignorance. He is H. L. Mencken's nemesis come to life, a "champion of popular opinion," or, perhaps more correctly, Limbaugh is an articulate spokesman for the shadows on the wall of Plato's cave.

52. Schumaker, *Wings of Illusion*, p. 50.

53. In the introduction to Nietzsche's *Ecce Homo*, Walter Kaufmann compares Nietzsche to Van Gogh. Nietzsche did, in fact, succumb to madness in 1890, much to the delight of his critics. Some philosophers argue that, to Nietzsche, the eternal return is really a clear manifestation of the absurdity of human life. And I would not argue the point except to say that, in the case of human subjectivity, I think the reverse is true. It is ironic that Nietzsche concluded that there are no final interpretations since an industry in academia has emerged to interpret his works. Nietzsche had some bizarre ideas, no doubt about it, but he was, hands down, one of the greatest bullshit detectors of all times.

54. Nietzsche, *The Portable Nietzsche*, p. 101.

55. Shaw, pp. xxxi-xxxii.

56. Attributed to Jean Paul Sartre.

Chapter Nine

1. Emerson, "Politics," in *Essays and Lectures*, p. 568.

2. Charles Derber. *The Wilding of America* (New York: St. Martin's Press, 1996), p. 9.

3. Ralph Waldo Emerson has been accused of being everything from an anti-rationalist to the architect of excessive individualism, mostly from people who've misread or have never read his work.

4. Even though the violent acts of many young people are vile beyond belief, the reality of the "super predator" appears to be little more than media illusion. This kind of behavior has been with us throughout history. What has changed is our ability to focus attention on it.

5. Follett, *Creative Experience* p. 47.

6. People who try to call our attention to water and air pollution and who call for the manufacturing of cars that get better gas mileage are often accused of being anti-business. Thus, the reasoning goes, they are anti-American.

7. Even though only a portion of the population will become expert technicians, we have far greater capacity to teach technical skills than traditional education would lead us to believe.

8. Postman, *Technopoly*, pp. 190-194.

9. Ibid., p. 188.

10. John Stuart Mill. "Utilitarianism," in vol. 43 of *Great Books of the Western World* (Chicago, IL: Encyclopaedia Britannica, 1952), p. 451.

11. George Lakoff. *Moral Politics* (Chicago, IL: University Press, 1996), p. 114.

12. Ibid., p. 115.

13. Wright, *The Moral Animal*, pp. 336-342.

14. Ibid., p. 344.

15. Thoreau, *The Portable Thoreau*, p. 328.

16. Juliet B. Schor. *The Overworked American* (New York: Basic Books, 1991), p. 126.

17. Adam Smith, *The Wealth of Nations*, p. 340.

18. Ronald Gross. *Peak Learning* (Los Angeles, CA: Jeremy P. Tarcher, 1991), p. xi.

19. Nicholas Negroponte. *Being Digital* (Alfred A. Knopf, 1995), p. 229.

20. Anderson, *Evolution Isn't What It Used To Be*, p. 194.

21. Nietzsche, *The Portable Nietzsche*, p. 42.

22. Richardson. *Emerson. Richardson used the subtitle, The Mind on Fire,* to characterize Emerson in this way.

23. Emerson, *Essays and Lectures*, pp. 952, 956, 958, 963, 967.

24. Krishnamurti, *The First and Last Freedom*, p. 20.

25. Humphrey, p. 37.

26. C. Owen Paepke. *The Evolution of Progress* (New York: Random House, 1993), p. 254.

27. Richard Garner. *Beyond Morality* (Philadelphia, PA: Temple University Press, 1994), p. 361.

28. Ibid., pp. 382-383.

29. Pirsig, *Lila*, p. 97.

30. Peter Singer. *How Are We to Live?* (New York: Prometheus Books, 1995), pp. 17-18.

31. Emerson, *Essays and Lectures*, p. 953.

32. Carl Sagan. *The Demon-Haunted World* (New York: Random House, 1995), p. 336.

Bibliography

Adams, James. *Conceptual Blockbusting*. Reading, MA: Addison-Wesley, 1986.

Adler, Mortimer J. *We Hold These Truths: Understanding the Ideas and Ideals of the Constitution*. New York: Macmillan, 1987.

Adler, Mortimer J. *Intellect: Mind Over Matter*. New York: Macmillan, 1990.

Adler, Mortimer J. *Haves Without Have-Nots*. New York: Macmillan, 1991.

Allman, William F. *The Stone Age Present*. New York: Simon & Schuster, 1994.

Allport, Gordon W. *The Nature of Prejudice*. Reading, MA: Addison-Wesley, 1954.

Anderson, Walter Truett. *Reality Isn't What It Used To Be*. San Francisco: Harper & Row, 1990.

Anderson, Walter Truett. *Evolution Isn't What It Used To Be*. New York: W. H. Freeman, 1996.

Anderson, Walter Truett, ed. *The Truth About the Truth*. New York: Tarcher/Putnam, 1995.

Arendt, Hannah. *Between Past and Future*. New York: Penguin Books, 1968.

Armstrong, Karen. *A History of God*. New York: Alfred A. Knopf, 1993.

Aurelius, Marcus. "The Meditations of Marcus Aurelius." Trans. George Long. Vol. 12 of *Great Books of the Western World*. Chicago: Encyclopaedia Britannica, 1952.

Ayer, A. J. *The Meaning of Life*. New York: Charles Scribner's Sons, 1990.

Asimov, Isaac. *Isaac Asimov's Book of Facts*. New York: Wings Books, 1979.

Asimov, Isaac. *On the Past, Present & Future*. New York: Barnes & Noble, 1987.

Barber, Benjamin R. *Jihad vs. McWorld*. New York: Times Books, 1995.

Barkow, Jerome H., Leda Cosmides, and John Tooby. *The Adapted Mind*. New York: Oxford University Press, 1992.

Baritz, Loren. *The Good Life*. New York: Alfred A. Knopf, 1989.

Barlett, Donald L., and James B. Steele. *America What Went Wrong?* Kansas City, MO: Andrews & McMeel, 1992.

Barrett, William. *The Illusion of Technique*. New York: Anchor Press/Doubleday, 1979.

Bateson, Mary Catherine. *Composing a Life*. New York: Penguin Books, 1989.

Beane, J.A., and R.A. Lipka. *Self-Concept, Self-Esteem, and the Curriculum*. New York: Teachers College Press, 1984.

Becker, Ernest. *The Denial of Death*. New York: The Free Press, 1973.

Bellah, Robert N., Richard Madsen, William M. Sullivan, Ann Swindler, and Steven M. Tipton. *The Good Society*. New York: Alfred A. Knopf, 1991.

Berger, Peter L., *The Capitalist Revolution: Fifty Propositions about Prosperity, Equality, and Liberty*. New York: Basic Books, 1986.

Berger, Peter L. and Thomas Luckmann. *The Social Construction of Reality: A Treatise in the Sociology of Knowledge*. Garden City, New York: Doubleday, 1966.

Berman, Morris. *The Reenchantment of the World*. New York: Bantam Books, 1981.

Berman, Morris. *Coming to Our Senses*. New York: Bantam Books, 1989.

Bloom, Harold. *The American Religion*. New York: Simon & Schuster, 1992.

Bode, Carl. *The American Lyceum*. Carbondale and Edwardsville, IL: Southern Illinois University Press, 1968.

Bohm, David, and Mark Edwards. *Changing Consciousness*. San Francisco: HarperCollins, 1991.

Boorstin, Daniel J. "The Amature Spirit" in *Living Philosophies*. Ed. Clifton Fadiman. New York: Doubleday, 1990.

Botkin, Daniel B. *Discordant Harmonies*. New York: Oxford University Press, 1990.

Bradshaw, John. *Bradshaw On the Family: A Revolutionary Way of Self-Discovery*. Deerfield Beach, FL: Health Communications, 1988.

Brand, Stewart. *The Media Lab: Inventing the Future at MIT.* New York: Viking, 1987.

Brands, H. W. *The Reckless Decade.* New York: St. Martin's Press, 1995.

Bridges, William. *Transitions: Making Sense of Life's Changes.* Reading, MA: Addison-Wesley, 1980.

Brown, Lester R., Alan Durning, Christopher Flavin, Hilary French, Jodi Jacobson, Marcia Lowe, Sandra Postel, Michael Renner, Linda Starke, and John Young. *State of the World: A Worldwatch Institute Report on Progress Toward a Sustainable Society.* New York: W. W. Norton, 1990.

Brundage, Fitzhugh W. *Lynching in the New South.* Chicago: University of Illinois Press, 1993.

Cahn, Edgar, and Jonathan Rowe. *Time Dollars.* Emmaus, PA: Rodale Press, 1992.

Campbell, Joseph. *Myths To Live By.* New York: Bantam Books, 1973.

Campbell, Joseph, Bill Moyers, and Betty Sue Flowers, eds. *The Power of Myth.* New York: Doubleday, 1988.

Carter, Stephen L. *The Culture of Disbelief.* New York: Basic Books, 1993.

Carville, James. *We're Right, They're Wrong.* New York: Simon & Schuster and Random House, 1996.

Cernic, David, and Linda Longmire, eds. *Know Thyself: Collected Readings on Identity.* Mahwah, NJ: Paulist Press, 1987.

Cetron, Marvin J. *Encounters with the Future: A Forecast.* New York: McGraw-Hill, 1982.

Cetron, Marvin, Alicia Pagano, and Otis Port. *The Future of American Business: The U.S. in World Competition.* New York: McGraw-Hill, 1985.

Chiariello, Michael. "Reopening the American Mind: Alternatives to Relativism and Absolutism," *Free Inquiry,* winter 1991/92, vol. 12, no. 1.

Chomsky, Noam. *Reflections on Language.* New York: Pantheon Books, 1975.

Collier, James Lincoln. *The Rise of Selfishness in America.* New York: Oxford University Press, 1991.

Combs, Arthur W. *Individual Behavior: A Perceptual Approach to Behavior.* New York: Harper, 1959.

Commager, Henry Steel. *Jefferson, Nationalism, and the Enlightenment.* New York: George Braziller, 1975.

Coontz, Stephanie. *The Way We Never Were*. New York: Basic Books, 1992.

Cousins, Norman. *Human Options*. New York: W. W. Norton, 1981.

Covey, Stephen R. *The Seven Habits of Highly Effective People*. New York: Simon & Schuster, 1989.

Crick, Francis "Thinking about the Brain," *Scientific American* offprint, 1984.

Crick, Francis. *The Astonishing Hypothesis*. New York: Charles Scribner's Sons, 1994.

Csikszentmihalyi, Mihaly. *Flow: The Psychology of Optimal Experience*. New York: Harper & Row, 1990.

Csikszentmihalyi, Mihaly. *The Evolving Self: A Psychology for the Third Millennium*. New York: HarperCollins, 1993.

Cuomo, Mario. *Reason to Believe*. New York: Simon & Schuster, 1995.

Darwin, Charles. *The Descent of Man, and Selection in Relation to Sex*. 1871. Princeton, NJ: Princeton Univerty Press, 1981.

Dalai Lama XIV. *The Power of Compassion*. San Francisco: Thorsons, 1995.

Daumal, René. *Mount Analogue*. Boston: Shambhala Books, 1986.

Dawkins, Richard. *The Selfish Gene*. New York: Oxford University Press, 1976.

De Bono, Edward. *De Bono's Thinking Course*. New York: Facts on File Publications, 1982.

De Bono, Edward. *I Am Right—You Are Wrong*. New York: Viking Penguin, 1990.

Deci, Edward L. *Intrinsic Motivation*. New York: Plenum Press, 1975.

Deci, Edward L. *The Psychology of Self-Determination*. Lexington, MA: Lexington Books, 1980.

Deming, W. Edwards. *Out of the Crisis*. Cambridge, MA: MIT Press, 1986.

Dennett, Daniel C. *Darwin's Dangerous Idea*. New York: Simon & Schuster, 1995.

Derber, Charles. *The Wilding of America*. New York: St. Martin's Press, 1996.

Descartes, René. *Descartes*. Trans. Elizabeth S. Haldane and G.R.T. Ross. Vol. 31 of *Great Books of the Western World*. Chicago: Encyclopaedia Britannica, 1952.

Dewey, John. *Human Nature and Conduct*. New York: The Modern Library, 1922.

Diamond, Jared. *The Third Chimpanzee*. New York: HarperCollins, 1992.

Dickens, Charles. *American Notes*. New York: Oxford University Press, 1989.

Dionne, E. J., Jr. *Why Americans Hate Politics*. New York: Simon & Schuster, 1991.

Dionne, E. J., Jr. *They Only Look Dead*. New York: Simon & Schuster, 1996.

Douglass, Frederick. "What to the Slave is the Fourth of July?" Speech given July 4, 1852.

Dobson, Linda. *The Art of Education*. Tonasket, WA: Home Education Press, 1995.

Draves, Bill. *The Free University: A Model for Lifelong Learning*. Chicago: Association Press, 1980.

Drucker, Peter F. *Toward the Next Economics and Other Essays*. New York: Harper & Row, 1981.

Drucker, Peter F. *Innovation and Entrepreneurship: Practice and Principles*. New York: Harper & Row, 1985.

Drucker, Peter F. *The Frontiers of Management: Where Tomorrow's Decisions are Being Shaped Today*. New York: Truman Talley Books/E.P. Dutton, 1986.

Drucker, Peter F. *The New Realities: In Government and Politics/ In Economics and Business/ In Society and World View*. New York: Harper & Row, 1989.

Drucker, Peter F. *Post-Capitalist Society*. New York: HarperCollins, 1993.

Drucker, Peter F. *Managing in a Time of Great Change*. New York: Dutton, 1995.

Druckman, Daniel, and Robert A. Bjork, eds. *In the Mind's Eye: Enhancing Human Performance*. Washington, D.C.: National Academy Press, 1991.

Dunbar, Leslie W. *Reclaiming Liberalism*. New York: W. W. Norton, 1991.

Durant, Will. *The Story of Philosophy: The Lives and Opinions of the Greatest Philosophers from Plato to John Dewey*. New York: Pocket Books/Simon & Schuster, 1953.

Durant, Will. *The Pleasures of Philosophy*. New York: Simon & Schuster, 1981.

Dychtwald, Ken, and Joe Flower. *Age Wave: The Challenges and Opportunities of an Aging America*. Los Angeles: Jeremy P. Tarcher, 1989.

Ehrenreich, Barbara. *Fear of Falling*. New York: Harper Perennial, 1989.

Ehrenreich, Barbara. *Blood Rites*. New York: Metropolitan Books, 1997.

Ehrlich, Paul R., *The Population Bomb*. New York: Ballantine Books, 1968.

Ehrlich, Paul R. and Anne H. Ehrlich. *The Population Explosion*. New York: Simon & Schuster, 1990.

Einstein, Albert. *Ideas and Opinions*. New York: Crown Publishers, 1954.

Elgin, Duane. *Voluntary Simplicity*. New York: Quill, 1993.

Emerson, Ralph Waldo. *The Portable Emerson*. Ed. by Carl Bode. New York: Penguin Books, 1981.

Emerson, Ralph Waldo. *Ralph Waldo Emerson: Selected Essays*. Ed. by Larzer Ziff. New York: Penguin Books, 1982.

Emerson, Ralph Waldo. *Essays and Lectures*. New York: The Library of America, 1983.

Erikson, Erik H. *Adulthood: Essays*. New York: W.W. Norton, 1976.

Etzioni, Amitai. *The Spirit of Community*. New York: Crown Publishers, 1993.

Etzioni, Amitai. *The New Golden Rule*. Basic Books, 1996.

Fadiman, Clifton, ed. *Living Philosophies*. New York: Doubleday, 1990.

Fallows, James. *More Like Us: Making America Great Again*. Boston: Houghton Mifflin, 1989.

Feller, W. *An Introduction to Probability Theory and Its Applications*. New York: Wiley, 1967.

Ferris, Timothy. *The Mind's Sky*. New York: Bantam Books, 1992.

Festinger, Leon. *A Theory of Cognitive Dissonance*. Stanford, CA: Stanford University Press, 1962.

Finsterbusch, Kurt, and George McKenna. *Taking Sides: Clashing Views on Controversial Social Issues*. Guilford, CT: Dushkin, 1988.

Fisher, James R., Jr. *The Worker Alone*. Tampa, FL: The Delta Group, 1995.

Fisher, James R., Jr. *The Taboo Against Being Your Own Best Friend*. Tampa, FL: The Delta Group, 1996.

Follett, Mary Parker. *The New State*. New York: Longmans, Green, 1918.

Follett, Mary Parker. *Creative Experience*. New York: Longmans, Green, 1924.

Foner, Eric. *Tom Paine and Revolutionary America*. New York: Oxford University Press, 1976.

Fox, Matthew. *The Reinvention of Work*. San Francisco: HarperSanFrancisco, 1994.

Frank, Robert H., and Philip J. Cook. *The Winner-Take-All Society*. New York: Free Press, 1996.

Frankl, Viktor E. *Man's Search for Meaning*. New York: Pocket Books, 1984.

French, Marilyn. *Beyond Power: On Women, Men and Morals*. New York: Ballantine Books, 1985.

Freud, Sigmund. *The Major Works of Sigmund Freud*. Vol. 54 of *Great Books of the Western World*. Chicago: Encyclopaedia Britannica, 1952.

Friedman, Milton, and Thomas S. Szasz. *On Liberty and Drugs*. Washington, DC: The Drug Policy Foundation, 1992.

Fromm, Erich. *The Sane Society*. New York: Holt, Rinehart & Winston, 1955.

Fromm, Erich. *To Have or To Be*. New York: Harper & Row, 1976.

Fromm, Erich. *On Disobedience and Other Essays*. New York: The Seabury Press, 1981.

Funiciello, Theresa. *Tyranny of Kindness*. New York: The Atlantic Monthly Press, 1993.

Fukuyama, Francis. *The End of History and the Last Man*. New York: The Free Press, 1992.

Fukuyama, Francis. *Trust*. New York: The Free Press, 1995.

Furlong, Monica. *Genuine Fake*. London: Unwin Hyman Ltd., 1986.

Galbraith, John Kenneth. *The Culture of Contentment*. New York: Houghton Mifflin, 1992.

Gandhi, Mohandas K. *The Words of Gandhi*. Selected by Richard Attenborough. New York: New Market Press, 1982.

Gans, Herbert J. *The War Against the Poor*. New York: Basic Books, 1995.

Gardner, Howard. *Frames of Mind*. New York: Basic Books, 1985.

Gardiner, W. Lambert. *The Ubiquitous Chip: The Human Impact of Electronic Technology*. Quebec, Canada: Scot & Siliclone, 1987.

Garner, Richard. *Beyond Morality*. Philadelphia, PA: Temple University Press, 1994.

Gergen, Kenneth J. *The Saturated Self*. New York: Basic Books, 1991.

Gilligan, Carol. *In a Different Voice*. Cambridge MA: Harvard University Press, 1982.

Gilovich, Thomas. *How We Know What Isn't So: The Fallibility of Human Reason in Everyday Life*. New York: Macmillan, 1991.

Gitlin, Todd. *The Twilight of Common Dreams*. New York: Metropolitan Books, 1995.

Gleick, James. *Chaos: Making a New Science*. New York: Viking, 1987.

Goble, Frank G. *The Third Force: The Psychology of Abraham Maslow*. New York: Simon & Schuster, 1971.

Goldberg, S.R., and F. Deutsch. *Life-Span: Individual and Family Development*. Monterey, CA: Brooks/Cole, 1977.

Goldberg, Steven. *When Wish Replaces Thought*. Buffalo, NY: Prometheus Books, 1991.

Goldsmith, Sir James. *The Trap*. New York: Carroll & Graf, 1994.

Goleman, Daniel. *Vital Lies, Simple Truths*. New York: Simon & Schuster, 1985.

Goleman, Daniel. *Emotional Intelligence*. New York: Bantam Books, 1995.

Gore, Al. *Earth in the Balance*. New York: Houghton Mifflin, 1992.

Gould, Stephen Jay. *Ever Since Darwin: Reflections in Natural History*. New York: W.W. Norton, 1977.

Gould, Stephen Jay. *The Mismeasure of Man*. New York: W.W. Norton, 1981.

Great Books of the Western World. 54 volumes. Ed. Robert M. Hutchins, and Mortimer J. Adler. Chicago: Encyclopaedia Britannica, 1952.

Greenberger, Martin, ed. *Electronic Publishing Plus: Media for a Technological Future*. White Plains, NY: Knowledge Industry Publications, 1985.

Greenfield, P.M. *Mind and Media: The Effects of Television, Video Games, and Computers*. Cambridge, MA: Harvard University Press, 1984.

Griffin, Susan. *A Chorus of Stones*. New York: Doubleday, 1992.

Gross, Ronald. *Peak Learning*. Los Angeles: Jeremy P. Tarcher, 1991.

Gross, Ronald. *The Independent Scholar's Handbook*. Berkely: Ten Speed Press, 1993.

Grossman, Lawwrence K. *The Electronic Republic*. New York: Viking, 1995.

Halal, W.E. *The New Capitalism*. New York: John Wiley & Sons, 1986.

Haldeman, H.R. *The Haldeman Diaries: Inside the Nixon White House*. New York: Berkley Books, 1994.

Hall, David L. *Richard Rorty: Prophet and Poet of the New Pragmatism*. Albany, NY: State University of New York Press, 1994.

Handy, Charles. *The Age of Unreason*. Boston, MA: Harvard Business School Press, 1989.

Handy, Charles. *The Age of Paradox*. Boston, MA: Harvard Business School Press, 1994.

Handy, Charles. *Beyond Certainty*. Boston, MA: Harvard Business School Press, 1996.

Hanson, F. Allan. *Testing, Testing*. Berkeley, CA: University of California Press, 1993.

Hardin, Garrett. *Living Within Limits: Ecology, Economics, and Population Taboos*. New York: Oxford University Press, 1993.

Harman, Willis. *Global Mind Change: The Promise of the Last Years of the Twentieth Century*. Indianapolis, IN: Knowledge Systems, 1988.

Harman, David. *Illiteracy: A National Dilemma*. New York: Cambridge Book Co., 1987.

Harris, Marvin. *Cows, Pigs, Wars and Witches: The Riddles of Culture*. New York: Vintage Books, 1974.

Harris, Marvin. *Cannibals and Kings: The Origins of Cultures*. New York: Vintage Books, 1978.

Harris, Marvin. *Our Kind*. New York: HarperCollins, 1989.

Hart, Leslie A. *Human Brain and Human Learning*. New York: Longman, 1983.

Hawken, Paul. *The Next Economy*. New York: Holt, Rinehart & Winston, 1983.

Hawking, Stephen W. *A Brief History of Time*. New York: Bantam Books, 1988.

Hayek, F.A., *The Road to Serfdom*. Chicago: University of Chicago Press, 1944.

Hayes, Charles D. *Self-University: The Price of Tuition Is the Desire to Learn. Your Degree Is a Better Life*. Wasilla, AK: Autodidactic Press, 1989.

Hayes, Charles D. *Proving You're Qualified: Strategies for Competent People without College Degrees*. Wasilla, AK: Autodidactic Press, 1995.

Hegel, Georg Wilhelm Friedrich. "The Philosophy of Right" and "The Philosophy of History." Vol. 46 of *Great Books of the Western World*. Chicago: Encyclopaedia Britannica, 1952.

Heidegger, Martin. *Being and Time*. 1953. Trans. Joan Stambaugh. New York: State University of New York Press, 1996.

Henderson, Hazel. *The Politics of the Solar Age: Alternatives to Economics*. Indianapolis, IN: Knowledge Systems, Inc., 1988.

Henderson, Hazel. *Paradigms in Progress*. Indianapolis, IN: Knowledge Systems, 1991.

Henry, William A., III. *In Defense of Elitism*. New York: Doubleday, 1994.

Herrmann, Ned. *The Creative Brain*. Lake Lure, NC: Brain Books, 1989.

Hesse, Hermann. *Siddhartha*. New York: New Directions Publishing, 1951.

Highwater, Jamake. *The Primal Mind*. New York: Harper & Row, 1981.

Himmelfarb, Gertrude. *On Looking into the Abyss*. New York: Vintage Books, 1994.

Hochschild, Jennifer L. *Facing Up to the American Dream*. Princeton, NJ: Princeton University Press, 1995.

Hoffer, Eric. *The True Believer: Thoughts on the Nature of Mass Movements*. New York: Harper & Row, 1951. Reset, First Perennial Library, 1989.

Hoffman, Edward. *The Right to be Human: A Biography of Abraham Maslow*. Los Angeles: Tarcher, 1988.

Hofstadter, Richard. *Anti-Intellectualism in American Life*. New York: Vantage Books, 1962.

Horgan, John. *The End of Science*. New York: Addison-Wesley, 1996.

Howard, Philip K., *The Death of Common Sense*. New York: Random House, 1994.

Hughes, Robert. *Culture of Complaint*. New York: Oxford University Press, 1993.

Hume, David. *A Treatise of Human Nature*. Ed. L.A. Selby-Bigge. London: Oxford at the Clarendon Press, 1888.

Humphrey, Nicholas. *Leaps of Faith*. New York: Basic Books, 1996.

Hunter, James Davison. *Culture Wars*. New York: Basic Books, 1991.

Huxley, Aldous. *Huxley and God*. Ed. by Jacqueline Hazard Bridgeman. New York: HarperCollins, 1992

Illich, Ivan, and Barry Sanders. *The Alphabetization of the Popular Mind*. San Francisco: North Point Press, 1988.

Illich, Ivan. *In the Vineyard of the Text*. Chicago: University of Chicago Press, 1993.

James, William. *Pragmatism: A New Name for Some Old Ways of Thinking*. New York: Longsman, Green, 1910.

James, William. "The Social Value of the College Bred." in *The Academy Classics Book of Modern Essays*. Ed. John M. Avent. New York: Allyn and Bacon, 1924

James, William. *The Writings of William James*. Ed. John J. McDermott. Chicago: University of Chicago Press, 1967.

Janos, A.C. *Politics and Paradigms*. Stanford, CA: Stanford University Press, 1986.

Jarvis, Peter. *Paradoxes of Learning*. San Francisco: Jossey-Bass, 1992.

Johnson, Paul. *Intellectuals*. New York: Harper & Row, 1988.

Johnston, Charles M. *Necessary Wisdom*. Seattle, WA: ICD Press in association with Celestial Arts, 1991.

Kaminer, Wendy. *I'm Dysfunctional, You're Dysfunctional*. New York: Addison-Wesley, 1992.

Kant, Immanuel. "The Critique of Pure Reason," "The critique of Practical Reason," and "The Metaphysic of Morals." Trans. J. M. D. Meiklejohn and W. Hastie. Vol. 42 of *Great Books of the Western World*. Chicago: Encyclopaedia Britannica, 1952.

Kanter, Donald L., and Philip H. Mirvis. *The Cynical Americans: Living and Working in an Age of Discontent and Disillusion*. San Francisco: Jossey-Bass, 1989.

Kanter, R. M. *Men and Women of the Corporation*. New York: Basic Books, 1977.

Katen, Thomas Ellis. *Doing Philosophy*. Englewood Cliffs, NJ: Prentice-Hall, 1973.

Kaus, Mickey. *The End of Equality*. New York: Basic Books, 1992.

Keen, Sam. *Fire in the Belly*. New York: Bantam Books, 1991.

Keiser, T.W., and J.L. Keiser. *The Anatomy of Illusion*. Springfield, IL: Charles C. Thomas, 1987.

Kemp, Nigel. *Information Technology and People: Designing for the Future*. Cambridge, MA: MIT Press, 1987.

Kennedy, Margrit. *Interest and Inflation Free Money*. Philadelphia: New Society Publishers, 1995.

Kinder, Melvyn. *Going Nowhere Fast*. New York: Prentice-Hall Press, 1990.

Knowles, Malcolm S. *Self-Directed Learning: A Guide for Learners and Teachers*. New York: The Adult Education Co., 1975.

Knowles, Malcolm S. *The Modern Practice of Adult Education: From Pedagogy to Andragogy*. Chicago: Follett, 1980.

Knowles, Malcolm S. *The Adult Learner: A Neglected Species*. Houston: Gulf Publishing, 1990.

Knox, Alan B. *Adult Development and Learning*. San Francisco: Jossey-Bass, 1977.

Kohlberg, Lawrence. *The Psychology of Moral Development*. San Francisco: Harper & Row, 1984.

Kohn, Alfie. *No Contest: The Case Against Competition*. Boston: Houghton Mifflin, 1986.

Kohn, Alfie. *The Brighter Side of Human Nature*. New York: Basic Books, 1990.

Kohn, Alfie. *Punished by Rewards*. New York: Houghton Mifflin, 1993.

Kozol, Jonathan. *Savage Inequalities*. New York: Crown, 1991.

Kozol, Jonathan. *Amazing Grace*. New York: Crown, 1995.

Krishnamurti, J. *You Are The World*. New York: Harper & Row 1972.

Krishnamurti, J. *The First and Last Freedom*. San Francisco: Harper & Row, 1975.

Kurtz, Paul. *The Transcendental Temptation*. New York: Prometheus Books, 1991.

LaBier, Douglas. *Modern Madness: The Emotional Fallout of Success*. Reading, MA: Addison-Wesley, 1986.

Lakoff, George. *Moral Politics: What Conservatives Know That Liberals Don't*. Chicago: University of Chicago Press, 1996.

Lamont, Corliss. *The Illusion of Immortality*. New York: Continuum, 1990.

Landman, Janet. *Regret: The Persistence of the Possible*. New York: Oxford University Press, 1993.

Langer, Ellen J. *Mindfulness*. Reading, MA: Addision-Wesley, 1989.

Lapham, Lewis H. *Money and Class in America: Notes and Observations on Our Civil Religion*. New York: Weidenfeld & Nicolson, 1988.

Lapham, Lewis H. *The Wish for Kings*. New York: Grove Press, 1993.

Lappe, Frances M., and Joseph Collins. *World Hunger: Ten Myths*. 4th ed. San Francisco: Institute for Food and Development Policy, 1982.

Larkin, Jack. *The Reshaping of Everyday Life 1790-1840*. New York: Harper & Row, 1988.

Lasch, Christopher. *The Culture of Narcissism: American Life in an Age of Diminishing Expectations*. New York: Warner Books, 1979.

Lasch, Christopher. *The True and Only Heaven: Progress and Its Critics*. New York: W.W. Norton, 1991.

Lasch, Christopher. *The Revolt of the Elites*. New York: W.W. Norton, 1995.

Lawson, Hilary. *Reflexivity*. La Salle, IL: Open Court, 1985.

Leach, William. *Land of Desire*. New York: Pantheon Books, 1993.

Lemann, Nicholas. *The Promised Land*. New York: Alfred A. Knopf, 1991.

Lerner, M.J. *The Belief in a Just World: A Fundamental Delusion*. New York: Plenum, 1980.

Lerner, Michael. *The Politics of Meaning*. New York: Addison-Wesley, 1996.

Lewis, D. *Thinking Better*. New York: Rawson, Wade, 1982.

Lewis, Michael. *The Culture of Inequality*. Amherst, MA: University of Massachusetts Press, 1978.

Levine, Art. "Child Prodigies." *U.S. News and World Report*, 29 December 1986, p. 93.

Liddon, Sim C. *The Dual Brain, Religion, and the Unconscious*. Buffalo, NY: Prometheus Books, 1989.

Lincoln, Abraham. "First Annual Message to Congress," December 3, 1861.

Lind, Michael. *The Next American Nation*. New York: The Free Press, 1995.

Lindeman, Eduard C. *The Meaning of Adult Education*. Montreal: Harvest House, 1961.

Linton, Ralph. "100 Percent American." In *Modern American Vistas*, Ed. Howard W. Hintz, and Bernard D. N. Grebanier. New York: Dryden Press, 1940.

Lipnack, Jessica, and Jeffrey Stamps. *The Networking Book: People Connecting with People*. New York: Routledge & Kegan Paul, 1986.

Loewen, James W. *Lies My Teacher Told Me*. New York: The New Press, 1995.

London, Jack. *The Call of the Wild*. New York: Scholastic Book Services, 1963.

Longman, Phillip. *The Return of Thrift*. New York: The Free Press, 1996.

Lowrance, William W. *Modern Science and Human Values*. New York: Oxford University Press, 1985.

Lowy, L., and D. O'Connor. *Why Education in the Later Years*. Lexington, MA: D.C. Heath & Co., 1986.

Lovelock, James. *The Ages of Gaia: A Biography of Our Living Earth*. New York: W.W. Norton, 1988.

Lukacs, John. *The End of the Twentieth Century and the End of the Modern Age*. New York: Ticknor & Fields, 1993.

Lundberg, Ferdinand. *The Myth of Democracy*. New York: Carol Publishing Group, 1989.

Lux, Kenneth. *Adam Smith's Mistake*. Boston, MA: Shambhala, 1990.

McPherson, James M. *Battle Cry of Freedom: The Civil War Era*. New York: Ballantine, 1989.

Madsen, K.B. *Modern Theories of Motivation*. New York: Halsted Press, 1974.

Magee, Bryan, *The Great Philosophers: An Introduction to Western Philosophy*. New York: Oxford University Press, 1987.

Magee, Bryan, ed. *Men of Ideas: Some Creators of Contemporary Philosophy*. London: British Broadcasting Co., 1978.

Magill, Frank N., ed. *Masterpieces of World Philosophy*. New York: HarperCollins Publishers, 1990.

Magnus, Bernd, Stanley Stewart, and Jean-Pierre Mileur. *Nietzsche's Case*. New York: Routledge, 1993.

Margolis, Howard. *Patterns, Thinking, and Cognition: A Theory of Judgment*. Chicago: University of Chicago Press, 1987.

Maslow, Abraham H. *The Farther Reaches of Human Nature*. New York: Viking Press, 1971.

Maslow, Abraham H. *The Psychology of Science*. New York: Harper & Row, 1966.

Maslow, Abraham H. *Religions, Values, and Peak Experiences*. New York: Penguin Books, 1987.

Maurois, André. *Illusions*. New York: Columbia University Press, 1968.

May, Rollo, Carl Rogers, Abraham Maslow, et al. *Politics and Innocence: A Humanistic Debate*. Dallas: Saybrook Publishers, 1986.

McCrone, John. *The Myth of Irrationality*. New York: Carroll & Graf, 1993.

McKibben, Bill. *The End of Nature*. New York: Random House, 1989.

McLuhan, Marshall. *The Gutenberg Galaxy*. Toronto: University of Toronto Press, 1962.

McLuhan, Marshall. *Understanding Media*. New York: McGraw-Hill, 1964.

Mencken, H. L. *H. L. Mencken's Smart Set Criticism*. Ed. Willam H. Nolte. Washington, DC: Regnery Gateway, 1987.

Mill, John Stuart. "On Liberty," "Representative Government," and "Utilitarianism." Vol. 43 of *Great Books of the Western World* Chicago: Encyclopaedia Britannica, 1952.

Miller, Arthur G., ed. *In the Eye of the Beholder: Contemporary Issues in Stereotyping*. New York: Praeger, 1982.

Montagu, Ashley. *Growing Young*. Granby, MA: Bergin & Garvey, 1989.

Montuori, Alfonso, and Isabella Conti. *From Power to Partnership*. San Francisco: HarperSanFrancisco, 1993.

Moyers, Bill, and Betty Sue Flowers, eds. *A World of Ideas*. New York: Doubleday, 1989.

Muller, Jerry Z. *Adam Smith: In His Time and Ours*. Princeton, NJ: Princeton University Press, 1993.

Murdoch, Iris. *Metaphysics as a Guide to Morals*. New York: Penguin Press, 1992.

Needleman, Jacob. *Money and the Meaning of Life*. New York: Doubleday/Currency, 1991.

Negroponte, Nicholas. *Being Digital*. New York: Alfred A. Knopf, 1995.

Nietzsche, Friedrich. *Beyond Good and Evil*. Ed. and trans. R. J. Hollingdale. New York: Penguin Books, 1973.

Nietzsche, Friedrich. *The Portable Nietzsche*. Ed. and trans. Walter Kaufmann. New York: Penguin Books, 1982.

Nietzsche. Friedrich. *On the Genealogy of Morals* and *Ecce Hommo*. Trans. Walter Kaufmann and R.J. Hollingdale. New York: Vintage Books, 1989.

Niktiforuk, Andrew. *The Fourth Horseman: A Short History of Epidemics, Plagues and Other Scourges*. London: Phoenix, 1991.

Nozick, Robert. *Anarchy, State and Utopia*. New York: Basic Books, 1974.

Olasky, Marvin. *The Tragedy of American Compassion*. Washington, DC: Regenery, 1992.

Olsen, Edward Gustave. *Life Centering Education*. Midland, MI: Pendell, 1977.

Ornstein, Robert E. *The Psychology of Consciousness*. New York: Viking Press, 1972.

Ornstein, Robert E. *The Mind Field*. New York: Grossman, 1976.

Ornstein, Robert E. *Multimind: A New Way of Looking at Human Behavior*. New York: Doubleday, 1986.

Ornstein, Robert E., ed. *The Nature of Human Consciousness: A Book of Readings*. San Francisco: W.H. Freeman, 1973.

Ornstein, Robert E., and Paul Ehrlich. *New World New Mind: Moving Toward Conscious Evolution*. New York: Doubleday, 1989.

Osborne, David, and Ted Gaebler. *Reinventing Government*. New York: Plume, 1992.

Osborne, Richard. *Philosophy for Beginners*. New York: Writers and Readers, 1992.

Overbye, Dennis. "Cosmologies in Conflict," *Omni*, October 1992.

Paepke, C. Owen. *The Evolution of Progress*. New York: Random House, 1993.

Pagels, Heinz R. *The Dreams of Reason: The Computer and the Rise of the Sciences of Complexity*. New York: Bantam Books, 1988.

Paine, Thomas. *Common Sense*. 1776. New York: Penguin Books, 1976.

Paine, Thomas. *The Age of Reason*. 1794. New York: Carol Publishing Group, 1995.

Patterson, James, and Peter Kim. *The Day America Told the Truth*. New York: Plume, 1991.

Patterson, Orlando. *Freedom in the Making of Western Culture*. New York: Basic Books, 1991.

Peck, M. Scott. *The Road Less Traveled: A New Psychology of Love, Traditional Values, and Spiritual Growth*. New York: Simon & Schuster, 1978.

Peled, Abraham. "The Next Computer Revolution." *Scientific American*, October 1987, pp. 56-64.

Peters, Tom. *Thriving on Chaos: Handbook for a Management Revolution*. New York: Alfred A. Knopf, 1987.

Peterson, Merrill D. *Thomas Jefferson: A Reference Biography*. New York: Charles Scribner & Sons, 1986.

Pifer, Alan, and Lydia Bronte, eds. *Our Aging Society: Paradox and Promise*. New York: W.W. Norton, 1986.

Pimentel, David. "Expert Says Only Hope To Feed World Is with Food Production Unlike That in U.S." *New York Times*, 8 December 1976.

Piirto, Rebecca. *Beyond Mind Games*. New York: American Demographics Books, 1991.

Pinker, Steven. *How the Mind Works*. New York: W.W. Norton, 1997.

Pirsig, Robert M. *Zen and the Art of Motorcycle Maintenance: An Inquiry into Values*. New York: Bantam Books, 1985.

Pirsig, Robert M. *Lila: An Inquiry into Morals*. New York: Bantam Books, 1991.

Pitts, Robert E. Jr., and Arch G. Woodside, eds. *Personal Values and Consumer Psychology*. Lexington, MA: Lexington Books, 1984.

Plato. "The Dialogues of Plato." Trans. Benjamin Jowett. Vol. 7 of *Great Books of the Western World*. Chicago: Encyclopaedia Britannica, 1952.

Postman, Neil. *Teaching as a Conserving Activity*. New York: Delacorte Press, 1979.

Postman, Neil. *Amusing Ourselves to Death*. New York: Viking Penguin, 1985.

Postman, Neil. *Conscientious Objections*. New York: Alfred A. Knopf, 1988.

Postman, Neil. *Technopoly*. New York: Alfred A. Knopf, 1992.

Postman, Neil. *The End of Education*. New York: Alfred A. Knopf, 1995.

Postman, Neil, and Charles Weingarten. *Teaching as a Subversive Activity*. New York: Dell, 1969.

Pozner, Vladimer. *Parting with Illusions*. New York: Avon Books, 1990.

Preston, Richard. *The Hot Zone*. New York: Random House, 1994.

Pugh, George Edgin. *The Biological Origin of Human Values*. New York: Basic Books, 1977.

Rachels, James. *The Elements of Moral Philosophy*. Philadelphia: Temple University Press, 1986.

Rachels, James. *The End of Life*. New York: Oxford University Press, 1986.

Rand, Ayn. *The Virtue of Selfishness*. New York: Signet Books, 1961.

Rawls, John. *A Theory of Justice*. Cambridge, MA: Belnap Press of Harvard University Press, 1971.

Rawls, John. *Political Liberalism*. New York: Columbia University Press, 1993.

Reich, Robert B. *The Resurgent Liberal (and Other Unfashionable Prophecies)*. New York: Times Books, 1989.

Reich, Robert B. *The Work of Nations*. New York: Alfred A. Knopf, 1991.

Restak, Richard M. *The Brain: The Last Frontier*. New York: Warner Books, 1980.

Richardson, Robert D., Jr. Emerson: *The Mind on Fire*. Berkeley, CA: University of California Press, 1995.

Rifkin, Jeremy. *Time Wars*. New York: Henry Holt, 1987.

Rifkin, Jeremy. *The End of Work*. New York: Tarcher/Putnam, 1995.

Robeach, Milton. *The Nature of Human Values*. New York: The Free Press, 1973.

Roderick, Rick. *Philosophy and Human Values*. Kearneysville, WV: The Teaching Company, 1991. Audio cassette series.

Roderick, Rick. *The Self Under Siege: Philosophy in the 20th Century*. Kearneysville, WV: The Teaching Company, 1993. Audio cassette series.

Roosevelt, Franklin D. *The Public Papers and Addresses of Franklin D. Roosevelt*. Ed. Samuel I. Rosenman. New York: Random House, 1938.

Roszak, Theodore. *The Cult of Information: The Folklore of Computers and the True Art of Thinking*. United Kingdom: Lutterworth Press, 1986.

Rubinstein, Joseph, and Brent Slife. *Taking Sides: Clashing Views on Controversial Psychological Issues*. Guilford, CT: Dushkin Publishing Group, 1988.

Rushkoff, Douglas. *Media Virus*. New York: Ballantine Books, 1994.

Russell, Bertrand. *Principles of Social Reconstruction*. London: George Allen & Unwin, 1916.

Sagan, Carl. *Broca's Brain*. New York: Ballantine, 1974.

Sagan, Carl. *The Demon-Haunted World*. New York: Random House, 1995.

Samples, Bob. *The Metaphoric Mind: A Celebration of Creative Consciousness*. Reading, MA: Addison-Wesley, 1976.

Sarkar, P. R. *Human Society*. Denver: Ananda Marga Press, 1967.

Schank, Roger, and Peter Childers. *The Creative Attitude*. New York: Macmillan, 1988.

Schlesinger, Arthur M. *The Disuniting of America*. New York: W.W. Norton, 1993.

Schiller, Herbert I. *Information Inequality*. New York: Routledge, 1996.

Schopenhauer, Arthur. *Studies in Pessimism*. Trans. T. Bailey Saunders. London: George Allen and Company, 1913.

Schopenhauer, Arthur. *Essays of Arthur Schopenhauer*. Comp. and trans. T. Bailey Saunders. New York: A.L. Bert, 1949.

Schor, Juliet B. *The Overworked American*. New York: Basic Books, 1991.

Schumacher, E.F. *Small Is Beautiful*. New York: Harper & Row, 1973.

Schumacher, E.F. *Good Work*. New York: Harper & Row, 1979.

Schumaker, John F. *Wings of Illusion: The Origin and Future of Paranormal Belief*. New York: Prometheus Books, 1990.

Schumaker, John F. "The Mental Health of Atheists." *Free Inquiry*, summer 1993.

Schwartz, Gail Garfield. *The Work Revolution*. New York: Rawson Associates, 1984.

Senge, Peter M. *The Fifth Discipline*. New York: Doubleday/Currency, 1990.

Sennet, Richard. *Authority*. New York: W.W. Norton, 1980.

Shaw, George Bernard. *Man and Superman*. New York: Brentano's, 1903.

Sheehy, Gail. *Passages: Predictable Crises of Adult Life*. Toronto, New York: Bantam Books, 1981.

Shenkman, Richard. *Legends, Lies and Cherished Myths of American History*. New York: William Morrow, 1988.

Sheppard, C. Stewart, and Donald C. Carroll, eds. *Working in the Twenty-First Century*. New York: Wiley, 1980.

Shermer, Michael. *Why People Believe Weird Things*. New York: W.H. Freeman, 1997.

Shi, David E. *The Simple Life*. New York: Oxford University Press, 1985.

Shore, Bill. *Revolution of the Heart*. New York: Riverhead Books, 1995.

Shorris, Earl. *The Oppressed Middle: Politics of Middle Management, Scenes from Corporate Life*. New York: Anchor Press, 1981.

Shorris, Earl. *A Nation of Salesmen*. New York: W.W. Norton, 1994.

Shorris, Earl. *New American Blues*. New York: W. W. Norton, 1997.

Sigel, Efrem, with Joseph Roisen, Colin McIntyre, and Max Wilkinson. *Videotext: Worldwide Prospects for Home/Office Electronic Information Services*. New York: Knowlege Industry Publications, 1980.

Simon, Julian L. *The State of Humanity*. Cambridge, MA: Blackwell, 1995.

Sinetar, Marsha. *Do What You Love, the Money Will Follow: Discovering Your Right Livelihood*. New York: Paulist Press, 1987.

Sinetar, Marsha. *Elegant Choices, Healing Choices*. New York: Paulist Press, 1988.

Singer, Benjamin D. "The Future-Focused Role-Image." In *Learning for Tomorrow*. New York: Random House, 1974.

Singer, Irving. *Meaning in Life: The Creation of Value*. New York: Macmillan, 1992.

Singer, Peter. *How Are We to Live?* New York: Prometheus Books, 1995.

Singer, Peter, ed. *A Companion to Ethics*. Cambridge, MA: Blackwell Reference, 1993

Skinner, B.F. *Science and Human Behavior*. New York: The Free Press, 1953.

Skinner, B.F. *Upon Further Reflection*. Englewood Cliffs, NJ: Prentice-Hall, 1987.

Slater, Philip. *Earthwalk*. New York: Anchor Press, 1974.

Slater, Philip. *Wealth Addiction*. New York: E.P. Dutton, 1980.

Slater, Philip. *The Pursuit of Loneliness*, 3rd ed. Boston, MA: Beacon Press Books, 1990.

Slater, Philip. *A Dream Deferred*. Boston, MA: Beacon Press Books, 1991.

Smith, Adam. *The Theory of Moral Sentiments*. New York: Oxford University Press, 1976.

Smith, Adam. "An Inquiry into the Nature and Causes of the Wealth of Nations." Vol. 39 of *Great Books of the Western World*. Chicago: Encyclopaedia Britannica, 1952.

Smith, Huston. *The Religions of Man*. New York: Harper & Row, 1986.

Smith, Huston. *Beyond the Post-Modern Mind*. New York: Crossroads Publishing, 1989.

Smith, Huston. *The World's Religions*. New York: Harper Collins, 1991.

Smith, Huston. *Huston Smith: Essays on World Religion*. ed. by M. Darrol Bryant. New York: Paragon House, 1992.

Smith, Page. *Killing the Spirit*. New York: Penguin Books, 1990.

Smith, Robert M. *Learning How to Learn: Applied Theory for Adults*. Chicago: Follett, 1982.

Solomon, Robert C., *A Passion for Justice*. New York: Addison-Wesley, 1990.

Solomon, Robert C., and Kathleen Higgins. *A Short History of Philosophy*. New York: Oxford University Press, 1996.

Spinoza, Benedict de. *The Ethics of Spinoza*. Trans. W. H. White and rev. A.H. Stirling. ed. by Robert Maynard Hutchins. Vol. 31 of *Great Books of the Western World*. Chicago: Encyclopaedia Britannica, 1952.

Stack, George J. *Nietzsche and Emerson*. Athens, OH: Ohio University Press, 1992.

Staguhn, Gerhard. *God's Laughter*. New York: HarperCollins Publishers, 1992.

Stearn, Gerald E., ed. *McLuhan: Hot and Cool*. New York: Dial Press, 1967.

Sternberg, Robert J. *The Triarchic Mind: A New Theory of Human Intelligence*. New York: Viking Penguin, 1988.

Stevenson, Leslie. *Seven Theories of Human Nature*. New York: Oxford University Press, 1987.

Stewart, David W. *Adult Learning in America: Eduard Lindeman and His Agenda for Lifelong Education*. Malabar, FL: Robert E. Krieger, 1987.

Stivers, Richard. *The Culture of Cynicism*. Cambridge, MA: Blackwell Publishers, 1994.

Storfer, Miles D. *Intelligence and Giftedness*. San Francisco: Jossey-Bass, 1990.

Sykes, Charles J. *A Nation of Victims*. New York: St. Martin's Press, 1992.

Tannen, Deborah. *You Just Don't Understand*. New York: William Morrow, 1990.

Taylor, Charles. *Sources of the Self*. Cambridge, MA: Harvard University Press, 1989.

Taylor, Shelly E. *Positive Illusions*. New York: Basic Books, 1989.

Terry, Roger. *Economic Insanity*. San Francisco: Berrett-Koehler, 1995.

Thoreau, Henry David. *The Portable Thoreau*. Ed. Carl Bode. New York: Penguin Books, 1947.

Thoreau, Henry David. *The Selected Works of Thoreau*. New York: Houghton Mifflin, 1975.

Thurow, Lester C. *The Future of Capitalism*. New York: William Morrow, 1996.

Tiger, Lionel. *Optimism: The Biology of Hope*. New York: Kodansha International, 1979.

Tocqueville, Alexis de. *Democracy in America*. Ed. Richard D. Heffner. New York: Mentor Books, 1956.

Toffler, Alvin. *Future Shock*. New York: Bantam Books, 1971.

Toffler, Alvin. *The Third Wave*. New York: Bantam Books/William Morrow, 1981.

Toffler, Alvin. *PowerShift: Knowledge, Wealth, and Violence at the Edge of the 21st Century*. New York: Bantam Books, 1990.

Toffler, Alvin, ed. *Learning for Tomorrow: The Role of the Future in Education*. New York: Random House, 1974.

Trebach, Arnold S. "The Drug Policy Letter," no. 28 (winter 1996).

Turner, Jonathan H. and David Musick. *American Dilemmas: A Sociological Interpretation of Enduring Social Issues*. New York: Columbia University Press, 1985.

Vetter, George B. *Magic and Religion*. New York: The Philosophical Library, 1958.

Voss, Hans-Georg, and Heidi Keller. *Curiosity and Exploration: Theories and Results*. New York: Academic Press, 1983.

Waterhouse, Philip. *Managing the Learning Process*. New York: McGraw-Hill, 1983.

Watts, Alan. *The Book on the Taboo Against Knowing Who You Are*. New York: Vintage Books, 1966.

Watts, Alan. *Does It Matter: Essays on Man's Relation to Materiality*. New York: Vintage Books, 1968.

Watts, Alan. *The Wisdom of Insecurity*. New York: Vintage Books, 1968.

Watts, Alan. *The Essential Alan Watts*. Berkley, CA: Celestial Arts, 1974.

Weatherford, Jack. *Savages and Civilization*. New York: Crown, 1994.

Weil, Simone. *Gravity and Grace*. London: Routledge and Kegan Paul, 1947.

Weiss, Richard. *The American Myth of Success*. New York: Basic Books, 1969.

West, Cornel. *Race Matters*. Boston: Beacon Press, 1993.

What Works: Research About Teaching and Learning. Washington, DC: U.S. Department of Education, 1986.

White, Mary Alice, ed. *The Future of Electronic Learning*. Hillsdale, NJ: Lawrence Erlbaum Associates, 1983.

Whitlock, Baird W. *Educational Myths I Have Known and Loved*. New York: Schocken Books, 1986.

Wilbur, Ken. *Sex, Ecology, Spirituality*. Boston: Shambhala, 1995.

Wilder, Thornton. *The Eighth Day*. New York: Harper & Row, 1967.

Wilkinson, Denys. *New Perspectives on Liberal Education*. Ed. Herbert Costner. Seattle, WA: University of Washington Press, 1989.

Williams, Frederick. *The Communications Revolution*. New York: New American Library, 1983.

Wills, Gary. *John Wayne's America*. New York: Simon & Schuster, 1997.

Wilson, Edward O. *The Diversity of Life*. Cambridge, MA: The Belknap Press of Harvard University Press, 1992.

Wilson, James Q. *The Moral Sense*. New York: The Free Press, 1993.

Winn, Denise. *The Manipulated Mind*. London: The Octagon Press, 1983.

Witmer, J. M. *Pathways to Personal Growth: Developing a Sense of Worth and Competence, A Holistic Education Approach*. Muncie, IN: Accelerated Development, 1985.

Wolf, Naomi. *The Beauty Myth*. New York: William and Morrow, 1991.

Wright, Robert. *The Moral Animal*. New York: Pantheon Books, 1994.

Wright, Robert. *Three Scientists and Their Gods*. New York: Perennial Library, 1989.

Wurman, Richard Saul. *Information Anxiety: What to Do When Information Doesn't Tell You What You Need to Know.* New York: Bantam Books, 1989.

Yankelovich, D. *New Rules.* New York: Random House, 1981.

Young, Michael. *The Rise of Meritocracy.* New York: Penguin Books, 1961.

Zinn, Howard. *A People's History of the United States.* New York: HarperCollins, 1995.

Zuboff, Shoshana. *In the Age of the Smart Machine.* New York: Basic Books, 1988.

Index

Lucas, Robert, 189
Lukacs, John, *End of the Twentieth Century*, 100
Lux, Kenneth, *Adam Smith's Mistake*, 203

M

Madison, James, *Federalist Paper No. 10*, 221
Malthus, Thomas, 8
Manifest Destiny, 12, 233
marketplace, global, 234
Marx, Karl, 86, 96-97, 149, 194, 249, 254-257
Marxist movement, 279
Maslow, Abraham, 38-41, 43, 45, 179, 219, 284, 292
Maurois, André, 172
McCrone, John, 71
McKinley, William, 12
meaning, 185; context and, 152; life and, 56, 74; search for, 247
media, 102-109
medical science, 75
meme, 64-65, 189; brotherly love as, 281; capitalism as, 205; self-interest as, 196
memory, 171
Mencken, H. L., 329n
menial tasks, 88
meritocracy, 18, 22
Mexico City, 121
Mexico, 11
Mill, John Stuart, 30, 46, 49, 280
mind and body, 71; relationship of, 76
mind-sets, 182
minority groups, 142-143
miracles, 121
Mizener, Wilson, 47
money, 84, 89, 166, 170, 206-210, 214-216, 247-248, 266
Montagu, Ashley, xiii, 242
moral authority, 45, 61
moral high ground, 49
moralists, 298
morality, 44, 233, 260, 287, 297-298; Christianity and, 282; concept of, 275; empathy and, 281; the public and, 109; virtue and, 60
moralizing, 300
moral law, 52, 128, 133, 195, 260
moral reminder, 261

morals, 43; development of, 284; dilemmas over, 120; inner compass and, 48, 195; principles and, 50-52
Morgan, J.P., 12
Morris, Desmond, 313n
Mother Teresa, 298
motivation, 59; external, 19; hierarchical, 125; intrinsic and extrinsic, 51, 128
Mott Haven, 121
mountain fever, 27-28
Mozart, W.A., 280
Muhammad, 258
Muller, Jerry A., 195
multiculturalism, 91, 135, 140
mutual respect, 137
mysticism, Eastern, 115

N

nationalism, 100, 102, 117, 133-134, 147, 296
Native Americans, 101, 152, 182
natural resources, 153
nature, estrangement from, 62
Needleman, Jacob, *Money and the Meaning of Life*, 265
needs, manufactured, 85
Negroponte, Nicholas, *Being Digital*, 288
net worth, 85
new ageism, 129
New Deal, 215
Nietzsche, Friedrich, 47, 50, 53, 57-59, 70-71, 95, 131, 165, 267-268, 282, 289-292; *Ecce Homo*, 329n; *On the Genealogy of Morals*, 316n
nihilism, 125
Nikiforuk, Andrew, *Fourth Horseman*, 54
Nixon, Richard, 210
Noddings, Nel, 271
nonbelievers, 118

O

obedience, 102, 129
objectification, 112-113
objectivists, 256
Oklahoma City bombing, 107

DATE DUE

MAR 0 1 2007			

GAYLORD

PRINTED IN U.S.A.